P9-CDL-639

PENGUIN BOOKS

THEODORE ROOSEVELT: AN AMERICAN MIND

Mario R. DiNunzio is a Professor of History at Providence College, Rhode Island. He is the author of *American Democracy and the Authoritarian Tradition of the West*.

THEODORE ROOSEVELT

AN AMERICAN MIND

A SELECTION FROM HIS WRITINGS

Edited and Introduced by
Mario R. DiNunzio

PENGUIN BOOKS

PENGUIN BOOKS
Published by the Penguin Group
Penguin Books USA Inc., 375 Hudson Street,
New York, New York 10014, U.S.A.
Penguin Books Ltd, 27 Wrights Lane,
London W8 5TZ, England
Penguin Books Australia Ltd,
Ringwood, Victoria, Australia
Penguin Books Canada Ltd, 10 Alcorn Avenue,
Toronto, Ontario, Canada M4V 3B2
Penguin Books (N.Z.) Ltd, 182–190 Wairau Road,
Auckland 10, New Zealand

Penguin Books Ltd, Registered Offices:
Harmondsworth, Middlesex, England

First published in the United States of America by St. Martin's Press, 1994
Reprinted by arrangement with St. Martin's Press
Published in Penguin Books 1995

5   7   9   10   8   6   4

Copyright © Mario R. DiNunzio, 1994
All rights reserved

Photographs courtesy of the Theodore Roosevelt Collection,
Harvard College Library.

THE LIBRARY OF CONGRESS HAS CATALOGUED THE HARDCOVER
AS FOLLOWS:
Roosevelt, Theodore, 1858–1919.
(Selections. 1994)
Theodore Roosevelt: an American mind: a selection from his writings/edited
and introduced by Mario R. DiNunzio.
p.   cm.
ISBN 0-312-10352-2 (hc.)
ISBN 0 14 02.4520 0 (pbk.)
1. United States—Politics and government—1865–1933.   2. United States—
Territorial expansion.   3. Outdoor life.   4. United States—History,
Military—To 1900.   5. Conservation of natural resources—United States.
6. West (U.S.)—History.   I. DiNunzio, Mario R., 1936–.   II. Title.
E660.R72   1994
973—dc20   93–26611

Printed in the United States of America
Set in Cochin
Designed by Digital Type & Design

Except in the United States of America, this book is sold subject to the condition that it shall not, by way of trade or otherwise, be lent, re-sold, hired
out, or otherwise circulated without the publisher's prior consent in
any form of binding or cover other than that in which it is
published and without a similar condition including this
condition being imposed on the subsequent purchaser.

— For Joan, Joseph, and Thomas —

CONTENTS

LIST OF ILLUSTRATIONS

PREFACE

The writings of Theodore Roosevelt mirror the man and, in some ways, the age in which he lived. He was, even as a young man, supremely self-confident about his vision of what was right in personal and public morality. He knew that he wrote well enough to reach a large audience. Such a vehicle for the moral and political education of that audience he could not resist. The teacher-preacher in him is evident throughout his works. Even in his hunting tales, and especially in his histories, he dramatizes those lessons that rose out of experiences his audience could share only indirectly. Because he insisted on instructing the reader in so many subjects, the body of his writing leaves few corners of his mind unexamined, few ideas unexpressed.

The effect on his contemporaries was generally positive. His histories earned the praise of historians, including Frederick Jackson Turner. His work as a naturalist impressed professionals in the field. His hunting and adventure stories, as his other work, won a wide audience in Britain as well as the United States. Had there been no political career, Roosevelt's name would still have survived through the twentieth century as a lesser historian and popular writer.

The judgment from a longer distance varies. Much of his writing is exciting, some brilliant, most lively. Some, however, seems rushed; he could be trite and at times repetitive; he sounds, on occasion, insufferably smug. One midcentury commentator with little sympathy for Roosevelt's political role in American history judges his writing full of "philistine conventionalities." The more generous and probably more objective assessment sees in his writings a sharp intelligence, a scientist's appreciation for the importance of detail, and a bookseller's understanding of audience. Not all his ideas were profound; much *was* conventional. Yet that his work should reflect the moral and social conventions of his class and his age should neither surprise nor disturb. More troublesome for the student of American thought, however, is the near unanimity with which his contemporary intellectuals and academicians shared most of his less attractive views of race and class. When they differed with his ideas, it was more often a consequence of a stylish agnosticism than the product of a more progressive or humane sensibility.

Nor is it useful to explain Roosevelt's ideas simply as a reflection of the artificial standards of a beleaguered patrician class. His audience was so large even before his military and political fame probably because he reflected the prejudices, tastes, and ambitions of so many Americans of his age. In contrast to his clear commitment to democracy and equal opportunity, Roosevelt did reveal in his writing many of the racist ideas that so dominated American attitudes at the turn of the century. He had no doubts about Nordic superiority and often wrote about strengths and weaknesses of bloodlines in history. He was an imperialist in an age of imperialism and a nationalist in an age of romantic nationalism. He showed persistent and, at times, undiscriminating patriotism in all he wrote. He associated "manliness" (a word he tended to overuse) with physical prowess, preferably exercised under conditions of one kind or another of combat or danger. He demanded uncompromising honesty in private and public affairs, but had no trouble describing that practical compromising which the tough world of politics demanded. He was as little concerned with serious theological argument as most Americans, and like most he was conventionally religious and recommended religious observance as fitting and proper. His autobiographical work shows he could laugh at himself, but in important matters he was often given to insistent self-justification. In much of this he was more typically American than is perhaps comfortable to contemplate at the end of the twentieth century. But the political, social, and moral confusions of the end of our century offer little to justify the smug superiority that often accompanies analysis of the past.

We must not take Roosevelt or his work out of time, but use his writing to understand him and his age. The work of few writers has been as revealing, prolific, and varied as the writing of Theodore Roosevelt, and with it he has bequeathed to us the detailed composite of an American mind.

This volume contains selections that represent the best and most important of Roosevelt's writing and that retain enduring interest. They are arranged topically, reflecting the varied roles and interests of TR's life, and the titles are his own. Where it has been deemed necessary to shorten the selections to a more suitable length, the editing has been done with an eye to preserving the selections' original sense and spirit. Deletions are indicated by 🌿 🌿 🌿.

I am indebted to Theodore Roosevelt, the study of whom taught me the folly of quick and simplistic judgment and the complexity of truth in history. In the preparation of this work I am obligated for advice and encouragement to colleagues who were generous with time and talent. I thank Brian Barbour, Rodney Delasanta, Suzanne Fournier, Richard Grace, Violet Halpert, and John Scanlan. Special thanks go to Simon Winder at St. Martin's Press and to Wallace Dailey, curator of the Theodore Roosevelt Collection of the Harvard College Library. Sylvia White was most patient and skillful in helping to prepare the manuscript. For their boundless confidence and constant support, I owe my gratitude to that trio to whom this effort is dedicated.

It is not the critic who counts; not the man who points out how the strong man stumbles, or where the doer of deeds could have done better. The credit belongs to the man who is actually in the arena, whose face is marred by dust and sweat and blood; who strives valiantly; . . . who spends himself in a worthy cause; who at the best knows in the end the triumph of high achievement, and who at the worst, if he fails, at least fails while daring greatly, so that his place shall never be with those cold and timid souls who know neither victory nor defeat.

—THEODORE ROOSEVELT,
from his address at the Sorbonne, 1910

THEODORE ROOSEVELT

AN AMERICAN MIND

THEODORE ROOSEVELT: AN AMERICAN LIFE

On St. Valentine's Day in 1884, Alice Lee Roosevelt died in the arms of her husband, Theodore, at their home in New York City. She was twenty-two years old. Alice had given birth to a healthy daughter on the twelfth, but Bright's disease and the helplessness of Victorian medicine cut the celebration short. On another floor of the same house only a few hours earlier, Theodore had stood by the bed as his mother, Martha Bulloch Roosevelt, died of typhoid fever. His pain was beyond expression. He mumbled of a curse on his house. His diary records for that day his despair, "The light has gone out of my life." In the days after the funeral, Roosevelt proceeded to excise the recorded memories of Alice. He destroyed their letters, cut pages from his scrapbooks, and discarded photographs until he had almost literally removed her from his life. It has been recounted that after this purging was completed, he never spoke her name again. Not once does Alice appear in the autobiography he wrote years later.

His was to be a private agony, and this very private chapter of his life stands in dramatic contrast to the otherwise voluble Theodore Roosevelt whose life was in many ways, almost literally, an open book. From his days as a youthful assemblyman in Albany to the end of his life, he raised his voice and his pen to instruct a less tutored and less sensitive world in the ways of proper conduct, right thinking, and good government. The result was a massive production of history, criticism, nature writing, political analysis, and moral and patriotic exhortation. Through this work we know a great deal of the thought and temper of this man. And yet he remains an elusive character. Historians still argue whether he is to be classed as a liberal reformer or a conservative elitist. He admired the skills and envied the power of the business tycoons of his day, but in another mood called them "malefactors" and feared their greed would bring revolution to the land. He defended the interests of capital, but like his distant relation Franklin, he would be called a traitor to his class. Ahead of his time he favored equality for women, especially in matters of education, so that they could be learned and sophisticated enough to fulfill effectively the duties of—wives and mothers. A supporter of black suffrage, he was host to Booker T. Washington at a White House dinner, an act of considerable courage and little political profit in turn-of-the-century America. Yet his ideas about blacks, immigration, and Anglo-Saxon superiority cause the reader at the end of the twentieth century to wince, though they were, alas, common enough in his day. A pioneer conservationist and skilled naturalist, he kept with pride long lists of game killed and trophies taken. He who was almost physically ill at the thought that the Spanish-American War might end before he could join the fighting was also the winner of the Nobel Prize for peacemaking.

Such a litany of the contrasts and contradictions in his life and thought can be extended at length. His life and his writings show us the tensions in his actions and thoughts that troubled others but gave Roosevelt little pause. He seldom doubted. Utterly conventional in conforming to the values and customs of his class and his age, he could shock his family and friends with unconventional enterprise. So they gasped when he announced his decision to enter state politics in 1881, a time when such a career was deemed inappropriate for the "best people." Throughout his career he railed against corruption, but more than infrequently he found it necessary and proper to cooperate with party "bosses." Almost obsessed with the need to develop physical strength, to confront and conquer the dangers of the wilderness, to cultivate and display "manly" qualities, he was also a successful scholar, loved bird watching, and greatly valued the intellectual life, qualities not usually identified closely with the body-building, big- game hunting, rancher-cowboy.

Perhaps the most intriguing contradiction about Roosevelt is how he could be both unique and yet so typically American. If Americans have been, as Michael Kammen has called them, a people of paradox, Roosevelt is indeed the quintessential American. His writing expresses many of the prejudices typical of his countrymen then and now. That these ideas and values were sometimes contradictory troubled Roosevelt as little as paradox has troubled his brothers and sisters. If much of his thought was typically American, the events of his life compose a portrait of a unique and remarkable man.

Theodore Roosevelt was born to "old money." His was the seventh generation of Roosevelts since the first arrived in New Amsterdam in the seventeenth century. The second child of Martha and Theodore, Sr., he entered the world on October 27, 1858, in the family home on East Twentieth Street in New York. Born to social and financial privilege, he would eventually inherit a trust that provided an annual income of some eight thousand dollars, a comfortable but not opulent income in late nineteenth-century America. Indeed, given his tastes and the needs of a growing family, he sought to supplement that income by his writing, which in part accounts for the great volume and variety of his work.

If his was silver spoon good fortune, he was less privileged in his physical inheritance. A somewhat frail and sickly child, he suffered so greatly from bouts with asthma that at times his family feared even for his survival. That weakness, like all weakness, was simply unacceptable to young Teedie, as he was called, and he resolved to strengthen and reshape his body with the most strenuous regimen of gymnastics, exercise, and outdoor exertions. He won the battle. Slowly, as his body responded, his lungs strengthened, and Roosevelt developed a toughness and stamina that one day would startle not only New York politicians, but Dakota cowboys and African game hunters.

His intellectual gifts needed no remedial program. He was an intelligent, endlessly curious child and, in time, a well-educated young man. Especially drawn to and precociously skilled in the study of nature, for a time he entertained the suggestion of a career in science. This calling never fully matured, but he sustained his interest in science throughout his life and made valuable contributions as a naturalist by avocation. A member of the Harvard class of 1880, he graduated with high honors after four eventful years in Cambridge that he lived, as always, with great zest.

It was during his junior year at Harvard that he met Alice Lee of Chestnut Hill, who was then only seventeen. He pursued her ceaselessly over the next two years. They married on his twenty-second birthday, and he thought himself the happiest of men. After a honeymoon trip to Europe, he brought his bride home to New York and began the study of law. Little seemed to stand in the way of a prosperous and untroubled life in New York society.

Family and friends were surprised and some were dismayed when Roosevelt announced that he planned an active role in politics. The reputation of politicians in the United States had enjoyed greater approbation in earlier times when those not required by fortune to work with their hands (or brains, for that matter) devoted themselves to public service as a matter of civic obligation. Those days were past, and after the Civil War the country had entered a period of political corruption and venality unchallenged until the 1920s and unmatched until the era of Watergate and assorted other national and local "gate" scandals. For Roosevelt this meant only that good men were needed more than ever in the political fray, and he joined that battle as he did everything, with apparently limitless energy.

As was true so often in Roosevelt's life, his timing was perfect. A squabble among Republican bosses in New York's twenty-first district left the leader of one faction looking for a clean face to run for the state assembly in the fall of 1881, and TR fit the need perfectly. It would not be the first time bosses boosted Roosevelt's political fortunes, nor the first time they would reap a harvest of regret for their efforts.

And so Roosevelt launched two careers simultaneously. He won election to the assembly as he was finishing his book on the navy during the War of 1812, which soon won the praise of historians and public alike. Both his election and the very favorable reviews of his book were most gratifying to him. He would continue his two careers as author and politician through most of his life.

In Albany, Roosevelt established a pattern for his political career. He knew when to be flexible and, indeed, worked with the party and its leadership even while recognizing their often less-than-noble motives. He was a party regular and loyalist. He had no patience with self-proclaimed reformers and mocked them as do-gooders. Yet the demands of conscience and conviction forced the inevitable clash with the interests of the machine, and Roosevelt was a reformer in spite of himself. He wanted to do what was right. He would join no organized antiparty or extraparty crusades, but he would, from the inside, push and pull the regulars in the direction of progressive change. At times he succeeded. As a result his less scrupulous colleagues thought him often annoying and occasionally dangerous.

Instinct and habit gave Roosevelt an advantage over his colleagues and competitors; he worked harder than anyone else. He knew more than most, and what he did not know he took the time to learn. He read rapidly and voluminously and forgot little. The result was a record of achievement and a grudging respect from the old party men who had greeted his arrival in Albany with amusement but few expectations. One sign of this growing stature came at the start of his second year in the legislature, when he was honored by his party caucus in the House with the nomination for the office of Speaker. The honor would have been significantly more beneficial had the Democrats not firmly controlled the House, making Roosevelt's chances of election amply remote. A year later when the Republicans won control of the House, the prize was given to another, and TR was deeply disappointed. One of Roosevelt's genuinely proud moments in Albany came when he succeeded in pressing the passage of a state civil service law, a success that was supported by help from Governor Grover Cleveland. This was one of the reform achievements that aided Cleveland's climb to the presidency in 1884. Despite party differences the two men would work together again during Cleveland's second term, also in the area of civil service.

It was early in the 1884 session when Roosevelt was called back to New York City by the news of impending tragedy at home. After burying his wife and mother and leaving his daughter in the care of his sister Anna, he returned to Albany and threw himself at full speed into the work of the legislature. He fought as hard as ever for what he thought should be done, but his pain was obvious to those who worked with him. He determined to work through the year's political season and then to seek escape and refuge in the West and the Badlands of Dakota.

The presidential election of 1884 was one of the more interesting of the age. The Republican star of the day was James G. Blaine of Maine: popular, talented, but with a reputation stained by rumors of an excessively friendly and profitable relationship with certain railroad lobbies. So unhappy were reform-minded Republicans with the prospect of Blaine as president that they let it be known they would vote for a Democrat if that party would nominate an honest man. For the Democrats, out of the White House for almost twenty-four years, it was an offer too tempting to decline. They found an honest man in Grover Cleveland, who was completing his second year as a reform governor cleaning up corruption in New York. That Cleveland had fathered a child out of wedlock weighed less heavily with the reformers than Blaine's supposed civic sins, and these Mugwumps, as they were called, bolted the party and voted for Cleveland. The episode offers another insight into the political character of Theodore Roosevelt.

Doubts about Blaine's fitness for the presidency visited Roosevelt, but he was not a Mugwump. At the Republican national convention, together with Henry Cabot Lodge, he worked with his customary vigor and attendant publicity for the nomination of one George F. Edmunds, a U.S. senator from Vermont. But when the convention nominated Blaine and the campaign began, Roosevelt, though tempted to bolt, still refused to join the rebellious reformers and dutifully campaigned for Blaine in the fall.

After Cleveland's election Roosevelt returned again to Dakota, leaving his baby daughter once more in the care of his sister in New York. The trip was an escape from politics and from memory. He loved the rough life of the Badlands, barely out of frontier conditions and still a territory, and he decided now to make them a part of his life. He invested heavily in cattle and by spring moved into a newly built ranch house at Elkhorn in what is now North Dakota. He threw himself into the physically punishing and often dangerous life of hunter-rancher, pausing from time to time to write of his adventures. The persistence, intensity, and fearlessness of his cowboy antics worried his old friends in the East and amazed and delighted his new friends in Dakota. His new life strengthened his body and eased, if it did not erase, his pain.

For the next two years, Roosevelt divided his time between Dakota and New York. While he loved his Dakota life, ranching turned out to be a financial disaster, and in 1886 his political career fared little better. He was persuaded to accept the Republican nomination for mayor of New York against what all conceded were long odds. It was a three-way race against Abram S. Hewitt for the Democrats and crusading reform writer Henry George. Though he knew the odds made victory doubtful, Roosevelt was surprised and embarrassed by placing third in the contest.

But Roosevelt's personal life took a happier turn. He had for months quietly courted Edith Carow on his trips to New York and long distance from Dakota. He married Edith, a lifelong family friend and his childhood playmate, in December after the election. Edith would bring him five more children and a lifetime of family happiness.

Having lost heavily in ranching and politics, Roosevelt devoted his energies more fully to his writing for the rest of the decade. He had already established a solid reputation with his naval history, and his book *Hunting Trips of a Ranchman* was a great success. Biographies of Thomas Hart Benton and Gouverneur Morris soon followed, and in 1889 he published the first of his multivolume study *The Winning of the West*, his longest and in some ways his most important historical work. His writing earned him plaudits on both sides of the Atlantic long before he won political fame.

Despite his literary successes, Roosevelt could not remain long out of politics. He had resolved after his graduation from Harvard to be part of the "governing class," and neither a lost election nor the lack of opportunity had changed his mind. Always a faithful party man, he campaigned for Benjamin Harrison in 1888 and, with victory, hoped for office. After some disappointing delays and with pressure from Lodge, Harrison finally appointed Roosevelt to the federal Civil Service Commission. He gave to this, as to all his pursuits, his driving energy. He fought with commission colleagues, angered cabinet officers, worried the president, but strove for the most honest and effective civil service administration possible. He was, in fact, so effective that Democrat Cleveland, on reclaiming the presidency in 1892, asked Roosevelt to stay on. TR was pleased to accept, for he loved his life in the seat of government and in Washington society. During these years he participated in Washington scientific meetings at the Cosmos Club; he continued to work on *The Winning of the West* and other writings; and he was especially delighted with a coterie of close friends including Lodge, John Hay, Henry Adams (who once described Roosevelt as "pure act"), and his English friend now in the British legation, Cecil Spring-Rice.

Despite substantial success in expanding and administering the civil service, Roosevelt grew restless in the post. In the spring of 1895 he sent inquiries to New York about an appointment as a police commissioner in the reform administration of Republican mayor William L. Strong, soon to take office. New York seemed perpetually to need reforming, a condition fated to continue, and Roosevelt saw the reshaping of the police department as an exciting challenge, for corruption in it was at its worst since the days of the Tweed Ring more than two decades earlier. The appointment came, and with it election as president of the New York City police commission. Another crusade by the reformer who sneered at reform movements was about to begin. Lincoln Steffens, then a reporter for the *Evening Post*, in his autobiography described the delight with which he and Jacob Riis, a reporter for the *Evening Sun* and already a friend of Roosevelt, greeted the new commissioner on his first day in office. TR did not disappoint them.

Like a Dakota tornado Roosevelt blew up the dust. He fought with the other members of the board; he showed great instinctive skill in manipulating press coverage of his actions to stir public support; and to the delight of New Yorkers, he took to the streets, incognito, often after midnight, to check on the performance and innovative pastimes of his men on the beat. He had difficulty finding some of them, and others he found in places and postures unbecoming officers of the law on duty. Details of these forays were duly reported in the press (TR had invited a friendly newsman, Riis, to join the patrol), and New York and Roosevelt were pleased. Roosevelt, however, drew heavy fire to himself by what many believed was excessively zealous enforcement of an old law banning the sale of liquor on Sunday. His squabbling with other commissioners who were less interested in reforming the department, with members of his own Republican party who feared his zeal would jeopardize election chances, and with Senator Thomas Platt, the powerful boss of the Republican state machine, showed that many had come to regret his appointment. Roosevelt had no regrets, only the frustration of having his reforms slowed and obstructed. Nevertheless, the morale, efficiency, and reputation of the New York City police all improved during Roosevelt's two-year tenure on the commission.

In the presidential campaign of 1896, Roosevelt volunteered to hit the stump for William McKinley, for he thought William Jennings Bryan, the nominee of both the Democrats and the Populists, would lead the country to class conflict and revolution. Patriotism and party loyalty were enough to bring him into the campaign; he was always ready for a good political scrap. But his enthusiasm for this effort masked a more personal motive as well. He knew the limits of his position on the police commission, and his unfailing political sense told him it was time to move on. Ambition, for himself and for the nation, pointed him toward the post of assistant secretary of the navy.

From the days of his writing *The Naval War of 1812*, published in 1882, Roosevelt had been an advocate of a stronger navy for the United States, and as the country took its first hesitant steps into the world of imperialism in the 1890s, his concern about naval power intensified. He knew and admired Alfred Thayer Mahan, whose book *The Influence of Sea Power Upon History* was massively influential on Roosevelt's generation with its central argument that no nation could hope to be a great power without a great navy. Roosevelt meant the United States to be a great power. With his close friend Henry Cabot Lodge, Mahan, and others, Roosevelt had for some years joined in lobbying efforts in behalf of building naval armaments. Now Roosevelt saw his opportunity to join that work not from the sidelines but from a seat of power. To that end he threw himself into the campaign to elect McKinley and, after the election, would send intermediaries to persuade the new president that the appropriate reward should follow.

There were obstacles. Normally an office seeker of Roosevelt's influence and stature in the party ought not to have encountered resistance. But Roosevelt's fulsome reputation may have been part of the problem, for it carried with it an impression of impetuosity and independence that gave McKinley pause. Roosevelt grew increasingly nervous as weeks passed after the inauguration in March without the desired result, but finally in April the nomination was made, and the Roosevelts headed for Washington again.

The appointment of Theodore Roosevelt as assistant secretary of the navy begins a chapter of American history that is at once bizarre, heroic, comic, and, as far as the McKinley administration was concerned, entirely unplanned. The irrepressible assistant secretary had in some ways more influence on the course of events concerning the Spanish-American War than the president himself.

The secretary of the navy was John D. Long, a gentle and genial former congressman, who enjoyed extended rest visits to his Massachusetts home. He was happy enough to leave the day-to-day work of the navy department to his assistant during the summer of 1897. While others fled the Washington heat, Roosevelt had the time of his life revivifying the fighting capacity of the United States. Early in June he gave a speech at the Naval War College in Newport, Rhode Island, that argued the necessity of preparedness with that refrain so familiar in the twentieth century: keeping the peace requires building a massive arsenal for war. The speech attracted immediate and somewhat worried attention throughout the government and in more than one foreign capital. Nor did the furious activity in the navy department that summer go unnoticed, save perhaps by Secretary Long relaxing in Massachusetts.

Roosevelt's words and actions were serious. Although the United States had been at peace for many years, increasing American sympathy for Cuban rebels against Spanish rule, fed by real and fabricated atrocity stories in the yellow press, made war thinkable. Roosevelt thought about it frequently. When the USS *Maine*, on a visit in Havana harbor, blew up, with heavy loss of life, he turned thought into preparatory action.

One afternoon in the tense days of diplomatic exchanges with Spain that followed, Secretary Long asked Roosevelt to tend to the affairs of the department while he kept a doctor's appointment. This he would regret. In a few hours Roosevelt issued fleet orders and put into action long-planned steps to put the navy on a war footing. The most famous of these acts was to cable Commodore George Dewey, commander of the American squadron in the Pacific, directing him to Hong Kong. The plan directed Dewey to sail to and take Manila should war be declared. The next day an astonished Secretary Long surrendered to what he now deemed inevitable and allowed all the orders to stand. Hopelessly late, he concluded that he ought not to leave Roosevelt in charge of the office.

Roosevelt's navy department antics were only the start of the story of this incredible year, 1898. Immediately when war was declared late in April, he made good his earlier promise to resign his post and volunteer for combat duty. He could not urge the necessity of war on others and stay at home in safety. Some had been skeptically amused by his announced intentions, but those who knew him well, including his wife, Edith, and his friend Lodge, knew he would not be stopped. That he was by now the father of six children, the youngest of whom was only months old, did not dampen his resolve or the zest with which he prepared for duty.

Within days Roosevelt was commissioned and joined his friend Leonard Wood in raising the First U.S. Volunteer Cavalry. As lieutenant colonel, he was second in command to Wood over the regiment soon to be known as the Rough Riders. He was a few months short of his fortieth birthday.

By the time Roosevelt left the navy department, Dewey had already taken Manila. The new colonel was triumphant though he had not yet fired a shot, and for that exercise he was anxiously impatient. On June 22 the Rough Riders landed in Cuba. Two days later Roosevelt led his men into the successful battle of Las Guasimas, driving Spanish troops out of their entrenched positions. Reporters filed stories quickly, and a reputation for heroism was already building for Roosevelt. Kettle Hill, San Juan Hill, and glory lay ahead.

The glory arrived with little delay on July 1. Promoted to colonel in command of a regiment, TR, against withering Spanish rifle fire, led a charge up Kettle Hill, remaining mounted on horseback lest his men doubt his courage and lose theirs. The Rough Riders took the hill, and, with barely a pause for second wind, Roosevelt led his troops down and across to San Juan Hill to help those units storming the summit. His Rough Riders regiment was among the units suffering the heaviest losses that day, but the colonel escaped with only scratches, despite repeated close calls and a stubborn reluctance to take cover. His troops and the accompanying reporters, and through them the public at home, were much impressed.

The smoke of battle had barely cleared when offers of political candidacy were telegraphed to Roosevelt in the field. The heaviest fighting was over, and disease became the greater threat. After a brief siege of Santiago, the Spanish had surrendered by mid-July. Early in August, Roosevelt and his men were ordered to sail for Montauk on Long Island for a period of quarantine before being mustered out of service. It would be a convenient time and place for Roosevelt and others to meditate on his future.

As so often was the case in Roosevelt's career, fortuitous timing of events worked in his favor. The Republicans were in trouble in New York in 1898, their prospects for retaining the governorship damaged by charges of mismanagement and corruption. Little was decided in the state party without the approval of Senator Thomas Platt, and the boss did not like Roosevelt, was unimpressed by his Cuban exploits, and cringed at the thought of to what higher office the governorship might lead him. Nevertheless, the party needed a winner, and in the end the logic of backing Roosevelt's candidacy pressed itself even on the reluctant boss Platt. Always a regular Republican, Roosevelt had little difficulty accepting the nomination from the party machine, all the while encouraging support from reform elements in the state.

With a handful of Rough Riders by his side, Roosevelt canvassed the state with promises of honest government, war stories from Cuba, and attacks on the Democrats. The party calculations were accurate. The Republicans took the governorship by little more than seventeen thousand votes, and it was clear to the pundits that only Roosevelt could have won the day.

Roosevelt had continued his writing career throughout the decade of the 1890s. Enlarging his reputation as a historian, he was genuinely proud of his multivolume *Winning of the West*, and he continued to write essays and criticism for literary and other journals. Now, in the weeks between the election and inauguration, he quickly produced what would be one of his best-selling and most profitable works—the story of his adventures in Cuba, *The Rough Riders*. When not writing he romped with the children at Oyster Bay. Roosevelt, the hunter-warrior, loved children and reveled in child's play, and children loved him as one of their own. More than one observer of the Roosevelts marveled at Edith's skill in managing a household of seven children: Alice, her own five, and Theodore. His friend Cecil Spring-Rice once affectionately remarked that one had always to keep in mind that Roosevelt's age was "about six."

The writing and the revelry paused with the dawn of 1899 and TR's inauguration as governor. Neither stopped completely in spite of the duties of office. Roosevelt was always ready to tussle with the children, and during his term as governor he wrote a biography of Oliver Cromwell and published a compilation of his essays, *The Strenuous Life*, outlining his views of personal and public morality. *Dolce far niente* was not among the ingredients listed in his prescription for the good life.

Roosevelt used some of that remarkable energy in hammering out a successful record in his first assembly session. The inevitable clash with boss Platt was delayed a few months, but came inexorably in a dispute over tax reform. Roosevelt thought the idea that corporations holding public franchises should pay taxes to be a matter of simple justice; Platt held such a scheme to be subversive of the Republic and a peril to the survival of the capitalist system. Drawing on all the experience and skill he had husbanded from his first days in the legislature through his military exploits, Roosevelt stunningly outmaneuvered Platt and his organization men in the legislature and won passage of a significant tax-reform act. His first term was also marked by successful passage of civil service reform legislation and a series of modestly progressive labor laws. Roosevelt scorned the label "reformer" but played that role with uncanny success.

With these reforms safely passed and the promise of more to come, Platt and his men were inspired with an ingenious idea. Given his "successes" as governor of New York and his growing national reputation, the boss concluded that Roosevelt deserved promotion—he ought to be vice president of the United States. What better place to bury Roosevelt than in the vice presidency—away from New York and effectively powerless? With great devotion New York Republicans worked tirelessly to win the party nomination for their governor. And win it they did.

Roosevelt, no novice to political games or to the New York rules for such antics, soon realized what the boss intended. But he suffered a certain ambivalence about the prospects of the vice presidency. He abhorred idleness, and no public office in the government was so spared the burden of serious labor as the vice presidency. And yet, given the realities of power in the legislature and the influence of the great corporations there, he knew how difficult it would be to work with Platt for another term as governor. He would risk appearing to sell out to the machine or suffer the frustration of failure in efforts to wring more progressive reform legislation from a reluctant and Platt-dominated assembly. More positively, he was attracted by life in Washington society and the proximity to issues larger than those available in state politics, even in New York. Which office would position him best for a run for the presidency in 1904? an idea his friends were already promoting. These contending thoughts must have in part accounted for his inability to make an unequivocal under-no-circumstances statement when approached about the possibility of his nomination.

He never did close that door, and, with the help of his diligent New York "supporters," he was the leading candidate for the nomination as the Republican national convention approached in June 1900. All were not equally enthusiastic. McKinley seemed to have doubts, though to the surprise of many and the distress of his friend and longtime advisor Mark Hanna, the president announced he would throw the choice entirely to the convention. Hanna was deeply disturbed. He despised Roosevelt and thought him unfit for the office, even suggesting a certain dangerous instability. The distance between Hanna's view and that of the public and most of the delegates at Philadelphia was astronomical. Roosevelt was easily nominated, prompting the famous line attributed to Hanna castigating his Republican colleagues, "Don't you realize that there's only one life between this madman and the Presidency?" With the choice settled, Hanna wrote to McKinley admonishing him that it was now his duty to the nation to remain living through his second term.

Hanna's worry reflected his confidence in a Republican victory in November. The McKinley-Roosevelt ticket easily defeated the Democrats, led again, as in 1896, by William Jennings Bryan. Roosevelt gave hundreds of stump speeches and suggested that the election of Bryan would be little better than a red revolution for the nation and perhaps a prelude to it. He had the solid comfort of sincerity in believing much of his campaign propaganda.

Having won the office, Roosevelt entertained renewed doubts about its utility. After inauguration in March, his duties presiding over the Senate ended in a few days. In those simpler times the Congress completed such work as it had and adjourned for the year in the early spring. This left Roosevelt in the unaccustomed position of being employed but unoccupied by duties. He retreated to Oyster Bay and his family, which was always a pleasure, vacationed in the West, and accepted a few speaking chores. It was a life of somewhat unwelcome leisure. Then, in September, all changed.

President McKinley had traveled to Buffalo for the Pan-American Exposition and, on September 6, was shaking hands at a reception in the Temple of Music. Too quickly for nearby Secret Service men to stop, a young anarchist intent on reform by murder shot the president twice at close range. One wound was superficial, but one of the bullets tore through the president's stomach and could not be located in the surgery that followed almost immediately. The first fears for McKinley's survival brought cabinet officers and Roosevelt hurrying to Buffalo. But the president quickly rallied and was soon thought to be out of danger. Roosevelt, in fact, was encouraged to leave as a gesture of public reassurance. He traveled to the Adirondacks to join a planned family vacation in the mountains. On the thirteenth Roosevelt climbed Mount Marcy, the highest peak in New York, pursued by a messenger who finally caught him near the summit with word that McKinley was close to death. Before Roosevelt reached Buffalo, he was president of the United States.

Washington was unaccustomed to having a young president with a family of young children. Roosevelt was a few weeks short of his forty-third birthday, and the children ranged in age from four to seventeen. The Roosevelts transformed the staid and aging White House into a lively mansion of youthful fun and (when the president joined in, as he frequently did) sometimes raucous play. Washington society brightened with frequent and sophisticated White House entertainment. Roosevelt also brought with him an interest in art, literature, science, and the life of the intellect that was unusual among presidents. One must look back as far as John Quincy Adams to find a president of such broad interests and to Jefferson for as active a writer. Aside from transforming the life of the White House with vitality and talent, politically the new president reshaped the agenda of the presidency and the nation.

The tensions of the formative years of his political life were the tensions of Roosevelt's presidency. He wanted to do what was right, but the realities of power and interest too often interfered. He wanted to reform but was reluctant to be identified with the professional reformers of his day, whom he considered naive, impractical, and at times dangerous. His political essays clearly and repeatedly reflect this prejudice. He was sympathetic to the hardships endured by the laboring classes and showed this in his term as governor, but he mistrusted labor unions and tended to identify any expression of organized power among the masses with radical revolution. He disdained the new rich, whose wealth had come through monopolistic and other manipulative or dishonest practices at the expense of the nation. But he admired their power and, given the demands of electoral politics, courted their support. The moguls, in turn, generally shared Hanna's suspicion of Roosevelt's stability, and their tentative romance with him was dictated more by their views on the ugliness of the alternatives (Bryanism or worse) than by affection for Roosevelt, "that damned cowboy in the White House." In matters of foreign affairs, his presidency was marked both by a period of peace and a passion for military and imperial power. The contending aims brought inevitable contradictions, but these disturbed the digestion of his enemies much more than they did the conscience or the confidence of Theodore Roosevelt.

In his first annual message to Congress in December 1901, Roosevelt warned of the growing danger from corporate mergers producing monopolistic giants. In March he ordered the Justice Department to bring suit to break up the Northern Securities Company, a recently formed rail monopoly controlled by J. P. Morgan, James J. Hill, and Edward H. Harriman. Up to this time the Sherman antitrust law of 1890 had been most notable for its failure to inflict even modest damage on monopolies and for its ingenious and much more effective application against labor unions. More stunning than the government's prosecution was the resulting victory in court. Roosevelt's initiative delighted and surprised some of the Progressives, who were suspicious of his history of working relationships with conservative Republican machines. At the same time the suspicions of big business interests about his reliability were confirmed.

And so Roosevelt won a reputation as a "trustbuster." Taft, and Wilson after him, prosecuted many more trust cases than did Roosevelt, but it was he who first challenged the power of the business barons; it was he who first used the presidency to bring the attention of the public to the problem of economic concentration; and it was he who, much more effectively than Taft or Wilson, was able to generate maximum press coverage and publicity for his actions. The president was not uniformly hostile to big business and was always ready to compromise when need demanded. In 1907, for example, he agreed to allow J. P. Morgan's United States Steel, already a billion-dollar corporation, to buy the Tennessee Coal and Iron Company, promising not to invoke antitrust action. That company was about to fail and take with it several key banks, jeopardizing, Roosevelt was told, the entire banking system. In using the office to shape public opinion, to challenge the power of capital, and to intervene in the economic life of the nation, Roosevelt was re-creating the presidency for the twentieth century. The antitrust effort is helpful in understanding the Roosevelt presidency, as is the coal strike of 1902.

Always suspicious of organized labor, Roosevelt was nevertheless open to instruction. In 1902 a great coal strike halted the production of that then-vital fuel. When winter drew nearer with no settlement, he used the prestige of his office to intervene. In October he called union leaders and management to a conference at the White House. Much to his surprise and annoyance, he found the union men much more reasonable and accommodating, and he described the mine operators as arrogantly stupid. Against the advice of some of his conservative cabinet, he brought pressure on the operators by threatening to take over the mines with federal troops. The mine owners agreed to arbitration and the strike was settled. The incident brought the president a revised view of labor in the United States and confirmed a long-standing fear that the greed and stupidity of capital could, if unchecked, lead to revolution.

Through his years in office, Roosevelt became more and more popular among Progressives, though he never broke his ties with the conservatives of his party, who were a dominant bloc in Congress. It was a tight rope to walk, and the performance left neither side completely happy. His reforming impulses kept conservatives shifting between anxiety and anger. His realistic recognition of the need to compromise with a reluctant Congress left him open to charges of betrayal and hypocrisy from Progressives. He saw himself as a mediator between contending classes and a trustee of the national interest. That attitude, a reluctance to admit error, and a sense of natural (and moral) superiority combined to make Roosevelt insufferable to his enemies and on occasion to his supporters as well. Such was the complexity of Roosevelt's character and leadership that argument about them persists, unsettled by historians for almost a century.

Whatever the interpretation, the record of his presidency is impressive. The Elkins Act of 1903 and the Hepburn Act of 1906 began the first real regulation of the railroads and affirmed a federal role in the regulation of business generally. Pure food and drug and meat inspection laws gave the government new responsibilities for public health. At Roosevelt's direction millions of acres of public lands were withdrawn from sale and the foundations were laid for a national park system. No president before and few since have moved the nation to an awareness of the need for conservation as did Roosevelt. He led the United States in adjusting its democratic government to the realities of modern capitalism. While much of the industrial world toyed with one kind or another of socialism, fascism, and communism, Roosevelt was the first architect of a structure of regulated capitalism that would be enlarged by Woodrow Wilson and especially by Franklin D. Roosevelt. As Americans continue to debate whether the government does too much or not enough, they are arguing about a system that essentially began with Theodore Roosevelt.

The emergence of the United States as a world power also had much to do with the career of Theodore Roosevelt. His role began, as we have seen, when he campaigned for a strong navy and continued in his work as assistant secretary. As president, he carried a big stick and spoke loudly. He was perhaps most proud of his achievements in foreign policy, though time has been less kind in assessing some of his initiatives. For bringing the Russians and the Japanese to the peace table at the Portsmouth Conference in 1905, he was awarded the Nobel Prize. Less generous was his conduct of relations with Latin America.

As the United States gradually assumed great-power status, it joined the imperialist world. That was the kind of world it was. Insurrection in the Philippines, taken from Spain, warned Americans of the dangers and costs of colonialism. American imperialism would thereafter pursue influence and power rather than occupation and possession. So it was in Latin America.

Roosevelt was deeply proud of his role in building the Panama Canal, but that adventure was not one of his most noble. In 1903 the United States entered into negotiations with Colombia for a canal project at the isthmus. When that country balked at what it believed, with some reason, was inadequate compensation, Roosevelt was outraged. He could have tried to accommodate Colombia with a better offer. Instead, Washington inspired the hitherto placid Panama's revolt for independence from Colombia. With record-breaking haste, Washington recognized the independence of the new nation. A contingent of U.S. Marines just happened to be on training maneuvers near Panama at the time, and they were landed between the Panamanians and an approaching Colombian force. Its security assured, the new government of Panama negotiated a most friendly treaty with the United States for the construction and operation of a canal. Many years later, during the debates over renegotiating the treaty by the Carter administration, one staunch defender of the American presence in Panama declared with more accuracy than humor, "We stole it fair and square, and we should keep it." When Woodrow Wilson proposed the payment of twenty-five million dollars to Colombia in compensation for the American role in Panama, Roosevelt was beside himself with rage. For him the American enterprise had been entirely honorable, and any suggestion of apology would be permanently damaging to American interests.

Roosevelt saw a special role for the United States in the hemisphere. When corruption and mismanagement in Latin American republics threatened European intervention for the collection of debts, as was the case in Santo Domingo in 1904, Roosevelt announced a novel expansion of the Monroe Doctrine. Known since as the Roosevelt Corollary, it reserved the right of the United States to intervene if a hemisphere republic placed itself in danger of losing its independence to a European power. When this danger seemed proximate in Santo Domingo, the United States took over the collection of import duties in that country. In a modestly short time, effective customs collections and administration resolved the indebtedness, and the danger of intervention passed. But the precedent for American intervention was established, and in hands other than Roosevelt's it would cause much mischief. Despite the precedent and the bluster, the full record shows Roosevelt much more restrained in intervening in the affairs of Latin American countries than the only apparently more benign Woodrow Wilson.

Roosevelt had long championed the cause of American expansion with few apologies. His work *The Winning of the West* and other essays had defended continental expansion and settlement with no trace of regret about the treatment of the Indians. That American influence and presence in the hemisphere and the world would spread he took as a matter of the historic destiny of a great people, and he framed his argument with unembarrassed claims of superior racial endowment.

His conduct of foreign policy, as well as his domestic political battles, made Roosevelt as controversial in his day as historians have found him in reviewing the record. He remained, however, a popular figure with the electorate. He was reelected in 1904 in a landslide and would probably have won again in 1908 had he not sworn to forgo the nomination because he had served almost two full terms. Instead, his designated successor, William Howard Taft, became president. Roosevelt, confident that Taft would continue his policies, decided he should leave the political arena entirely to the new president. This allowed him to indulge his long-standing wish—to go big-game hunting in Africa.

With his son Kermit, Roosevelt spent months in 1909 hunting and traveling through Africa, collecting museum specimens and keeping detailed records of the hundreds of animal and bird kills on the safari. He allowed few experiences to go unrecorded, and his account of the adventure, *African Game Trails*, was published in 1910. He returned from Africa by way of Europe, where he was feted everywhere he went and treated as royalty by the crowned heads of the Continent. He was at this point quite possibly the most famous man in the world. At least one would have thought so from his reception by great crowds in June when he returned to New York, which welcomed him home with a huge Manhattan parade.

Though happy to be home and delighted with his reception, Roosevelt was not nearly so pleased by the political realities of party and nation. Roosevelt had supported Taft for president knowing him to be a loyal supporter and believing that the work he had started would be continued and fulfilled. But necessary reforms seemed to be lagging under the Taft administration, and even while he was still in Africa, reports reached him from friends in Washington that Taft was being subservient to big-business interests, sacrificing even important national conservation efforts.

Also while he hunted in Africa a friend sent him a book, *The Promise of American Life*, by Herbert Croly. The work was a critique of American

Progressivism with a prescription for the future. Croly argued that Progressive reformers were too closely tied to those ideas of Thomas Jefferson that emphasized states' rights and small government, ideas that were outdated and could not deal with the problems of a modern industrial society. Croly insisted that the problem of the trusts was not their size, but the absence of public influence over their activities. His prescription for this and other modern problems called for strong governments headed by strong leaders who could define a national agenda and fulfill a national destiny. Croly could have been writing about a Roosevelt presidency, and the point was not lost on the reader. Roosevelt had long been critical of Jefferson, and Croly's vision of modern government matched his own remarkably closely.

It was impossible for Roosevelt to remain silent for long. He wrote on political and other subjects as a contributing editor of *The Outlook* magazine and made speeches around the country. In August, touring western states, Roosevelt called for drastic changes in the country's direction. He described the courts as tools and defenders of corporate power at the expense of the public welfare. It was at Osawatomie, Kansas, that Roosevelt, borrowing a phrase from Croly, called for a "New Nationalism" that would put national need before personal advantage, that would see the executive as a steward of the public welfare, and that would support a government with sufficient regulatory power to deal with modern problems. His attack on corporate abuses and his argument for the subordination of property rights to human and community need were the boldest he had ever made.

These speeches were thinly veiled attacks on Taft, so thinly veiled that the target was clear to all. Henry Cabot Lodge cautioned his old friend to stop these attacks and to temper his language lest he endanger the unity of the party. For a time Roosevelt followed the advice, but not for long. His criticism of Taft and the party's Old Guard continued over the next year and more. The truth was that Roosevelt wanted to be president again, and, as many Progressives urged him to make the run, in the end he could not resist. Hesitation turned to resolution, and in February 1912 Roosevelt announced his candidacy for the Republican nomination. As he campaigned, the program he announced showed how far he had moved toward the Progressive vision of what the nation needed. Beyond his attack on the courts and the corporations, he spoke of the rights of workers in a way that would have startled the young Roosevelt and shocked many of his old Republican colleagues. He called for child labor laws, federal workmen's compensation, income and inheritance taxes, support for labor, and fulsome regulation of corporations.

Roosevelt's following was large and enthusiastic but did not extend to the controlling powers in the Republican party. The nominating convention in

Chicago remained firmly in the hands of Taft men, who included Roosevelt's old friends Lodge and Elihu Root, and Taft remained the party's choice. Citing irregularities in convention procedure, Roosevelt charged that the rules had been unfairly manipulated by the Old Guard and, with some justification, argued that a fair and open meeting would have nominated him. Many delegates committed to him were denied seats by the credentials committee, and Taft men were recognized in their place. Roosevelt said he was cheated out of the opportunity for a fair contest, and on those grounds he justified his next move. He bolted the party and called for a new convention of Progressives.

In August the hastily organized Bull Moose Progressive party nominated Roosevelt and made him the hero of a movement that had won his occasional cooperation for a dozen years or more, but with which he had never fully identified himself. Always a party regular working from within and usually disdainful of the label "reformer," he now led a third party and a reform movement.

The election returns showed the country in the mood for change. Roosevelt and Democrat Wilson advocated progressive change; Taft represented a conservative defense of things as they were. Taft finished a weak third with 3.4 million votes; Roosevelt gathered 4.1 million; and Wilson 6.2 million. Though far short of a majority, Wilson's total produced a clean electoral college win, and he became only the second Democrat in the White House since James Buchanan before the Civil War.

Withdrawing temporarily from politics, Roosevelt took time to write his autobiography and, in 1913, to embark on another wilderness hunting adventure, this time in the jungles of Brazil. He accepted a challenging opportunity to explore a portion of the interior and to chart a river whose full course was yet unknown but that he found connected eventually to the Amazon. Roosevelt was fifty-five years old; the journey was clearly dangerous; and he was cautioned by friends and family hoping to restrain him. As usual, the pleas went unheeded. He was determined to go because, he said, he thought it would be his last chance "to be a boy again." The trip was indeed dangerous. The exploring party traveled for months through steaming jungle cut repeatedly by gorges and rapids that made rowing and portage much more difficult than had been expected. An injury to Roosevelt's leg became seriously infected, and at one point he was so sick with fever there was concern for his survival. He did, of course, survive to complete both the journey and the charting of the river that now bears his name, an honor bestowed on him by the Brazilian government. *Through the Brazilian Wilderness* was written on his return, recording details of this remarkable and perilous adventure.

His return to the United States was a return to politics. Roosevelt continued as a leader of the Progressive party, but never completely cut his ties to
the Republicans. His ambivalence was not unique; many of the Progressives
in the years immediately after 1912 could not decide whether to rejoin the
Republicans or take the gamble on success with a new party. By 1916
Roosevelt was ready to return fully to Republican ranks. He came to
despise Wilson, and, when the world war broke out in 1914, with blistering
criticism he added weakness in the conduct of foreign policy and inaction
toward military preparedness to the list of Wilsonian sins. For a time he
dreamed of the White House again and did the letter writing and speech
making necessary to test the chances of nomination and election. He was
confident he could be elected; it was the nomination that was out of reach.
The party was in the hands of the regulars who had not bolted in 1912, and
they could not forgive Roosevelt, who had. A remnant of the 1912 Progressive
party nominated Roosevelt, but seeing the cause as hopeless, he declined to
accept. Instead Roosevelt returned to the fold and campaigned for the
Republican nominee, Charles Evans Hughes, giving dozens of speeches
filled with fierce attacks on Wilson, especially on his policy toward the war.

Roosevelt thought Wilson weak. He believed the Germans had given
more than necessary provocation, but Wilson had not acted, and, when
Wilson spoke of the necessity of peace without victory in Europe, Roosevelt
feared the president would never be persuaded to declare war. But the war
did come for the United States when the Germans declared unrestricted
submarine warfare and began to sink American ships early in 1917. At
Wilson's request Congress declared war in the first week of April. Roosevelt
was ready.

He applauded as his sons volunteered, and he himself began a campaign
for a commission to lead a volunteer force to France. He desperately wanted
to fight again. He tried every avenue he could think of, including direct
appeal to the president, but neither the army nor the commander-in-chief
could sanction such a quixotic gesture by the aging Roosevelt. He was a
year short of sixty now and his health had suffered, especially since his
Brazilian experience. Nevertheless, Roosevelt was determined to go once
more into battle. One reading of his plan saw a triumphal return as from
Cuba and a run for the elusive presidential prize in 1920. More likely the
reason was simpler. This was war; the bugle had sounded and the old
warhorse could not restrain himself. Even pride was set aside. Repressing
his personal feelings toward Wilson, he requested and received an audience
so he could present his plea to the president face to face. Wilson was cordial;
the meeting was friendly, but in the end the effort failed. Little in Roosevelt's

life left him as frustrated and bitter as this rebuff, and his hostility toward Wilson, whom he once described as "that old gray skunk in the White House," turned to something very much like hatred.

So Roosevelt stayed at home, doing what he could to help the war effort. He toured the country, speaking to encourage volunteers and writing for newspapers and periodicals. He was proud that all four of his boys were in the fight and looked for their letters. Then in July 1918 came the crushing news from the front. His youngest son, Quentin, a fighter pilot, was shot down and killed in a dogfight. The body was recovered by the Germans, who, upon learning his identity, buried him with full military honors. His father's pride was, if anything, stronger, but mixed now with unspeakable pain.

Grief now contributed to existing problems with his health, which caused his family growing concern. He seemed suddenly older than his sixty years and was bothered by a variety of ailments, including recurrent fevers, a legacy of Brazil. The fall of 1918 brought several ailments that weakened him further and required hospitalization, but he was able to return to his beloved Sagamore Hill on Christmas Day. On Sunday, January 5, 1919, Roosevelt retired near midnight after feeling unwell earlier in the evening. He had complained to Edith of having some difficulty breathing, but this had passed. His wife looked in on him later and found him comfortably asleep. Then, in the early hours before dawn, Theodore Roosevelt, who lived a life so full of risk taking and dangerous adventure, died in his sleep.

The Rough Rider victorious — back from Cuba at Montauk,
New York, 1898.

1

THE ROUGH RIDER

THE CAVALRY AT SANTIAGO

*I*n the weeks of training, preparation, and waiting before he sailed to Cuba during the Spanish-American War, TR lived with the most intense anxiety that the fighting would be over before he arrived. He had often dreamed and written about proving one's courage and manliness with the test of battle. That he was at the time the father of six young children gave him little pause, for he had determined he would go to Cuba if war came, and he volunteered for combat duty at the instant the war began. His fearlessness in battle blurred the distinction between courage and recklessness and amazed his own troops as much as the enemy. The account of his experiences in Cuba was first published in Scribner's in January-June 1899 and then in book form as The Rough Riders.

On June 30th we received orders to hold ourselves in readiness to march against Santiago, and all the men were greatly overjoyed, for the inaction was trying. The one narrow road, a mere muddy track along which the army was encamped, was choked with the marching columns. As always happened when we had to change camp, everything that the men could not carry, including, of course, the officers' baggage, was left behind.

About noon the Rough Riders struck camp and drew up in column beside the road in the rear of the First Cavalry. Then we sat down and waited for hours before the order came to march, while regiment after regiment passed by, varied by bands of tatterdemalion Cuban insurgents, and by mule-trains with ammunition. Every man carried three days' provisions. We had succeeded in borrowing mules sufficient to carry along the dynamite-gun and the automatic Colts. At last, toward mid-afternoon, the First and Tenth Cavalry, ahead of us, marched, and we followed. . . . Every few minutes there would be a stoppage in front, and at the halt I would make the men sit or lie down beside the track, loosening their packs. The heat was intense as we passed through the still, close jungle, which formed a wall on either hand. Occasionally we came to gaps or open spaces, where some regiment was camped, and now and then one of these regiments, which apparently had been left out of its proper place, would file into the road, breaking up our line of march. As a result, we finally found ourselves following merely the tail of the regiment ahead of us, an infantry regiment being thrust into the interval. Once or twice we had to wade streams. Darkness came on, but we still continued to march. It was about eight o'clock when we turned to the left and climbed El Poso Hill, on whose summit there was a ruined ranch and sugar factory, now, of course, deserted. Here I found General Wood, who was arranging for the camping of the brigade. Our own arrangements for the night were simple. I extended each troop across the road into the jungle, and then the men threw down their belongings where they stood and slept on their arms. Fortunately, there was no rain.

❧ ❧ ❧

As the sun rose the men fell in, and at the same time a battery of field-guns was brought up on the hillcrest just beyond, between us and toward Santiago. It was a fine sight to see the great horses straining under the lash as they whirled the guns up the hill and into position.

Our brigade was drawn up on the hither side of a kind of half basin, a big band of Cubans being off to the left. As yet we had received no orders, except that we were told that the main fighting was to be done by Lawton's infantry division, which was to take El Caney, several miles to our right, while we were simply to make a diversion. This diversion was to be made mainly with the artillery, and the battery which had taken position immediately in front of us was to begin when Lawton began.

It was about six o'clock that the first report of the cannon from El Caney came booming to us across the miles of still jungle. It was a very lovely morning, the sky of cloudless blue, while the level, shimmering rays from the just-risen sun brought into fine relief the splendid palms which here and there towered above the lower growth. The lofty and beautiful mountains hemmed in the Santiago plain, making it an amphitheatre for the battle.

Immediately our guns opened, and at the report great clouds of white smoke hung on the ridge crest. For a minute or two there was no response. Wood and I were sitting together, and Wood remarked to me that he wished our brigade could be moved somewhere else, for we were directly in line of any return fire aimed by the Spaniards at the battery. Hardly had he spoken when there was a peculiar whistling, singing sound in the air, and immediately afterward the noise of something exploding over our heads. It was shrapnel from the Spanish batteries. We sprung to our feet and leaped on our horses. Immediately afterward a second shot came which burst directly above us; and then a third. From the second shell one of the shrapnel bullets dropped on my wrist, hardly breaking the skin, but raising a bump about as big as a hickory-nut. The same shell wounded four of my regiment, one of them being Mason Mitchell, and two or three of the regulars were also hit, one losing his leg by a great fragment. . . . I at once hustled my regiment over the crest of the hill into the thick underbrush, where I had no little difficulty in getting them together again into column.

Meanwhile the firing continued for fifteen or twenty minutes, until it gradually died away. As the Spaniards used smokeless powder, their artillery had an enormous advantage over ours, and, moreover, we did not have the best type of modern guns, our fire being slow.

As soon as the firing ceased, Wood formed his brigade, with my regiment in front, and gave me orders to follow behind the First Brigade, which was just moving off the ground. In column of fours we marched down the trail toward the ford of the San Juan River. We passed two or three regiments of infantry, and were several times halted before we came to the ford. . . .

Our orders had been of the vaguest kind, being simply to march to the right and connect with Lawton—with whom, of course, there was no chance of our connecting. No reconnaissance had been made, and the exact position and strength of the Spaniards was not known. A captive balloon was up in the air at this moment, but it was worse than useless. A previous proper reconnaissance and proper lookout from the hills would have given us exact information. As it was, Generals Kent, Sumner, and Hawkins had to be their own reconnaissance, and they fought their troops so well that we won anyhow.

I was now ordered to cross the ford, march half a mile or so to the right, and then halt and await further orders; and I promptly hurried my men across, for the fire was getting hot, and the captive balloon, to the horror of everybody, was coming down to the ford. I got my men across before it reached the ford. There it partly collapsed and remained, causing severe loss of life, as it indicated the exact position where the Tenth and the First Cavalry, and the infantry, were crossing.

As I led my column slowly along, under the intense heat, through the high grass of the open jungle, the First Brigade was to our left and the firing between it and the Spaniards on the hills grew steadily hotter and hotter. After a while I came to a sunken lane, and as by this time the First Brigade had stopped and was engaged in a stand-up fight, I halted my men and sent back words for orders. As we faced toward the Spanish hills my regiment was on the right with next to it and a little in advance the First Cavalry, and behind them the Tenth. In our front the Ninth held the right, the Sixth the centre, and the Third the left; but in the jungle the lines were already overlapping in places. Kent's infantry were coming up, farther to the left.

Captain Mills was with me. The sunken lane, which had a wire fence on either side, led straight up toward, and between, the two hills in our front, the hill on the left, which contained heavy blockhouses, being farther away from us than the hill on our right, which we afterward grew to call Kettle Hill, and which was surmounted merely by some large ranch buildings or haciendas, with sunken brick-lined walls and cellars. I got the men as well sheltered as I could. Many of them lay close under the bank of the lane, others slipped into the San Juan River and crouched under its hither bank, while the rest lay down behind the patches of bushy jungle in the tall grass. The heat was intense, and many of the men were already showing signs of exhaustion. The sides of the hills in front were bare; but the country up to them was, for the most part, covered with such dense jungle that in charging through it no accuracy of formation could possibly be preserved.

The fight was now on in good earnest, and the Spaniards on the hills were engaged in heavy volley firing. The Mauser bullets drove in sheets through the trees and the tall jungle grass, making a peculiar whirring or rustling sound; some of the bullets seemed to pop in the air, so that we thought they were explosive; and, indeed, many of those which were coated with brass did explode, in the sense that the brass coat was ripped off, making a thin plate of hard metal with a jagged edge, which inflicted a ghastly wound. These bullets were shot from a .45- caliber rifle carrying smokeless powder, which was much used by the guerillas and irregular Spanish troops. The Mauser bullets themselves made a small, clean hole, with the result that the wound healed in a most astonishing manner. One or two of our men who were shot in the head had the skull blown open, but elsewhere the wounds from the minute steel-coated bullet, with its very high velocity, were certainly nothing like as serious as those made by the old large-caliber, low-power rifle. If a man was shot through the heart, spine, or brain he was, of course, killed instantly; but very few of the wounded died—even under the appalling conditions which prevailed, owing to the lack of attendance and supplies in the field-hospitals with the army.

ᘜ ᘜ ᘜ

The most serious loss that I and the regiment could have suffered befell just before we charged. Bucky O'Neill was strolling up and down in front of his men, smoking his cigarette, for he was inveterately addicted to the habit. He had a theory that an officer ought never to take cover—a theory which was, of course, wrong, though in a volunteer organization the officers certainly expose themselves very fully, simply for the effect on the men; our regimental toast on the transport running: "The officers; may the war last until each is killed, wounded, or promoted." As O'Neill moved to and fro, his men begged him to lie down, and one of the sergeants said: "Captain, a bullet is sure to hit you." O'Neill took his cigarette out of his mouth, and blowing out a cloud of smoke laughed and said: "Sergeant, the Spanish bullet isn't made that will kill me." A little later he discussed for a moment with one of the regular officers the direction from which the Spanish fire was coming. As he turned on his heel a bullet struck him in the mouth and came out at the back of his head; so that even before he fell his wild and gallant soul had gone out into the darkness.

My orderly was a brave young Harvard boy, Sanders, from the quaint old Massachusetts town of Salem. The work of an orderly on foot, under the blazing sun, through the hot and matted jungle, was very severe, and finally the heat overcame him. He dropped; nor did he ever recover fully, and later he died from fever. In his place I summoned a trooper whose name I did not know. Shortly afterward, while sitting beside the bank, I directed him to go back and ask whatever general he came across if I could not advance, as my men were being much cut up. He stood up to salute and then pitched forward across my knees, a bullet having gone through his throat, cutting the carotid.

❧ ❧ ❧

I sent messenger after messenger to try to find General Sumner or General Wood and get permission to advance, and was just about making up my mind that in the absence of orders I had better "march toward the guns," when Lieutenant Colonel Dorst came riding up through the storm of bullets with the welcome command "to move forward and support the regulars in the assault on the hills in front." General Sumner had obtained authority to advance from Lieutenant Miley, who was representing General Shafter at the front, and was in the thick of the fire. The general at once ordered the first brigade to advance on the hills, and the second to support it. He himself was riding his horse along the lines, superintending the fight. Later I overheard a couple of my men talking together about him. What they said illustrates the value of a display of courage among the officers in hardening their soldiers; for their theme was how, as they were lying down under a fire which they could not return, and were in consequence feeling rather nervous, General Sumner suddenly appeared on horseback, sauntering by quite unmoved; and, said one of the men: "That made us feel all right. If the general could stand it, we could."

The instant I received the order I sprang on my horse and then my "crowded hour" began. The guerillas had been shooting at us from the edges of the jungle and from their perches in the leafy trees, and as they used smokeless powder, it was almost impossible to see them, though a few of my men had from time to time responded. We had also suffered from the hill on our right front, which was held chiefly by guerillas, although there were also some Spanish regulars with them, for we found their dead. I formed my men in column of troops, each troop extended in open skirmishing order, the right resting on the wire fences which bordered the sunken lane. Captain Jenkins led the first squadron, his eyes literally dancing with joyous excitement.

I started in the rear of the regiment, the position in which the colonel should theoretically stay. Captain Mills and Captain McCormick were both with me as aides; but I speedily had to send them off on special duty in getting the different bodies of men forward. I had intended to go into action on foot as at Las Guasimas, but the heat was so oppressive that I found I should be quite unable to run up and down the line and superintend matters unless I was mounted; and, moreover, when on horseback, I could see the men better and they could see me better.

❧ ❧ ❧

I soon found that I could get that line, behind which I personally was, faster forward than the one immediately in front of it, with the result that the two rearmost lines of the regiment began to crowd together; so I rode through them both, the better to move on the one in front. This happened with every line in succession, until I found myself at the head of the regiment.

Both lieutenants of B Troop from Arizona had been exerting themselves greatly, and both were overcome by the heat; but Sergeants Campbell and Davidson took it forward in splendid shape. Some of the men from this troop and from the other Arizona troop (Bucky O'Neill's) joined me as a kind of fighting tail.

The Ninth Regiment was immediately in front of me, and the First on my left, and these went up Kettle Hill with my regiment. The Third, Sixth, and Tenth went partly up Kettle Hill (following the Rough Riders and the Ninth and First), and partly between that and the blockhouse hill, which the infantry were assailing. General Sumner in person gave the Tenth the order to charge the hills; and it went forward at a rapid gait. The three regiments went forward more or less intermingled, advancing steadily and keeping up a heavy fire. Up Kettle Hill Sergeant George Berry, of the Tenth, bore not only his own regimental colors but those of the Third, the color-sergeant of the Third having been shot down; he kept shouting, "Dress on the colors, boys, dress on the colors!" as he followed Captain Ayres, who was running in advance of his men, shouting and waving his hat. The Tenth Cavalry lost a greater proportion of its officers than any other regiment in the battle— eleven out of twenty-two.

By the time I had come to the head of the regiment we ran into the left wing of the Ninth regulars, and some of the First regulars, who were lying down; that is, the troopers were lying down, while the officers were walking to and fro. The officers of the white and colored regiments alike took the greatest pride in seeing that the men more than did their duty; and the mortality among them was great.

I spoke to the captain in command of the rear platoons, saying that I had been ordered to support the regulars in the attack upon the hills, and that in my judgment we could not take these hills by firing at them, and that we must rush them. He answered that his orders were to keep his men lying where they were, and that he could not charge without orders. I asked where the colonel was, and as he was not in sight, said, "Then I am the ranking officer here and I give the order to charge"—for I did not want to keep the men longer in the open suffering under a fire which they could not effectively return. Naturally the captain hesitated to obey this order when no word had been received from his own colonel. So I said, "Then let my men through, sir," and rode on through the lines, followed by the grinning Rough Riders, whose attention had been completely taken off the Spanish bullets, partly by my dialogue with the regulars, and partly by the language I had been using to themselves as I got the lines forward, for I had been joking with some and swearing at others, as the exigencies of the case seemed to demand. When we started to go through, however, it proved too much for the regulars, and they jumped up and came along, their officers and troops mingling with mine, all being delighted at the chance. When I got to where the head of the left wing of the Ninth was lying, through the courtesy of Lieutenant Hartwick, two of whose colored troopers threw down the fence, I was enabled to get back into the lane, at the same time waving my hat, and giving the order to charge the hill on our right front. Out of my sight, over on the right, Captains McBlain and Taylor, of the Ninth, made up their minds independently to charge at just about this time; and at almost the same moment Colonels Carroll and Hamilton, who were off, I believe, to my left where we could see neither them nor their men, gave the order to advance. But of all this I knew nothing at the time. The whole line, tired of waiting, and eager to close with the enemy, was straining to go forward; and it seems that different parts slipped the leash at almost the same moment. The First Cavalry came up the hill just behind, and partly mixed with my regiment and the Ninth. As already said, portions of the Third, Sixth, and Tenth followed, while the rest of the members of these three regiments kept more in touch with the infantry on our left.

By this time we were all in the spirit of the thing and greatly excited by the charge, the men cheering and running forward between shots, while the delighted faces of the foremost officers, like Captain C. J. Stevens, of the Ninth, as they ran at the head of their troops, will always stay in my mind. As soon as I was in the line I galloped forward a few yards until I saw that the men were well started, and then galloped back to help Goodrich, who was in command of his troop, get his men across the road so as to attack the hill from that side. Captain Mills had already thrown three of the other troops of the regiment across this road for the same purpose. Wheeling around, I then again galloped toward the hill, passing the shouting, cheering, firing men, and went up the lane, splashing through a small stream; when I got abreast of the ranch buildings on the top of Kettle Hill, I turned and went up the slope. Being on horseback I was, of course, able to get ahead of the men on foot, excepting my orderly, Henry Bardshar, who had run ahead very fast in order to get better shots at the Spaniards, who were now running out of the ranch buildings. Sergeant Campbell and a number of the Arizona men, and Dudley Dean, among others, were very close behind. Stevens, with his platoon of the Ninth, was abreast of us; so were McNamee and Hartwick. Some forty yards from the top I ran into a wire fence and jumped off little Texas, turning him loose. He had been scraped by a couple of bullets, one of which nicked my elbow, and I never expected to see him again. As I ran up to the hill, Bardshar stopped to shoot, and two Spaniards fell as he emptied his magazine. These were the only Spaniards I actually saw fall to aimed shots by any one of my men, with the exception of two guerillas in trees.

Almost immediately afterward the hill was covered by the troops, both Rough Riders and the colored troopers of the Ninth, and some men of the First.

ⓦ ⓦ ⓦ

No sooner were we on the crest than the Spaniards from the line of the hills in our front, where they were strongly entrenched, opened a very heavy fire upon us with their rifles. They also opened upon us with one or two pieces of artillery, using time fuses which burned very accurately, the shells exploding right over our heads.

On the top of the hill was a huge iron kettle, or something of the kind, probably used for sugar-refining. Several of our men took shelter behind this. We had a splendid view of the charge on the San Juan blockhouse to our left, where the infantry of Kent, led by Hawkins, were climbing the hill. Obviously the proper thing to do was to help them, and I got the men together and started them volley-firing against the Spaniards in the San Juan blockhouse and in the trenches around it. We could only see their heads; of course this was all we ever could see when we were firing at them in their trenches. Stevens was directing not only his own colored troopers, but a number of Rough Riders; for in a melee good soldiers are always prompt to recognize a good officer, and are eager to follow him.

We kept up a brisk fire for some five or ten minutes; meanwhile we were much cut up ourselves. Gallant Colonel Hamilton, than whom there was never a braver man, was killed, and equally gallant Colonel Carroll wounded. When near the summit Captain Mills had been shot through the head, the bullet destroying the sight of one eye permanently and of the other temporarily. He would not go back or let any man assist him, sitting down where he was waiting until one of the men brought him word that the hill was stormed. Colonel Veile planted the standard of the First Cavalry on the hill, and General Sumner rode up. He was fighting his division in great form, and was always himself in the thick of the fire. As the men were much excited by the firing, they seemed to pay very little heed to their own loses.

Suddenly, above the cracking of the carbines, rose a peculiar drumming sound, and some of the men cried: "The Spanish machine-guns!" Listening, I made out that it came from the flat ground to the left, and jumped to my feet, smiting my hand on my thigh, and shouting aloud with exultation: "It's the Gatlings, men, our Gatlings!" Lieutenant Parker was bringing his four Gatlings into action, and shoving them nearer and nearer the front. Now and then the drumming ceased for a moment; then it would resound again, always closer to San Juan Hill, which Parker, like ourselves, was hammering to assist the infantry attack. Our men cheered lustily. We saw much of Parker after that, and there was never a more welcome sound than his Gatlings as they opened. It was the only sound which I ever heard my men cheer in battle.

The infantry got nearer and nearer the crest of the hill. At last we could see the Spaniards running from the rifle-pits as the Americans came on in their final rush. Then I stopped my men for fear they should injure their comrades, and called to them to charge the next line of trenches, on the hills in our front, from which we had been undergoing a good deal of punishment. Thinking that the men would all come, I jumped over the wire fence in front of us and started at the double; but, as a matter of fact, the troopers were so excited, what with shooting and being shot, and shouting and cheering, that they did not hear, or did not heed me; and after running about a hundred yards I found I had only five men along with me. Bullets were ripping the grass all around us, and one of the men, Clay Green, was mortally wounded; another, Winslow Clark, a Harvard man, was shot first in the leg and then through the body. He made not the slightest murmur, only asking me to put his water canteen where he could get at it, which I did; he ultimately recovered. There was no use going on with the remaining three men, and I bade them stay where they were while I went back and brought up the rest of the brigade. This was a decidedly cool request, for there was really no possible point in letting them stay there while I went back; but at the moment it seemed perfectly natural to me, and apparently so to them, for they cheerfully nodded, and sat down in the grass, firing back at the line of trenches from which the Spaniards were shooting at them. Meanwhile, I ran back, jumped over the wire fence, and went over the crest of the hill, filled with anger against the troopers, and especially those of my own regiment, for not having accompanied me. They, of course, were quite innocent of wrong-doing; and even while I taunted them bitterly for not having followed me, it was all I could do not to smile at the look of injury and surprise that came over their faces, while they cried out: "We didn't hear you, we didn't see you go, Colonel; lead on now, we'll sure follow you." I wanted the other regiments to come too, so I ran down to where General Sumner was and asked him if I might make the charge; and he told me to go and that he would see that the men followed. By this time everybody had his attention attracted, and when I leaped over the fence again, with Major Jenkins beside me, the men of the various regiments which were already on the hill came with a rush, and we started across the wide valley which lay between us and the Spanish entrenchments. Captain Dimmick, now in command of the Ninth, was bringing it forward; Captain McBlain had a number of Rough Riders mixed with his troop, and led them all together; Captain Taylor had been severely wounded. The long-legged men like Greenway, Goodrich, Sharp-shooter Proffit, and others, outstripped the rest of us, as we had a considerable distance to go. Long before we got near them the Spaniards ran, save a few here and there, who either surrendered or were shot down. When we reached the trenches we found them filled with dead bodies in the light blue and white uniform of the Spanish regular army. There were very few wounded. Most of the fallen had little holes in their heads from which their brains were oozing; for they were covered from the neck down by the trenches.

🌿 🌿 🌿

There was very great confusion at this time, the different regiments being completely intermingled—white regulars, colored regulars, and Rough Riders . . .

While I was reforming the troops on the chain of hills, one of General Sumner's aides, Captain Robert Howze—as dashing and gallant an officer as there was in the whole gallant cavalry division, by the way—came up with orders to me to halt where I was, not advancing farther, but to hold the hill at all hazards. Howze had his horse, and I had some difficulty in making him take proper shelter; he stayed with us for quite a time, unable to make up his mind to leave the extreme front, and meanwhile jumping at the chance to render any service, of risk or otherwise, which the moment developed.

I now had under me all the fragments of the six cavalry regiments which were at the extreme front, being the highest officer left there, and I was in immediate command of them for the remainder of the afternoon and that night.

🌿 🌿 🌿

Our artillery made one or two efforts to come into action on the firing-line of the infantry, but the black powder rendered each attempt fruitless.

The Spanish guns used smokeless powder, so that it was difficult to place them. In this respect they were on a par with their own infantry and with our regular infantry and dismounted cavalry; but our only two volunteer regiments, the Second Massachusetts and the Seventy-first New York, and our artillery, all had black powder. This rendered the two volunteer regiments, which were armed with the antiquated Springfield, almost useless in the battle, and did practically the same thing for the artillery wherever it was formed within rifle-range. When one of the guns was discharged a thick cloud of smoke shot out and hung over the place, making an ideal target, and in a half-minute every Spanish gun and rifle within range was directed at the particular spot thus indicated; the consequence was that after a more or less lengthy stand the gun was silenced or driven off. We got no appreciable help from our guns on July 1st. Our men were quick to realize the defects of our artillery, but they were entirely philosophic about it, not showing the least concern at its failure. On the contrary, whenever they heard our artillery open they would grin as they looked at one another and remark, "There go the guns again; wonder how soon they'll be shut up," and shut up they were sure to be. The light battery of Hotchkiss one-pounders, under Lieutenant J. B. Hughes, of the Tenth Cavalry, was handled with conspicuous gallantry.

On the hill slope immediately around me I had a mixed force composed of members of most of the cavalry regiments, and a few infantrymen. There were about fifty of my Rough Riders with Lieutenants Goodrich and Carr. Among the rest were perhaps a score of colored infantrymen, but, as it happened, at this particular point without any of their officers. No troops could have behaved better than the colored soldiers had behaved so far; but they are, of course, peculiarly dependent upon their white officers. Occasionally they produce non-commissioned officers who can take the initiative and accept responsibility precisely like the best class of whites; but this cannot be expected normally, nor is it fair to expect it. With the colored troops there should always be some of their own officers; whereas, with the white regulars, as with my own Rough Riders, experience showed that the non-commissioned officers could usually carry on the fight by themselves if they were once started, no matter whether their officers were killed or not.

At this particular time it was trying for the men, as they were lying flat on their faces, very rarely responding to the bullets, shells, and shrapnel which swept over the hilltop, and which occasionally killed or wounded one of their number. Major Albert G. Forse, of the First Cavalry, a noted Indian fighter, was killed about this time. One of my best men, Sergeant

Greenly, of Arizona, who was lying beside me, suddenly said: "Beg pardon, Colonel; but I've been hit in the leg." I asked: "Badly?" He said: "Yes, Colonel; quite badly." After one of his comrades had helped him fix up his leg with a first-aid-to-the-injured bandage, he limped off to the rear.

None of the white regulars or Rough Riders showed the slightest sign of weakening; but under the strain the colored infantrymen (who had none of their officers) began to get a little uneasy and to drift to the rear, either helping wounded men, or saying that they wished to find their own regiments. This I could not allow, as it was depleting my line, so I jumped up, and walking a few yards to the rear, drew my revolver, halted the retreating soldiers, and called out to them that I appreciated the gallantry with which they had fought and would be sorry to hurt them, but that I should shoot the first man who, on any pretense whatever, went to the rear. My own men had all sat up and were watching my movements with utmost interest; so was Captain Howze. I ended my statement to the colored soldiers by saying, "Now, I shall be very sorry to hurt you, and you don't know whether or not I will keep my word, but my men can tell you that I always do"; whereupon my cow-punchers, hunters, and miners solemnly nodded their heads and commented in chorus exactly as if in a comic opera: "He always does; he always does!"

This was the end of the trouble, for the "smoked Yankees"— as the Spaniards called the colored soldiers—flashed their white teeth at one another, as they broke into broad grins, and I had no more trouble with them, they seeming to accept me as one of their own officers. The colored cavalrymen had already so accepted me; in return, the Rough Riders, although for the most part southwesterners, who have a strong color prejudice, grew to accept them with hearty good-will as comrades, and were entirely willing, in their own phrase, "to drink out of the same canteen." Where all the regular officers did so well, it is hard to draw any distinction; but in the cavalry division a peculiar meed of praise should be given to the officers of the Ninth and Tenth for their work, and under their leadership the colored troops did as well as any soldiers could possibly do.

In the course of the afternoon the Spaniards in our front made the only offensive movement which I saw them make during the entire campaign; for what were ordinarily called "attacks" upon our lines consisted merely of heavy firing from their trenches and from their skirmishers. In this case they did actually begin to make a forward movement, their cavalry coming up as well as the marines and reserve infantry, while their skirmishers, who were always bold, redoubled their activity. It could not be called a charge, and not only was it not pushed home, but it was stopped almost as soon as it began, our men immediately running forward to the crest of the hill with shouts of delight at seeing their enemies at last come into the open. A few seconds' firing stopped their advance and drove them into the cover of the trenches.

They kept up a very heavy fire for some time longer, and our men again lay down, only replying occasionally. Suddenly we heard on our right the peculiar drumming sound which had been so welcome in the morning, when the infantry were assailing the San Juan blockhouse. The Gatlings were up again! I started over to inquire, and found that Lieutenant Parker, not content with using his guns in support of the attacking forces, had thrust them forward to the extreme front of the fighting-line, where he was handling them with great effect. From this time on, throughout the fighting, Parker's Gatlings were on the right of my regiment, and his men and mine fraternized in every way. He kept his pieces at the extreme front, using them on every occasion until the last Spanish shot was fired. Indeed, the dash and efficiency with which the Gatlings were handled by Parker was one of the most striking features of the campaign; he showed that a first-rate officer could use machine-guns, on wheels, in battle and skirmish, in attacking and defending trenches, alongside of the best troops, and to their great advantage.

As night came on, the firing gradually died away. Before this happened, however, Captains Morton and Boughton, of the Third Cavalry, came over to tell me that a rumor had reached them to the effect that there had been some talk of retiring and that they wished to protest in the strongest manner. I had been watching them both, as they handled their troops with the cool confidence of the veteran regular officer, and had been congratulating myself that they were off toward the right flank, for as long as they were there, I knew I was perfectly safe in that direction. I had heard no rumor about retiring, and I cordially agreed with them that it would be far worse than a blunder to abandon our position.

To attack the Spaniards by rushing across open ground, or through wire entanglements and low, almost impossible jungle, without the help of artillery, and to force unbroken infantry, fighting behind earthworks and armed with the best repeating weapons, supported by cannon, was one thing; to repel such an attack ourselves, or to fight our foes on anything like even terms in the open, was quite another thing. No possible number of Spaniards coming at us from in front could have driven us from our position, and there was not a man on the crest who did not eagerly and devoutly hope that our opponents would make the attempt, for it would surely have been followed, not merely by a repulse, but by our immediately taking the city. There was not an officer or a man on the firing-line, so far as I saw them, who did not feel this way. . . .

Soon after dark, General Wheeler, who in the afternoon had resumed command of the cavalry division, came to the front. A very few words with General Wheeler reassured us about retiring. He had been through too much heavy fighting in the Civil War to regard the present fight as very serious, and he told us not to be under any apprehension, for he had sent word that there was no need whatever of retiring, and was sure we would stay where we were until the chance came to advance. He was second in command; and to him more than to any other one man was due the prompt abandonment of the proposal to fall back—a proposal which, if adopted, would have meant shame and disaster.

Shortly afterward General Wheeler sent us orders to entrench. The men of the different regiments were now getting in place again and sifting themselves out. All of our troops who had been kept at Kettle Hill came forward and rejoined us after nightfall. During the afternoon Greenway, apparently not having enough to do in the fighting, had taken advantage of a lull to explore the building himself, and had found a number of Spanish entrenching tools, picks, and shovels, and these we used in digging trenches along our line. The men were very tired, indeed, but they went cheerfully to work, all the officers doing their part.

Crockett, the ex-revenue officer from Georgia, was a slight man, not physically very strong. He came to me and told me he didn't think he would be much use in digging, but that he had found a lot of Spanish coffee and would spend his time making coffee for the men, if I approved. I did approve very heartily, and Crockett officiated as cook for the next three or four hours until the trench was dug, his coffee being much appreciated by all of us.

🌿 🌿 🌿

We finished digging the trench soon after midnight, and then the worn-out men laid down in rows on their rifles and dropped heavily to sleep. About one in ten of them had blankets taken from the Spaniards. Henry Bardshar, my orderly, had procured one for me. He, Goodrich, and I slept together. If the men without blankets had not been so tired that they fell asleep anyhow, they would have been very cold, for, of course, we were all drenched with sweat, and above the waist had on nothing but our flannel shirts, while the night was cool, with a heavy dew. Before anyone had time to wake from the cold, however, we were all awakened by the

Spaniards, whose skirmishers suddenly opened fire on us. Of course, we could not tell whether or not this was the forerunner of a heavy attack, for our cossack posts were responding briskly. It was about three o'clock in the morning, at which time men's courage is said to be at the lowest ebb, but the cavalry division was certainly free from any weakness in that direction. At the alarm everybody jumped to his feet and the stiff, shivering, haggard men, their eyes only half opened, all clutched their rifles and ran forward to the trench on the crest of the hill.

The sputtering shots died away and we went to sleep again. But in another hour dawn broke and the Spaniards opened fire in good earnest. There was a little tree only a few feet away, under which I made my headquarters, and while I was lying there, with Goodrich and Keyes, a shrapnel burst among us, not hurting us in the least, but with the sweep of its bullets killing or wounding five men in our rear, one of whom was a singularly gallant young Harvard fellow, Stanley Hollister. An equally gallant young fellow from Yale, Theodore Miller, had already been mortally wounded. Hollister also died.

The Second Brigade lost more heavily than the First; but neither its brigade commander nor any of its regimental commanders were touched, while the commander of the First Brigade and two of its three regimental commanders had been killed or wounded.

In this fight our regiment had numbered four hundred and ninety men, as, in addition to the killed and wounded of the first fight, some had to go to the hospital for sickness and some had been left behind with the baggage, or were detailed on other duty. Eighty-nine were killed and wounded: the heaviest loss suffered by any regiment in the cavalry division. The Spaniards made a stiff fight, standing firm until we charged home. They fought much more stubbornly than at Las Guasimas. We ought to have expected this, for they have always done well in holding entrenchments. On this day they showed themselves to be brave foes, worthy of honor for their gallantry.

In the attack on the San Juan hills our forces numbered about six thousand six hundred. There were about four thousand five hundred Spaniards against us. Our total loss in killed and wounded was one thousand and seventy-one. Of the cavalry division there were, all told, some two thousand three hundred officers and men, of whom three hundred and seventy-five were killed and wounded. In the division over a fourth of the officers were killed or wounded, their loss being relatively half as great again as that of the enlisted men—which was as it should be.

I think we suffered more heavily than the Spaniards did in killed and wounded (though we also captured some scores of prisoners). It would have been very extraordinary if the reverse was the case, for we did the charging; and to carry earthworks on foot with dismounted cavalry, when these earthworks are held by unbroken infantry armed with the best modern rifles, is a serious task.

Assistant secretary of the navy, 1898.

2

THE HISTORIAN

THE WINNING OF THE WEST
The Spread of the English-Speaking Peoples

*T*he Winning of the West *is the longest and in some ways the most arresting of TR's historical writing. Dedicated to historian of the West Francis Parkman, the work was originally published in four volumes between 1889 and 1896 by G. P. Putnam's Sons. The focus on race, racial differences, and what TR calls "race-history" should be understood in the context of the attitudes toward race among intellectuals of the late nineteenth century, which today can only be called racism. The impact of a distorted Darwinism, a generation of pseudo-scientific treatises contending Nordic superiority, and a certain discomfort with the increasingly massive immigration to the United States from southern and eastern Europe, areas that were thought to have produced less fit "breeds," convinced that generation of university scholars and others that national and personal destinies were determined by racial stock. This theme recurs again and again in TR's writing as a fascinating counter-point (somewhat odd to the mind of the late twentieth century) to his commitment to democracy and civil equality. Even while conceding outrageous incidents, TR defended the taking of western lands without apology.*

♦◊♦

During the past three centuries the spread of the English-speaking peoples over the world's waste spaces has been not only the most striking feature in the world's history, but also the event of all others most far-reaching in its effects and its importance.

The tongue which Bacon feared to use in his writings, lest they should remain forever unknown to all but the inhabitants of a relatively unimportant insular kingdom, is now the speech of two continents. The Common Law which Coke jealously upheld in the southern half of a single European island is now the law of the land throughout the vast regions of Australasia, and of America north of the Rio Grande. The names of the plays that Shakespeare wrote are household words in the mouths of mighty nations whose wide domains were to him more unreal than the realm of Prester John. Over half the descendants of their fellow countrymen of that day now dwell in lands which, when these three Englishmen were born, held not a single white inhabitant; the race which, when they were in their prime, was hemmed in between the North and the Irish seas, to-day holds sway over worlds whose endless coasts are washed by the waves of the three great oceans.

There have been many other races that at one time or another had their great periods of race expansion—as distinguished from mere conquest—but there has never been another whose expansion has been either so broad or so rapid. At one time, many centuries ago, it seemed as if the Germanic peoples, like their Celtic foes and neighbors, would be absorbed into the all-conquering Roman power, and merging their identity in that of the victors, would accept their law, their speech, and their habits of thought. But this danger vanished forever on the day of the slaughter by the Teutoburger Wald, when the legions of Vaus were broken by the rush of Hermann's wild warriors.

Two or three hundred years later the Germans, no longer on the defensive, themselves went forth from their marshy forests, conquering and to conquer. For century after century they swarmed out of the dark woodland east of the Rhine and north of the Danube; and as their force spent itself, the movement was taken up by their brethren who dwelt along the coasts of the Baltic and the North Atlantic. From the Volga to the Pillars of Hercules, from Sicily to Britain, every land in turn bowed to the warlike prowess of the stalwart sons of Odin. Rome and Novgorod, the imperial city of Italy as well as the squalid capital of Muscovy, acknowledged the sway of kings of Teutonic or Scandinavian blood.

In most cases, however, the victorious invaders merely intruded themselves among the original and far more numerous owners of the land, ruled over them, and were absorbed by them. This happened to both Teuton and

Scandinavian—to the descendants of Alaric as well as to the children of Rurik. The Dane in Ireland became a Celt; the Goth of the Iberian peninsula became a Spaniard; Frank and Norwegian alike were merged into the mass of Romance-speaking Gauls, who themselves finally grew to be called by the names of their masters. Thus it came about that though the German tribes conquered Europe they did not extend the limits of Germany nor the sway of the German race. On the contrary, they strengthened the hands of the rivals of the people from whom they sprang. They gave rulers—kaisers, kings, barons, and knights—to all the lands they overran; here and there they imposed their own names on kingdoms and principalities—as in France, Normandy, Burgundy, and Lombardy; they grafted the feudal system on the Roman jurisprudence, and interpolated a few Teutonic words in the Latin dialects of the peoples they had conquered; but, hopelessly outnumbered, they were soon lost in the mass of their subjects, and adopted from them their laws, their culture, and their language. As a result, the mixed races of the south—the Latin nations as they are sometimes called— strengthened by the infusion of northern blood, sprang anew into vigorous life, and became for the time being the leaders of the European world.

There was but one land whereof the winning made a lasting addition to Germanic soil; but this land was destined to be of more importance in the future of the Germanic peoples than all their continental possessions, original and acquired, put together. The day when the keels of the Low Dutch sea-thieves first grated on the British coast was big with the doom of many nations. There sprang up in conquered southern Britain, when its name had been significantly changed to England, that branch of the Germanic stock which was in the end to grasp almost literally world-wide power, and by its over-shadowing growth to dwarf into comparative insignificance all its kindred folk. At the time, in the general wreck of the civilized world, the making of England attracted but little attention. Men's eyes were riveted on the empires conquered by the hosts of Alaric, Theodoric, and Clovis, not on the swarm of little kingdoms and earldoms founded by the nameless chiefs who led each his band of hard-rowing, hard-fighting henchmen across the stormy waters of the German Ocean. Yet the rule and the race of Goth, Frank, and Burgund have vanished from off the earth, while the sons of the unknown Saxon, Anglian, and Friesic warriors now hold in their hands the fate of the coming years.

After the great Teutonic wanderings were over, there came a long lull, until, with the discovery of America, a new period of even vaster race expansion began. During this lull the nations of Europe took on their present shapes. Indeed, the so-called Latin nations—the French and Spaniards, for instance—may be said to have been born after the first set of migrations ceased. Their national history, as such, does not really begin until about that time, whereas that of the Germanic peoples stretches back unbroken to the days when we first hear of their existence. It would be hard to say which one of half a dozen races that existed in Europe during the early centuries of the present era should be considered as especially the ancestor of the modern Frenchman or Spaniard. When the Romans conquered Gaul and Iberia they did not in any place drive out the ancient owners of the soil; they simply Romanized them, and left them as the base of the population. By the Frankish and Visigothic invasions another strain of blood was added, to be speedily absorbed, while the invaders took the language of the conquered people, and established themselves as the ruling class. Thus the modern nations who sprang from this mixture derive portions of their governmental system and general policy from one race, most of their blood from another, and their language, law, and culture from a third.

The English race, on the contrary, has a perfectly continuous history. When Alfred reigned, the English already had a distinct national being; when Charlemagne reigned, the French, as we use the term to-day, had no national being whatever. The Germans of the mainland merely overran the countries that lay in their path; but the sea-rovers who won England to a great extent actually displaced the native Britons. The former were absorbed by the subject-races; the latter, on the contrary, slew or drove off or assimilated the original inhabitants. Unlike all the other Germanic swarms, the English took neither creed nor custom, neither law nor speech, from their beaten foes. At the time when the dynasty of the Capets had become firmly established at Paris, France was merely part of a country where Latinized Gauls and Basques were ruled by Latinized Franks, Goths, Burgunds, and Normans; but the people across the Channel then showed little trace of Celtic or Romance influence. It would be hard to say whether Vercingetorix or Caesar, Clovis or Syagrius, has the better right to stand as the prototype of a modern French general. There is no such doubt in the other case. The average Englishman, American, or Australian of to-day who wishes to recall the feats of power with which his race should be credited in the shadowy dawn of its history, may go back to the half-mythical glories of Hengist and Horsa, perhaps to the deeds of Civilis the Batavian, or to those of the hero of the Teutoburger fight, but certainly to the wars neither of the Silurian chief Caractacus nor of his conqueror, the Emperor Vespasian.

Nevertheless, when, in the sixteenth century, the European peoples began to extend their dominions beyond Europe, England had grown to differ profoundly from the Germanic countries of the mainland. A very large

Celtic element had been introduced into the English blood, and, in addition, there had been a considerable Scandinavian admixture. More important still were the radical changes brought by the Norman conquest; chief among them the transformation of the old English tongue into the magnificent language which is now the common inheritance of so many wide-spread peoples. England's insular position, moreover, permitted it to work out its own fate comparatively unhampered by the presence of outside powers; so that it developed a type of nationality totally distinct from the types of the European mainland.

All this is not foreign to American history. The vast movement by which this continent was conquered and peopled cannot be rightly understood if considered solely by itself. It was the crowning and greatest achievement of a series of mighty movements, and it must be taken in connection with them. Its true significance will be lost unless we grasp, however roughly, the past race-history of the nations who took part therein.

When, with the voyages of Columbus and his successors, the great period of extra-European colonization began, various nations strove to share in the work. Most of them had to plant their colonies in lands across the sea; Russia, alone, was by her geographical position enabled to extend her frontiers by land, and, in consequence, her comparatively recent colonization of Siberia bears some resemblance to our own work in the Western United States. The other countries of Europe were forced to find their outlets for conquest and emigration beyond the ocean, and, until the colonists had taken firm root in their new homes, the mastery of the seas thus became a matter of vital consequence.

Among the lands beyond the ocean America was the first reached and the most important. It was conquered by different European races, and shoals of European settlers were thrust forth upon its shores. These sometimes displaced and sometimes merely overcame and lived among the natives. They also, to their own lasting harm, committed a crime whose short-sighted folly was worse than its guilt, for they brought hordes of African slaves, whose descendants now form immense populations in certain portions of the land. Throughout the continent we therefore find the white, red, and black races in every stage of purity and intermixture. One result of this great turmoil of conquest and immigration has been that, in certain parts of America, the lines of cleavage of race are so far from coinciding with the lines of cleavage of speech that they run at right angles to them — as in the four communities of Ontario, Quebec, Hayti, and Jamaica.

Each intruding European power, in winning for itself new realms beyond the seas, had to wage a twofold war, overcoming the original inhabitants with one hand, and with the other warding off the assaults of the kindred nations that were bent on the same schemes. Generally, the contests of the latter kind were much the most important. The victories by which the struggles between the European conquerors themselves were ended deserve lasting commemoration. Yet, sometimes, even the most important of them, sweeping though they were, were in parts less sweeping than they seemed. It would be impossible to overestimate the far-reaching effects of the over-throw of the French power in America; but Lower Canada, where the fatal blow was given, itself suffered nothing but a political conquest, which did not interfere in the least with the growth of a French state along both sides of the lower St. Lawrence. In a somewhat similar way Dutch communities have held their own, and indeed have sprung up, in South Africa.

All the European nations touching on the Atlantic seaboard took part in the new work, with very varying success—Germany alone, then rent by many feuds, having no share therein. Portugal founded a single state, Brazil. The Scandinavian nations did little; their chief colony fell under the control of the Dutch. The English and the Spaniards were the two nations to whom the bulk of the new lands fell, the former getting much the greater portion. The conquests of the Spaniards took place in the sixteenth century. The West Indies and Mexico, Peru and the limitless grass plains of what is now the Argentine Confederation—all these and the lands lying between them had been conquered and colonized by the Spaniards before there was a sin-gle English settlement in the New World, and while the fleets of the Catholic king still held for him the lordship of the ocean. Then the cumbrous Spanish vessels succumbed to the attacks of the swift warships of Holland and England, and the sun of the Spanish world-dominion set as quickly as it had risen. Spain at once came to a standstill; it was only here and there that she even extended her rule over a few neighboring Indian tribes, while she was utterly unable to take the offensive against the French, Dutch, and English. But it is a singular thing that these vigorous and powerful newcom-ers, who had so quickly put a stop to her further growth, yet wrested from her very little of what was already hers. They plundered a great many Spanish cities and captured a great many Spanish galleons, but they made no great or lasting conquest of Spanish territory. Their mutual jealousies, and the fear each felt of the others, were among the main causes of this state of things; and hence it came about that after the opening of the seventeenth century the wars they waged against one another were of far more ultimate consequence than the wars they waged against the former mistress of the western world. England in the end drove both France and Holland from the field; but it was under the banner of the American Republic, not under that of the British monarchy, that the English-speaking peoples first won vast stretches of land from the descendants of the Spanish conquerors.

❧ ❧ ❧

It is of vital importance to remember that the English and Spanish conquests in America differed from each other very much as did the original conquests which gave rise to the English and the Spanish nations. The English had exterminated or assimilated the Celts of Britain, and they substantially repeated the process with the Indians of America; although of course in America there was very little, instead of very much, assimilation. The Germanic strain is dominant in the blood of the average Englishman, exactly as the English strain is dominant in the blood of the average American. Twice a portion of the race has shifted its home, in each case undergoing a marked change, due both to outside influence and to internal development; but in the main retaining, especially in the last instance, the general race characteristics.

It was quite otherwise in the countries conquered by Cortes, Pizarro, and their successors. Instead of killing or driving off the natives as the English did, the Spaniards simply sat down in the midst of a much more numerous aboriginal population. The process by which Central and South America became Spanish bore very close resemblance to the process by which the lands of southeastern Europe were turned into Romance-speaking countries. The bulk of the original inhabitants remained unchanged in each case. . . .

The settlement of the United States and Canada, throughout most of their extent, bears much resemblance to the later settlement of Australia and New Zealand. The English conquest of India and even the English conquest of South Africa come in an entirely different category. The first was a mere political conquest, like the Dutch conquest of Java or the extension of the Roman Empire over parts of Asia. South Africa in some respects stands by itself, because there the English are confronted by another white race which it is as yet uncertain whether they can assimilate, and, what is infinitely more important, because they are there confronted by a very large native population with which they cannot mingle, and which neither dies out nor recedes before their advance. It is not likely, but it is at least within the bounds of possibility, that in the course of centuries the whites of South Africa will suffer a fate akin to that which befell the Greek colonists in the Tauric Chersonese, and be swallowed up in the overwhelming mass of black barbarism.

On the other hand, it may fairly be said that in America and Australia the English race has already entered into and begun the enjoyment of its great inheritance. When these continents were settled they contained the largest tracts of fertile, temperate, thinly peopled country on the face of the globe. We cannot rate too highly the importance of their acquisition. Their successful settlement was a feat which by comparison utterly dwarfs all the European wars of the last two centuries; just as the importance of the issues at stake in the wars of Rome and Carthage completely overshadowed the interests for which the various contemporary Greek kingdoms were at the same time striving.

⁂

The extension of the English, westward through Canada, since the War of the Revolution has been in its essential features merely a less important repetition of what has gone on in the northern United States. The goldminer, the transcontinental railway, and the soldier have been the pioneers of civilization. The chief point of difference, which was but small, arose from the fact that the whole of western Canada was for a long time under the control of the most powerful of all the fur companies, in whose employ were very many French *voyageurs* and *coureurs de bois*. From these there sprang up in the valleys of the Red River and the Saskatchewan a singular race of halfbreeds, with a unique semicivilization of their own. It was with these halfbreeds, and not, as in the United States, with the Indians, that the settlers of north-western Canada had their main difficulties.

In what now forms the United States, taking the country as a whole, the foes who had to be met and overcome were very much more formidable. The ground had to be not only settled but conquered, sometimes at the expense of the natives, often at the expense of rival European races. As already pointed out, the Indians themselves formed one of the main factors in deciding the fate of the continent. They were never able in the end to avert the white conquest, but they could often delay its advance for a long spell of years. The Iroquois, for instance, held their own against all comers for two centuries. Many other tribes stayed for a time the oncoming white flood, or even drove it back; in Maine, the settlers were for a hundred years confined to a narrow strip of seacoast. Against the Spaniards, there were even here and there Indian nations who definitely recovered the ground they had lost.

When the whites first landed, the superiority and, above all, the novelty of their arms gave them a very great advantage. But the Indians soon became accustomed to the newcomers' weapons and style of warfare. By the time the English had consolidated the Atlantic colonies under their rule, the Indians had become what they have remained ever since, the most formidable savage foes ever encountered by colonists of European stock. Relatively to their numbers, they have shown themselves far more to be dreaded than the Zulus or even the Maoris.

Their presence had caused the process of settlement to go on at unequal rates of speed in different places; the flood has been hemmed in at one point, or has been forced to flow round an island of native population at another. Had the Indians been as helpless as the native Australians were, the continent of North America would have had an altogether different history. It would not only have been settled far more rapidly, but also on very different lines. Not only have the red men themselves kept back the settlements, but they have also had a very great effect upon the outcome of the struggles between the different intrusive European peoples. Had the original inhabitants of the Mississippi valley been as numerous and unwarlike as the Aztecs, De Soto would have repeated the work of Cortes, and we would very possibly have been barred out of the greater portion of our present domain. Had it not been for their Indian allies, it would have been impossible for the French to prolong, as they did, their struggle with their much more numerous English neighbors.

The Indians have shrunk back before our advance only after fierce and dogged resistance. They were never numerous in the land, but exactly what their numbers were when the whites first appeared is impossible to tell. Probably an estimate of half a million for those within the limits of the present United States is not far wrong; but in any such calculation there is of necessity a large element of mere rough guesswork. Formerly writers greatly overestimated their original numbers, counting them by millions. Now it is the fashion to go to the other extreme, and even to maintain they have not decreased at all. This last is a theory that can only be upheld on the supposition that the whole does not consist of the sum of the parts; for whereas we can check off on our fingers the tribes that have slightly increased, we can enumerate scores that have died out almost before our eyes. Speaking broadly, they have mixed but little with the English (as distinguished from the French and Spanish) invaders. They are driven back, or die out, or retire to their own reservations; but they are not often assimilated. Still, on every frontier, there is always a certain amount of assimilation going on, much more than is commonly admitted, and whenever a French or Spanish community has been absorbed by the energetic Americans, a certain amount of Indian blood has been absorbed also. There seems to be a chance that in one part of our country, the Indian Territory, the Indians, who are continually advancing in civilization, will remain as the ground element of the population, like the Creoles in Louisiana, or the Mexicans in New Mexico.

❦ ❦ ❦

[I]t is well always to remember that at the day when we began our career as a nation we already differed from our kinsmen of Britain in blood as well as in name; the word American already had more than a merely geographical signification. Americans belong to the English race only in the sense in which Englishmen belong to the German. The fact that no change of language has accompanied the second wandering of our people, from Britain to America, as it accompanied their first, from Germany to Britain, is due to the further fact that when the second wandering took place the race possessed a fixed literary language, and, thanks to the ease of communication, was kept in touch with the parent stock. The change of blood was probably as great in one case as in the other. The modern Englishman is descended from a Low-Dutch stock, which, when it went to Britain, received into itself an enormous infusion of Celtic, a much smaller infusion of Norse and Danish, and also a certain infusion of Norman-French blood. When this new English stock came to America it mingled with and absorbed into itself immigrants from many European lands, and the process has gone on ever since. It is to be noted that, of the new blood thus acquired, the greatest proportion has come from the Dutch and German sources, and the next greatest from Irish, while the Scandinavian element comes third, and the only other of much consequence is French Huguenot. Thus it appears that no new element of importance has been added to the blood. Additions have been made to the elemental race-strains in much the same proportion as these were originally combined.

Some latter-day writers deplore the enormous immigration to our shores as making us a heterogeneous instead of a homogeneous people; but as a matter of fact we are less heterogeneous at the present day than we were at the outbreak of the Revolution. Our blood was as much mixed a century ago as it is now. No State now has a smaller proportion of English blood than New York or Pennsylvania had in 1775. Even in New England, where the English stock is the purest, there was a certain French and Irish mixture; in Virginia there were Germans in addition. In the other colonies, taken as a whole, it is not probable that much over half of the blood was English; Dutch, French, German, and Gaelic communities abounded.

But all were being rapidly fused into one people. As the Celt of Cornwall and the Saxon of Wessex are now alike Englishmen, so in 1775 Hollander and Huguenot, whether in New York or South Carolina, had become Americans, undistinguishable from the New Englanders and Virginians, the descendants of the men who followed Cromwell or charged behind Rupert.

When the great Western movement began we were already a people by ourselves. Moreover, the immense immigration from Europe that has taken place since had little or no effect on the way in which we extended our boundaries; it only began to be important about the time when we acquired our present limits. These limits would in all probability be what they are now even if we had not received a single European colonist since the Revolution.

Thus the Americans began their work of Western conquest as a separate and individual people, at the moment when they sprang into national life. It has been their great work ever since.

A Note on Helen Hunt Jackson and Other Writers on Relations with the Indians

In a concluding note to his chapter on the Algonquins in The Winning of the West, *TR shows his disdain for historians who write polemics and for those he describes as "foolish sentimentalist" reformers and "amiable but maudlin fanatics" who "misread" the past. His chapter about the Indian Wars of 1784 to 1787 is a distinctly unsentimental (TR would have said realistic) view of relations with the Indians.*

It is greatly to be wished that some competent person would write a full and true history of our national dealings with the Indians. Undoubtedly the latter have often suffered terrible injustice at our hands. A number of instances, such as the conduct of the Georgians to the Cherokees in the early part of the present century [nineteenth], or the whole treatment of Chief Joseph and his Nez Perces, might be mentioned, which are indelible blots on our fair fame; and yet, in describing our dealings with the red men as a whole, historians do us much less than justice.

It was wholly impossible to avoid conflicts with the weaker race, unless we were willing to see the American continent fall into the hands of some other strong power; and even had we adopted such a ludicrous policy, the Indians themselves would have made war upon us. It cannot be too often insisted that they did not own the land; or, at least, that their ownership was merely such as that claimed often by our own white hunters. If the Indians really owned Kentucky in 1775, then in 1776 it was the property of Boone and his associates and to dispossess one party was as great a wrong as to dispossess the other. To recognize the Indian ownership of the limitless prairies and forests of this continent—that is, to consider the dozen squalid savages who hunted at long intervals over a territory of a thousand square miles as owning it outright—necessarily implies a similar recognition of the claims of every white hunter, squatter, horse thief, or wandering cattleman. Take as an example the country round the Little Missouri. When the cattlemen, the first actual settlers, came into this land in 1882, it was already scantily peopled by a few white hunters and trappers. The latter were extremely jealous of intrusion; they had held their own in spite of the Indians, and, like the Indians, the inrush of settlers and the consequent destruction of the game meant their own undoing; also, again like the Indians, they felt that their having hunted over the soil gave them a vague prescriptive right to its sole occupation, and they did their best to keep actual settlers out. In some cases, to avoid difficulty, their nominal claims were bought up; generally, and rightly, they were disregarded. Yet they certainly had as good a right to the Little Missouri country as the Sioux have to most of the land on their present reservations. In fact, the mere statement of the case is sufficient to show the absurdity of asserting that the land really belonged to the Indians. The different tribes have always been utterly unable to define their own boundaries. Thus the Delawares and Wyandots, in 1785, though entirely separate nations, claimed and, in a certain sense, occupied almost exactly the same territory.

Moreover, it was wholly impossible for our policy to be always consistent. Nowadays we undoubtedly ought to break up the great Indian reservations, disregard the tribal governments, allot the land in severalty (with, however, only a limited power of alienation), and treat the Indians as we do other citizens, with certain exceptions for their sakes as well as ours. But this policy, which it would be wise to follow now, would have been wholly impracticable a century since. Our central government was then too weak either effectively to control its own members or adequately to punish aggressions made upon them; and even if it had been strong, it would probably have proved impossible to keep entire order over such a vast, sparsely peopled frontier, with such turbulent element on both sides. The Indians could not be treated as individuals at that time. There was no possible alternative, therefore, to treating their tribes as nations, exactly as the French and English had done before us. Our difficulties were partly inherited from these, our predecessors, were partly caused by our own misdeeds, but were mainly the inevitable result of the conditions under which the problem had to be solved; no human wisdom or virtue could have worked out a peaceable solution. As a nation, our Indian policy is to be blamed, because of the weakness it displayed, because of its short-sightedness, and its occasional leaning to the policy of the sentimental humanitarians; and we have often promised what was impossible to perform; but there has been little willful wrongdoing. Our government almost always tried to act fairly by the tribes; the governmental agents (some of whom have been dishonest, and others foolish, but who, as a class, have been greatly traduced), in their reports, are far more apt to be unjust to the whites than to the reds; and the federal authorities, though unable to prevent much of the injustice, still did check and control the white borderers very much more effectually than the Indian sachems and war-chiefs controlled their young braves. The tribes were warlike and bloodthirsty, jealous of each other and of the whites; they claimed the land for their hunting-grounds, but their claims all conflicted with one another; their knowledge of their own boundaries was so indefinite that they were always willing, for inadequate compensation, to sell land to which they had merely the vaguest title; and yet, when once they had received the goods, were generally reluctant to make over even what they could; they coveted the goods and scalps of the whites, and the young warriors were always on the alert to commit outrages when they could do it with impunity. On the other hand, the evil-disposed whites regarded the Indians as fair game for robbery and violence of any kind; and the far larger number of well-disposed men, who would not willingly wrong any Indian, were themselves maddened by the memories of hideous injuries received. They bitterly resented the action of the government, which, in their eyes, failed to properly protect them and yet sought to keep them out of waste, uncultivated lands which they did not regard as being any more the property of the Indians than of their own hunters. With the best intentions, it was wholly impossible for any government to evolve order out of such a chaos without resort to the ultimate arbitrator—the sword.

The purely sentimental historians take no account of the difficulties under which we labored nor of the countless wrongs and provocations we endured, while grossly magnifying the already lamentably large number of injuries for which we really deserve to be held responsible. To get a fair idea of the Indians of the present day, and of our dealings with them, we have fortunately one or two excellent books, notably *Hunting Grounds of the Great West* and *Our Wild Indians*, by Colonel Richard I. Dodge (Hartford, 1882); and *Massacres of the Mountains*, by J. P. Dunn (New York, 1886). As types of the opposite class, which are worse than valueless, and which nevertheless might cause some hasty future historian, unacquainted with the facts, to fall into grievous error, I may mention *A Century of Dishonor*, by Mrs. Helen Hunt Jackson, and *Our Indian Wards* (George W. Manypenny). The latter is a mere spiteful diatribe against various army officers, and neither its manner nor its matter warrants more than an allusion. Mrs. Jackson's book is capable of doing more harm because it is written in good English, and because the author, who had lived a pure and noble life, was intensely in earnest in what she wrote, and had the most praiseworthy purpose—to prevent our committing any more injustice to the Indians. This was all most proper; every good man or woman should do whatever is possible to make the government treat the Indians of the present time in the fairest and most generous spirit, and to provide against any repetition of such outrages as were inflicted upon the Nez Perces and upon part of the Cheyennes, or the wrongs with which the civilized nations of the Indian Territory are sometimes threatened. The purpose of the book is excellent, but the spirit in which it is written cannot be called even technically honest. As a polemic, it is possible that it did not do harm (though the effect of even a polemic is marred by hysterical indifference to facts). As a history it would be beneath criticism, were it not that the high character of the author and her excellent literary work in other directions have given it a fictitious value and made it much quoted by the large class of amiable but maudlin fanatics concerning whom it may be said that the excellence of their intentions but indifferently atones for the invariable folly and ill effect of their actions. It is not too much to say that the book is thoroughly untrustworthy from cover to cover, and that not a single statement it contains should be accepted without independent proof; for even those that are not absolutely false are often as bad on account of so much of the truth having been suppressed. One effect of this is, of course, that the author's recitals of the many real wrongs of Indian tribes utterly fail to impress us, because she lays quite as much stress on those that are nonexistent, and on the equally numerous cases where the wrong-doing was wholly the other way. To get an idea of the value of the work, it is only necessary to compare her statements about almost any tribe with the real facts, choosing at random; for instance, compare her accounts of the Sioux and the plains tribes generally with those given by Colonel Dodge in his two books; or her recital of the Sandy Creek massacre with the facts as stated by Mr. Dunn — who is apt, if anything, to lean to the Indian's side.

These foolish sentimentalists not only write foul slanders about their own countrymen, but are themselves the worst possible advisers on any point touching Indian management. They would do well to heed General Sheridan's bitter words, written when many easterners were clamoring against the army authorities because they took partial vengeance for a series of brutal outrages: "I do not know how far these humanitarians should be excused on account of their ignorance; but surely it is the only excuse that can give a shadow of justification for aiding and abetting such horrid crimes."

The Indian Wars, 1784-1787

In this chapter from The Winning of the West *TR writes of war with the Indians from the perspective of the winners, unmoved by the "sentimentality" he attacks in other writings on relations with the Indians.*

After the close of the Revolution there was a short, uneasy lull in the eternal border warfare between the white men and the red. The Indians were, for the moment, daunted by a peace which left them without allies, and the feeble Federal Government attempted for the first time to aid and control the West by making treaties with the most powerful frontier tribes. Congress raised a tiny regular army and several companies were sent to the upper Ohio to garrison two or three small forts which were built upon its banks. Commissioners (one of whom was [explorer] George Rogers Clark himself) were appointed to treat with both the Northern and Southern Indians. Councils were held in various places. In 1785 and early in 1786 utterly fruitless treaties were concluded with the Shawnees, Wyandots, and Delawares, at one or other of the little forts.

About the same time, in the late fall of 1785, another treaty somewhat more noteworthy, but equally fruitless, was concluded with the Cherokees at Hopewell, on Keowee, in South Carolina. In this treaty, the commissioners promised altogether too much. They paid little heed to the rights and needs of the settlers. Neither did they keep in mind the powerlessness of the Federal Government to enforce against these settlers what their treaty promised the Indians. The pioneers along the upper Tennessee and the Cumberland had made various arrangements with bands of the Cherokees, sometimes acting on their own initiative, and sometimes on behalf of the State of North Carolina. Many of these different agreements were entered into by the whites with honesty and good faith, but were violated at will by the Indians. Others were violated by the whites, or were repudiated by the Indians as well, because of some real or fancied unfairness in the making. Under them large quantities of land had been sold or allotted, and hundreds of homes had been built on the lands thus won by the whites or ceded by the Indians. As with all Indian treaties, it was next to impossible to say exactly who had authority to represent the tribes. The commissioners paid little heed to these treaties, and drew the boundary so that quantities of land which had been entered under regular grants, and were covered by the homesteads of the frontiersmen, were declared to fall within the Cherokee line. Moreover, they even undertook to drive all settlers off these lands.

Of course, such a treaty excited the bitter anger of the frontiersmen, and they scornfully refused to obey its provisions. They hated the Indians, and, as a rule, were brutally indifferent to their rights, while they looked down on the Federal Government as impotent. Nor was the ill will to the treaty confined to the rough borderers. Many men of means found that land grants which they had obtained in good faith and for good money were declared void. Not only did they denounce the treaty, and decline to abide by it, but they denounced the motives of the commissioners, declaring, seemingly without justification, that they had ingratiated themselves with the Indians to further land speculations of their own.

As the settlers declined to pay any heed to the treaty, the Indians naturally became as discontented with it as the whites. In the following summer the Cherokee chiefs made solemn complaint that, instead of retiring from the disputed ground, the settlers had encroached yet farther upon it, and had come to within five miles of the beloved town of Chota. The chiefs added that they had now made several such treaties, each of which established boundaries that were immediately broken, and that indeed it had been their experience that after a treaty the whites settled even faster on their lands than before. Just before this complaint was sent to Congress the same chiefs had been engaged in negotiations with the settlers themselves who advanced radically different claims. The fact was that in this unsettled time the bond of governmental authority was almost as lax among the whites as among the Indians, and the leaders on each side who wished for peace were hopelessly unable to restrain their fellows who did not. Under such circumstances, the sword, or rather the tomahawk, was ultimately the only possible arbiter.

The treaties entered into with the northwestern Indians failed for precisely the opposite reason. The treaty at Hopewell promised so much to the Indians that the whites refused to abide by its terms. In the councils on the Ohio the Americans promised no more than they could and did perform; but the Indians themselves broke the treaties at once, and in all probability never for a moment intended to keep them, merely signing from a greedy desire to get the goods they were given as an earnest. They were especially anxious for spirit, for they far surpassed even the white borderers in their crazy thirst for strong drink. "We have smelled your liquor and it is very good; we hope you will give us some little kegs to carry home," said the spokesmen of a party of Chippewas, who had come from the upper Great Lakes. These frank savages, speaking thus in behalf of their far Northern brethren, uttered what was in the minds of most of the Indians who attended the councils held by the United States commissioners. They came to see what they could get by begging, or by promising what they had nei-ther the will nor the power to perform. Many of them, as in the case of the Chippewas, were from lands so remote that they felt no anxiety about white encroachments, and were lured into hostile encounter with the Americans chiefly by their own overmastering love of plunder and bloodshed.

Nevertheless, there were a few chiefs and men of note in the tribes who sincerely wished peace. One of these was Cornplanter the Iroquois. The power of the Six Nations had steadily dwindled; moreover, they did not, like the more Western tribes, lie directly athwart the path which the white advance was at the moment taking. Thus they were not drawn into open warfare, but their continual uneasiness, and the influence they still pos-sessed with the other Indians, made it an object to keep on friendly terms with them. Cornplanter, a valiant and able warrior, who had both taken and given hard blows in warring against the Americans, was among the chiefs and ambassadors who visited Fort Pitt during the troubled lull in the fron-tier war which succeeded the news of the peace of 1783. His speeches showed, as his deeds had already shown, in a high degree, that loftiness of courage, and stern, uncomplaining acceptance of the decrees of a hostile fate, which so often ennobled the otherwise gloomy and repellent traits of the Indian character. He raised no plaint over what had befallen his race; "the Great Spirit above directs us so that whatever hath been said or done must be good and right," he said in a spirit of strange fatalism well known to certain creeds, both Christian and heathen.

☙ ☙ ☙

Some of the Algonquin chiefs, notably Molunthee the Shawnee, likewise sincerely endeavored to bring about a peace. But the Western tribes, as a whole, were bent on war. They were constantly excited and urged on by the British partisan leaders, such as Simon Girty, Elliot, and Caldwell. These leaders took part in the great Indian councils, at which even tribes west of the Mississippi were represented; and though they spoke without direct authority from the British commanders at the lake posts, yet their words carried weight when they told the young red warriors that it was better to run the risk of dying like men than of starving like dogs. Many of the old men among the Wyandots and Delawares spoke against strife; but the young men were for war, and among the Shawnees, the Wabash Indians, and the Miamis, the hostile party was still stronger. A few Indians would come to one of the forts and make a treaty on behalf of their tribe, at the very moment that the other members of the same tribe were murdering and ravaging among the exposed settlements or were harrying the boats that went down the Ohio. All the tribes that entered into the treaties of peace were represented among the different parties of marauders. Over the outlaw bands there was no pretense of control; and their successes, and the numerous scalps and quantities of plunder they obtained, made them very dangerous examples to the hot-blooded young warriors everywhere. Perhaps the most serious of all obstacles to peace was the fact that the British still kept the lake posts.

The Indians who did come in to treat were sullen, and at first always insisted on impossible terms. They would finally agree to mutual concessions, would promise to keep their young men from marauding, and to allow surveys to be made, provided the settlers were driven off all lands which the Indians had not yielded; and, after receiving many gifts, would depart. The representatives of the Federal Government would then at once set about performing their share of the agreement, the most important part of which was the removal of the settlers who had built cabins on the Indian lands west of the Ohio. The Federal authorities, both military and civil, disliked the intruders as much as they did the Indians, stigmatizing them as "a banditti who were a disgrace to human nature." There was no unnecessary harshness exercised by the troops in removing the trespassers; but the cabins were torn down and the sullen settlers themselves were driven back across the river, though they protested and threatened resistance. Again and again this was done; not alone in the interest of the Indians, but in part also because Congress wished to reserve the lands for sale, with the purpose of paying off the public debt. At the same time surveying-parties were sent out. But in each case, no sooner had the Federal commissioners and their subordinates begun to perform their part of the agreement, than they were stopped by tidings of fresh outrages on the part of the very Indians with whom they had made the treaty; while the surveying-parties were driven in and forced to abandon their work.

The truth was that while the Federal Government sincerely desired peace, and strove to bring it about, the northwestern tribes were resolutely bent on war; and the frontiersmen themselves showed nearly as much inclination for hostility as the Indians. They were equally anxious to intrude on the government and on the Indian lands; for they were adventurous, the lands were valuable, and they hated the Indians, and looked down on the weak Federal authority. They often made what were legally worthless "tomahawk claims," and objected almost as much as the Indians to the work of the regular government surveyors. Even the men of note, men like George Rogers Clark, were often engaged in schemes to encroach on the land north of the Ohio; drawing on themselves the bitter reproaches not only of the

Federal authorities, but also of the Virginia government, for their cruel readiness to jeopardize the country by incurring the wrath of the Indians. The more lawless whites were as little amenable to authority as the Indians themselves; and at the very moment when a peace was being negotiated one side or the other would commit some brutal murder. While the chiefs and old Indians were delivering long-winded speeches to the Peace Commissioners, bands of young braves committed horrible ravages among the lonely settlements. Now a drunken Indian at Fort Pitt murdered an innocent white man, the local garrison of regular troops saving him with difficulty from being lynched; now a band of white ruffians gathered to attack some peaceable Indians who had come in to treat; again a white man murdered an unoffending Indian, and was seized by a Federal officer, and thrown into chains, to the great indignation of his brutal companions; and yet again another white man murdered an Indian, and escaped to the woods before he could be arrested.

Under such conditions the peace negotiations were doomed from the outset. The truce on the border was of the most imperfect description; murders and robberies by the Indians, and acts of vindictive retaliation or aggression by the whites, occurred continually and steadily increased in number.

☙ ☙ ☙

The more far-sighted and resolute among all the Indians, Northern and Southern, began to strive for a general union against the Americans. In 1786, the northwestern Indians almost formed such a union. Two thousand warriors gathered at the Shawnee towns and agreed to take up the hatchet against the Americans; British agents were present at the council; and even before the council was held, war-parties were bringing into the Shawnee towns the scalps of American settlers, and prisoners, both men and women, who were burned at the stake. But the jealousy and irresolution of the tribes prevented the actual formation of a league.

The Federal Government still feebly hoped for peace; and in the vain endeavors to avoid irritating the Indians forbade all hostile expeditions into the Indian country—though these expeditions offered the one hope of subduing the savages and preventing their inroads. By 1786, the settlers generally, including all their leaders, such as Clark, had become convinced that the treaties were utterly futile, and that the only right policy was one of resolute war.

In truth the war was unavoidable. The claims and desires of the two parties were irreconcilable. Treaties and truces were palliatives which did not touch the real underlying trouble. The white settlers were unflinchingly bent on seizing the land over which the Indians roamed, but which they did not in any true sense own or occupy. In return, the Indians were determined at all costs and hazards to keep the men of chain and compass, and of axe and rifle, and the forest-felling settlers who followed them, out of their vast and lonely hunting-grounds. Nothing but the actual shock of battle could decide the quarrel. The display of overmastering, overwhelming force might have cowed the Indians; but it was not possible for the United States, or for any European power, ever to exert or display such force far beyond the limits of the settled country. In consequence, the warlike tribes were not then, and never have been since, quelled, save by actual hard fighting, until they were overawed by the settlement of all the neighboring lands.

Nor was there any alternative to these Indian wars. It is idle folly to speak of them as being the fault of the United States Government; and it is even more idle to say that they could have been averted by treaty. Here and there, under exceptional circumstances or when a given tribe was feeble and unwarlike, the whites might gain the ground by a treaty entered into of their own free will by the Indians, without the least duress; but this was not possible with warlike and powerful tribes when once they realized that they were threatened with serious encroachment on their hunting-grounds. Moreover, looked at from the standpoint of the ultimate result, there was little real difference to the Indian whether the land was taken by treaty or by war. In the end the Delaware fared no better at the hands of the Quaker than the Wampanoag at the hands of the Puritan; the methods were far more humane in the one case than in the other, but the outcome was the same in both. No treaty could be satisfactory to the whites, no treaty served the needs of humanity and civilization, unless it gave the land to the Americans as unreservedly as any successful war.

As a matter of fact, the lands we have won from the Indians have been won as much by treaty as by war; but it was almost always war, or else the menace and possibility of war, that secured the treaty. In these treaties we have been more than just to the Indians; we have been abundantly generous, for we have paid them many times what they were entitled to; many times what we would have paid any civilized people whose claim was as vague and shadowy as theirs. By war or threat of war, or purchase, we have won from great civilized nations, from France, Spain, Russia, and Mexico, immense tracts of country already peopled by many tens of thousands of families; we have paid many millions of dollars to these nations for the land we took; but for every dollar thus paid to these great and powerful civilized commonwealths, we have paid ten, for lands less valuable, to the chiefs and warriors of the red tribes. No other conquering and colonizing nation has ever treated the original savage owners of the soil with such generosity as has the United States. Nor is the charge that the treaties with the Indians have been broken of weight itself; it depends always on the individual case. Many of the treaties were kept by the whites and broken by the Indians; others were broken by the whites themselves; and sometimes they did right. No treaties, whether between civilized nations or not, can ever be regarded as binding in perpetuity; with changing conditions, circumstances may arise which render it not only expedient, but imperative and honorable, to abrogate them.

Whether the whites won the land by treaty, by armed conquest, or, as was actually the case, by a mixture of both, mattered comparatively little so long as the land was won. It was all-important that it should be won, for the benefit of civilization and in the interests of mankind. It is, indeed, a warped, perverse, and silly morality which would forbid a course of conquest that has turned whole continents into the seats of mighty and flourishing civilized nations. All men of sane and wholesome thought must dismiss with impatient contempt the plea that these continents should be reserved for the use of scattered savage tribes, whose life was but a few degrees less meaningless, squalid, and ferocious than that of the wild beasts with whom they held joint ownership. It is as idle to apply to savages the rules of international morality which obtain between stable and cultured communities, as it would be to judge the fifth-century English conquest of Britain by the standards of to-day. Most fortunately, the hard, energetic, practical men who do the rough pioneer work of civilization in barbarous lands are not prone to false sentimentality. The people who are, are the people who stay at home. Often these stay-at-homes are too selfish and indolent, too lacking in imagination, to understand the race-importance of the work which is done by their pioneer brethren in wild and distant lands; and they judge them by standards which would only be applicable to quarrels in their own townships and parishes. Moreover, as each new land grows old, it misjudges the yet newer lands, as once it was itself misjudged. The home-staying Englishman of Britain grudges to the Africander [*sic*] his conquest of Matabeleland; and so the home-staying American of the Atlantic States dislikes to see the Western miners and cattlemen win for the use of their people the Sioux hunting-grounds. Nevertheless, it is the men actually on the borders of the longed-for ground, the men actually in contact with the savages, who in the end shape their own destinies.

The most ultimately righteous of all wars is a war with savages, though it is apt to be also the most terrible and inhuman. The rude, fierce settler who drives the savage from the land lays all civilized mankind under a debt to him. American and Indian, Boer and Zulu, Cossack and Tartar, New

Zealander and Maori—in each case the victor, horrible though many of his deeds are, has laid deep the foundations for the future greatness of a mighty people. The consequences of struggles for territory between civilized nations seem small by comparison. Looked at from the standpoint of the ages, it is of little moment whether Lorraine is part of Germany or of France, whether the northern Adriatic cities pay homage to Austrian Kaiser or Italian King; but it is of incalculable importance that America, Australia, and Siberia should pass out of the hands of their red, black, and yellow aboriginal owners, and become the heritage of the dominant world races.

༄ ༄ ༄

The men of Kentucky and of the infant Northwest could have found their struggle with the Indians dangerous enough in itself; but there was an added element of menace in the fact that back of the Indians stood the British. It was for this reason that the frontiersmen grew to regard as essential to their well-being the possession of the lake posts; so that it became with them a prime object to wrest from the British, whether by force of arms or by diplomacy, the forts they held at Niagara, Detroit, and Michilimackinac. Detroit was the most important, for it served as the headquarters for the Western Indians, who formed, for the time being, the chief bar to American advance. The British held the posts with a strong grip, in the interest of their traders and merchants. To them the land derived its chief importance from the fur trade. This was extremely valuable, and, as it steadily increased in extent and importance, the consequence of Detroit, the fitting-out town for the fur traders, grew in like measure. It was the center of a population of several thousand Canadians, who lived by the chase and by the rude cultivation of their long, narrow farms; and it was held by a garrison of three or four hundred British regulars, with auxiliary bands of American Loyalists and French-Canadian rangers, and, above all, with a formidable but fluctuating reserve force of Indian allies.

It was to the interest of the British to keep the American settlers out of the land; and therefore their aims were at one with those of the Indians. All the tribes between the Ohio and the Missouri were subsidized by them, and paid them a precarious allegiance.

༄ ༄ ༄

The British officers and the American border leaders found themselves face to face in the wilderness as rivals of one another. Sundered by interest and ambition, by education and habits of thought, trained to widely different ways of looking at life, and with the memories of the hostile past fresh in their minds, they were in no humor to do justice to one another. Each side regarded the other with jealousy and dislike, and often with bitter hatred. Each often unwisely scorned the other. Each kept green in mind the wrongs suffered at the other's hands, and remembered every discreditable fact in the other's recent history—every failure, every act of cruelty or stupidity, every deed that could be held as the consequence of the worst moral and mental shortcomings. Neither could appreciate the other's many and real virtues. The policies for which they warred were hostile and irreconcilable; the interests of the nations they represented were, as regards the northwestern wilderness, not only incompatible, but diametrically opposed. The commanders of the British posts, and the men who served under them, were moved by a spirit of stern loyalty to the empire, the honor of whose flag they upheld, and endeavored faithfully to carry out the behests of those who shaped that empire's destinies; in obedience to the will of their leaders at home they warred to keep the Northwest a wilderness, tenanted only by the Indian hunter and the white fur trader. The American frontiersmen warred to make this wilderness the heart of the greatest of all republics; they obeyed the will of no superior, they were not urged onward by any action of the supreme authorities of the land; they were moved only by the stirring ambition of a masterful people, who saw before them a continent which they claimed as their heritage. The Americans succeeded, the British failed; for the British fought against the stars in their courses, while the Americans battled on behalf of the destiny of the race.

THE CHARGE AT GETTYSBURG

This account of battle in the Civil War was one chapter TR wrote for a book co-authored with his friend Henry Cabot Lodge for the Century Company in 1895. Hero Tales from American History proved a popular work and was reprinted in many editions. It is not surprising that Roosevelt's relish of glory in battle shows through in his accounts of battlefield heroics.

The battle of Chancellorsville marked the zenith of Confederate good fortune. Immediately afterward, in June, 1863, Lee led the victorious army of northern Virginia into Pennsylvania. The South was now the invader, not the invaded, and its heart beat proudly with hopes of success; but these hopes went down in bloody wreck on July 4, when word was sent to the world that the high valor of Virginia had failed at last on the field of Gettysburg, and that in the far West, Vicksburg had been taken by the army of the "silent soldier."

At Gettysburg Lee had under him some seventy thousand men, and his opponent, Meade, about ninety thousand. Both armies were composed mainly of seasoned veterans, trained to the highest point by campaign after campaign and battle after battle; and there was nothing to choose between them as to the fighting power of the rank and file. The Union army was the larger, yet most of the time it stood on the defensive; for the difference between the generals, Lee and Meade, was greater than could be bridged by twenty thousand men. For three days the battle raged. No other battle of recent time has been so obstinate and so bloody. The victorious Union army lost a greater percentage in killed and wounded than the allied armies of England, Germany, and the Netherlands lost at Waterloo. Four of its seven corps suffered each a greater relative loss than befell the world-renowned British infantry on the day that saw the doom of the French emperor. The defeated Confederates at Gettysburg lost, relatively, as many men as the defeated French at Waterloo; but whereas the French army became a mere rabble, Lee withdrew his formidable soldiery with their courage unbroken, and their fighting power only diminished by their actual losses in the field.

The decisive moment of the battle, and perhaps of the whole war, was in the afternoon of the third day, when Lee sent forward his choicest troops in a last effort to break the middle of the Union line. The centre of the attacking force was Pickett's division, the flower of the Virginia infantry, but many other brigades took part in the assault, and the column, all told, numbered over fifteen thousand men. At the same time the Confederates attacked, the

Union left to create a diversion. The attack was preceded by a terrific cannonade, Lee gathering one hundred and fifteen guns, and opening a fire on the centre of the Union line. In response, Hunt, the Union chief of artillery, and Tyler, of the artillery reserves, gathered eighty guns on the crest of the gently sloping hill, where attack was threatened. For two hours, from one till three, the cannonade lasted, and the batteries on both sides suffered severely. In both the Union and Confederate lines caissons were blown up by the fire, riderless horses dashed hither and thither, the dead lay in heaps, and throngs of wounded streamed to the rear. Every man lay down and sought what cover he could. It was evident that the Confederate cannonade was but a prelude to a great infantry attack, and at three o'clock Hunt ordered the fire to stop, that the guns might cool, to be ready for the coming assault. The Confederates thought that they had silenced the hostile artillery, and for a few minutes their firing continued; then, suddenly, it ceased, and there was a lull.

The men on the Union side who were not at the point directly menaced peered anxiously across the space between the lines to watch the next move, while the men in the divisions which it was certain were about to be assaulted lay hugging the ground and gripping their muskets, excited, but confident and resolute. They saw the smoke clouds rise slowly from the opposite crest, where the Confederate army lay, and the sunlight glinted again on the long line of brass and iron guns which had been hidden from view during the cannonade. In another moment, out of the lifting smoke there appeared, beautiful and terrible, the picked thousands of the Southern army coming on to the assault. They advanced in three lines, each over a mile long, and in perfect order. Pickett's Virginians held the centre, with on their left the North Carolinians of Pender and Pettigrew, and on their right the Alabama regiments of Wilcox; and there were also Georgian and Tennessee regiments in the attacking force. Pickett's division, however, was the only one able to press its charge home. After leaving the woods where they started, the Confederates had nearly a mile and a half to go in their charge. As the Virginians moved, they bent slightly to the left, so as to leave a gap between them and the Alabamians on the right.

The Confederate lines came on magnificently. As they crossed the Emmetsburg Pike the eighty guns on the Union crest, now cool and in good shape, opened upon them, first with host and then with shell. Great gaps were made every second in the ranks, but the gray-clad soldiers closed up to the centre, and the color-bearers leaped to the front, shaking and waving the flags. The Union infantry reserved their fire until the Confederates were within easy range, when the musketry crashed out with a roar, and the big guns began to fire grape and canister. On came the Confederates, the men falling by hundreds, the colors fluttering in front like a little forest; for as fast as a color-bearer was shot some one else seized the flag from his hand before it fell. The North Carolinians were more exposed to the fire than any other portion of the attacking force, and they were broken before they reached the line. There was a gap between the Virginians and the Alabama troops, and this was taken advantage of by Stannard's Vermont brigade and a demi-brigade under Gates, of the Twentieth New York, who were thrust forward into it. Stannard changed front with his regiments and fell on Pickett's forces in flank, and Gates continued the attack. When thus struck in the flank, the Virginians could not defend themselves, and they crowded off toward the centre to avoid the pressure. Many of them were killed or captured; many were driven back; but two of the brigades, headed by General Armistead, forced their way forward to the stone wall on the crest, where the Pennsylvania regiments were posted under Gibbon and Webb.

The Union guns fired to the last moment, until of the two batteries immediately in front of the charging Virginians every officer but one had been struck. One of the mortally wounded officers was young Cushing, a brother of the hero of the *Albemarle* fight. He was almost cut in two, but holding his body together with one hand, with the other he fired his last gun, and fell dead, just as Armistead, pressing forward at the head of his men, leaped the wall, waving his hat on his sword. Immediately afterward the battle-flags of the foremost confederate regiments crowned the crest; but their strength was spent. The Union troops moved forward with the bayonet, and the remnant of Pickett's division, attacked on all sides, either surrendered or retreated down the hill again. Armistead fell, dying, by the body of the dead Cushing. Both Gibbon and Webb were wounded. Of Pickett's command two-thirds were killed, wounded or captured, and every brigade commander and every field-officer, save one, fell. The Virginians tried to rally, but were broken and driven again by Gates, while Stannard repeated, at the expense of the Alabamians, the movement he had made against the Virginians, and reversing his front, attacked them in flank. Their lines were torn by the batteries in front, and they fell back before the Vermonters' attack, and Stannard reaped a rich harvest of prisoners and of battle-flags.

The charge was over. It was the greatest charge in any battle of modern times, and it had failed. It would be impossible to surpass the gallantry of those that made it, or the gallantry of those that withstood it. Had there been in command of the Union army a general like Grant, it would have been followed by a counter-charge, and in all probability the war would have been shortened by nearly two years; but no counter-charge was made.

As the afternoon waned, a fierce cavalry fight took place on the Union right. Stuart, the famous Confederate cavalry commander, had moved forward to turn the Union right, but he was met by Gregg's cavalry, and there followed a contest, at close quarters with "the white arm." It closed with a desperate melee, in which the Confederates, charging under General Wade Hampton and Fitz Lee, were met in mid career by the Union generals Custer and McIntosh. All four fought, sabre in hand, at the head of their troopers, and every man on each side was put into the struggle. Custer, his yellow hair flowing, his face aflame with the eager joy of battle, was in the thick of the fight, rising in his stirrups as he called to his famous Michigan swordsmen: "Come on, you Wolverines, come on!" All that the Union infantry, watching eagerly from their lines, could see, was a vast dust-cloud where flakes of light shimmered as the sun shone upon the swinging sabres. At last the Confederate horsemen were beaten back, and they did not come forward again or seek to renew the combat; for Pickett's charge had failed, and there was no longer hope of Confederate victory.

When night fell, the Union flags waved in triumph on the field of Gettysburg; but over thirty thousand men lay dead or wounded, strewn through wood and meadow, on field and hill, where the three days' fight had surged.

NEW YORK HISTORY
1860-1890

Roosevelt wrote a history of New York in 1891 for a series on historic towns published by Longmans, Green and Co. He reveals here a view of society he would sustain for many years. He hated and feared the mob or any sign of trouble rising from the lower classes, but with equal disdain he attacked the corruption of the capitalist too blinded by "ferocious greed" to see the danger of provoking revolution among the masses. These twin hates had much to do with his vision of his own political role as a disinterested leader and just mediator between contending classes in society. His description of the qualities and character necessary in those who ought to take up the responsibilities of civic leadership can be read without strain to the imagination as a near self-portrait.

The contrast drawn in this piece between the "coarse-grained" surface of the city and its often-displayed generosity and civic spirit will not be entirely unfamiliar to New Yorkers a century later.

In 1860, New York had over eight hundred thousand inhabitants. During the thirty years that have since passed, its population has nearly doubled. If the city limits were enlarged, like those of London and Chicago, so as to take in the suburbs, the population would amount to some three millions. Recently there has been a great territorial expansion northward, beyond the Haarlem, by the admission of what is known as the Annexed District. The growth of wealth has fully kept pace with the growth of population. The city is one of the two or three greatest commercial and manufacturing centres of the world.

The ten years between 1860 and 1870 form the worst decade in the city's political annals, although the sombre picture is relieved by touches of splendid heroism, martial prowess, and civic devotion. At the outbreak of the Civil War the city was—as it has since continued to be—the stronghold of the Democratic party in the North; and unfortunately, during the Rebellion, while the Democratic party contained many of the loyal, it also contained all of the disloyal, elements. A Democratic victory at the polls, hardly, if at all, less than a Confederate victory in the field, meant a Union defeat. A very large and possibly controlling element in the city Democracy was at heart strongly disunion in sentiment, and showed the feeling whenever it dared.

At the outset of the Civil War there was even an effort made to force the city into active rebellion. The small local Democratic leaders, of the type of Isaiah Rynders, the brutal and turbulent ruffians who led the mob and controlled the politics of the lower wards, openly and defiantly threatened to make common cause with the South, and to forbid the passage of Union troops through the city. The mayor, Fernando Wood, in January, 1861, proclaimed disunion to be "a fixed fact" in a message to the Common Council, and proposed that New York should herself secede and become a free city, with but a nominal duty upon imports. The independent commonwealth was to be named "Tri-Insula," as being composed of three islands — Long, Staten, and Manhattan. The Common Council, a corrupt body as disloyal as Wood himself, received the message enthusiastically, and had it printed and circulated wholesale.

But when Sumter was fired on the whole current changed like magic. There were many more good men than bad in New York; but they had been supine, or selfish, or indifferent, or undecided, and so the bad had had it all their own way. The thunder of Sumter's guns waked the heart of the people to passionate loyalty. The bulk of the Democrats joined with the Republicans to show by word and act their fervent and patriotic devotion to the Union. Huge mass-meetings were held, and regiment after regiment was organized and sent to the front. Shifty Fernando Wood, true to his nature, went with the stream, and was loudest in proclaiming his horror of rebellion. The city, through all her best and bravest men, pledged her faithful and steadfast support to the government at Washington. The Seventh Regiment of the New York National Guards, by all odds the best regiment in the United States militia, was the first in the whole country to go to the front and reach Washington, securing it against any sudden surprise.

The Union men of New York kept their pledge of loyalty in spirit and letter. Taking advantage of the intensity of the loyal excitement, they even elected a Republican mayor. The New Yorkers of means were those whose part was greatest in sustaining the nation's credit, while almost every high-spirited young man in the city went into the army. The city, from the beginning to the end of the war, sent her sons to the front by scores of thousands. Her troops alone would have formed a large army; and on a hundred battle-fields, and throughout the harder trails of the long, dreary campaigns, they bore themselves with high courage and stern, unyielding resolution. Those who by a hard lot were forced to stay at home busied themselves in caring for the men at the front, or for their widows and orphans; and the Sanitary Commission, the Allotment Commission, and other kindred organizations which did incalculable good, originated in New York.

Yet the very energy with which New York sent her citizen soldiery to the front, left her exposed to a terrible danger. Much of the low foreign element, as well as the worst among the native-born roughs, had been hostile to the war all along, and a ferocious outbreak was produced by the enforcement of the draft in July, 1863. The mob, mainly foreign, especially Irish, but reinforced by all the native rascality of the city, broke out for three days in what are known as the draft riots. They committed the most horrible outrages, their hostility being directed especially against the unfortunate negroes, many of whom they hung or beat to death with lingering cruelty; and they attacked various charitable institutions where negroes were cared for. They also showed their hatred to the national government and its defenders in every way, and even set out to burn down a hospital filled with wounded Union soldiers, besides mobbing all government officials. From attacking government property they speedily went to assailing private property as well, burning and plundering the houses of rich and poor alike, and threatened to destroy the whole city in their anarchic fury—the criminal classes, as always in such a movement, taking the control into their own hands. Many of the baser Democratic politicians, in order to curry favor with the mob, sought to prevent effective measures being taken against it; and even the Democratic governor, Seymour, an estimable man of high private character, but utterly unfit to grapple with the times that tried men's souls, took refuge in temporizing, half measures, and concessions. The Roman Catholic archbishop and priests opposed and denounced the rioters with greater or less boldness, according to their individual temperaments.

But the governing authorities, both national and municipal, acted with courage and energy. The American people are good-natured to the point of lax indifference; but once roused, they act with the most straightforward and practical resolution. Much fear had been expressed lest the large contingent of Irish among the police and State troops would be lukewarm or doubtful, but throughout the crisis they showed to the full as much courage and steadfast loyalty as their associates of native origin. One of the most deeply mourned victims of the mob was the gallant Colonel O'Brien of the Eleventh New York Volunteers, who had dispersed a crowd of rioters with considerable slaughter, and was afterward caught by them when alone, and butchered under circumstances of foul and revolting brutality.

Most of the real working men refused to join with the rioters, except when overawed and forced into their ranks; and many of them formed themselves into armed bodies, and assisted to restore order. The city was bare of troops, for they had all been sent to the front to face Lee at Gettysburg; and the police at first could not quell the mob. As regiment after regiment was hurried back to their assistance desperate street-fighting took place. The troops and police were thoroughly aroused, and attacked the rioters with the most wholesome desire to do them harm. In a very short time after the forces of order put forth their strength the outbreak was stamped out, and a lesson inflicted on the lawless and disorderly which they never entirely forgot. Two millions of property had been destroyed, and many valuable lives lost. But over twelve hundred rioters were slain—an admirable object-lesson to the remainder.

It was several years before the next riot occurred. This was of a race or religious character. The different nationalities of New York are in the habit of parading on certain days—a particularly senseless and objectionable custom. The Orangemen on this occasion paraded on the anniversary of the Battle of the Boyne, with the usual array of flags and banners, covered with mottoes especially insulting to the Celtic Irish; the latter threatened to stop the procession, and made the attempt; but the militia had been called out, and after a moment's sharp fighting, in which three of their number and seventy or eighty rioters were slain, the mob was scattered to the four winds. For the last twenty years no serious riots have occurred, and no mob has assembled which the police could not handle without the assistance of the State troops. The outbreaks that have taken place have almost invariably been caused by strikes or other labor troubles. Yet the general order and peacefulness should not blind us to the fact that there exists ever in our midst a slumbering "volcano under the city," as under all other large cities of the civilized world. This danger must continue to exist as long as our rich men look at life from a standpoint of silly frivolity, or else pursue a commercial career in a spirit of ferocious greed and disregard of justice, while the poor feel with sullen anger the pressure of many evils—some of their own making, and some not—and are far more sensible of the wrongs they suffer than of the folly of trying to right them under the lead of ignorant visionaries or criminal demagogues.

For several years after the war there was a perfect witches' Sabbath of political corruption in New York City, which culminated during the mayoralty of Oakey Hall, who was elected in 1869. The Democratic party had absolute control of the municipal government; and this meant that the city was at the mercy of the ring of utterly unscrupulous and brutal politicians who then controlled that party, and who in time of need had friends among some of their so-called Republican opponents on whom they could always rely. Repeating, ballot-box stuffing, fraudulent voting and counting of votes, and every kind of violence and intimidation at the polls turned the elections into criminal farces. The majorities by which the city was carried for the

Democratic presidential candidate Seymour in 1868 represented the worst electoral frauds which the country ever witnessed—far surpassing even those by which Polk had been elected over Clay.

This was also the era of gigantic stock-swindling. The enormously rich stock speculators of Wall Street in their wars with one another and against the general public, found ready tools and allies to be hired for money in the State and city politicians, and in judges who were acceptable alike to speculators, politicians, and mob. There were continual contests for the control of railway systems, and "operations" in stocks which barely missed being criminal, and which branded those who took part in them as infamous in the sight of all honest men; and the courts and legislative bodies became parties to the iniquity of men composing that most dangerous of all classes, the wealthy criminal class.

Matters reached their climax in the feats of the "Tweed Ring." William M. Tweed was the master spirit among the politicians of his own party, and also secured a hold on a number of the local Republican leaders of the baser sort. He was a coarse, jovial, able man, utterly without scruple of any kind; and he organized all of his political allies and adherents into a gigantic "ring" to plunder the city. Incredible sums of money were stolen, especially in the construction of the new court-house. When the frauds were discovered, Tweed, secure in his power, asked in words that have become proverbial: "What are you going to do about it?" But the end came in 1871. Then the decent citizens, irrespective of party, banded together, urged on by the newspapers, especially the *Times* and *Harper's Weekly*—for the city press deserves the chief credit for the defeat of Tweed. At the fall elections the ring candidates were overwhelmingly defeated; and the chief malefactors were afterward prosecuted, and many of them imprisoned, Tweed himself dying in a felon's cell. The offending judges were impeached, or resigned in time to escape impeachment.

For the last twenty years our politics have been better and purer, though with plenty of corruption and jobbery left still. There are shoals of base, ignorant, vicious "heelers" and "ward workers," who form a solid, well-disciplined army of evil, led on by abler men whose very ability renders them dangerous. Some of these leaders are personally corrupt; others are not, but do almost as much harm as if they were, because they divorce political from private morality. As a prominent politician recently phrased it, they believe that "the purification of politics is an iridescent dream; the decalogue and the golden rule have no place in a political campaign." The cynicism, no less silly than vicious, with which such men regard political life is repaid by the contemptuous anger with which they themselves are regarded by all men who are proud of their country and wish her well.

If the citizens can be thoroughly waked up, and a plain, naked issue of right and wrong presented to them, they can always be trusted. The trouble is that in ordinary times the self-seeking political mercenaries are the only persons who both keep alert and understand the situation; and they commonly reap their reward. The mass of vicious and ignorant voters—especially among those of foreign origin—forms a trenchant weapon forged ready to their hand, and presents a standing menace to our prosperity; and the selfish and short-sighted indifference of decent men is only one degree less dangerous. Yet of recent years there has been among men of character and good standing a steady growth of interest in, and of a feeling of responsibility for, our politics. This otherwise most healthy growth has been at times much hampered and warped by the political ignorance and bad judgment of the leaders in the government. Too often the educated men who without having had any practical training as politicians yet turn their attention to politics, are and remain utterly ignorant of the real workings of our governmental system, and in their attitude toward our public men oscillate between excessive credulity concerning their idol of the moment and jealous, ignorant prejudice against those with whom they temporarily disagree. They forget, moreover, that the man who really counts in the world is the doer, not the mere critic—the man who actually does the work, even if roughly and imperfectly, not the man who only talks or writes about how it ought to be done.

Neither the unintelligent and rancorous partisan, nor the unintelligent and rancorous independent, is a desirable member of the body politic; and it is unfortunately true of each of them that he seems to regard with special and sour hatred, not the bad man, but the good man with whom he politically differs.

Above all, every young man should realize that it is a disgrace to him not to take active part in some way in the work of governing the city. Whoever fails to do this, fails notably in his duty to the Commonwealth.

The character of the immigration to the city is changing. The Irish, who in 1860 formed three-fifths of the foreign-born population, have come in steadily lessening numbers, until the Germans stand well at the head; while increasing multitudes of Italians, Poles, Bohemians, Russian Jews, and Hungarians—both Slavs and Magyars—continually arrive. The English and Scandinavian elements among the immigrants have likewise increased. At the present time four-fifths of New York's population are of foreign birth or parentage; and among them there has been as yet but little race intermixture, though the rising generation is as a whole well on the way to complete Americanization. Certainly hardly a tenth of the people are of old

Revolutionary American stock. The Catholic Church has continued to grow at a rate faster than the general rate of increase. The Episcopalian and Lutheran are the only Protestant churches whereof the growth has kept pace with that of the population.

The material prosperity of the city has increased steadily. There has been a marked improvement in architecture; and one really great engineering work, the bridge across the East River, was completed in 1883. The stately and beautiful Riverside Drive, skirting the Hudson, along the hills which front the river, from the middle of the island northward, is well worth mention. It is one of the most striking roads or streets of which any city can boast, and the handsome houses that are springing up along it bid fair to make the neighborhood the most attractive portion of New York. Another attractive feature of the city is Central Park, while many other parks are being planned and laid out beyond where the town has as yet been built up. There are large numbers of handsome social clubs, such as the Knickerbocker, Union, and University, and many others of a politico-social character—the most noted of them, alike for its architecture, political influence, and its important past history, being the Union League Club.

There are many public buildings which are extremely interesting as showing the growth of a proper civic spirit, and of a desire for a life with higher possibilities than money-making. There has been an enormous increase in the number of hospitals, many of them admirably equipped and managed; and the numerous Newsboys' Lodging Houses, Night Schools, Working Girls' Clubs and the like, bear witness to the fact that many New Yorkers who have at their disposal time or money are alive to their responsibilities, and are actively striving to help their less fortunate fellows to help themselves. The Cooper Union building, a gift to the city for the use of all its citizens, in the widest sense, keeps alive the memory of old Peter Cooper, a man whose broad generosity and simple kindliness of character, while not rendering him fit for the public life into which he at times sought entrance, yet inspired in New Yorkers of every class a genuine regard such as they felt for no other philanthropist. Indeed, uncharitableness and lack of generosity have never been New York failings; the citizens are keenly sensible to any real, tangible distress or need. A blizzard in Dakota, an earthquake in South Carolina, a flood in Pennsylvania—after any such catastrophe hundreds of thousands of dollars are raised in New York at a day's notice, for the relief of the sufferers; while, on the other hand, it is a difficult matter to raise money for a monument or a work of art.

❧ ❧ ❧

In science and art, in musical and literary development, much remains to be wished for; yet something has already been done. The building of the Metropolitan Museum of Art, of the American Museum of Natural History, of the Metropolitan Opera House, the gradual change of Columbia College into a University— all show a development which tends to make the city more and more attractive to people of culture; and the growth of literary and dramatic clubs, such as the Century and the Players, is scarcely less significant. The illustrated monthly magazines—the *Century, Scribner's,* and *Harper's*—occupy an entirely original position of a very high order in periodical literature.

❧ ❧ ❧

Grim dangers confront us in the future, yet there is more ground to believe that we shall succeed than that we shall fail in overcoming them. Taking into account the enormous mass of immigrants, utterly unused to self-government of any kind, who have been thrust into our midst, and are even yet not assimilated, the wonder is not that universal suffrage has worked so badly, but that it has worked so well. We are better, not worse off than we were a generation ago. There is much gross civic corruption and commercial and social selfishness and immorality, upon which we are in honor bound to wage active and relentless war. But honesty and moral cleanliness are the rule; and under the laws order is well preserved, and all men are kept secure in the possession of life, liberty and property. The sons and grandsons of the immigrants of fifty years back have as a whole become good Americans, and have prospered wonderfully, both as regards their moral and material well-being. There is no reason to suppose that the condition of the working classes as a whole has grown worse, though there are enormous bodies of them whose condition is certainly very bad. There are grave social dangers and evils to meet, but there are plenty of earnest men and women who devote their minds and energies to meeting them. With many very serious shortcomings and defects, the average New Yorker yet possesses courage, energy, business capacity, much generosity of a practical sort, and shrewd, humorous common sense. The greedy tyranny of the unscrupulous rich and the anarchic violence of the vicious and ignorant poor are ever-threatening dangers; but though there is every reason why we should realize the gravity of the perils ahead of us, there is none why we should not face them with confident and resolute hope, if only each of us, according to the measure of his capacity, will with manly honesty and good faith do his full share of the all-important duties incident to American citizenship.

THE NAVAL WAR OF 1812

His book The Naval War of 1812 *was one of TR's most important and successful writing efforts. The work had its origins in his study of the subject while still an undergraduate at Harvard. First published in 1882 by G. P. Putnam's Sons, it went through four editions by 1889. It was reprinted frequently thereafter, and more than a century after its writing it is still listed as a useful and important piece of historical writing, despite its occasional display of rather intense patriotic fervor. Roosevelt's research and writing undoubtedly had an enduring affect on his views about naval power and influenced his extraordinary and sustained efforts to increase U.S. naval armaments in the years before the Spanish-American War and during his presidency. The following are four excerpts from TR's history of the naval war.*

At the Beginning of the War

During the early years of this century [nineteenth] England's naval power stood at a height never reached before or since by that of any other nation. On every sea her navies rode, not only triumphant, but with none to dispute their sway. The island folk had long claimed the mastery of the ocean, and they had certainly succeeded in making their claim completely good during the time of bloody warfare that followed the breaking out of the French Revolution. Since the year 1792 each European nation, in turn, had learned to feel bitter dread of the weight of England's hand. In the Baltic, Sir Samuel Hood had taught the Russians that they must needs keep in port when the English cruisers were in the offing. The descendants of the Vikings had seen their whole navy destroyed at Copenhagen. No Dutch fleet ever put out after the day when, off Camperdown, Lord Duncan took possession of Van Winter's shattered ships. But a few years before 1812, the greatest sea-fighter of all time [Lord Nelson] had died in Trafalgar Bay, and in dying had crumbled to pieces the navies of France and of Spain.

From that day England's task was but to keep in port such of her foes' vessels as she had not destroyed. France alone still possessed fleets that could be rendered formidable, and so, from the Scheldt to Toulon, her harbors were watched and her coasts harried by the blockading squadrons of the English. Elsewhere the latter had no fear of their power being seriously assailed; but their vast commerce and numerous colonies needed ceaseless protection. Accordingly in every sea their cruisers could be found, of all sizes, from the stately ship of the line, with her tiers of heavy cannon and her many hundreds of men, down to the little cutter carrying but a score of souls and a couple of light guns. All these cruisers, but especially those of the lesser rates, were continually brought into contact with such of the hostile vessels as had run through the blockade, or were too small to be affected by it. French and Italian frigates were often fought and captured when they were skirting their own coasts, or had started off on a plundering cruise through the Atlantic, or to the Indian Ocean; and though the Danes had lost their larger ships they kept up a spirited warfare with brigs and gunboats. So the English marine was in constant exercise, attended with almost invariable success.

Such was Great Britain's naval power when the Congress of the United States declared war upon her. While she could number her thousand sail, the American navy included but half a dozen frigates, and six or eight sloops and brigs; and it is small matter for surprise that the British officers should have regarded their new foe with contemptuous indifference. Hitherto the American seamen had never been heard of except in connection with two or three engagements with French frigates, and some obscure skirmishes against the Moors of Tripoli; none of which could possibly attract attention in the years that saw Abourkir, Copenhagen, and Trafalgar. And yet these same petty wars were the school which raised our marines to the highest standard of excellence. A continuous course of victory, won mainly by seamanship, had made the English sailor overweeningly self-confident, and caused him to pay but little regard to maneuvering or even to gunnery. Meanwhile the American learned, by receiving hard knocks, how to give them, and belonged to a service too young to feel an overconfidence in itself. One side had let its training relax, while the other had carried it to the highest possible point. Hence our ships proved, on the whole, victorious in the apparently unequal struggle, and the men who had conquered the best seamen of Europe were now in turn obliged to succumb. Compared with the great naval battles of the preceding few years, our bloodiest conflicts were mere skirmishes, but they were skirmishes between the hitherto acknowledged kings of the ocean and new men who yet proved to be more than their equals.

❦ ❦ ❦

The first point to be remembered in order to write a fair account of this war is that the difference in fighting skill, which certainly existed between the two parties, was due mainly to training, and not to the nature of the men. It seems certain that the American had in the beginning somewhat the

advantage, because his surroundings, partly physical and partly social and
political, had forced him into habits of greater self-reliance. Therefore, on
the average, he offered rather the best material to start with; but the difference was very slight, and totally disappeared under good training. The combatants were men of the same race, differing but little from one another. On
the New England coast the English blood was as pure as in any part of
Britain; in New York and New Jersey it was mixed with that of the Dutch
settlers—and the Dutch are by race nearer to the true old English of Alfred
and Harold than are, for example, the thoroughly Anglicized Welsh of
Cornwall. Otherwise, the infusion of new blood into the English race on this
side of the Atlantic has been chiefly from three sources—German, Irish, and
Norse; and these three sources represent the elemental parts of the composite English stock in about the same proportions in which they were originally combined—mainly Teutonic, largely Celtic, and with a Scandinavian
admixture. The descendant of the German becomes as much an Anglo-
American as the descendant of the Strathclyde Celt has already become an
Anglo-Briton. Looking through names of the combatants it would be difficult to find any of one navy that could not be matched in the other—Hull or
Lawrence, Allen, Perry, or Stewart. And among all the English names on
both sides will be found many Scotch, Irish, or Welsh— Macdonough,
O'Brien, or Jones. Still stranger ones appear: the Huguenot Tattnall is one
among the American defenders of the *Constellation,* and another Huguenot
Tattnall is among the British assailants at Lake Borgne. It must always be
kept in mind that the Americans and the British are two substantially similar
branches of the great English race, which both before and after their separation have assimilated, and made Englishmen of many other peoples. The
lessons taught by the war can hardly be learned unless this identity is kept
in mind.

To understand aright the efficiency of our navy, it is necessary to take a
brief look at the character and antecedents of the officers and men who
served in it.

When war broke out the United States navy was but a few years old, yet
it already had a far from dishonorable history. The captains and lieutenants
of 1812 had been taught their duties in a very practical school, and the flag
under which they fought was endeared to them already by not a few glorious traditions—though these, perhaps, like others of their kind, had lost
none of their glory in the telling. A few of the older men had served in the
war of the Revolution, and all still kept fresh in mind the doughty deeds of
the old-time privateering war-craft. Men still talked of Biddle's daring
cruises and Barney's stubborn fights, or told of Scotch Paul and the grim

work they had who followed his fortunes. Besides these memories of an older generation, most of the officers had themselves taken part, when younger in years and rank, in deeds not a whit less glorious. Almost every man had had a share in some gallant feat, to which he, in part at least, owed his present position. The captain had perhaps been a midshipman under Truxton when he took the *Vengeance,* and had been sent aboard the captured French frigate with the prize-master; the lieutenant had borne a part in the various attacks on Tripoli, and had led his men in the desperate hand-to-hand fights in which the Yankee cutlass proved an overmatch for the Turkish and Moorish scimitars. Nearly every senior officer had extricated himself by his own prowess or skill from the dangers of battle or storm; he owed his rank to the fact that he had proved worthy of it. Thrown upon his own resources, he had learned self-reliance; he was a first-rate practical seaman, and prided himself on the way his vessel was handled. Having reached his rank by hard work, and knowing what real fighting meant, he was careful to see that his men were trained in the *essentials* of discipline, and that they knew how to handle the guns in battle as well as polish them in peace. Beyond almost any of his countrymen, he worshipped the "Gridiron Flag," and, having been brought up in the navy, regarded its honor as his own. It was, perhaps, the navy alone that thought itself a match, ship against ship, for Great Britain. The remainder of the nation pinned its faith to the army, or rather to that weakest of weak reeds, the militia. The officers of the navy, with their strong *esprit de corps,* their jealousy of their own name and record, and the knowledge, by actual experience, that the British ships sailed no faster and were no better handled than their own, had no desire to shirk a conflict with any foe, and having tried their bravery in actual service, they made it doubly formidable by cool, wary skill. Even the younger men, who had never been in action, had been so well trained by the tried veterans over them that the lack of experience was not sensibly felt.

The sailors comprising the crews of our ships were well worthy of their leaders. There was no better seaman in the world than the American Jack; he had been bred to his work from infancy, and had been off in a fishing dory almost as soon as he could walk. When he grew older, he shipped on a merchantman or whaler, and in those warlike times, when our large merchant marine was compelled to rely pretty much on itself for protection, each craft *had* to be well handled; all who were not were soon weeded out by a process of natural selection, of which the agents were French picaroons, Spanish buccaneers, and Malay pirates. It was a rough school, but it taught Jack to be both skillful and self-reliant; and he was all the better fitted to become a man-of-war's man, because he knew more about firearms than

most of his kind in foreign lands. At home he had used his ponderous duck-
ing gun with good effect on the flocks of canvasbacks in the reedy flats of
the Chesapeake, or among the sea-coots in the rough water off the New
England cliffs; and when he went on a sailing voyage the chances were even
that there would be some use for the long guns before he returned, for the
American merchant sailor could trust to no armed escort.

The wonderful effectiveness of our seamen at the date of which I am writing as well as long subsequently to it was largely due to the curious condition of things in Europe. For thirty years all the European nations had been
in a state of continuous and very complicated warfare, during the course of
which each nation in turn fought almost every other, England being usually
at loggerheads with all. One effect of this was to force an enormous proportion of the carrying trade of the world into American bottoms. The old
Massachusetts town of Salem was then one of the main depots of the East
India trade; the Baltimore clippers carried goods into the French and
German ports with small regard to the blockade; New Bedford and Sag
Harbor fitted out whalers for the Arctic seas as well as for the South Pacific;
the rich merchants of Philadelphia and New York sent their ships to all
parts of the world; and every small port had some craft in the coasting trade.
On the New England seaboard but few of the boys would reach manhood
without having made at least one voyage to the Newfoundland Banks after
codfish; and in the whaling towns of Long Island it used to be an old saying
that no man could marry till he struck his whale. The wealthy merchants of
the large cities would often send their sons on a voyage or two before they
let them enter their counting-houses. Thus it came about that a large portion
of our population was engaged in seafaring pursuits of a nature strongly
tending to develop a resolute and hardy character in the men that followed
them. The British merchantmen sailed in huge convoys, guarded by men-of-
war, while, as said before, our vessels went alone, and relied for protection
on themselves. If a fishing-smack went to the Banks it knew that it ran a
chance of falling in with some not overscrupulous Nova Scotian privateer.
The barks that sailed from Salem to the Spice Islands kept their men well
trained both at great guns and musketry, so as to be able to beat off either
Malay proas or Chinese junks. The New York ships, loaded for the West
Indies, were prepared to do battle with the picaroons that swarmed in the
Spanish Main; while the fast craft from Baltimore could fight as well as they
could run. Wherever an American seaman went, he not only had to contend
with all the legitimate perils of the sea, but he had also to regard almost
every stranger as a foe. Whether this foe called himself pirate or privateer
mattered but little. French, Spaniards, Algerines, Malays, from all alike our

commerce suffered, and against all our merchants were forced to defend themselves. The effect of such a state of things, which made commerce so remunerative that the bolder spirits could hardly keep out of it, and so hazardous that only the most skillful and daring could succeed in it, was to raise up as fine a set of seamen as ever manned a navy. The stern school in which the American was brought up forced him into habits of independent thought and action which it was impossible that the more protected Briton could possess. He worked more intelligently and less from routine, and while perfectly obedient and amenable to discipline, was yet able to judge for himself in an emergency. He was more easily managed than most of his kind—being shrewd, quiet, and, in fact, comparatively speaking, rather moral than otherwise; if he was a New Englander, when he retired from a sea life he was not unapt to end his days as a deacon. Altogether there could not have been better material for a fighting crew than cool, gritty American Jack. Moreover, there was a good nucleus of veterans to begin with, who were well fitted to fill the more responsible positions, such as captains of guns, etc. These were men who had cruised in the little *Enterprise* after French privateers, who had been in the *Constellation* in her two victorious fights, or who, perhaps, had followed Decatur when with only eighty men he cut out the *Philadelphia,* manned by fivefold his force and surrounded by hostile batteries and warvessels—one of the boldest expeditions of the kind on record.

It is to be noted, furthermore, in this connection, that by a singular turn of fortune, Great Britain, whose system of impressing American sailors had been one of the chief causes of the war, herself became, in consequence of that very system, in some sort a nursery for the seamen of the young Republican navy. The American sailor feared nothing more than being impressed on a British ship—dreading beyond measure the hard life and cruel discipline aboard of her; but once there, he usually did well enough, and in course of time often rose to be of some little consequence. For years before 1812, the number of these impressed sailors was in reality greater than the entire number serving in the American navy, from which it will readily be seen that they formed a good stock to draw upon. Very much to their credit, they never lost their devotion to the home of their birth, more than two thousand of them being imprisoned at the beginning of the war because they refused to serve against their country. When Commodore Decatur captured the *Macedonian,* that officer, as we learn from Marshall's *Naval Biography,* stated that most of the seamen of his own frigate, the *United States,* had served in British war-vessels, and that some had been with Lord Nelson in the *Victory,* and had even been bargemen to the great Admiral—a pretty sure proof that the American sailors did not show at a disadvantage when compared with others.

Good seaman as the impressed American proved to be, yet he seldom missed an opportunity to escape from the British service, by desertion or otherwise. In the first place, the life was very hard, and, in the second, the American seaman was very patriotic. He had an honest and deep affection for his own flag, while, on the contrary, he felt a curiously strong hatred for England, as distinguished from Englishmen. This hatred was partly an abstract feeling, cherished through a vague traditional respect for Bunker Hill, and partly something very real and vivid, owing to the injuries he, and others like him, had received. Whether he lived in Maryland or Massachusetts, he certainly knew men whose ships had been seized by British cruisers, their goods confiscated, and the vessels condemned. Some of his friends had fallen victims to the odious right of search, and had never been heard of afterward. He had suffered many an injury to friend, fortune, or person, and some day he hoped to repay them all; and when the war did come, he fought all the better because he knew it was his own quarrel. But, as I have said, this hatred was against England, not against Englishmen. Then, as now, sailors were scattered about over the world without any great regard for nationality; and the resulting intermingling was especially great in those of Britain and America, whose people spoke the same tongue and wore the same aspect. When chance drifted the American into Liverpool or London, he was ready enough to ship in an Indiaman or whaler, caring little for the fact that he served under the British flag; and the Briton, in turn, who found himself in New York or Philadelphia, willingly sailed in one of the clipper-built barks, whether it floated the Stars and Stripes or not. When Captain Porter wrought such havoc among the British whalers in the South Seas, he found that no inconsiderable portion of their crews consisted of Americans, some of whom enlisted on board his own vessel; and among the crews of the American whalers were many British. In fact, though the skipper of each ship might brag loudly of his nationality, yet in practical life he knew well enough that there was very little to choose between a Yankee and a Briton. Both were bold and hardy, cool and intelligent, quick with their hands, and showing at their best in an emergency. They looked alike and spoke alike; when they took the trouble to think, they thought alike; and when they got drunk, which was not an unfrequent occurrence, they quarreled alike.

On the Ocean

The year 1812, on the ocean, ended as gloriously as it had begun. In four victorious fights the disparity in loss had been so great as to sink the disparity of force into insignificance. Our successes had been unaccompanied by any important reverse. Nor was it alone by the victories, but by the cruises, that the year was noteworthy. The Yankee men-of-war sailed almost in sight of the British coast and right in the track of the merchant fleets and their armed protectors. Our vessels had shown themselves immensely superior to their foes.

The reason of these striking and unexpected successes was that our navy in 1812 was the exact reverse of what our navy is now, in 1882. I am not alluding to the personnel, which still remains excellent; but, whereas we now have a large number of worthless vessels, standing very low down in their respective classes, we then possessed a few vessels, each unsurpassed by any foreign ship of her class. To bring up our navy to the condition in which it stood in 1812 it would not be *necessary* (although in reality both very wise and in the end very economical) to spend any more money than at present; only instead of using it to patch up a hundred antiquated hulks, it should be employed in building half a dozen ships on the most effective model. If in 1812 our ships had borne the same relation to the British ships that they do now, not all the courage and skill of our sailors would have won us a single success. As it was, we could only cope with the lower rates, and had no vessels to oppose to the great "liners"; but to-day there is hardly any foreign ship, no matter how low its rate, that is not superior to the corresponding American ones. It is too much to hope that our political short-sightedness will ever enable us to have a navy that is first-class in point of size; but there certainly seems no reason why what ships we have should not be of the very best quality. The effect of a victory is twofold, moral and material. Had we been as roughly handled on water as we were on land during the first year of the war, such a succession of disasters would have had a most demoralizing effect on the nation at large. As it was, our victorious sea-fights, while they did not inflict any material damage upon the colossal sea-might of England, had the most important results in the feelings they produced at home and even abroad. Of course they were magnified absurdly by most of our writers at the time; but they do not need to be magnified, for as they are any American can look back upon them with the keenest national pride. For a hundred and thirty years England had had no equal on the sea; and now she suddenly found one in the untried navy of an almost unknown power.

Lake Erie

Captain Oliver Hazard Perry had assumed command of Erie and the upper lakes, acting under Commodore Chauncy. With intense energy he at once began creating a naval force which should be able to contend successfully with the foe. As already said, the latter in the beginning had exclusive control of Lake Erie; but the Americans had captured the *Caledonia*, brig, and purchased three schooners, afterward named the *Somers*, *Tigress*, and *Ohio*, and a sloop, the *Trippe*. These at first were blockaded in the Niagara, but after the fall of Fort George and retreat of the British forces, Captain Perry was enabled to get them out, tracking them up against the current by the most arduous labor. They ran up to Presque Isle (now called Erie), where two 20-gun brigs were being constructed under the directions of the indefatigable captain. Three other schooners, the *Ariel*, *Scorpion*, and *Porcupine*, were also built.

The harbor of Erie was good and spacious, but had a bar on which there was less than 7 feet of water. Hitherto this had prevented the enemy from getting in; now it prevented the two brigs from getting out. Captain Robert Heriot Barclay had been appointed commander of the British forces on Lake Erie; and he was having built at Amherstburg a 20-gun ship. Meanwhile he blockaded Perry's force, and as the brigs could not cross the bar with their guns in, or except in smooth water, they of course could not do so in his presence. He kept a close blockade for some time; but on the 2d of August he disappeared. Perry at once hurried forward everything; and on the 4th, at 2 P.M., one brig, the *Lawrence*, was towed to that point of the bar where the water was deepest. Her guns were whipped out and landed on the beach, and the brig got over the bar by a hastily improvised "camel."

❧ ❧ ❧

Just as the *Lawrence* had passed the bar, at 8 A.M. on the 5th, the enemy reappeared, but too late; Captain Barclay exchanged a few shots with the schooners and then drew off. The *Niagara* crossed without difficulty. There were still not enough men to man the vessels, but a draft arrived from Ontario, and many of the frontiersmen volunteered, while soldiers also were sent on board. The squadron sailed on the 18th in pursuit of the enemy, whose ship was now ready. After cruising about some time the *Ohio* was sent down the lake, and the other ships went into Put-in Bay. On the 9th of September Captain Barclay put out from Amherstburg, being so short of provisions that he felt compelled to risk an action with the superior force opposed.

❦ ❦ ❦

At daylight on September 10th Barclay's squadron was discovered in the N.W., and Perry at once got under way; the wind soon shifted to the N.E., giving us the weather-gauge, the breeze being very light. Barclay lay to in a close column, heading to the S.W. in the following order: *Chippeway,* Master's Mate J. Campbell; *Detroit,* Captain R. H. Barclay; *Hunter,* Lieutenant G. Bignell; *Queen Charlotte,* Captain R. Finnis; *Lady Prevost,* Lieutenant Edward Buchan; and *Little Belt,* by whom commanded is not said. Perry came down with the wind on his port beam, and made the attack in column ahead, obliquely. First in order came the *Ariel,* Lieutenant John H. Packet, and *Scorpion,* Sailing-master Stephen Champlain, both being on the weather-bow of the *Lawrence,* Captain O. H. Perry; next came the *Caledonia,* Lieutenant Daniel Turner; *Niagara,* Captain Jesse D. Elliott; *Somers,* Lieutenant A. H. M. Conklin; *Porcupine,* Acting-master George Serrat; *Tigress,* Sailing-master Thomas C. Almy; and *Trippe,* Lieutenant Thomas Holdup.

As, amid light and rather baffling winds, the American squadron approached the enemy, Perry's straggling line formed an angle of about 15 with the more compact one of his foes. At 11:45 the *Detroit* opened the action by a shot from her long 24, which fell short; at 11:50 she fired a second which went crashing through the *Lawrence,* and was replied to by the *Scorpion's* long 32. At 11:55 the *Lawrence,* having shifted her port bow-chaser, opened with both the long 12s, and at meridian began with her carronades, but the shot from the latter all fell short. At the same time the action became general on both sides, though the rearmost American vessels were almost beyond the range of their own guns, and quite out of range of the guns of their antagonists. Meanwhile the *Lawrence* was already suffering considerably as she bore down on the enemy. It was twenty minutes before she succeeded in getting within good carronade range, and during that time the action at the head of the line was between the long guns of the *Chippeway* and *Detroit,* throwing 123 pounds, and those of the *Scorpion, Ariel,* and *Lawrence,* throwing 104 pounds. As the enemy's fire was directed almost exclusively at the *Lawrence* she suffered a great deal. The *Caledonia, Niagara,* and *Somers* were meanwhile engaging, at long range, the *Hunter* and *Queen Charlotte,* opposing from their long guns 96 pounds to the 39 pounds of their antagonists, while from a distance the three other American gun-vessels engaged the *Prevost* and *Little Belt.* By 12:20 the *Lawrence* had worked down to close quarters, and at 12:30 the action was going on with great fury between her and her antagonists, within canister range. The raw and inexperienced American crews committed the same fault the British so often fell into on the ocean, and overloaded their carronades. In consequence, that of the *Scorpion* upset down the hatchway in the middle of the action, and the sides of the *Detroit* were dotted with marks from shot that did not penetrate. One of the *Ariel's* long 12s also burst. Barclay fought the *Detroit* exceedingly well, her guns being most excellently aimed, though they actually had to be discharged by flashing pistols at the touch-holes, so deficient was the ship's equipment. Meanwhile the *Caledonia* came down too, but the *Niagara* was wretchedly handled, Elliott keeping at a distance which prevented the use either of his carronades or of those of the *Queen Charlotte*, his antagonist; the latter, however, suffered greatly from the long guns of the opposing schooners, and lost her gallant commander, Captain Finnis, and first lieutenant, Mr. Stokes, who were killed early in the action; her next in command, Provincial-Lieutenant Irvine, perceiving that he could do no good, passed the *Hunter* and joined in the attack on the *Lawrence*, at close quarters. The *Niagara*, the most efficient and best manned of the American vessels, was thus almost kept out of the action by her captain's misconduct. At the end of the line the fight went on at long range between the *Somers, Tigress, Porcupine*, and *Trippe* on one side, and *Little Belt* and *Lady Prevost* on the other; the *Lady Prevost* making a very noble fight, although her 12-pound carronades rendered her almost helpless against the long guns of the Americans. She was greatly cut up, her commander, Lieutenant Buchan, was dangerously, and her acting first lieutenant, Mr. Roulette, severely, wounded, and she began falling gradually to leeward.

The fighting at the head of the line was fierce and bloody to an extraordinary degree. The *Scorpion, Ariel, Lawrence*, and *Caledonia*, all of them handled with the most determined courage, were opposed to the *Chippeway, Detroit, Queen Charlotte*, and *Hunter*, which were fought to the full as bravely. At such close quarters the two sides engaged on about equal terms, the Americans being superior in weight of metal, and inferior in number of men. But the *Lawrence* had received such damage in working down as to make the odds against Perry. On each side almost the whole fire was directed at the opposing large vessel or vessels; in consequence the *Queen Charlotte* was almost disabled, and the *Detroit* was also frightfully shattered, especially by the raking fire of the gunboats, her first lieutenant, Mr. Garland, being mortally wounded, and Captain Barclay so severely injured that he was obliged to quit the deck, leaving his ship in the command of Lieutenant George Inglis. But on board the *Lawrence* matters had gone even worse, the combined fire of her adversaries having made the grimmest carnage on her decks. Of the 103 men who were fit for duty when she began the action, 83, or over four-fifths, were killed or wounded. The vessel was shallow, and the ward-room, used as a cockpit, to which the wounded were taken, was mostly above water, and the shot came through it continually, killing and wounding many men under the hands of the surgeon.

The first lieutenant, Yarnall, was three times wounded, but kept to the deck through all; the only other lieutenant on board, Brooks, of the marines, was mortally wounded. Every brace and bowline was shot away, and the brig almost completely dismantled; her hull was shattered to pieces, many shot going completely through it, and the guns on the engaged side were by degrees all dismounted. Perry kept up the fight with splendid courage. As the crew fell one by one, the commodore called down through the skylight for one of the surgeon's assistants; and this call was repeated and obeyed till none was left; then he asked, "Can any of the wounded pull a rope?" and three or four of them crawled up on deck to lend a feeble hand in placing the last guns. Perry himself fired the last effective heavy gun, assisted only by the purser and chaplain. A man who did not possess his indomitable spirit would have then struck. Instead, however, although failing in the attack so far, Perry merely determined to win by new methods, and remodeled the line accordingly. Mr. Turner, in the *Caledonia*, when ordered to close, had put his helm up, run down on the opposing line, and engaged at very short range, though the brig was absolutely without quarters. The *Niagara* had thus become the next in the line astern of the *Lawrence* and the sloop *Trippe*, having passed the three schooners in front of her, was next ahead. The *Niagara* now, having a breeze, steered for the head of Barclay's line, passing over a quarter of a mile to windward of the *Lawrence*, on her port beam. She was almost uninjured, having so far taken very little part in the combat, and to her Perry shifted his flag. Leaping into a row-boat, with his brother and four seamen, he rowed to the fresh brig, where he arrived at 2:30, and at once sent Elliott astern to hurry up the three schooners. The *Trippe* was now very near the *Caledonia*. The *Lawrence*, having but 14 sound men left, struck her colors, but could not be taken possession of before the action recommenced. She drifted astern, the *Caledonia* passing between her and her foes. At 2:45 the schooners having closed up, Perry in his fresh vessel bore up to break Barclay's line.

The British ships had fought themselves to a standstill. The *Lady Prevost* was crippled and sagged to leeward, though ahead of the others. The *Detroit* and *Queen Charlotte* were so disabled that they could not effectually oppose fresh antagonists. There could thus be but little resistance to Perry, as the *Niagara* stood down, and broke the British line, firing her port guns into the *Chippeway, Little Belt*, and *Lady Prevost*, and the starboard ones into the *Detroit, Queen Charlotte*, and *Hunter*, raking on both sides. Too disabled to tack, the

Detroit and *Charlotte* tried to wear, the latter running up to leeward of the former; and, both vessels having every brace and almost every stay shot away, they fell foul. The *Niagara* luffed athwart their bows, within half pistol-shot, keeping up a terrific discharge of great guns and musketry, while on the other side the British vessels were raked by the *Caledonia* and the schooners so closely that some of their grape-shot, passing over the foe, rattled through Perry's spars. Nothing further could be done, and Barclay's flag was struck at 3 P.M., after three and a quarter hours' most gallant and desperate fighting. The *Chippeway* and *Little Belt* tried to escape, but were overtaken and brought to respectively by the *Trippe* and *Scorpion*, the commander of the latter, Mr. Stephen Champlin, firing the last, as he had the first, shot of the battle. "Captain Perry has behaved in the most humane and attentive manner, not only to myself and officers, but to all the wounded," writes Captain Barclay.

The American squadron had suffered severely, more than two-thirds of the loss falling upon the *Lawrence*, which was reduced to the condition of a perfect wreck, her starboard bulwarks being completely beaten in. . . . The total loss was 123; 27 were killed and 96 wounded, of whom 3 died.

The British loss, falling most heavily on the *Detroit* and *Queen Charlotte*, amounted to 41 killed. . . . and 94 wounded. . . . in all 145. The first and second in command on every vessel were killed or wounded, a sufficient proof of the desperate nature of the defense.

The victory of Lake Erie was most important, both in its material results and in its moral effect. It gave us complete command of all the upper lakes, prevented any fears of invasion from that quarter, increased our prestige with the foe and our confidence in ourselves, and insured the conquest of upper Canada; in all these respects its importance has not been overrated. But the "glory" acquired by it most certainly *has* been estimated at more than its worth. Most Americans, even the well educated, if asked which was the most glorious victory of the war, would point to this battle. Captain Perry's name is more widely known than that of any other commander. Every schoolboy reads about *him*, if of no other sea-captain; yet he certainly stands on a lower grade than either Hull or Macdonough, and not a bit higher than a dozen others. On Lake Erie our seamen displayed great courage and skill; but so did their antagonists. The simple truth is that, where on both sides the officers and men were equally brave and skillful, the side which possessed the superiority in force, in the proportion of three to two, could not well help winning. The courage with which the *Lawrence* was defended has hardly ever been surpassed, and may fairly be called heroic; but equal praise belongs to the men on board the *Detroit*, who had to discharge the great guns by flashing pistols at the touch-holes, and yet made such a terribly effective defense. Courage is only one of the many elements which go to make up the character of a first-class commander; something more than bravery is needed before a leader can be really called great.

🌿 🌿 🌿

And it must always be remembered that a victory, honorably won, if even over a weaker foe, *does* reflect credit on the nation by whom it is gained. It was creditable to us as a nation that our ships were better made and better armed than the British frigates, exactly as it was creditable to them that a few years before their vessels had stood in the same relation to the Dutch ships. It was greatly to our credit that we had been enterprising enough to fit out such an effective little flotilla on Lake Erie, and for this Perry deserves the highest praise.

Summary

The concluding operations of the war call for much the same comments as those of the preceding years. The balance of praise certainly inclines toward the Americans. Captain John Hayes's squadron showed great hardihood, perseverance, and judgment, which was rewarded by the capture of the *President*; and Decatur's surrender seems decidedly tame. But as regards the action between the *President* and *Endymion* (taking into account the fact that the former fought almost under the guns of an overwhelming force, and was therefore obliged to expose herself far more than she otherwise would have), it showed nearly as great superiority on the side of the Americans as the frigate actions of 1812 did—in fact, probably quite as much as in the case of the *Java*. Similarly, while the *Cyane* and *Levant* did well, the *Constitution* did better; and Sir George Collier's ships certainly did not distinguish themselves when in chase of *Old Ironsides*. So with the *Hornet* in her two encounters; no one can question the pluck with which the *Penguin* was fought, but her gunnery was as bad as that of the *Cornwallis* subsequently proved. And though the skirmish between the *Peacock* and *Nautilus* is not one to which an American cares to look back, yet, regarding it purely from a fighting standpoint, there is no question which crew was the better trained and more skillful.

[Seven] ships first put to sea in this year. For the first time in her history the United States possessed line-of-battle ships; and for the first time in all history, the steam frigate appeared on the navy list of a nation. The *Fulton*, with her clumsy central wheel, concealed from shot by the double hull, with such thick scanting that none but heavy guns could harm her, and relying for offensive weapons not on a broadside of 30 guns of small caliber but on 2 pivotal 100-pounder columbiads, or, perhaps, if necessary, on blows from her hog snout—the *Fulton* was the true prototype of the modern steam iron-clad, with its few heavy guns and ram. Almost as significant is the presence of the *Torpedo*. I have not chronicled the several efforts made by the Americans to destroy British vessels with torpedoes; some very nearly succeeded, and although they failed it must not be supposed that they did no good. On the contrary, they made the British in many cases very cautious about venturing into good anchorage (especially in Long Island Sound and the Chesapeake), and by the mere terror of their name prevented more than one harrying expedition. The *Fulton* was not got into condition to be fought until just as the war ended; had it continued a few months, it is more than probable that the deeds of the *Merrimac* and the havoc wrought by the Confederate torpedoes would have been forestalled by nearly half a century. As it was, neither of these engines of war attracted much attention. For ten or fifteen years the *Fulton* was the only war-vessel of her kind in existence, and then her name disappears from our lists. The torpedoes had been tried in the Revolutionary War, but their failure prevented much notice from being taken of them, and besides, at that time there was a strong feeling that it was dishonorable to blow a ship up with a power-can concealed *under* the water, though highly laudable to burn her by means of a fire-raft floating on the water—a nice distinction in naval ethics that has since disappeared.

In summing up the results of the struggle on the ocean it is to be noticed that very little was attempted, and nothing done, by the American navy that could *materially* affect the result of the war. Commodore Rodgers's expedition after the Jamaica plate fleet failed; both the efforts to get a small squadron into the East Indian waters also miscarried; and otherwise the whole history of the struggle on the ocean is, as regards the Americans, only the record of individual cruises and fights. The material results were not very great, at least in their effect on Great Britain, whose enormous navy did not feel in the slightest degree the loss of a few frigates and sloops. But morally the result was of inestimable benefit to the United States. The victories kept up the spirits of the people, cast down by the defeats on land; practically decided in favor of the Americans the chief question in dispute— Great Britain's right of search and impressment—and gave the navy, and thereby the country, a world-wide reputation. I doubt if ever before a nation gained so much honor by a few single-ship duels. For there can be no question which side came out of the war with the greatest credit. The damage inflicted by each on the other was not very unequal in amount, but the balance was certainly in favor of the Untied States. . . . [B]ut the comparative material loss gives no idea of the comparative honor gained. The British navy, numbering at the outset a thousand cruisers, had accomplished less than the American, which numbered but a dozen. Moreover, most of the loss suffered by the former was in single fight, while this had been but twice the case with the Americans, who had generally been overwhelmed by numbers. The *President* and *Essex* were both captured by more than double their force simply because they were disabled before the fight began, otherwise they would certainly have escaped. With the exceptions of the *Chesapeake* and *Argus* (both of which were taken fairly, because their antagonists, though of only equal force, were better fighters), the remaining loss of the Americans was due to the small cruisers stumbling from time to time across the path of some one of the innumerable British heavy vessels. Had Congressional forethought been sufficiently great to have allowed a few line-of-battle ships to have been in readiness some time previous to the war, results of weight might have been accomplished. But the only activity ever exhibited by Congress in materially increasing the navy previous to the war, had been in partially carrying out President Jefferson's ideas of having an enormous force of very worthless gunboats—a scheme whose wisdom was about on a par with some of that statesman's political and military theories.

Of the twelve single-ship actions, two (those of the *Argus* and *Chesapeake*) undoubtedly redounded most to the credit of the British, in two (that of the *Wasp* with the *Reindeer*, and that of the *Enterprise* with the *Boxer*) the honors were nearly even, and in the other eight the superiority of the Americans was very manifest. In three actions (those with the *Penguin*, *Frolic*, and *Shannon*) the combatants were about equal in strength, the Americans having slightly the advantage; in all the others but two, the victors combined superiority of force with superiority of skill. In but two cases, those of the *Argus* and *Epervier*, could any lack of courage be imputed to the vanquished. The second year alone showed to the advantage of the British; the various encounters otherwise were as creditable to the Americans at the end as the beginning of the war. This is worth attending to, because many authors speak as if the successes of the Americans were confined to the first year. It is true that no frigate was taken after the first year, but this was partly because the strictness of the blockade kept the American frigates more in port, while the sloops put out to sea at pleasure, and partly because after that year the British 18-pounder frigates either cruised in couples, or, when single, invariably refused, by order of the Board of Admiralty, an encounter with a 24-pounder; and though much of the American success was unquestionably to be attributed to more men and heavier guns, yet much of it was not.

The Republic of the United States owed a great deal to the excellent make and armament of its ships, but it owed still more to the men who were in them. The massive timbers and heavy guns of *Old Ironsides* would have availed but little had it not been for her able commanders and crews. Of all the excellent single-ship captains, British or American, produced by the war, the palm should be awarded to Hull. The deed of no other man (except Macdonough) equaled his escape from Broke's five ships, or surpassed his half-hour's conflict with the *Guerriere*. After him, almost all the American captains deserve high praise — Decatur, Jones, Blakely, Biddle, Bainbridge, Lawrence, Burrows, Allen, Warrington, Stewart, Porter. It is no small glory to a country to have had such men upholding the honor of its flag. On a par with the best of them are Broke, Manners, and also Byron and Blythe. It must be but a poor-spirited American whose veins do not tingle with pride when he reads of the cruises and fights of the sea-captains, and their grim prowess, which kept the old Yankee flag floating over the waters of the Atlantic for three years, in the teeth of the mightiest naval power the world has ever seen.

THE FORMATION OF THE NATIONAL CONSTITUTION

During the 1880s and 1890s, TR's income from his political offices and his trust was inadequate to sustain his standard of living. To supplement his income, TR continued his historical writing, which also gave him a vehicle by which to broadcast his views on politics, patriotism, and the public interest. He contributed to Houghton Mifflin's "American Stastesmen" series with a biography of Jacksonian-era senator Thomas Hart Benton of Missouri (1887) and a study of Pennsylvania statesman and constitutional convention delegate Gouverneur Morris (1888). TR's prejudices in favor of strong government, his dislike for Jefferson and Jeffersonianism, and his tendency, like many of his generation, to see democratic sympathy as an "inborn" trait especially in the Anglo-Saxon "race" are all explicit in his work on Morris, from which this excerpt on the constitution is taken.

No sooner was peace declared, and the immediate and pressing danger removed, than the confederation relapsed into a loose knot of communities, as quarrelsome as they were contemptible. The States'-rights men for the moment had things all their own way, and speedily reduced us to the level afterward reached by the South American republics. Each commonwealth set up for itself, and tried to press its neighbors; not one had a creditable history for the next four years; while the career of Rhode Island in particular can only be properly described as infamous. We refused to pay our debts, we would not even pay our army; and mob violence flourished rankly. As a natural result, the European powers began to take advantage of our weakness and division.

All our great men saw the absolute need of establishing a National Union — not a league or a confederation — if the country was to be saved. None felt this more strongly than Morris, and no one was more hopeful of the final result. Jay had written to him as to the need of "raising and maintaining a national spirit in America"; and he wrote in reply, at different times: "Much of convulsion will yet ensue, yet it must terminate in giving to government that power without which government is but a name. . . . This country has never yet been known to Europe, and God knows whether it ever will be. To England it is less known than to any other part of Europe, because they constantly view it through a medium of either prejudice or faction. True it is that the general government wants energy, and equally true it is that the want will eventually be supplied. A national spirit is the natural result of national existence; *and although some of the present generation may feel the result of colonial oppositions of opinion; that generation will die away and give place to a race of Americans*. [Italics are TR's.] On this occasion, as on others, Great Britain is our best friend; and, by seizing the critical moment when we were about to divide, she has shown us the dreadful consequences of division. . . . Indeed, my friend, nothing can do us so much good as to convince the eastern and southern States how necessary it is to give proper force to the federal government, and nothing will so soon operate that conviction as foreign efforts to restrain the navigation of the one and the commerce of the other." The last sentence referred to the laws aimed at our trade by Great Britain, and by other powers as well—symptoms of outside hostility which made us at once begin to draw together again.

Money troubles grew apace, and produced the usual crop of crude theories and of vicious and dishonest legislation in accordance therewith. Lawless outbreaks became common, and in Massachusetts culminated in actual rebellion. The mass of the people were rendered hostile to any closer union by their ignorance, their jealousy, and the general particularistic bent of their minds—this last being merely a vicious graft on, or rather outgrowth of, the love of freedom inborn in the race. Their leaders were enthusiasts of pure purpose and unsteady mental vision; they were followed by the mass of designing politicians, who feared that their importance would be lost if their sphere of action should be enlarged. Among these leaders the three most important were, in New York, George Clinton, and, in Massachusetts and Virginia, two much greater men—Samuel Adams and Patrick Henry. All three had done excellent service at the beginning of the Revolutionary troubles. Patrick Henry lived to redeem himself, almost in his last hour, by the noble stand he took in aid of Washington against the Democratic nullification agitation of Jefferson and Madison; but the usefulness of each of the other two was limited to the early portion of his career.

Like every other true patriot and statesman, Morris did all in his power to bring into one combination the varied interests favorable to the formation of a government that should be strong and responsible as well as free. The public creditors and the soldiers of the army—whose favorite toasts were, "A hoop to the barrel," and "Cement to the union"—were the two classes most sensible of the advantages of such a government; and to each of these Morris addressed himself when he proposed to consolidate the public debt, both to private citizens and to the soldiers, and to make it a charge on the United States, and not on the several separate States.

In consequence of the activity and ability with which he advocated a firmer union, the extreme States'-rights men were especially hostile to him;

and certain of their number assailed him with bitter malignity, both then and afterward. One accusation was that he had improper connections with the public creditors. This was a pure slander, absolutely without foundation, and not supported by even the pretense of proof. Another accusation was that he favored the establishment of a monarchy. This was likewise entirely untrue. Morris was not a sentimental political theorist; he was an eminently practical—that is, useful—statesman, who saw with unusual clearness that each people must have a government suited to its own individual character, and to the stage of political and social development it had reached. He realized that a nation must be governed according to the actual needs and capacities of its citizens, not according to any abstract theory or set of ideal principles. He would have dismissed with contemptuous laughter the ideas of those Americans who at the present day believe that Anglo-Saxon democracy can be applied successfully to a half-savage negroid people in Hayti, or of those Englishmen who consider seriously the proposition to renovate Turkey by giving her representative institutions and a parliamentary government. He understood and stated that a monarchy "did not consist with the taste and temper of the people" in America, and he believed in establishing a form of government that did. Like almost every other statesman of the day, the perverse obstinacy of the extreme particularist section at times made him downhearted, and caused him almost to despair a good government being established; and like every sensible man he would have preferred almost any strong orderly government to the futile anarchy toward which the ultra States'-rights men or separatists tended.

❦ ❦ ❦

Our very doctrinaires have usually acted much more practically than they have talked. Jefferson, when in power, adopted most of the Federalist theories, and became markedly hostile to the nullification movements at whose birth he had himself officiated. We have often blundered badly in the beginning, but we have always come out well in the end. The Dutch, when they warred for freedom from Spanish rule, showed as much short-sighted selfishness and bickering jealousy as even our own Revolutionary ancestors, and only a part remained faithful to the end: as a result, but one section won independence, while the Netherlands were divided, and never grasped the power that should have been theirs. As for the Spanish-Americans, they split up hopelessly almost before they were free, and, though they bettered their condition a little, yet lost nine-tenths of what they had gained. Scotland and Ireland, when independent, were nests of savages. All the follies our forefathers committed can be paralleled elsewhere, but their successes are unique.

So it was in the few years immediately succeeding the peace by which we won our independence. The mass of the people wished for no closer union than was to be found in a lax confederation; but they had the good sense to learn the lesson taught by the weakness and lawlessness they saw around them; they reluctantly made up their minds to the need of a stronger government, and when they had once come to their decision, neither demagogue nor doctrinaire could swerve them from it.

The national convention to form a constitution met in May, 1787; and rarely in the world's history has there been a deliberative body which contained so many remarkable men, or produced results so lasting and far-reaching. The Congress whose members signed the Declaration of Independence had but cleared the ground on which the framers of the Constitution were to build. Among the delegates in attendance, easily first stood Washington and Franklin—two of that great American trio in which Lincoln is the third. Next came Hamilton from New York, having as colleagues a couple of mere obstructionists sent by the Clintonians to handicap him. From Pennsylvania came Robert Morris and Gouverneur Morris; from Virginia, Madison; from South Carolina, Rutledge and the Pinckneys; and so on through the other States. Some of the most noted statesmen were absent, however. Adams and Jefferson were abroad. Jay was acting as secretary for foreign affairs, in which capacity, by the way, he had shown most unlooked-for weakness in yielding to Spanish demands about the Mississippi.

❦ ❦ ❦

The deliberations of the convention in their result illustrated in a striking manner the truth of the American principle, that—for deliberative, not executive, purposes—the wisdom of many men is worth more than the wisdom of any one man. The Constitution that the members assembled in convention finally produced was not only the best possible one for America at that time, but it was also, in spite of its short-comings, and taking into account its fitness for our own people and conditions, as well as its accordance with the principles of abstract right, probably the best that any nation has ever had, while it was beyond question a very much better one than any single member could have prepared. . . .

It is impossible to read through the debates of the convention without being struck by the innumerable shortcomings of each individual plan proposed by the several members, as divulged in their speeches, when compared with the plan finally adopted. Had the result been in accordance with the views of the strong-government men like Hamilton on the one hand, or of the weak-government men like Franklin on the other, it would have been equally disastrous for the country. The men who afterward naturally became the chiefs of the Federalist party, and who included in their number the bulk of the great Revolutionary leaders, were the ones to whom we mainly owe our present form of government; certainly we owe them more, both on this and on other points, than we do their rivals, the after-time Democrats. Yet there were some articles of faith in the creed of the latter so essential to our national well-being, and yet so counter to the prejudices of the Federalists, that it was inevitable they should triumph in the end. Jefferson led the Democrats to victory only when he had learned to acquiesce thoroughly in some of the fundamental principles of Federalism, and the government of himself and his successors was good chiefly in so far as it followed out the theories of the Hamiltonians; while Hamilton and the Federalists fell from power because they could not learn the one great truth taught by Jefferson—that in America a statesman should trust the people, and should endeavor to secure to each man all possible individual liberty, confident that he will use it aright. The old-school Jeffersonian theorists believed in "a strong people and a weak government." Lincoln was the first who showed how a strong people might have a strong government and yet remain the freest on the earth. He seized—half unwittingly—all that was best and wisest in the traditions of Federalism; he was the true successor of the Federalist leaders; but he grafted on their system a profound belief that the great heart of the nation beat for truth, honor, and liberty.

This fact, that in 1787 all the thinkers of the day drew out plans that in some respects went very wide of the mark, must be kept in mind, or else we shall judge each particular thinker with undue harshness when we examine his utterances without comparing them with those of his fellows. But one partial exception can be made. In the Constitutional Convention Madison, a moderate Federalist, was the man who, of all who were there, saw things most clearly as they were, and whose theories most closely corresponded with the principles finally adopted; and although even he was at first dissatisfied with the result, and both by word and by action interpreted the Constitution in widely different ways at different times, still this was Madison's time of glory; he was one of the statesmen who do extremely useful work, but only at some single given crisis. While the Constitution was being formed and adopted, he stood in the very front; but in his later career he sunk his own individuality, and became a mere pale shadow of Jefferson.

Morris played a very prominent part in the convention. He was a ready speaker, and among all the able men present there was probably no such really brilliant thinker. In the debates he spoke more often than any one else, although Madison was not far behind him; and his speeches betrayed, but with marked and exaggerated emphasis, both the virtues and the shortcomings of the Federalist school of thought. They show us, too, why he never rose to the first rank of statesmen. His keen, masterful mind, his far-sightedness, and the force and subtlety of his reasoning were all marred by his incurable cynicism and deep-rooted distrust of mankind. He throughout appears as *advocatus diaboli*; he puts the lowest interpretation upon every act, and frankly avows his disbelief in all generous and unselfish motives. His continual allusions to the overpowering influence of the baser passions, and to their mastery of the human race at all times, drew from Madison, although the two men generally acted together, a protest against his "forever inculcating the utter political depravity of men, and the necessity for opposing one vice and interest as the only possible check to another vice and interest."

Morris championed a strong national government, wherein he was right; but he also championed a system of class representation, leaning toward aristocracy, wherein he was wrong. Not Hamilton himself was a firmer believer in the national idea. His one great object was to secure a powerful and lasting Union, instead of a loose federal league. It must be remembered that in the convention the term "federal" was used in exactly the opposite sense to the one in which it was taken afterward; that is, it was used as the antithesis of "national," not as its synonym. The States'-rights men used it to express a system of government such as that of the old federation of the thirteen colonies; while their opponents called themselves Nationalists, and only took the title of Federalists after the Constitution had been formed, and then simply because the name was popular with the masses. They thus appropriated their adversaries' party name, bestowing it on the organization most hostile to their adversaries' party theories. Similarly, the term "Republican party," which was originally in our history merely another name for the Democracy, has in the end been adopted by the chief opponents of the latter. The difficulties for the convention to surmount seemed insuperable; on almost every question that came up, there were clashing interests. Strong government and weak government, pure democracy or a modified aristocracy, small States and large States, North and South, slavery and freedom, agricultural sections as against commercial sections—on each of twenty points the delegates split into hostile camps, that could only be reconciled by concessions from both sides. The Constitution was not one compromise; it was a bundle of compromises, all needful.

Morris, like every other member of the convention, sometimes took the right and sometimes the wrong side on the successive issues that arose. But on the most important one of all he made no error; and he commands our entire sympathy for his thoroughgoing nationalism. As was to be expected, he had no regard whatever for States' rights. He wished to deny to the small States the equal representation in the Senate finally allowed them; and he was undoubtedly right theoretically. No good argument can be adduced in support of the present system on that point. Still, it has thus far worked no harm; the reason being that our States have merely artificial boundaries, while those of small population have hitherto been distributed pretty evenly among the different sections, so that they have been split up like the others on every important issue, and thus have never been arrayed against the rest of the country.

Though Morris and his side were defeated in their efforts to have the States represented proportionally in the Senate, yet they carried their point as to representation in the House. Also, on the general question of making a national government, as distinguished from a league or federation, the really vital point, their triumph was complete. The Constitution they drew up and had adopted no more admitted of legal or peaceable rebellion—whether called secession or nullification—on the part of the State than on the part of a country or an individual.

Morris expressed his own views with his usual clear-cut, terse vigor when he asserted that "state attachments and state importance had been the bane of the country," and that he came, not as a mere delegate from one section, but "as a representative of America—a representative in some degree of the whole human race, for the whole human race would be affected by the outcome of the convention." And he poured out the flood of his biting scorn on those gentlemen who came there "to truck and bargain for their respective States," asking what man there was who could tell with certainty the State wherein he—and even more wherein his children—would live in the future; and reminding the small States, with cavalier indifference, that, "if they did not like the Union, no matter—they would have to come in, and that was all there was about it; for if persuasion did not unite the country, then the sword would." His correct language and distinct enunciation—to which Madison has borne witness—allowed his grim truths to carry their full weight; and he brought them home to his hearers with a rough, almost startling, earnestness and directness.

Many of those present must have winced when he told them that it would matter nothing to America "if all the charters and constitutions of the States were thrown into the fire, and all the demagogues into the ocean," and asserted that "any particular State *ought* to be injured, for the sake of a majority of the people, in case its conduct showed that it deserved it." He held that we should create a national government, to be the one and only supreme power in the land—one which, unlike a mere federal league, such as we then lived under, should have complete and compulsive operation, and he instanced the examples as well of Greece as of Germany and the United Netherlands, to prove that local jurisdiction destroyed every tie of nationality.

𝓌 𝓌 𝓌

On the question as to whether the Constitution should be made absolutely democratic or not, Morris took the conservative side. On the suffrage his views are perfectly defensible: he believed that it should be limited to freeholders. He rightly considered the question as to how widely it should be extended to be one of expediency merely. It is simply idle folly to talk of suffrage as being an "inborn" or "natural" right. There are enormous communities totally unfit for its exercise; while true universal suffrage has never been, and never will be, seriously advocated by any one. There must always be an age limit, and such a limit must necessarily be purely arbitrary. The wildest Democrat of Revolutionary times did not dream of doing away with the restrictions of race and sex which kept most American citizens from the ballot-box; and there is certainly much less abstract right in a system which limits the suffrage to people of a certain color than there is in one which limits it to people who come up to a given standard of thrift and intelligence. On the other hand, our experience has not proved that men of wealth make any better use of their ballots than do, for instance, mechanics and other handicraftsmen. No plan could be adopted so perfect as to be free from all drawbacks. On the whole, however, and taking our country in its length and breadth, manhood suffrage has worked well, better than would have been the case with any other system; but even here there are certain localities where its results have been evil, and must simply be accepted as the blemishes inevitably attendant upon, and marring, any effort to carry out a scheme that will be widely applicable.

Morris contended that his plan would work no novel or great hardship, as the people in several States were already accustomed to freehold suffrage. He considered the freeholders to be the best guardians of liberty, and maintained that the restriction of the right to them was only creating a necessary safeguard "against the dangerous influence of those people, without property or principle, with whom, in the end, our country, like all other countries, was sure to abound." He did not believe that the ignorant and dependent could be trusted to vote. Madison supported him heartily, likewise thinking the freeholders the safest guardians of our rights; he indulged in some gloomy (and fortunately hitherto unverified) forebodings as to our future, which sound strangely coming from one who was afterward an especial pet of the Jeffersonian democracy. He said: "In future times a great majority of the people will be without landed or any other property. They will then either combine under the influence of their common situation — in which case the rights of property and the public safety will not be safe in their hands — or, as is more probable, they will become the tools of opulence and ambition."

❦ ❦ ❦

His views as to the power and functions of the national Executive were in the main sound, and he succeeded in having most of them embodied in the Constitution. He wished to have the President hold office during good behavior; and, though this was negatived, he succeeded in having him made re-eligible to the position. He was instrumental in giving him a qualified veto over legislation, and in providing for his impeachment for misconduct; and also in having him made commander-in-chief of the forces of the Republic, and in allowing him the appointment of governmental officers. The especial service he rendered, however, was his successful opposition to the plan whereby the President was to be elected by the legislature. This proposition he combated with all his strength, showing that it would take away greatly from the dignity of the Executive, and would render his election a matter of cabal and faction, "like the election of the pope by a conclave of cardinals." He contended that the President should be chosen by the people at large, by the citizens of the United States, acting through electors whom they had picked out. . . .

On the judiciary his views were also sound. He upheld the power of the judges, and maintained that they should have absolute decision as to the constitutionality of any law. By this means he hoped to provide against the encroachments of the popular branch of the government, the one from which danger was to be feared, as "virtuous citizens will often act as legislators in a way of which they would, as private individuals, afterward be ashamed." He wisely disapproved of low salaries for the judges, showing that the amounts must be fixed from time to time in accordance with the manner and style of living in the country; and that good work on the bench, where it was especially needful, like good work everywhere else, could only be insured by a high rate of recompense. On the other hand, he approved of introducing into the national Constitution the foolish New York State inventions of a Council of Revision and an Executive Council.

His ideas of the duties and powers of Congress were likewise very proper on the whole. Most citizens of the present day will agree with him that "the excess rather than the deficiency of laws is what we have to dread." He opposed the hurtful provision which requires that each congressman should be a resident of his own district, urging that congressmen represented the people at large, as well as their own small localities; and he also objected to making officers of the army and navy ineligible. He laid much stress on the propriety of passing navigation acts to encourage American bottoms and seamen, as a navy was essential to our security, and the shipping business was always one that stood in peculiar need of public patronage. Also, like Hamilton and most other Federalists, he favored a policy of encouraging domestic manufactures. Incidentally he approved of Congress having power to lay an embargo, although he has elsewhere recorded his views as to the general futility of such kinds of "commercial warfare." He believed in having a uniform bankruptcy law, approved of abolishing all religious tests as qualifications for office, and was utterly opposed to the "rotation-in-office" theory.

One curious incident in the convention was the sudden out-cropping, even thus early, of a "Native American" movement against all foreigners, which was headed by Butler, of South Carolina, who himself was of Irish parentage. He strenuously insisted that no foreigners whosoever should be admitted to our councils—a rather odd proposition, considering that it would have excluded quite a number of the eminent men he was the addressing. Pennsylvania in particular—whose array of native talent has always been far from imposing—had a number of foreigners among her delegates, and loudly opposed the proposition, as did New York. These States wished that there should be no discrimination whatever between native and foreign born citizens; but finally a compromise was agreed to, by which the latter were excluded only from the presidency, but were admitted to all other rights after a seven years' residence—a period that was certainly none too long.

A much more serious struggle took place over the matter of slavery, quite as important then as ever, for at that time the negroes were a fifth of our population, instead of, as now, an eighth. The question, as it came before the convention, had several sides to it; the especial difficulty arising over the representation of the slave States in Congress, and the importation of additional slaves from Africa. No one proposed to abolish slavery offhand; but an influential though small number of delegates, headed by Morris, recognized it as a terrible evil, and were very loath either to allow the South additional representation for the slaves, or to permit the foreign trade in them to go on. When the Southern members banded together on the issue, and made it evident that it was the one which they regarded as almost the most important of all, Morris attacked them in a telling speech, stating with his usual boldness facts that most Northerners only dared hint at, and summing up with the remark that, if he was driven to the dilemma of doing injustice to the Southern States or to human nature, he would have to do it to the former; certainly he would not encourage the slave trade by allowing representation for negroes. Afterward he characterized the proportional representation of the blacks even more strongly, as being "a bribe for the importation of slaves."

In advocating the proposal, first made by Hamilton, that the representation should in all cases be proportioned to the number of free inhabitants, Morris showed the utter lack of logic in the Virginian proposition, which was that the slave States should have additional representation to the extent of three-fifths of their negroes. If negroes were to be considered as inhabitants, then they ought to be added in their entire number; if they were to be considered as property, then they ought to be counted only if all other wealth was likewise included. The position of the Southerners was ridiculous: he tore their arguments to shreds; but he was powerless to alter the fact that they were doggedly determined to carry their point, while most of the Northern members cared comparatively little about it.

In another speech he painted in the blackest colors the unspeakable misery and wrong wrought by slavery, and showed the blight it brought upon the land. "It was the curse of Heaven on the States where it prevailed." He contrasted the prosperity and happiness of the Northern States with the misery and poverty which overspread the barren wastes of those where slaves were numerous. "Every step you take through the great region of slavery presents a desert widening with the increasing number of these wretched beings." He indignantly protested against the Northern States being bound to march their militia for the defense of the Southern States against the very slaves of whose existence the Northern men complained. "He would sooner submit himself to a tax for paying for all the negroes in the United States than saddle posterity with such a Constitution."

Some of the high-minded Virginian statesmen were quite as vigorous as he was in their denunciation of the system. One of them, George Mason, portrayed the effect of slavery upon the people at large with bitter emphasis, and denounced the slave traffic as "infernal," and slavery as a national sin that would be punished by a national calamity—stating therein the exact and terrible truth. In shameful contrast, many of the Northerners championed the institution; in particular, Oliver Ellsworth, of Connecticut, whose name should be branded with infamy because of the words he then uttered. He actually advocated the free importation of negroes into the south Atlantic States, because the slaves "died so fast in the sickly rice-swamps" that it was necessary ever to bring fresh ones to labor and perish in the places of their predecessors; and, with a brutal cynicism, peculiarly revolting from its mercantile baseness, he brushed aside the question of morality as irrelevant, asking his hearers to pay heed only to the fact that "what enriches the part enriches the whole."

The Virginians were opposed to the slave trade; but South Carolina and Georgia made it a condition of their coming into the Union. It was accordingly agreed that it should be allowed for a limited time—twelve years; and this was afterward extended to twenty by a bargain made by Maryland and the three south Atlantic States with the New England States, the latter getting in return the help of the former [with] certain provisions respecting commerce. One of the main industries of the New England of that day was the manufacture of rum; and its citizens cared more for their distilleries than for all the slaves held in bondage throughout Christendom. The rum was made from molasses which they imported from the West Indies, and they carried there in return the fish taken by their great fishing fleets; they also carried the slaves into the Southern ports. Their commerce was what they especially relied on; and to gain support for it they were perfectly willing to make terms with even such a black Mammon of unrighteousness as the Southern slave-holding system. Throughout the contest, Morris and a few other stout anti-slavery men are the only ones who appear to advantage; the Virginians, who were honorably anxious to minimize the evils of slavery, come next; then the other Southerners who allowed pressing self-interest to overcome their scruples; and, last of all, the New Englanders whom a comparatively trivial self-interest made them willing allies of the extreme slaveholders. These last were the only Northerners who yielded anything to the Southern slaveholders that was not absolutely necessary; and yet they were the forefathers of the most determined and effective foes that slavery ever had.

❧ ❧ ❧

The fierceness of the opposition to the adoption of the Constitution, and the narrowness of the majority by which Virginia and New York decided in its favor, while North Carolina and Rhode Island did not come in at all until absolutely forced, showed that the refusal to compromise on any one of the points at issue would have jeopardized everything. Had the slavery interest been in the least dissatisfied, or had the plan of government been a shade less democratic, or had the smaller States not been propitiated, the Constitution would have been rejected offhand; and the country would have had before it decades, perhaps centuries, of misrule, violence, and disorder.

Madison paid a very just compliment to some of Morris's best points when he wrote, anent his services in the convention: "To the brilliancy of his genius he added, what is too rare, a candid surrender of his opinions when the light of discussion satisfied him that they had been too hastily formed, and a readiness to aid in making the best of measures in which he had been overruled." Although so many of his own theories had been rejected, he was one of the warmest advocates of the Constitution; and it was he who finally drew up the document and put the finish to its style and arrangement, so that, as it now stands, it comes from his pen.

HISTORY AS LITERATURE

*In 1912 TR was president of the American Historical Association,
and the following is his address to the annual meeting in Boston.
His commonsense response to the endless debate about history—
as science or art—and his view of the role of the historian hold
up very well even after so many years have passed.*

There has been much discussion as to whether history should not henceforth be treated as a branch of science rather than of literature. As with most such discussions, much of the matter in dispute has referred merely to terminology. Moreover, as regards part of the discussion, the minds of the contestants have not met, the propositions advanced by the two sides being neither mutually incompatible nor mutually relevant. There is, however, a real basis for conflict in so far as science claims exclusive possession of the field.

There was a time—we see it in the marvelous dawn of Hellenic life—when history was distinguished neither from poetry, from mythology, nor from the first dim beginnings of science. There was a more recent time, at the opening of Rome's brief period of literary splendor, when poetry was accepted by a great scientific philosopher as the appropriate vehicle for teaching the lessons of science and philosophy. There was a more recent time still—the time of Holland's leadership in arms and arts—when one of the two or three greatest world painters put his genius at the service of anatomists.

In each case the steady growth of specialization has rendered such combination now impossible. Virgil left history to Livy; and when Tacitus had become possible Lucan was a rather absurd anachronism. The elder Darwin, when he endeavored to combine the functions of scientist and poet, may have thought of Lucretius as a model; but the great Darwin was incapable of such a mistake. The surgeons of to-day would prefer the services of a good photographer to those of Rembrandt—even were those of Rembrandt available. No one would now dream of combining the history of the Trojan War with a poem on the wrath of Achilles. Beowulf's feats against the witch who dwelt under the water would not now be mentioned in the same matter-of-fact way that a Frisian or Frankish raid is mentioned. We are long past the stage when we would accept as parts of the same epic Siegfried's triumphs over dwarf and dragon and even a distorted memory of the historic Hunnish king in whose feast-hall the Burgundian heroes held their last revel and made their death fight. We read of the loves of the Hound of Muirthemne and Emer the Fair without attributing to the chariot-riding heroes who "fought over the ears of their horses," and to their fierce lady-loves more than a symbolic reality. The Roland of the Norman trouveres, the Roland who blew the ivory horn at Roncesvalles, is to our minds wholly distinct from the actual Warden of the Marches who fell in a rear-guard skirmish with the Pyrenean Basques.

As regards philosophy, as distinguished from material science and from history, the specialization has been incomplete. Poetry is still used as a vehicle for the teaching of philosophy. Goethe was as profound a thinker as Kant. He has influenced the thought of mankind far more deeply than Kant because he was also a great poet. Robert Browning was a real philosopher, and his writings have had a hundredfold the circulation and the effect of those of any similar philosopher who wrote in prose, just because, and only because, what he wrote was not merely philosophy but literature. The form in which he wrote challenged attention and provoked admiration. That part of his work which some of us—which I myself, for instance—most care for is merely poetry. But in that part of his work which has exercised most attraction and has given him the widest reputation, the poetry, the form of expression, bears to the thought expressed much the same relation that the expression of Lucretius bears to the thought of Lucretius. As regards this, the great mass of his product, he is primarily a philosopher, whose writings surpass in value those of other similar philosophers precisely because they are not only philosophy but literature. In other words, Browning the philosopher is read by countless thousands to whom otherwise philosophy would be a sealed book, for exactly the same reason that Macaulay the historian is read by countless thousands to whom otherwise history would be a sealed book; because both Browning's works and Macaulay's works are material additions to the great sum of English literature. Philosophy is a science just as history is a science. There is need in one case as in the other for vivid and powerful presentation of scientific matter in literary form.

This does not mean that there is the like need in the two cases. History can never be truthfully presented if the presentation is purely emotional. It can never be truthfully or usefully presented unless profound research, patient, laborious, painstaking, has preceded the presentation. No amount of self-communion and of pondering on the soul of mankind, no gorgeousness of literary imagery, can take the place of cool, serious, widely extended study. The vision of the great historian must be both wide and lofty. But it must be sane, clear, and based on full knowledge of the facts and of their interrelations. Otherwise we get merely a splendid bit of serious romance-writing, like Carlyle's *French Revolution.* Many hard-working students, alive to the deficiencies of this kind of romance-writing, have grown to distrust not only all historical writing that is romantic, but all historical writing that is vivid. They feel that complete truthfulness must never be sacrificed to color. In this they are right. They also feel that complete truthfulness is incompatible with color. In this they are wrong. The immense importance of full knowledge of a mass of dry facts and gray details has so impressed them as to make them feel that the dryness and the grayness are in themselves meritorious.

These students have rendered invaluable service to history. They are right in many of their contentions. They see how literature and the science have specialized. They realize that scientific methods are as necessary to the proper study of history as to the proper study of astronomy or zoology. They know that in many, perhaps in most, of its forms, literary ability is divorced from the restrained devotion to the actual fact which is as essential to the historian as to the scientist. They know that nowadays science ostentatiously disclaims any connection with literature. They feel that if this is essential for science, it is no less essential for history.

There is much truth in all these contentions. Nevertheless, taking them all together, they do not indicate what these hard-working students believed that they indicate. Because history, science, and literature have all become specialized, the theory now is that science is definitely severed from literature and that history must follow suit. Not only do I refuse to accept this as true for history, but I do not even accept it as true for science.

Literature may be defined as that which has permanent interest because both of its substance and its form, aside from the mere technical value that inheres in a special treatise for specialists. For a great work of literature there is the same demand now that there always has been; and in any great work of literature the first element is great imaginative power. The imaginative power demanded for a great historian is different from that demanded for a great poet; but it is no less marked. Such imaginative power is in no sense incompatible with minute accuracy. On the contrary, very accurate, very real and vivid, presentation of the past can come only from one in whom the imaginative gift is strong. The industrious collector of dead facts bears to such a man precisely the relation that a photographer bears to Rembrandt. There are innumerable books, that is, innumerable volumes of printed matter between covers, which are excellent for their own purposes, but in which imagination would be as wholly out of place as in the blueprints of a sewer system or in the photographs taken to illustrate a work on comparative osteology. But the vitally necessary sewer system does not take the place of the cathedral of Rheims or of the Parthenon; no quantity of photographs will ever be equivalent to one Rembrandt; and the greatest mass of data, although indispensable to the work of a great historian, is in no shape or way a substitute for that work.

History, taught for a directly and immediately useful purpose to pupils and the teachers of pupils, is one of the necessary features of a sound education in democratic citizenship. A book containing such sound teaching, even if without any literary quality, may be as useful to the student and as creditable to the writer as a similar book on medicine. I am not slighting such a book when I say that, once it has achieved its worthy purpose, it can be permitted to lapse from human memory as a good book on medicine, which has outlived its usefulness, lapses from memory. But the historical work which does possess literary quality may be a permanent contribution to the sum of man's wisdom, enjoyment and inspiration. The writer of such a book must add wisdom to knowledge, and the gift of expression to the gift of imagination.

It is a shallow criticism to assert that imagination tends to inaccuracy. Only a distorted imagination tends to inaccuracy. Vast and fundamental truths can be discerned and interpreted only by one whose imagination is as lofty as the soul of a Hebrew prophet. When we say that the great historian must be a man of imagination, we use the word as we use it when we say that the great statesman must be a man of imagination. Moreover, together with imagination must go the power of expression. The great speeches of statesmen and the great writings of historians can live only if they possess the deathless quality that inheres in all great literature. The greatest literary historian must of necessity be a master of the science of history, a man who has at his finger-tips all the accumulated facts from the treasure-houses of the dead past. But he must also possess the power to marshal what is dead so that before our eyes it lives again.

Many learned people seem to feel that the quality of readableness in a book is one which warrants suspicion. Indeed, not a few learned people seem to feel that the fact that a book is interesting is proof that it is shallow. This is particularly apt to be the attitude of scientific men. Very few great scientists have written interestingly, and these few have usually felt apologetic about it. Yet sooner or later the time will come when the mighty sweep of modern scientific discovery will be placed, by scientific men with the gift of expression, at the service of intelligent and cultivated laymen. Such service will be inestimable. Another writer of *Canterbury Tales*, another singer of *Paradise Lost*, could not add more to the sum of literary achievements than the man who may picture to us the phases of the age-long history of life on this globe, or make vivid before our eyes the tremendous march of the worlds through space.

❧ ❧ ❧

Do not misunderstand me. In the field of historical research an immense amount can be done by men who have no literary power whatever. Moreover, the most painstaking and laborious research, covering long periods of years, is necessary in order to accumulate the material for any history worth writing at all. There are important bypaths of history, moreover, which hardly admit of treatment that would make them of interest to any but specialists. All this I fully admit. In particular I pay high honor to the patient and truthful investigator. He does an indispensable work. My claim is merely that such work should not exclude the work of the great master who can use the materials gathered, who has the gift of vision, the quality of the seer, the power himself to see what has happened and to make what he has seen clear to the vision of others.

ভ ভ ভ

The great historian of the future will have easy access to innumerable facts patiently gathered by tens of thousands of investigators, whereas the great historian of the past had very few facts, and often had to gather most of these himself. The great historian of the future cannot be excused if he fails to draw on the vast storehouses of knowledge that have been accumulated, if he fails to profit by the wisdom and work of other men, which are now the common property of all intelligent men. He must use the instruments which the historians of the past did not have ready to hand. Yet even with these instruments he cannot do as good work as the best of the elder historians unless he has vision and imagination, the power to grasp what is essential and to reject the infinitely more numerous non-essentials, the power to embody ghosts, to put flesh and blood on dry bones, to make dead men living before our eyes. In short, he must have the power to take the science of history and turn it into literature.

Those who wish history to be treated as a purely utilitarian science often decry the recital of the mighty deeds of the past, the deeds which always have aroused, and for a long period to come are likely to arouse, most interest. These men say that we should study not the unusual but the usual. They say that we profit most by laborious research into the drab monotony of the ordinary, rather than by fixing our eyes on the purple patches that break it. Beyond all question the great historian of the future must keep ever in mind the relative importance of the usual and the unusual. If he is a really great historian, if he possesses the highest imaginative and literary quality, he will be able to interest us in the gray tints of the general landscape no less than in the flame hues of the jutting peaks. It is even more essential to have such quality in writing of the commonplace than in writing of the exceptional.

Otherwise no profit will come from study of the ordinary; for writings are useless unless they are read, and they cannot be read unless they are readable. Furthermore, while doing full justice to the importance of the usual, of the commonplace, the great historian will not lose sight of the importance of the heroic.

It is hard to tell just what it is that is most important to know. The wisdom of one generation may seem the folly of the next. This is just as true of the wisdom of the dry-as-dusts as of the wisdom of those who write interestingly. Moreover, while the value of the by-products of knowledge does not readily yield itself to quantitative expression, it is none the less real. A utilitarian education should undoubtedly be the foundation of all education. But it is far from advisable, it is far from wise, to have it the end of all education. Technical training will more and more be accepted as the prime factor in our educational system, a factor as essential for the farmer, the blacksmith, the seamstress, and the cook, as for the lawyer, the doctor, the engineer, and the stenographer. For similar reasons the purely practical and technical lessons of history, the lessons that help us to grapple with our immediate social and industrial problems, will also receive greater emphasis than ever before. But if we are wise we will no more permit this practical training to exclude knowledge of that part of literature which is history than of that part of literature which is poetry. Side by side with the need for the perfection of the individual in the technic of his special calling goes the need of broad human sympathy, and the need of lofty and generous emotion in that individual. Only thus can the citizenship of the modern state rise level to the complex modern social needs.

❧ ❧ ❧

The great historian must be able to paint for us the life of the plain people, the ordinary men and women, of the time of which he writes. He can do this only if he possesses the highest kind of imagination. Collections of figures no more give us a picture of the past than the reading of a tariff report on hides or woolens gives us an idea of the actual lives of the men and women who live on ranches or work in factories. The great historian will in as full measure as possible present to us the every-day life of the men and women of the age which he describes. Nothing that tells of this life will come amiss to him. The instruments of their labor and the weapons of their warfare, the wills that they wrote, the bargains that they made, and the songs that they sang when they feasted and made love: he must use them all. He must tell us of the toil of the ordinary times, and of the play by which that ordinary toil was broken. He must never forget that no event stands out entirely isolated. He must trace from its obscure and humble beginnings each of the movements that in its hour of triumph has shaken the world.

Yet he must not forget that the times that are extraordinary need especial portrayal. In the revolt against the old tendency of historians to deal exclusively with the spectacular and the exceptional, to treat only of war and oratory and government, many modern writers have gone to the opposite extreme. They fail to realize that in the lives of nations as in the lives of men there are hours so fraught with weighty achievement, with triumph or defeat, with joy or sorrow, that each such hour may determine all the years that are to come thereafter, or may outweigh all the years that have gone before. In the writings of our historians, as in the lives of our ordinary citizens, we can neither afford to forget that it is the ordinary every-day life which counts most; nor yet that seasons come when ordinary qualities count for but little in the face of great contending forces of good and of evil, the outcome of whose strife determines whether the nation shall walk in the glory of the morning or in the gloom of spiritual death.

The historian must deal with the days of common things, and deal with them so that they shall interest us in reading of them as our own common things interest us as we live among them. He must trace the changes that come almost unseen, the slow and gradual growth that transforms for good or for evil the children and grandchildren so that they stand high above or far below the level on which their forefathers stood. He must also trace the great cataclysms that interrupt and divert this gradual development. He can no more afford to be blind to one class of phenomena than to the other. He must ever remember that while the worst offense of which he can be guilty is to write vividly and inaccurately, yet that unless he writes vividly he cannot write truthfully; for no amount of dull, painstaking detail will sum up as the whole truth unless the genius is there to paint the truth.

The political campaigner at Providence, Rhode Island, 1902.

3

ON POLITICS AND POLITICAL CAMPAIGNS

THE MENACE OF THE DEMAGOGUE

No political season could pass without Roosevelt stumping for cause and candidate. He campaigned hard for McKinley in 1896, hoping his reward would lead him back to Washington. Never reluctant to employ the hyperbolic for political purposes, TR, in this speech given in October in Chicago, indicts McKinley's opponent, William Jennings Bryan, and the Democrats as virtual enemies of the Republic. It is clear from this speech that negative campaigning has a long history in American politics.

◆◇◆

It is not merely schoolgirls that have hysterics; very vicious mob-leaders have them at times and so do well-meaning demagogues when their heads are turned by the applause of men of little intelligence and their minds inflated with the possibility of acquiring solid leadership in the country. The dominant note in Mr. [William Jennings] Bryan's utterances and in the campaign waged in his behalf is the note of hysteria. Messrs. Bryan, [Illinois governor John Peter] Altgeld, ["Pitchfork" Ben] Tillman, [Eugene V.] Debs, [Jacob] Coxey, and the rest have not the power to rival the deeds of Marat, Barrere, and Robespierre, but they are strikingly like the leaders of the Terror of France in mental and moral attitude, plus an added touch of the grotesque rising from the utter folly as well as the base dishonesty of their trying to play such a role in such a country as ours. For Mr. Bryan we can feel the contemptuous pity always felt for the small man unexpectedly thrust into a big place. He does not look well in a lion's skin, but that is chiefly the fault of those who put the skin on him. But in Mr. Altgeld's case we see all too clearly the jaws and hide of the wolf through the fleecy covering. Mr. Altgeld is a much more dangerous man than Mr. Bryan. He is much slyer, much more intelligent, much less silly, much more free from all the restraints of some public morality. The one is unscrupulous from vanity, the other from calculation.

❦ ❦ ❦

Our foes are waging a campaign which is at bottom waged primarily against morality and ability. They hate the men who pay their debts and obey the laws, exactly as they hate the men who win success in life or who cause the laws to be enforced. They use free silver as a cry because they hope therewith for the moment to mislead some honest men and to bribe some dishonest men; but they really care little for any particular form of policy as regards the currency. At bottom what they most desire is to strike down the men who by virtue of leadership in any walk of life, whether it be in business or theology or law or literature or science, tend by their efforts to raise the whole community upward. The forces which they have rallied behind them and which give them their only real power are the dark and mean hostility and envy felt for all men of ability by those unworthy men who care more to see their brethren fail than themselves to win success by earning and deserving it. Mr. Bryan and his followers rail at every form of enterprise and thrift and at all the countless manifestations of intelligence and of organized effort which go to make up civilization. He attacks business men as such. He attacks clergymen as such.

It is only natural that he should rail also at those who have spent part of their youth in striving to train their minds. He and his compeers who assail success in any form and strive to rouse the jealousy and malice of the less able against the more able, of the less fortunate against the more fortunate, show that they are ignorant of the first principles of our American social life. These principles demand that a man shall be treated for what he is, be he rich or be he poor. It is as un-American to deride and attack the man of means because he is well-to-do or the man of letters because he has a trained mind as it would be to attack his poorer brother who has had no chance to win the wealth or learning. The baseness of the latter attack is such that no American who thinks as we do would dream of making it; but Mr. Bryan and his kind have shown us that there are unfortunately some Americans who need to be taught the baseness and folly of the attack on those who have worked, who have studied, who have won success in letters or science or business.

❧ ❧ ❧

Instead of a government of the people, for the people, and by the people, which we now have, Mr. Bryan would substitute a government of a mob, by the demagogue, for the shiftless and disorderly and the criminal and the semicriminal. The fight for free silver, that is, the fight for that species of dishonest money which its advocates euphoniously call cheap money, is after all only one phase of the fight against civilization which is being waged by the opponents of decent government in this campaign. There are, of course, many sincere and honest men who follow Mr. Bryan's standard because they believe that the coinage of free silver would help the economic situation and consider this the overshadowing issue of the campaign. But these men by themselves would not be formidable foes. They do not make up the bulk even of those who follow Mr. Bryan on the financial issue alone.

With the majority of the men who want cheap money the silver dollar is desired, not because of any abstruse theories about the benefits of bimetallism, but because it is the first step toward that money. Mr. Bland, Mr. Weaver, and all the old-time Greenbackers, or soft-money men, whose motto was "to wipe out the national debt as with a sponge," form the backbone of those supporters of Mr. Bryan who are drawn to him by his financial theories. These men champion a silver dollar because it is cheaper than the gold dollar, just as they would champion a copper dollar rather than one of silver if copper could be made an issue at the moment. What they really want is irredeemable paper money. In other words these curious beings, who sometimes possess good hearts and sometimes not, but who always possess foggy brains, think that the money is of value precisely in the ratio of its being valueless. Gold and its equivalents possessing the greatest value, and forming, therefore, the currency of all the prosperous civilized communities, seem to them undesirable. They want money that is cheap; that is not so valuable. They like a silver dollar, as compared to a gold dollar, because it is worth only half as much; but they like a paper dollar even more because it is not worth anything. They seem to have a curious inverted idea that the minute we can get money that is not worth anything it will turn out to be able to purchase everything.

If there was anything in their theory one of the most prosperous communities that ever existed should have been the Confederate States just before the collapse of the confederacy. There was any amount of money, such as it was, in the Confederacy then and prices were on a scale which should surely have satisfied all who wished to see them high. A pair of boots cost three thousand dollars, and a carpenter's wife who went marketing had to fill her basket entirely full of flat money if she expected to bring it home half full of anything else. Nevertheless, the people were in a condition of wretchedness and starvation such as we now can hardly conceive. It really does not matter much as to the quantity of the money in a country. It is the quality of the money that is of importance and the circumstances of the people. The real point is that the credit of the country should be good and that it should contain those things of which money is merely the measure of value.

But the Bryanites do not depend and cannot depend only upon the cry for cheap money. Dishonest finance is only one of their rallying cries; they wish also a debased judiciary and an executive pledge not to interfere with violent mobs. What they appeal to is the spirit of social unrest, the spirit of discontent. They have invoked the aid of the mean and sombre vices of envy, of hatred for the well-to-do, and of class and of sectional jealousy. Mr. Bryan and the men who stand at his right and his left hands—Atgeld, Tillman, Coxey, Debs, and the rest of the crew—are fit representatives of those forces which simmer beneath the surface of every civilized community, and which, if they could break out, would destroy not only property and civilization but finally even themselves, leaving after them a mere burnt-out waste, as a cooled lava overflow becomes mere slag and cinders. They seek to rally to their banners all the forces that make for social disorder and national destruction. They hold out lures to the honest man who, through no fault of his own, has met with crushing disaster, and who strikes at what he calls the conditions of society with the same unreasonable anger that makes a child strike at the table or door against which it has hurt itself. They dazzle the eye of the visionary social reformer (well known to every man who has struggled for practical reform as one of his greatest enemies); the being who reads Tolstoy, or, if he possesses less intellect, Bellamy and Henry George;

who studies Karl Marx and Proudhon, and believes that at this stage of the world's progress it is possible to make every one happy by an immense social revolution, just as other enthusiasts of similar mental caliber believe in the possibility of constructing a perpetual-motion machine. They bid for the support of the knaves who see their profit in social convulsion, hoping to find it, if they be demagogues, in the shape of high office; or if they are more vulgar wrong-doers, in the opportunities offered by a general relaxation of the laws. They attract to their standard of the sullen men without very much intellect or very much strength of character, who are given to emotional bursts, both of good and evil, who are apt to think themselves injured because they do not get along as well as their more thrifty or harder working or more intelligent neighbors, and who can be readily led by demagogues into an agitation of which they will ultimately be themselves the most help-less victim.

ᘓ ᘓ ᘓ

Mr. Bryan conducts a campaign of denunciation. He is especially fond of denouncing non-producers. Does he mean by non-producers men who do not work with their hands? Lincoln and Grant, Sherman and Farragut, ren-dered the country some service at a time when they were not working with their hands. So, in another way, did Emerson and Lowell and Hawthorne; and yet in another way did Fulton and Morse and Edison. Does Mr. Bryan really believe that all these men were useless to the country? Is he so lost to all sense of patriotism that he does not glory in their service to the nation? Take again his denunciation of capitalists. There are good capitalists and bad capitalists, just as there are good working men and bad working men, honest bank cashiers and dishonest bank cashiers, reputable and disrep-utable newspaper men, straight and crooked politicians. A bad capitalist is worse than a bad man without capital because he can do more mischief; just as a bad man of ability is worse than a bad man of no ability. This no more justifies a general assault on all men of ability. There are in this country but a very small number of great capitalists. I am not concerned in them. I am concerned for the great body of our people, because I know that the people cannot afford to go wrong. I wish them to refrain from wronging others, chiefly because by so doing they would wrong no one so much as them-selves. What is a capitalist anyhow? Every man who saves money is a capi-talist. A good capitalist who employs his money and his leisure aright is often the most useful man in the community. The extreme Socialist, the champion of the type of government which found its highest expression in the Paris commune, objects to the man who puts a few dollars a month in a savings-bank on the ground that he thereby becomes a capitalist. Mr. Bryan is well on his way toward this position. Moreover, the capitalist and the wage-earner are often one. Seventy per cent of the people in the United States earn wages and receive salaries. Mr. Bryan's success would at one blow strike off here the value of the earnings of these men.

✿ ✿ ✿

We believe that the campaign should be waged on the moral, even more than the material, issue. Mr. Bryan and Mr. Altgeld are the embodiments of the two principles which our adversaries desire to see triumph; and in their ultimate analysis those principles are merely the negations of the two commandments, "Thou shalt not steal" and "Thou shalt do no murder." Mr. Bryan champions that system of dishonesty which would steal from the creditors of the nation half of what they have in good faith loaned and from the working men of the nation half of what by their honest toil they have earned. Mr. Altgeld condones and encourages the most infamous of murders and denounces the Federal Government and the Supreme Court for interfering to put a stop to the bloody lawlessness which would result in worse than murder. Both of them would substitute for the government of Washington and Lincoln, for the system of orderly liberty which we inherit from our forefathers and which we desire to bequeath to our sons, a red welter of lawlessness and dishonesty as fantastic and as vicious as the Paris commune itself. Turning aside from the American principles of government, repudiating everything which has made the name a symbol of hope among nations, they seek to substitute a crazy fabric, patched up from the worn-out theories of every European dreamer and European agitator. We appeal to no class and to no section; we appeal to all the citizens of this land alike, merely as Americans. Easterner and Westerner, Northerner and Southerner, merchant and working man, we ask you to stand together as Americans, jealous of the honor of your country and indignant at those who propose to drag that honor in the dust. We ask you to stand for decent government and the honest payment of debts. We ask you to set your faces against the spirit of lawless mob violence which could in the end produce nothing but anarchy; anarchy, the handmaiden and sure herald of tyranny. We ask you to vote against Mr. Bryan, not merely because his success would mean the impoverishment of the poor and the trouble of the rich, the breaking up of homes, the despair of strong men and the hungry misery of the women and children, but because the laws of right and justice bid you oppose them. We ask you to declare for the payment of honest debts and for the suppression of lawless mobs not merely because it is expedient but because it is right. No nation can long hold its place in the world if it does not strive to live up to a lofty moral ideal; and we ask you to join in the overthrow of the enemies of American honor and of American liberty because every principle of sound morality bids you take such action.

HOW NOT TO HELP OUR POORER BROTHERS

To the frustration of historians eager to classify him, TR at times struck conservative postures and at times looked like a genuine progressive reformer. In this essay, which was pub-lished in Review of Reviews *in 1897, he offers a deeply conser-vative political testament. It is an attitude his presidential experience would modify and one much different from the Progressive candidate of 1912.*

There are plenty of ugly things about wealth and its possessors in the present age, and I suppose there have been in all ages. There are many rich people who so utterly lack patriotism, or show such sordid and selfish traits of character, or lead such mean and vacuous lives, that all right-minded men must look upon them with angry contempt; but, on the whole, the thrifty are apt to be better citizens than the thriftless; and the worst capitalist cannot harm laboring men as they are harmed by demagogues. As the people of a State grow more and more intelligent the State itself may be able to play a larger and larger part in the life of the community, while at the same time individual effort may be given freer and less restricted movement along cer-tain lines; but it is utterly unsafe to give the State more than the minimum of power just so long as it contains masses of men who can be moved by the pleas and denunciations of the average Socialist leader of to-day. There may be better schemes of taxation than those at present employed; it may be wise to devise inheritance taxes, and to impose regulations on the kinds of busi-ness which can be carried on only under the special protection of the State; and where there is a real abuse by wealth it needs to be, and in this country generally has been, promptly done away with; but the first lesson to teach the poor man is that, as a whole, the wealth in the community is distinctly beneficial to him; that he is better off in the long run because other men are well off and that the surest way to destroy what measure of prosperity he may have is to paralyze industry and the well-being of those men who have achieved success.

I am not an empiricist; I would no more deny that sometimes human affairs can be much bettered by legislation than I would affirm that they can always be so bettered. I would no more make a fetish of unrestricted indi-vidualism than I would admit the power of the State offhand and radically to reconstruct society. It may become necessary to interfere even more than we have done with the right of private contract, and to shackle cunning as we have shackled force. All I insist upon is that we must be sure of our ground before trying to get any legislation at all, and that we must not expect too much from this legislation, nor refuse to better ourselves a little because we cannot accomplish everything at a jump. Above all, it is criminal to excite anger and discontent without proposing a remedy, or only proposing a false remedy. The worst foe of the poor man is the labor leader, whether philanthropist or politician, who tries to teach him that he is a victim of conspiracy and injustice, when in reality he is merely working out his fate with blood and sweat as the immense majority of men who are worthy of the name always have done and always will have to do.

The difference between what can and what cannot be done by law is well exemplified by our experience with the Negro problem. . . . The Negroes were formerly held in slavery. This was a wrong which legislation could remedy, and which could not be remedied except by legislation. Accordingly they were set free by law. This having been done, many of their friends believed that in some way, by additional legislation, we could at once put them on an intellectual, social, and business equality with the whites. The effort has failed completely. In large sections of the country the Negroes are not treated as they should be treated, and politically in particular the frauds upon them have been so gross and shameful as to awaken not merely indignation but bitter wrath; yet the best friends of the Negro admit that his hope lies, not in legislation, but in the constant working of those often unseen forces of the national life which are greater than all legislation.

It is but rarely that great advances in general social well-being can be made by the adoption of some far-reaching scheme, legislative or otherwise; normally they come only by gradual growth, and by incessant effort to do first one thing, then another, and then another. Quack remedies of the universal cure-all type are generally as noxious to the body politic as to the body corporal.

Often the head-in-the-air social reformers, because people of sane and wholesome minds will not favor their wild schemes, themselves decline to favor schemes for practical reform. For the last two years there has been an honest effort in New York to give the city good government, and to work intelligently for better social conditions, especially in the poorest quarters. We have cleaned the streets; we have broken the power of the ward boss and the saloon-keeper to work injustice; we have destroyed the most hideous of the tenement houses in which poor people are huddled like swine in a sty; we have made parks and playgrounds for the children in the crowded quarters; in every possible way we have striven to make life easier and healthier, and to give man and woman a chance to do their best work;

while at the same time we have warred steadily against the pauper-producing, maudlin philanthropy of the free soup-kitchen and tramp lodging-house kind. In all this we have had practically no help from either the parlor socialists or the scarcely more noxious beer-room socialists who are always howling about the selfishness of the rich and their unwillingness to do anything for those who are less well off.

There are certain labor unions, certain bodies of organized labor— notably those admirable organizations which include the railway conductors, the locomotive engineers and the firemen—which to my mind embody almost the best hope that there is for healthy national growth in the future; but bitter experience has taught men who work for reform in New York that the average labor leader, the average demagogue who shouts for a depreciated currency, or for the overthrow of the rich, will not do anything to help those who honestly strive to make better our civic conditions. There are immense numbers of workingmen to whom we can appeal with perfect confidence; but too often we find that a large proportion of the men who style themselves leaders of organized labor are influenced only by sullen short-sighted hatred of what they do not understand, and are deaf to all appeals, whether to their national or to their civic patriotism.

What I most grudge in all this is the fact that sincere and zealous men of high character and honest purpose . . . such as are to be found in all strata of our society, from the employer to the hardest-worked day laborer, go astray in their methods, and are thereby prevented from doing the full work for good they ought to. When a man goes on the wrong road himself he can do very little to guide others aright, even though these others are also on the wrong road. There are many wrongs to be righted; there are many measures of relief to be pushed; and it is a pity that when we are fighting what is bad and championing what is good, the men who ought to be our most effective allies should deprive themselves of usefulness by the wrong-headedness of their position. Rich men and poor men both do wrong on occasions, and whenever a specific instance of this can be pointed out all citizens alike should join in punishing the wrong-doer. Honesty and right-mindedness should be the tests; not wealth or poverty.

In our municipal administration here in New York we have acted with an equal hand toward wrong-doers of high and low degree. The Board of Health condemns the tenement-house property of the rich landowner, whether this landowner be priest or layman, banker or railroad president, lawyer or manager of a real estate business; and it pays no heed to the intercession of any politician, whether this politician be Catholic or Protestant, Jew or Gentile. At the same time the Police Department promptly suppresses, not only the criminal, but the rioter. In other words, we do strict justice. We feel we are defrauded of help to which we are entitled when men who ought to assist in any work to better the conditions of the people decline to aid us because their brains are turned by dreams only worthy of a European revolutionist.

Many workingmen look with distrust upon laws which really would help them; laws for the intelligent restriction of immigration, for instance. I have no sympathy with mere dislike of immigrants; there are classes and even nationalities of them which stand at least on an equality with the citizens of native birth, as the last election showed. But in the interest of our workingmen we must in the end keep out laborers who are ignorant, vicious, and with low standards of life and comfort just as we have shut out the Chinese.

Often labor leaders and the like denounce the present conditions of society, and especially of our political life, for shortcomings which they themselves have been instrumental in causing. In our cities the misgovernment is due, not to the misdeeds of the rich, but to the low standard of honesty and morality among citizens generally; and nothing helps the corrupt politician more than substituting either wealth or poverty for honesty as the standard by which to try a candidate. A few months ago a socialistic reformer in New York was denouncing the corruption caused by rich men because a certain judge was suspected of giving information in advance as to a decision in a case involving the interests of a great corporation. Now this judge had been elected some years previously, mainly because he was supposed to be a representative of the "poor man"; and the socialistic reformer himself, a year ago, was opposing the election of Mr. Beaman as judge because he was one of the firm of Evarts & Choate, who were friends of various millionaires and were counsel for various corporations. But if Mr. Beaman had been elected judge no human being, rich or poor, would have dared so much as hint at his doing anything improper.

Something can be done by good laws; more can be done by honest administration of the laws; but most of all can be done by frowning resolutely upon the preachers of vague discontent; and by upholding the true doctrine of self-reliance, self-help, and self-mastery. This doctrine sets forth many things. Among them is the fact that though a man can occasionally be helped when he stumbles, yet that it is useless to try to carry him when he will not or cannot walk; and worse than useless to try to bring down the work and reward of the thrifty and intelligent to the level of the capacity of the weak, the shiftless, and the idle. It further shows that the maudlin philanthropist and the maudlin sentimentalist are almost as noxious as the demagogue, and that it is even more necessary to temper mercy with justice than justice with mercy.

The worst lesson that can be taught a man is to rely upon others and to whine over his sufferings. If an American is to amount to anything he must rely upon himself, and not upon the State; he must take pride in his own work, instead of sitting idle to envy the luck of others; he must face life with resolute courage, win victory if he can, and accept defeat if he must, without seeking to place on his fellow-men a responsibility which is not theirs.

ON BUSINESS AND LABOR

*The views TR held on business and labor as a new president in
1901 and as a retiring executive in 1908 are remarkably far
apart. The distance is clear in comparing his tentative and
heavily buffered criticisms of the great corporations in his First
Annual Message with the confident and robust critique he delivered in his last message. TR's prescriptions for the federal regulation of corporations and for worker benefits forecast his program
as a Progressive candidate in the 1912 campaign. His call for
a strong central government to harness the power of capital was
an important step in setting the focus of twentieth-century
political debate in the United States.*

First Annual Message to Congress [1901]

During the last five years business confidence has been restored, and the
nation is to be congratulated because of its present abounding prosperity. Such
prosperity can never be created by law alone, although it is easy enough to
destroy any country, if flood or drought comes, human wisdom is powerless to
avert the calamity. Moreover, no law can guard us against the consequences of
our own folly. The men who are idle or credulous, the men who seek gains not
by genuine work with head or hand but by gambling in any form, are always a
source of menace not only to themselves but to others. If the business world
loses its head, it loses what legislation cannot supply. Fundamentally, the welfare of each citizen, and therefore, the welfare of the aggregate of citizens
which makes the nation, must rest upon individual thrift and energy, resolution, and intelligence. Nothing can take the place of this individual capacity;
but wise legislation and honest and intelligent administration can give it the
fullest scope, the largest opportunity to work to good effect.

The tremendous and highly complex industrial development which went on
with ever-accelerated rapidity during the latter half of the nineteenth century
brings us face to face, at the beginning of the twentieth, with very serious
social problems. The old laws, and the old customs which had almost the binding force of law, were once quite sufficient to regulate the accumulation and
distribution of wealth. Since the industrial changes which have so enormously
increased the productive power of mankind, they are no longer sufficient.

The growth of cities has gone on beyond comparison faster than the
growth of the country, and the upbuilding of the great industrial centres has
meant a startling increase, not merely in the aggregate of wealth, but in the

number of very large individual, and especially of very large corporate, fortunes. The creation of these great corporate fortunes has not been due to the
tariff nor to any other governmental action, but to natural causes in the
business world, operating in other countries as they operate in our own.

The process has aroused much antagonism, a great part of which is
wholly without warrant. It is not true that as the rich have grown richer the
poor have grown poorer. On the contrary, never before has the average
man, the wage-worker, the farmer, the small trader, been so well off as in
this country and at the present time. There have been abuses connected with
the accumulation of wealth; yet it remains true that a fortune accumulated in
legitimate business can be accumulated by the person specially benefitted
only on condition of conferring immense incidental benefits upon others.
Successful enterprise, of the type which benefits all mankind, can only exist
if the conditions are such as to offer great prizes as the rewards of success.

The captains of industry who have driven the railway systems across this
continent, who have built up our commerce, who have developed our manufactures, have on the whole done great good to our people. Without them
the material development of which we are so justly proud could never have
taken place. Moreover, we should recognize the immense importance of this
material development—of leaving as unhampered as is compatible with the
public good the strong and forceful men upon whom the success of business
operations inevitably rests. The slightest study of business conditions will
satisfy anyone capable of forming a judgment that the personal equation is
the most important factor in a business operation; that the business ability of
the man at the head of any business concern, big or little, is usually the factor which fixes the gulf between striking success and hopeless failure.

An additional reason for caution in dealing with corporations is to be
found in the international commercial conditions of to-day. The same business conditions which have produced the great aggregations of corporate
and individual wealth have made them very potent factors in international
commercial competition. Business concerns which have the largest means at
their disposal and are managed by the ablest men are naturally those which
take the lead in the strife for commercial supremacy among the nations of
the world. America has only just begun to assume that commanding position
in the international business world which we believe will more and more be
hers. It is of the utmost importance that this position be not jeopardized,
especially at a time when the over-flowing abundance of our own natural
resources and the skill, business energy, and mechanical aptitude of our people
make foreign markets essential. Under such conditions it would be most
unwise to cramp or to fetter the youthful strength of our nation.

Moreover, it cannot too often be pointed out that to strike with ignorant violence at the interests of one set of men almost inevitably endangers the interests of all. The fundamental rule in our national life—the rule which underlies all others—is that, on the whole, and in the long run, we shall go up or down together. There are exceptions; and in times of prosperity some will prosper far more, and in times of adversity, some will suffer far more, than others; but speaking generally, a period of good times means that all share more or less in them, and in a period of hard times all feel the stress to a greater or less degree. It surely ought not to be necessary to enter into any proof of this statement; the memory of the lean years which began in 1893 is still vivid, and we can contrast them with the conditions in this very year which is now closing. Disaster to great business enterprises can never have its effects limited to the men at the top. It spreads throughout, and while it is bad for everybody, it is worst for those farthest down. The capitalist may be shorn of his luxuries; but the wage-worker may be deprived of even bare necessities.

The mechanism of modern business is so delicate that extreme care must be taken not to interfere with it in a spirit of rashness or ignorance. Many of those who have made it their vocation to denounce the great industrial combinations which are popularly, although with technical inaccuracy, known as "trusts," appeal especially to hatred and fear. These are precisely the two emotions, particularly when combined with ignorance, which unfit men for the exercise of cool and steady judgment. In facing new industrial conditions, the whole history of the world shows that legislation will generally be both unwise and ineffective unless undertaken after calm inquiry and with sober self-restraint. Much of the legislation directed at the trusts would have been exceedingly mischievous had it not also been entirely ineffective. In accordance with a well-known sociological law, the ignorant or reckless agitator has been the really effective friend of the evils which he has been nominally opposing. In dealing with business interests, for the government to undertake by crude and ill-considered legislation to do what may turn out to be bad would be to incur the risk of such far-reaching national disaster that it would be preferable to undertake nothing at all. The men who demand the impossible or the undesirable serve as the allies of the forces with which they are nominally at war, for they hamper those who would endeavor to find out in rational fashion what the wrongs really are and to what extent and in what manner it is practicable to apply remedies.

All this is true; and yet it is also true that there are real and grave evils, one of the chief being overcapitalization because of its many baleful consequences; and a resolute and practical effort must be made to correct these evils.

There is a wide-spread conviction in the minds of the American people that the great corporations known as trusts are in certain of their features and tendencies hurtful to the general welfare. This springs from no spirit of envy or uncharitableness, nor lack of pride in the great industrial achievements that have placed this country at the head of the nations struggling for commercial supremacy. It does not rest upon a lack of intelligent appreciation of the necessity of meeting changing and changed conditions of trade with new methods, nor upon ignorance of the fact that combination of capital in the effort to accomplish great things is necessary when the world's progress demands the great things to be done. It is based upon sincere conviction that combination and concentration should be, not prohibited, but supervised and within reasonable limits controlled; and in my judgment this conviction is right.

♦ ♦ ♦

When the Constitution was adopted, at the end of the eighteenth century, no human wisdom could foretell the sweeping changes, alike in industrial and political conditions, which were to take place by the beginning of the twentieth century. At that time it was accepted as a matter of course that the several States were the proper authorities to regulate, so far as was then necessary, the comparatively insignificant and strictly localized corporate bodies of the day. The conditions are now wholly different and wholly different action is called for. I believe that a law can be framed which will enable the National Government to exercise control along the lines above indicated, profiting by the experience gained through the passage and administration of the Interstate Commerce Act. If, however, the judgment of the Congress is that it lacks the constitutional power to pass such an act, then a constitutional amendment should be submitted to confer the power.

♦ ♦ ♦

With the sole exception of the farming interest, no one matter is of such vital moment to our whole people as the welfare of the wage-workers. If the farmer and the wage-worker are well off, it is absolutely certain that all others will be well off too. It is therefore a matter for hearty congratulation that on the whole wages are higher to-day in the United States than ever before in our history, and far higher than in any other country. The standard of living is also higher than ever before. Every effort of legislator and administrator should be bent to secure the permanency of this condition of things and its improvement wherever possible. Not only must our labor be protected by the tariff, but it should also be protected so far as it is possible from the presence in this country of any laborers brought over by contract, or of those who, coming freely, yet represent a standard of living so depressed that they can undersell our men in the labor market and drag them to a lower level. I regard it as necessary with this end in view, to re-enact immediately the law excluding Chinese laborers and to strengthen it wherever necessary in order to make its enforcement entirely effective.

The National Government should demand the highest quality of service from its employees; and in return it should be a good employer. If possible legislation should be passed, in connection with the Interstate Commerce Law, which will render effective the efforts of different States to do away with the competition of convict contract labor in the open labor market. So far as practicable under the conditions of government work, provision should be made to render the enforcement of the eight-hour law easy and certain. In all industries carried on directly or indirectly for the United States Government women and children should be protected from excessive hours of labor, from night-work, and from work under unsanitary conditions. The government should provide in its contracts that all work should be done under "fair" conditions, and in addition to setting a high standard should uphold it by proper inspection, extending if necessary to the subcontractors. The government should forbid all night-work for women and children, as well as excessive overtime. For the District of Columbia a good factory law should be passed; and, as a powerful indirect aid to such laws, provision should be made to turn the inhabited alleys, the existence of which is a reproach to our capital city, into minor streets, where the inhabitants can live under conditions favorable to health and morals.

American wage-workers work with their heads as well as their hands. Moreover, they take a keen pride in what they are doing; so that, independent of the reward, they wish to turn out a perfect job. This is the great secret of our success in competition with the labor of foreign countries.

The most vital problem with which this country, and for that matter the whole civilized world, has to deal, is the problem which has for one side the betterment of social conditions, moral and physical, in large cities, and for another side the effort to deal with that tangle of far-reaching questions which we group together when we speak of "labor." The chief factor in the success of each man—wage-worker, farmer, and capitalist alike—must ever be the sum total of his own individual qualities and abilities. Second only to this comes the power of acting in combination or association with others. Very great good has been and will be accomplished by associations or unions of wage-workers, when managed with fore-thought, and when they combine insistence upon their own rights with law-abiding respect for the rights of others. The display of these qualities in such bodies is a duty to the nation no less than to the associations themselves. Finally, there must also in many cases be action by the government in order to safeguard the rights and interests of all. Under our constitution there is much more scope for such action by the State and the municipality than by the nation. But on points such as those touched on above the National Government can act.

When all is said and done, the rule of brotherhood remains as the indispensable prerequisite to success in the kind of national life for which we strive. Each man must work for himself, and unless he so works no outside help can avail him; but each man must remember also that he is indeed his brother's keeper, and that while no man who refuses to walk can be carried with advantage to himself or anyone else, yet that each at times stumbles or halts, that each at times needs to have the helping hand outstretched to him. To be permanently effective, aid must always take the form of helping a man to help himself; and we can all best help ourselves by joining together in the work that is of common interest to all.

Eighth Annual Message to Congress [1908]

As regards the great corporations engaged in interstate business, and especially the railroad, I can only repeat what I have already again and again said in my messages to the Congress. I believe that under the interstate clause of the Constitution the United States has complete and paramount right to control all agencies of interstate commerce; and I believe that the National Government alone can exercise this right with wisdom and effectiveness so as both to secure justice from, and to do justice to, the great corporations which are the most important factors in modern business. I believe that it is worse than folly to attempt to prohibit all combinations as is done by the Sherman antitrust law, because such a law can be enforced only imperfectly and unequally, and its enforcement works almost as much hardship as good. I strongly advocate that instead of an unwise effort to prohibit all combinations there shall be substituted a law which shall expressly permit combinations which are in the interest of the public, but shall at the same time give to some agency of the National Government full power of control and supervision over them. One of the chief features of this control should be securing entire publicity in all matters which the public has a right to know, and furthermore, the power, not by judicial but by executive action, to prevent or put a stop to every form of improper favoritism or other wrong-doing.

The railways of the country should be put completely under the Interstate Commerce Commission and removed from the domain of the antitrust law. The power of the commission should be made thoroughgoing, so that it could exercise complete supervision and control over the issue of securities as well as over the raising and lowering of rates. As regards rates, at least, this power should be summary. The power to investigate the financial operations and accounts of the railways has been one of the most valuable features in recent legislation. Power to make combinations and traffic agreements should be explicitly conferred upon the railroads, the permission of the commission being first gained and the combination or agreement being published in all its details. In the interest of the public the representatives of the public should have complete power to see that the railroads do their duty by the public, and as a matter of course this power should also be exercised so as to see that no injustice is done to the railroads. The shareholders, the employees, and the shippers all have interests that must be guarded. It is to the interest of all of them that no swindling stock speculation should be allowed, and that there should be no improper issuance of securities. The guiding intelligences necessary for the successful building and successful management of railroads should receive ample remuneration; but no man should be allowed to make money in connection with railroads out of fraudulent overcapitalization and kindred stock-gambling performances; there must be no defrauding of investors, oppression of the farmers and business men who ship freight, or callous disregard of the rights and needs of the employees. In addition to this the interests of the shareholders, of the employees, and of the shippers should all be guarded as against one another. To give any one of the them undue and improper consideration is to do injustice to the others. Rates must be made as low as is compatible with giving proper returns to all the employees of the railroad, from the highest to the lowest, and proper returns to the shareholders; but they must not, for instance, be reduced in such fashion as to necessitate a cut in the wages of the employees or the abolition of the proper and legitimate profits of honest shareholders.

Telegraph and telephone companies engaged in interstate business should be put under the jurisdiction of the Interstate Commerce Commission.

It is very earnestly to be wished that our people, through their representatives, should act in this matter. It is hard to say whether most damage to the country at large would come from entire failure on the part of the public to supervise and control the actions of the great corporations, or from the exercise of the necessary governmental power in a way which would do injustice and wrong to the corporations. Both the preachers of an unrestricted individualism, and the preachers of an oppression which would deny to able men of business the just reward of their initiative and business sagacity, are advocating policies that would be fraught with the gravest harm to the whole country. To permit every lawless capitalist, every law-defying corporation, to take any action, no matter how iniquitous, in the effort to secure an improper profit and to build up privilege, would be ruinous to the Republic and would mark the abandonment of the effort to secure in the industrial world the spirit of democratic fair dealing. On the other hand, to attack these wrongs in that spirit of demagogy which can see wrong only when committed by the man of wealth, and is dumb and blind in the presence of wrong committed against men of property or by men of no property, is exactly as evil as corruptly to defend the wrong-doing of men of wealth. The war we wage must be waged against misconduct, against wrong-doing wherever it is found; and we must stand heartily for the rights of every decent man, whether he be a man of great wealth or a man who earns his livelihood as a wage-worker or a tiller of the soil.

ピ ピ ピ

The opposition to government control of these great corporations makes its most effective effort in the shape of an appeal to the old doctrine of States' rights. Of course there are many sincere men who now believe in unrestricted individualism in business, just as there were formerly many sincere men who believed in slavery—that is, in the unrestricted right of an individual to own another individual. These men do not by themselves have great weight, however. The effective fight against adequate government control and supervision of individual, and especially of corporate, wealth engaged in interstate business is chiefly done under cover; and especially under cover of an appeal to States' rights. It is not at all infrequent to read in the same speech a denunciation of predatory wealth fostered by special privilege and defiant of both the public welfare and law of the land, and a denunciation of centralization in the centralized and organized wealth. Of course the policy set forth in such twin denunciations amounts to absolutely nothing, for the first half is nullified by the second half. The chief reason, among the many sound and compelling reasons, that led to the formation of the National Government was the absolute need that the Union, and not the several States, should deal with interstate and foreign commerce; and the power to deal with interstate commerce was granted absolutely and plenarily to the central government and was exercised completely as regards the only instruments of interstate commerce known in those days—the waterways, the highroads, as well as the partnerships of individuals who then conducted all of what business there was. Interstate commerce is now chiefly conducted by railroads; and the great corporation has supplanted the mass of small partnerships or individuals. The proposal to make the National Government supreme over, and therefore to give it complete control over, the railroads and other instruments of interstate commerce is merely a proposal to carry out to the letter one of the prime purposes, if not the prime purpose, for which the Constitution was founded. It does not represent centralization. It represents merely the acknowledgement of the patent fact that centralization has already come in business. If this irresponsible outside business power is to be controlled in the interest of the general public it can only be controlled in one way—by giving adequate power of control to the one sovereignty capable of exercising such power—the National Government. Forty or fifty separate State governments cannot exercise that power over corporations doing business in most or all of them; first, because they absolutely lack the authority to deal with interstate business in any form; and second, because of the inevitable conflict of authority sure to arise in the effort to enforce different kinds of State regulation, often inconsistent with one another and sometimes oppressive in themselves. Such divided authority cannot regulate commerce with wisdom and effect. The central government is the only power which, without oppression, can nevertheless thoroughly and adequately control and supervise the large corporations. To abandon the effort for national control means to abandon the effort for all adequate control and yet to render likely continual bursts of action by State legislatures, which cannot achieve the purpose sought for, but which can do a great deal of damage to the corporation without conferring any real benefit on the public.

I believe that the more far-sighted corporations are themselves coming to recognize the unwisdom of the violent hostility they have displayed during the last few years to regulation and control by the National Government of combinations engaged in interstate business. The truth is that we who believe in this movement of asserting and exercising a genuine control, in the public interest, over these great corporations have to contend against two sets of enemies, who, though nominally opposed to one another, are really allies in preventing a proper solution of the problem. There are, first, the big corporation men, and the extreme individualists among business men, who genuinely believe in utterly unregulated business—that is, in the reign of plutocracy; and, second, the men who, being blind to the economic movements of the day, believe in a movement of repression rather than of regulation of corporations, and who denounce both the power of the railroads and the exercise of the Federal power which alone can really control the railroads. Those who believe in efficient national control, on the other hand, do not in the least object to combinations; do not in the least object to concentration in business administration. On the contrary, they favor both, with the all-important proviso that there shall be such publicity about their workings, and such thoroughgoing control over them, as to insure their being in the interest, and not against the interest, of the general public. We do not object to the concentration of wealth and administration; but we do believe in the distribution of the wealth in profits to the real owners, and in securing to the public the full benefit of the concentrated administration. We believe that with concentration in administration there can come both the advantage of a larger ownership and of a more equitable distribution of profits, and at the same time a better service to the commonwealth. We believe that the administration should be for the benefit of the many; and that greed and rascality, practiced on a large scale, should be punished as relentlessly as if practiced on a small scale.

🌿 🌿 🌿

This administration is nearing its end; and, moreover, under our form of government the solution of the problem depends upon the action of the States as much as upon the action of the nation. Nevertheless, there are certain considerations which I wish to set before you, because I hope that our people will more and more keep them in mind. A blind and ignorant resistance to every effort for the reform of abuses and for the readjustment of society to modern industrial conditions represents not true conservatism, but an incitement to the wildest radicalism; for wise radicalism and wise conservatism go hand in hand, one bent on progress, the other bent on seeing that no change is made unless in the right direction. I believe in a steady effort, or perhaps it would be more accurate to say in steady efforts in many different directions, to bring about a condition of affairs under which the men who work with hand or with brain, the laborers, the superintendents, the men who produce for the market and the men who find a market for the articles produced, shall own a far greater share than at present of the wealth they produce, and be enabled to invest it in the tools and instruments by which all work is carried on. As far as possible I hope to see a frank recognition of the advantages conferred by machinery, organization, and division of labor, accompanied by an effort to bring about a larger share in the ownership by wage-worker of railway, mill, and factory. In farming, this simply means that we wish to see the farmer own his own land; we do not wish to see the farms so large that they become the property of absentee landlords who farm them by tenants, nor yet so small that the farmer becomes like a European peasant. Again, the depositors in our savings-banks now number over one-tenth of our entire population. These are all capitalists, who through the savings-banks loan their money to the workers—that is, in many cases to themselves—to carry on their various industries. The more we increase their number, the more we introduce the principle of co-operation into our industry. Every increase in the number of small stockholders in corporations is a good thing, for the same reasons; and where the employees are the stockholders the result is particularly good. Very much of this movement must be outside of anything that can be accomplished by legislation; but legislation can do a good deal. Postal savings-banks will make it easy for the poorest to keep their savings in absolute safety. The regulation of the national highways must be such that they shall serve all people with equal justice. Corporate finances must be supervised so as to make it far safer than at present for the man of small means to invest his money in stocks. There must be prohibition of child labor, diminution of woman labor, shortening of hours of all mechanical labor; stock watering should be prohibited, and stock gambling so far as is possible discouraged. There should be a progressive inheritance tax on large fortunes. Industrial education should be encouraged. As far as possible we should lighten the burden of taxation on the small man. We should put a premium upon thrift, hard work, and business energy; but these qualities cease to be the main factors in accumulating a fortune long before that fortune reaches a point where it would be seriously affected by any inheritance tax such as I propose. It is eminently right that the nation should fix the terms upon which the great fortunes are inherited. They rarely do good and they often do harm to those who inherit them in their entirety.

The above is the merest sketch, hardly even a sketch in outline, of the reforms for which we should work. But there is one matter with which the Congress should deal at this session. There should no longer be any paltering with the question of taking care of the wage-workers who, under our present industrial system, become killed, crippled, or worn out as part of the regular incidents of a given business. The majority of wage-workers must have their rights secured for them by State action; but the National Government should legislate in thoroughgoing and far-reaching fashion not only for all employees of the National Government, but for all persons engaged in interstate commerce. The object sought for could be achieved to a measurable degree, as far as those killed or crippled are concerned, by proper employers' liability laws. As far as concerns those who have been worn out, I call your attention to the fact that definite steps toward providing old-age pensions have been taken in many of our private industries. These may be indefinitely extended through voluntary association and contributory schemes, or through the agency of savings-banks, as under the recent Massachusetts plan. To strengthen these practical measures should be our immediate duty; it is not at present necessary to consider the larger and more general governmental schemes that most European governments have found themselves obliged to adopt.

Our present system, or rather no system, works dreadful wrong, and is of benefit to only one class of people—the lawyers. When a workman is injured what he needs is not an expensive and doubtful lawsuit, but the certainty of relief through immediate administrative action. The number of accidents which result in the death or crippling of wage-workers in the Union at large is simply appalling; in a very few years it runs up a total far in excess of the aggregate of the dead and wounded in any modern war. No academic theory about "freedom of contract" or "constitutional liberty to contract" should be permitted to interfere with this and similar movements. Progress in civilization has everywhere meant a limitation and regulation of contract. I call your especial attention to the bulletin of the Bureau of Labor which gives a statement of the methods of treating the unemployed in European countries, as this is a subject which in Germany, for instance, is treated in connection with making provision for worn-out and crippled workmen.

ᴿ ᴿ ᴿ

In this respect the generosity of the United States toward its employees compares most unfavorably with that of every country in Europe—even the poorest.

THE NEW NATIONALISM [1910]

The most important speech of his career after he left the presidency was TR's address at Osawatomie, Kansas, on August 31, 1910. It served, in fact, to begin his campaign to return to the White House. His call for a "New Nationalism" (the slogan for the campaign) excited the Progressives and convinced conservative Republicans that their long-standing fears of Roosevelt's unreliability were justified. When he argued that the commonweal retained the right to regulate the use of property "to whatever degree the public welfare may require," he pushed ahead of most of his countrymen and many Progressives. The prescription of strong leaders heading a central government to confront the concentrated power of modern capital represented a long journey from his earlier tentative and carefully hedged criticism of corporate wrongdoing. His support for changes in election laws to encourage more direct popular participation also signaled a more intensely liberal TR.

We come here to-day to commemorate one of the epoch-making events of the long struggle for the rights of man—the long struggle for the uplift of humanity. Our country—this great Republic—means nothing unless it means the triumph of a real democracy, the triumph of popular government, and, in the long run, of an economic system under which each man shall be guaranteed the opportunity to show the best that there is in him. That is why the history of America is now the central feature of the history of the world; for the world has set its face hopefully toward our democracy; and, O my fellow citizens, each one of you carries on your shoulders not only the burden of doing well for the sake of your own country, but the burden of doing well and of seeing that this nation does well for the sake of mankind.

There have been two great crises in our country's history: first, when it was formed, and then, again, when it was perpetuated; and, in the second of these great crises—in the time of stress and strain which culminated in the Civil War, on the outcome of which depended the justification of what had been done earlier, you men of the Grand Army, you men who fought through the Civil War, not only did you justify your generation, not only did you render life worth living for our generation, but you justified the wisdom of Washington and Washington's colleagues. If this Republic had been founded by them only to be split asunder into fragments when the strain came, then the judgment of the world would have been that Washington's work was not worth doing. It was you who crowned Washington's work, as you carried to achievement the high purpose of Abraham Lincoln.

🌾 🌾 🌾

I do not speak of this struggle of the past merely from the historic stand-point. Our interest is primarily in the application to-day of the lessons taught by the contest of half a century ago. It is of little use for us to pay lip-loyalty to the mighty men of the past unless we sincerely endeavor to apply to the problems of the present precisely the qualities which in other crises enabled the men of that day to meet those crises. It is half melancholy and half amusing to see the way in which well-meaning people gather to do honor to the men who, in company with John Brown, and under the lead of Abraham Lincoln, faced and solved the great problems of the nineteenth century, while, at the same time, these same good people nervously shrink from, or frantically denounce, those who are trying to meet the problems of the twentieth century in the spirit which was accountable for the successful solution of the problems of Lincoln's time.

Of that generation of men to whom we owe so much, the man to whom we owe most is, of course, Lincoln. Part of our debt to him is because he forecast our present struggle and saw the way out. He said:

"I hold that while man exists it is his duty to improve not only his own condition, but to assist in ameliorating mankind."

And again:

"Labor is prior to, and independent of, capital. Capital is only the fruit of labor, and could never have existed if labor had not first existed. Labor is the superior of capital, and deserves much the higher consideration."

If that remark was original with me, I should be even more strongly denounced as a Communist agitator than I shall be anyhow. It is Lincoln's. I am only quoting it; and that is one side; that is the side the capitalist should hear. Now, let the working man hear his side.

"Capital has its rights, which are as worthy of protection as any other rights. . . . Nor should this lead to a war upon the owners of property. Property is the fruit of labor; . . . property is desirable; is a positive good in the world."

And then comes a thoroughly Lincoln-like sentence:

"Let not him who is houseless pull down the house of another, but let him work diligently and build one for himself, thus by example assuring that his own shall be safe from violence when built."

It seems to me that, in these words, Lincoln took substantially the attitude that we ought to take; he showed the proper sense of proportion in his relative estimates of capital and labor, of human rights and property rights. Above all, in this speech, as in many others, he taught a lesson in wise kindliness and charity; an indispensable lesson to us of to-day. But this wise kindliness and charity never weakened his arm or numbed his heart. We cannot afford weakly to blind ourselves to the actual conflict which faces us to-day. The issue is joined, and we must fight or fail.

In every wise struggle for human betterment one of the main objects, and often the only object, has been to achieve in large measure equality of opportunity. In the struggle for this great end, nations rise from barbarism to civilization, and through it people press forward from one stage of enlightenment to the next. One of the chief factors in progress is the destruction of special privilege. The essence of any struggle for healthy liberty has always been, and must always be, to take from some one man or class of men the right to enjoy power, or wealth, or position, or immunity, which has not been earned by service to his or their fellows. That is what you fought for in the Civil War, and that is what we strive for now.

At many stages in the advance of humanity, this conflict between the men who possess more than they have earned and the men who have earned more than they possess is the central condition of progress. In our day it appears as the struggle of freemen to gain and hold the right of self-government as against the special interests, who twist the methods of free government into machinery for defeating the popular will. At every stage, and under all circumstances, the essence of the struggle is to equalize opportunity, destroy privilege, and give to the life and citizenship of every individual the highest possible value both to himself and to the commonwealth.

🌿 🌿 🌿

Practical equality of opportunity for all citizens, when we achieve it, will have two great results. First, every man will have a fair chance to make of himself all that in him lies; to reach the highest point to which his capacities, unassisted by special privilege of his own and unhampered by the special privilege of others, can carry him, and to get for himself and his family substantially what he has earned. Second, equality of opportunity means that the commonwealth will get from every citizen the highest service of which he is capable. No man who carries the burden of the special privileges of another can give to the commonwealth that service to which it is fairly entitled.

I stand for the square deal. But when I say that I am for the square deal, I mean not merely that I stand for fair play under the present rules of the game, but that I stand for having those rules changed so as to work for a more substantial equality of opportunity and of reward for equally good service. One word of warning, which, I think, is hardly necessary in Kansas. When I say I want a square deal for the poor man, I do not mean that I want a square deal for the man who remains poor because he has not got the energy to work for himself. If a man who has had a chance will not make good, then he has got to quit. . . . Now, this means that our government, National and State, must be freed from the sinister influence or control of special interests. Exactly as the special interests of cotton and slavery threatened our political integrity before the Civil War, so now the great special business interests too often control and corrupt the men and methods of government for their own profit. We must drive the special interests out of politics. That is one of our tasks to-day. Every special interest is entitled to justice—full, fair, and complete—and, now, mind you, if there were any attempt by mob-violence to plunder and work harm to the special interest, whatever it may be, that I most dislike, and the wealthy man, whomsoever he may be, for whom I have the greatest contempt, I would fight for him, and you would if you were worth your salt. He should have justice. For every special interest is entitled to justice, but not one is entitled to a vote in Congress, to a voice on the bench, or to representation in any public office. The Constitution guarantees protection to property, and we must make that promise good. But it does not give the right of suffrage to any corporation. The true friend of property, the true conservative, is he who insists that property shall be the servant and not the master of the commonwealth; who insists that the creature of man's making shall be the servant and not the master of the man who made it. The citizens of the United States must effectively control the mighty commercial forces which they have themselves called into being.

There can be no effective control of corporations while their political activity remains. To put an end to it will be neither a short nor an easy task, but it can be done.

We must have complete and effective publicity of corporate affairs, so that the people may know beyond peradventure whether the corporations obey the law and whether their management entitles them to the confidence of the public. It is necessary that laws should be passed to prohibit the use of corporate funds directly or indirectly for political purposes; it is still more necessary that such laws should be thoroughly enforced. Corporate expenditures for political purposes, and especially such expenditures by public-service corporations, have supplied one of the principal sources of corruption in our political affairs.

It has become entirely clear that we must have government supervision of the capitalization, not only of public-service corporations, including, particularly, railways, but of all corporations doing an interstate business. I do not wish to see the nation forced into the ownership of the railways if it can possibly be avoided, and the only alternative is thoroughgoing and effective regulation, which shall be based on a full knowledge of all the facts, including a physical valuation of property. This physical valuation is not needed, or, at least, is very rarely needed, for fixing rates; but it is needed as the basis of honest capitalization.

We have come to recognize that franchises should never be granted except for a limited time, and never without proper provision for compensation to the public. It is my personal belief that the same kind and degree of control and supervision which should be exercised over public-service corporations should be extended also to combinations which control necessaries of life, such as meat, oil, and coal, or which deal in them on an important scale. I have no doubt that the ordinary man who has control of them is much like ourselves. I have no doubt he would like to do well, but I want to have enough supervision to help him realize that desire to do well.

I believe that the officers, and, especially, the directors, of corporations should be held personally responsible when any corporation breaks the law.

Combinations [trusts] in industry are the result of an imperative economic law which cannot be repealed by political legislation. The effort at prohibiting all combination has substantially failed. The way out lies, not in attempting to prevent such combinations, but in completely controlling them in the interest of the public welfare. For that purpose the Federal Bureau of Corporations is an agency of first importance. Its powers, and, therefore, its efficiency, as well as that of the Interstate Commerce Commission, should be largely increased. We have a right to expect from the Bureau of Corporations and from the Interstate Commerce Commission a very high grade of public service. We should be as sure of the proper conduct of the interstate railways and the proper management of interstate business as we are now sure of the conduct and management of the national banks, and we should have as effective supervision in one case as in the other. The Hepburn Act, and the amendment to the act in the shape in which it finally passed Congress at the last session, represent a long step in advance, and we must go yet further.

There is a wide-spread belief among our people that, under the methods of making tariffs which have hitherto obtained, the special interests are too influential. Probably this is true. . . .

The absence of effective State, and, especially, national, restraint upon unfair money-getting has tended to create a small class of enormously wealthy and economically powerful men, whose chief object is to hold and increase their power. The prime need is to change the conditions which enable these men to accumulate power which it is not for the general welfare that they should hold or exercise. We grudge no man a fortune which represents his own power and sagacity, when exercised with entire regard to the welfare of his fellows. . . . It is not even enough that it should have been gained without doing damage to the community. We should permit it to be gained only so long as the gaining represents benefit to the community. This, I know, implies a policy of a far more active government interference with social and economic conditions in this country than we have yet had, but I think we have got to face the fact that such an increase in governmental control is now necessary.

No man should receive a dollar unless that dollar has been fairly earned. Every dollar received should represent a dollar's worth of service rendered—not gambling in stocks, but service rendered. The really big fortune, the swollen fortune, by the mere fact of its size acquires qualities which differentiate it in kind as well as in degree from what is possessed by men of relatively small means. Therefore, I believe in a graduated income tax on big fortunes, and in another tax which is far more easily collected and far more effective—a graduate inheritance tax on big fortunes, properly safeguarded against evasion and increasing rapidly in amount with the size of the estate.

The people of the United States suffer from periodical financial panics to a degree substantially unknown among the other nations which approach us in financial strength. There is no reason why we should suffer what they escape. It is of profound importance that our financial system should be promptly investigated, and so thoroughly and effectively revised as to make it certain that hereafter our currency will no longer fail at critical times to meet our needs.

It is hardly necessary for me to repeat that I believe in an efficient army and a navy large enough to secure for us abroad that respect which is the surest guaranty of peace. A word of special warning to my fellow citizens who are as progressive as I hope I am. I want them to keep up their interest in our internal affairs; and I want them also continually to remember Uncle Sam's interests abroad. Justice and fair dealing among nations rest upon principles identical with those which control justice and fair dealing among the individuals of which nations are composed, with the vital exception that each nation must do its own part in international police work. If you get into trouble here, you can call for the police; but if Uncle Sam gets into trouble, he has got to be his own policeman, and I want to see him strong enough to encourage the peaceful aspirations of other peoples in connection with us. I believe in national friendships and heartiest good-will to all nations; but national friendships, like those between men, must be founded on respect as well as on liking, on forbearance as well as upon trust. I should be heartily ashamed of any American who did not try to make the American Government act as justly toward the other nations in international relations as he himself would act toward any individual in private relations. I should be heartily ashamed to see us wrong a weaker power, and I should hang my head forever if we tamely suffered wrong from a stronger power.

Of conservation I shall speak more at length elsewhere. Conservation means development as much as it does protection. I recognize the right and duty of this generation to develop and use the natural resources of our land; but I do not recognize the right to waste them, or to rob, by wasteful use, the generations that come after us. I ask nothing of the nation except that it so behave as each farmer here behaves with reference to his own children. That farmer is a poor creature who skins the land and leaves it worthless to his children. The farmer is a good farmer who, having enabled the land to support himself and to provide for the education of his children, leaves it to them a little better than he found it himself. I believe the same thing of a nation.

Moreover, I believe that the natural resources must be used for the benefit of all our people, and not monopolized for the benefit of the few, and here again is another case in which I am accused of taking a revolutionary attitude. People forget now that one hundred years ago there were public men of good character who advocated the nation selling its public lands in great quantities, so that the nation could get the most money out of it, and giving it to the men who could cultivate it for their own uses. We took the proper democratic ground that the land should be granted in small sections to the men who were actually to till it and live on it. Now, with the water-power, with the forests, with the mines, we are brought face to face with the fact that there are many people who will go with us in conserving the resources only if they are to be allowed to exploit them for their benefit. That is one of the fundamental reasons why the special interests should be driven out of politics. Of all the questions which can come before this nation, short of the actual preservation of its existence in a great war, there is none which compares in importance with the great central task of leaving this land even a better land for our descendants than it is for us, and training them into a better race to inhabit the land and pass it on. Conservation is a great moral issue, for it involves the patriotic duty of insuring the safety and continuance of the nation. Let me add that the health and vitality of our people are at least as well worth conserving as their forests, waters, lands, and minerals, and in this great work the national government must bear most important part.

❦ ❦ ❦

Nothing is more true than that excess of every kind is followed by reaction; a fact which should be pondered by reformer and reactionary alike. We are face to face with new conceptions of the relations of property to human welfare, chiefly because certain advocates of the rights of property as against the rights of men have been pushing their claims too far. The man who wrongly holds that every human right is secondary to his profit must now give way to the advocate of human welfare, who rightly maintains that every man holds his property subject to the general right of the community to regulate its use to whatever degree the public welfare may require it.

But I think we may go still further. The right to regulate the use of wealth in the public interest is universally admitted. Let us admit also the right to regulate the terms and conditions of labor, which is the chief element of wealth, directly in the interest of the common good. The fundamental thing to do for every man is to give him a chance to reach a place in which he will make the greatest possible contribution to the public welfare. Understand what I say there. Give him a chance, not push him up if he will not be pushed. Help any man who stumbles; if he lies down, it is a poor job to try to carry him; but if he is a worthy man, try your best to see that he gets a chance to show the worth that is in him. No man can be a good citizen unless he has a wage more than sufficient to cover the bare cost of living, and hours of labor short enough so that after his day's work is done he will have time and energy to bear his share in the management of the community, to help in carrying the general load. We keep countless men from being good citizens by the conditions of life with which we surround them. We need comprehensive workmen's compensation acts, both State and national laws to regulate child labor and work for women, and, especially, we need in our common schools not merely education in book-learning, but also practical training for daily life and work. We need to enforce better sanitary conditions for our workers and to extend the use of safety appliances for our workers in industry and commerce, both within and between the States. Also, friends, in the interest of the working man himself we need to set our faces like flint against mob-violence just as against corporate greed; against violence and injustice and lawlessness by wage-workers just as much as against lawless cunning and greed and selfish arrogance of employers.

❦ ❦ ❦

National efficiency has many factors. It is a necessary result of the principle of conservation widely applied. In the end it will determine our failure or success as a nation. National efficiency has to do, not only with natural resources and with men, but it is equally concerned with institutions. The State must be made efficient for the work which concerns only the people of the State; and the nation for that which concerns all the people. There must remain no neutral ground to serve as a refuge for lawbreakers, and especially for lawbreakers of great wealth, who can hire the vulpine legal cunning which will teach them how to avoid both jurisdictions. It is a misfortune when the national legislature fails to do its duty in providing a national remedy, so that the only national activity is the purely negative activity of the judiciary in forbidding the State to exercise power in the premises.

I do not ask for overcentralization; but I do ask that we work in a spirit of broad and far-reaching nationalism when we work for what concerns our people as a whole. We are all Americans. Our common interests are as broad as the continent. I speak to you here in Kansas exactly as I would speak in New York or Georgia, for the most vital problems are those which affect us all alike. The National Government belongs to the whole American people, and where the whole American people are interested, that interest can be guarded effectively only by the National Government. The betterment which we seek must be accomplished, I believe, mainly through the National Government.

The American people are right in demanding that New Nationalism, without which we cannot hope to deal with new problems. The New Nationalism puts the national need before sectional or personal advantage. It is impatient of the utter confusion that results from local legislatures attempting to treat national issues as local issues. It is still more impatient of the impotence which springs from overdivision of governmental powers, the impotence which makes it possible for local selfishness or for legal cunning, hired by wealthy special interests, to bring national activities to a deadlock. This New Nationalism regards the executive power as the steward of the public welfare. It demands of the judiciary that it shall be interested primarily in human welfare rather than in the property, just as it demands that the representative body shall represent all the people rather than any one class or section of the people.

I believe in shaping the ends of government to protect property as well as human welfare. Normally, and in the long run, the ends are the same; but whenever the alternative must be faced, I am for men and not for property, as you were in the Civil War. I am far from underestimating the importance of dividends; but I rank dividends below human character. Again, I do not have any sympathy with the reformer who says he does not care for dividends. Of course, economic welfare is necessary, for a man must pull his own weight and be able to support his family. I know well that the reformers must not bring upon the people economic ruin, or the reforms themselves will go down in the ruin. But we must be ready to face temporary disaster, whether or not brought on by those who will war against us to the knife. Those who oppose all reform will do well to remember that ruin in its worst form is inevitable if our national life brings us nothing better than swollen fortunes for the few and the triumph in both politics and business of a sordid and selfish materialism.

If our political institutions were perfect, they would absolutely prevent the political domination of money in any part of our affairs. We need to make our political representatives more quickly and sensitively responsive to the people whose servants they are. More direct action by the people in their own affairs under proper safeguards is vitally necessary. The direct primary is a step in this direction, if it is associated with a corrupt-practices act effective to prevent the advantage of the man willing recklessly and unscrupulously to spend money over his more honest competitor. It is particularly important that all moneys received or expended for campaign purposes should be publicly accounted for, not only after election, but before election as well. Political action must be made simpler, easier, and freer from confusion for every citizen. I believe that the prompt removal of unfaithful or incompetent public servants should be made easy and sure in whatever way experience shall show to be most expedient in any given class of cases.

One of the fundamental necessities in a representative government such as ours is to make certain that the men to whom the people delegate their power shall serve the people by whom they are elected, and not the special interests. I believe that every national officer, elected or appointed, should be forbidden to perform any service or receive any compensation, directly or indirectly, from interstate corporations, and a similar provision could not fail to be useful within the States.

The object of government is the welfare of the people. The material progress and prosperity of a nation are desirable chiefly so far as they lead to the moral and material welfare of all good citizens. Just in proportion as the average man and woman are honest, capable of sound judgment and high ideals, active in public affairs—but, first of all, sound in their home life, and the father and mother of healthy children whom they bring up well— just so far, and no farther, we may count our civilization a success. We must have—I believe we have already—a genuine and permanent moral awakening, without which no wisdom of legislation or administration really means anything; and, on the other hand, we must try to secure the social and economic legislation without which any improvement due to purely moral agitation is necessarily evanescent. . . . No matter how honest and decent we are in our private lives, if we do not have the right kind of law and the right kind of administration of the law, we cannot go forward as a nation. That is imperative; but it must be an addition to, and not a substitution for, the qualities that make us good citizens. In the last analysis, the most important elements in any man's career must be the sum of those qualities which, in the aggregate, we speak of as character. If he has not got it, then no law that the wit of man can devise, no administration of the law by the boldest and strongest executive, will avail to help him. We must have the right kind of character—character that makes a man, first of all, a good man in the home, a good father, a good husband—that makes a man a good neighbor. You must have that, and, then, in addition, you must have the kind of law and the kind of administration of the law which will give to those qualities in the private citizen the best possible chance for development. The prime problem of our nation is to get the right type of good citizenship, and, to get it, we must have progress, and our public men must be genuinely progressive.

A CONFESSION OF FAITH [1912]

*Convinced that conservative Republicans, dominated by big
business interests that never fully trusted him, had unfairly
denied him the party's nomination in 1912, Roosevelt abandoned the tightrope he had walked as president between Old
Guard and progressive elements of the party. Now he stood
squarely on the reform platform of the new Bull Moose
Progressives. How far the spirit of his New Nationalism had
carried TR is revealed in his address to the national convention
of the Progressive party in Chicago on August 6, 1912. While
he had long supported strong executive leadership, he was now
more expansive about his vision of dynamic leadership using
the power of government to harness the power of capital while
regulating the economic life of the nation. His support of worker
rights and benefits goes much farther than anything the young
Roosevelt would have endorsed, and his critique of the courts
and their defense of property values at the expense of human
values was shared by radicals of his day. So many of the
specifics outlined in the address anticipate Franklin Roosevelt's
New Deal that TR could hardly have been disappointed in the
work of his kinsman, had he lived to witness it.*

To you men and women who have come here to this great city of this great
State formally to launch a new party, a party of the people of the whole
Union, the National Progressive party, I extend my hearty greeting. You are
taking a bold and a greatly needed step for the service of our beloved country. The old parties are husks, with no real soul within either, divided on
artificial lines, boss-ridden and privilege-controlled, each a jumble of incongruous elements, and neither daring to speak out wisely and fearlessly what
should be said on the vital issues of the day.

🕊 🕊 🕊

Neither the Republican nor the Democratic platform contains the slightest promise of approaching the great problems of to-day either with understanding or good faith; and yet never was there greater need in this nation
than now of understanding and of action taken in good faith, on the part of
the men and the organizations shaping our governmental policy. Moreover,
our needs are such that there should be coherent action among those
responsible for the conduct of national affairs and those responsible for the

conduct of State affairs; because our aim should be the same in both State and nation; that is, to use the government as an efficient agency for the practical betterment of social and economic conditions throughout this land. There are other important things to be done, but this is the most important thing. It is preposterous to leave such a movement in the hands of men who have broken their promises as have the present heads of the Republican organization (not of the Republican voters, for they in no shape represent the rank and file of the Republican voters). These men by their deeds give the lie to their words. There is no health in them, and they cannot be trusted. But the Democratic party is just as little to be trusted.

$$\text{🌿 🌿 🌿}$$

If this country is really to go forward along the path of social and economic justice, there must be a new party of nation-wide and non-sectional principles, a party where the titular national chiefs and the real State leaders shall be in genuine accord, a party in whose counsels the people shall be supreme, a party that shall represent in the nation and the several States alike the same cause, the cause of human rights and of governmental efficiency. At present both the old parties are controlled by professional politicians in the interests of the privileged classes, and apparently each has set up as its ideal of business and political development a government by financial despotism tempered by make-believe political assassination. Democrat and Republican alike, they represent government of the needy many by professional politicians in the interests of the rich life. This is class government, and class government of a peculiarly unwholesome kind.

It seems to me, therefore, that the time is ripe, and over-ripe, for a genuine Progressive movement, nation-wide and justice-loving, sprung from and responsible to the people themselves, and sundered by a great gulf from both of the old party organizations, while representing all that is best in the hopes, beliefs, and aspirations of the plain people who make up the immense majority of the rank and file of both the old parties.

The first essential in the Progressive programme is the right of the people to rule. But a few months ago our opponents were assuring us with insincere clamor that it was absurd for us to talk about desiring that the people should rule, because, as a matter of fact, the people actually do rule. Since that time the actions of the Chicago [Republican] Convention, and to an only less degree of the Baltimore [Democratic] Convention, have shown in striking fashion how little the people do rule under our present conditions.

We should provide by national law for presidential primaries. We should provide for the election of United States senators by popular vote. . . . There must be stringent and efficient corruption-practices acts . . . and there should be publicity of campaign contributions during the campaign.

We should provide throughout this Union for giving the people in every state the real right to rule themselves, and really and not nominally to control their public servants and their agencies for doing the public business. . . .

❦ ❦ ❦

The entire Wall Street press at this moment is vigorously engaged in denouncing the direct primary system and upholding the old convention system, or, as they call it, the "old representative system." They are doing so because they know that the bosses and the powers of special privilege have tenfold the chance under the convention system that they have when the rank and file of the people can express themselves at the primaries. The nomination of Mr. Taft at Chicago was a fraud upon the rank and file of the Republican party; it was obtained only by defrauding the rank and file of the party of their right to express their choice; and such fraudulent action does not bind a single honest member of the party.

Well, what the national committee and the fraudulent majority of the national convention did at Chicago in misrepresenting the people has been done again and again in Congress, perhaps especially in the Senate, and in the State legislatures. Again and again laws demanded by the people have been refused to the people because the representatives of the people misrepresented them.

Now, my proposal is merely that we shall give to the people the power, to be used not wantonly but only in exceptional cases, themselves to see to it that the governmental action taken in their name is really the action that they desire.

The American people, and not the courts, are to determine their own fundamental policies. The people should have power to deal with the effect of the acts of all their governmental agencies. This must be extended to include the effects of judicial acts as well as the acts of the executive and legislative representatives of the people. . . . Our prime concern is that in dealing with the fundamental law of the land, in assuming finally to interpret it, and therefore finally to make it, the acts of the courts should be subject to and not above the final control of the people as a whole. I deny that the American people have surrendered to any set of men, no matter what their position or their character, the final right to determine those fundamental questions upon which free self-government ultimately depends. The people themselves must be the ultimate makers of their own Constitution, and where their agents differ in their interpretations of the Constitution the people themselves should be given the chance, after full and deliberate judgment, authoritatively to settle what interpretation it is that their representatives shall thereafter adopt as binding.

❧ ❧ ❧

We in America have peculiar need thus to make the acts of the courts subject to the people, because, owing to causes which I need not now discuss, the courts have here grown to occupy a position unknown in any other country, a position of superiority over both the legislature and the Executive. Just at this time, when we have begun in this country to move toward social and industrial betterment and true industrial democracy, this attitude on the part of the courts is of grave portent, because privilege has entrenched itself in many courts just as it formerly entrenched itself in many legislative bodies and in many executive offices.

❧ ❧ ❧

I am well aware that every upholder of privilege, every hired agent or beneficiary of the special interests, including many well-meaning parlor reformers, will denounce all this as "Socialism" or "anarchy"—the same terms they used in the past in denouncing the movements to control the railways and to control public utilities. As a matter of fact, the propositions I make constitute neither anarchy nor Socialism, but on the contrary, a corrective to Socialism and an antidote to anarchy.

I especially challenge the attention of the people to the need of dealing in far-reaching fashion with our human resources, and therefore our labor power. In a century and a quarter as a nation the American people have subdued and settled the vast reaches of a continent; ahead lies the greater task of building up on this foundation, by themselves, for themselves, and with themselves, an American commonwealth which in its social and economic structure shall be four square with democracy.

❧ ❧ ❧

In the last twenty years an increasing percentage of our people have come to depend on industry for their livelihood, so that to-day the wage-workers in industry rank in importance side by side with the tillers of the soil. As a people we cannot afford to let any group of citizens or any individual citizen live or labor under conditions which are injurious to the common welfare. Industry, therefore, must submit to such public regulation as will make it a means of life and health, not of death or inefficiency. We must protect the crushable elements at the base of our present industrial structure.

The first charge on the industrial statesmanship of the day is to prevent human waste. The dead weight of orphanage and depleted craftsmanship, of crippled workers and workers suffering from trade diseases, of casual labor, of insecure old age, and of household depletion due to industrial conditions are, like our depleted soils, our gashed mountainsides and flooded river-bottoms, so many strains upon the national structure, draining the reserve strength of all industries and showing beyond all peradventure the public element and public concern in industrial health.

※ ※ ※

We hold that under no industrial order, in no commonwealth, in no trade, and in no establishment should industry be carried on under conditions inimical to the social welfare. The abnormal, ruthless, spendthrift industry of establishment tends to drag down all to the level of the least considerate.

Here the sovereign responsibility of the people as a whole should be placed beyond all quibble and dispute.

The public needs have been well summarized as follows:

1. We hold that the public has a right to complete knowledge of the facts of work.
2. On the basis of these facts and with the recent discoveries of physicians and neurologists, engineers and economists, the public can formulate minimum occupational standards below which, demonstrably, work can be prosecuted only at a human deficit.
3. In the third place, we hold that all industrial conditions which fall below such standards should come within the scope of governmental action and control in the same way that subnormal sanitary conditions are subject to public regulation and for the same reason—because they threaten the general welfare.

To the first end, we hold that the constituted authorities should be empowered to require all employers to file with them for public purposes such wage scales and other data as the public element in industry demands. The movement for honest weights and measures has its counterpart in industry. All tallies, scales, and check systems should be open to public inspection and inspection of committees of the workers concerned. All deaths, injuries, and diseases due to industrial operation should be reported to public authorities.

To the second end, we hold that minimum wage commissions should be established in the nation and in each State to inquire into wages paid in various industries and to determine the standard which the public ought to sanction as a minimum; and we believe that, as a present installment of what we hope for in the future, there should be at once established in the nation and its several States minimum standards for the wages of women, taking the present Massachusetts law as a basis from which to start and on which to improve.

We pledge the Federal Government to an investigation of industries along the lines pursued by the Bureau of Mines with the view to establishing standards of sanitation and safety; we call for the standardization of mine and factory inspection by interstate agreement or the establishment of a Federal standard. We stand for the passage of legislation in the nation and in all States providing standards of compensation for industrial accidents and death, and for diseases clearly due to the nature of conditions of industry, and we stand for the adoption by law of a fair standard of compensation for casualties resulting fatally which shall clearly fix the minimum compensation in all cases.

In the third place, certain industrial conditions fall clearly below the levels which the public to-day sanction.

We stand for a living wage. Wages are subnormal if they fail to provide a living for those who devote their time and energy to industrial occupations. The monetary equivalent of a living wage varies according to local conditions, but must include enough to secure the elements of a normal standard of living—a standard high enough to make morality possible, to provide for education and recreation, to care for immature members of the family, to maintain the family during periods of sickness, and to permit of reasonable saving for old age.

Hours are excessive if they fail to afford the worker sufficient time to recuperate and return to his work thoroughly refreshed. We hold that the night labor of women and children is abnormal and should be prohibited; we hold that the employment of women over forty-eight hours per week is abnormal and should be prohibited. We hold that the seven-day working week is abnormal, and we hold that one day of rest in seven should be provided by law. We hold that the continuous industries, operating twenty-four hours out of twenty-four, are abnormal, and where, because of public necessity or of technical reasons (such as molten metal), the twenty-four hours must be divided into two shifts of twelve hours or three shifts of eight, they should by law be divided into three of eight.

Safety conditions are abnormal when, through unguarded machinery, poisons, electrical voltage, or otherwise, the workers are subjected to unnecessary hazards of life and limb; and all such occupations should come under governmental regulation and control.

Home life is abnormal when tenement manufacture is carried on in the household. It is a serious menace to health, education, and childhood, and should therefore be entirely prohibited. Temporary construction camps are abnormal homes and should be subjected to governmental sanitary regulation.

The premature employment of children is abnormal and should be prohibited; so also the employment of women in manufacturing, commerce, or other trades where work compels standing constantly; and also any employment of women in such trades for a period of at least eight weeks at time of childbirth.

Our aim should be to secure conditions which will tend everywhere toward regular industry, and will do away with the necessity for rush periods, followed by out-of-work seasons, which put so severe a strain on wage-workers.

It is abnormal for any industry to throw back upon the community the human wreckage due to its wear and tear, and the hazards of sickness, accident, invalidism, involuntary unemployment, and old age should be provided for through insurance. This should be made a charge in whole or in part upon the industries, the employer, the employee, and perhaps the people at large to contribute severally in some degree. Wherever such standards are not met by given establishments, by given industries, are unprovided for by a legislature, or are balked by unenlightened courts, the workers are in jeopardy, the progressive employer is penalized, and the community pays a heavy cost in lessened efficiency and in misery. What Germany has done in the way of old-age pensions or insurance should be studied by us, and the system adapted to our uses, with whatever modifications are rendered necessary by our different ways of life and habits of thought.

Working women have the same need to combine for protection that working men have; the ballot is as necessary for one class as for the other; we do not believe that with the two sexes there is identity of function; but we do believe that there should be equality of right; and therefore we favor woman suffrage. Surely, if women could vote, they would strengthen the hands of those who are endeavoring to deal in efficient fashion with evils such as the white-slave traffic; evils which can in part be dealt with nationally, but which in large part can be reached only by determined local action, such as insisting on the wide-spread publication of the names of the owners, the landlords, of houses used for immoral purposes.

❦ ❦ ❦

The welfare of the farmer is a basic need of this nation. It is the men from the farm who in the past have taken the lead in every great movement within this nation, whether in time of war or in time of peace. It is well to have our cities prosper, but it is not well if they prosper at the expense of the country. . . .

The government must co-operate with the farmer to make the farm more productive. There must be no skinning of the soil. The farm should be left to the farmer's son in better, and not worse, condition because of its cultivation. Moreover, every invention and improvement, every discovery and economy, should be at the service of the farmer in the work of production; and, in addition, he should be helped to co-operate in business fashion with his fellows, so that the money paid by the consumer for the product of the soil shall, to as large a degree as possible, go into the pockets of the man who raised that product from the soil. So long as the farmer leaves co-operative activities with their profit-sharing to the city man of business, so long will the foundations of wealth be undermined and the comforts of enlightenment be impossible in the country as in the city.

🌾 🌾 🌾

We Progressives stand for the rights of the people. When these rights can best be secured by insistence upon States' rights, then we are for States' rights; when they can best be secured by insistence upon national rights, then we are for national rights. Interstate commerce can be effectively controlled only by the nation. The States cannot control it under the Constitution, and to amend the Constitution by giving them control of it would amount to a dissolution of the government. The worst of the big trusts have always endeavored to keep alive the feeling in favor of having the States themselves, and not the nation, attempt to do this work, because they know that in the long run such effort would be ineffective. There is no surer way to prevent all successful effort to deal with the trusts than to insist that they be dealt with by the States rather than by the nation, or to create a conflict between the States and the nation on the subject. The well-meaning ignorant man who advances such a proposition does as much damage as if he were hired by the trusts themselves, for he is playing the game of every big crooked corporation in the country. The only effective way in which to regulate the trusts is through the exercise of the collective power of our people as a whole through the governmental agencies established by the Constitution for this very purpose. Grave injustice is done by the Congress when it fails to give the National Government complete power in this matter; and still graver injustice by the Federal courts when they endeavor in any way to pare down the right of the people collectively to act in this matter as they deem wise; such conduct does itself tend to cause the creation of a twilight zone in which neither the nation nor the States have power. . . . It is utterly hopeless to attempt to control the trust merely by the antitrust law, or by any law the same in principle, no matter what the modifications may be in detail. In the first place, these great corporations cannot possibly be controlled merely by a succession of lawsuits. The administrative branch of the government must exercise such control.

        ❧ ❧ ❧

I believe in a protective tariff, but I believe in it as a principle, approached from the standpoint of the interests of the whole people, and not as a bundle of preferences to be given to favored individuals. In my opinion, the American people favor the principle of a protective tariff, but they desire such a tariff to be established primarily in the interests of the wage-worker and the consumer. . . . To accomplish this the tariff to be levied should as nearly as is scientifically possible approximate the differential between the cost of production at home and abroad. This differential is chiefly, if not wholly, in labor cost. No duty should be permitted to stand as regards any industry unless the workers receive their full share of the benefits of that duty. In other words, there is no warrant for protection unless a legitimate share of the benefits gets into the pay-envelope of the wage-worker.

        ❧ ❧ ❧

We believe that there exists an imperative need for prompt legislation for the improvement of our national currency system. The experience of repeated financial crises in the last forty years has proved that the present method of issuing through private agencies, notes secured by government bonds is both harmful and unscientific. This method was adopted as a means of financing the government during the Civil War through furnishing a domestic market for government bonds. It was largely successful in fulfilling that purpose; but that need is long past, and the system has outlived this feature of its usefulness. The issue of currency is fundamentally a governmental function. The system to be adopted should have as its basic principles soundness and elasticity. . . .

There can be no greater issue than that of conservation in this country. Just as we must conserve our men, women, and children, so we must conserve the resources of the land on which they live. We must conserve the soil so that our children shall have a land that is more and not less fertile than that our fathers dwelt in. We must conserve the forests, not by disuse but by use, making them more valuable at the same time that we use them. We must conserve the mines. Moreover, we must insure so far as possible the use of certain types of great natural resources for the benefit of the people as a whole. The public should not alienate its fee in the water-power which will be of incalculable consequence as a source of power in the immediate future.

The nation and the States within their several spheres should by immediate legislation keep the fee of the water-power, leasing its use only for a reasonable length of time on terms that will secure the interests of the public. Just as the nation has gone into the work of irrigation in the West, so it should go into the work of helping reclaim the swamp-lands of the South. We should undertake the complete development and control of the Mississippi as a national work, just as we have undertaken the work of building the Panama Canal. We can use the plant, and we can use the human experience, left free by the completion of the Panama Canal in so developing the Mississippi as to make it a mighty highroad of commerce, and a source of fructification and not of death to the rich and fertile lands lying along its lower length.

In the West, the forests, the grazing-lands, the reserves of every kind, should be so handled as to be in the interests of the actual settler, the actual home-maker. He should be encouraged to use them at once, but in such a way as to preserve and not exhaust them. We do not intend that our natural resources shall be exploited by the few against the interests of the many, nor do we intend to turn them over to any man who will wastefully use them by destruction, and leave to those who come after us a heritage damaged by just so much.

❧ ❧ ❧

In international affairs this country should behave toward other nations exactly as an honorable private citizen behaves toward other private citizens. We should do no wrong to any nation, weak or strong, and we should submit to no wrong. Above all, we should never in any treaty make any promise which we do not intend in good faith to fulfill. I believe it essential that our small army should be kept at a high pitch of perfection, and in no way can it be so damaged as by permitting it to become the plaything of men in Congress who wish to gratify either spite or favoritism, or to secure to localities advantages to which those localities are not entitled. The navy should be steadily built up; and the process of upbuilding must not be stopped until—and not before—it proves possible to secure by international agreement a general reduction of armaments. The Panama Canal must be fortified. It would have been criminal to build it if we were not prepared to fortify it and to keep our navy at such a pitch of strength as to render it unsafe for any foreign power to attack us and get control of it.

❧ ❧ ❧

Now, friends, this is my confession of faith. I have made it rather long because I wish you to know what my deepest convictions are on the great questions of to-day, so that if you choose to make me your standard-bearer in the fight you shall make your choice understanding exactly how I feel — and if, after hearing me, you think you ought to choose some one else, I shall loyally abide by your choice. . . .

Surely there never was a fight better worth making than the one in which we are engaged. It little matters what befalls any one of us who for the time being stands in the forefront of the battle. I hope we shall win, and I believe that if we can wake the people to what the fight really means we shall win. But, win or lose, we shall not falter. Whatever fate may at the moment overtake any of us, the movement itself will not stop. Our cause is based on the eternal principle of righteousness; and even though we who now lead may for the time fail, in the end the cause itself shall triumph. Six weeks ago, here in Chicago, I spoke to the honest representatives of a convention which was not dominated by honest men; a convention wherein sat, alas! a majority of men who, with sneering indifference to every principle of right, so acted as to bring to a shameful end a party which had been founded over a half-century ago by men in whose souls burned the fire of lofty endeavor. Now to you men, who, in your turn, have come together to spend and be spent in the endless crusade against wrong, to you who face the future resolute and confident, to you who strive in a spirit of brotherhood for the betterment of our nation, to you who gird yourselves for this great new fight in the never-ending warfare for the good of humankind, I say in closing what in that speech I said in closing: We stand at Armageddon, and we battle for the Lord.

THE HEROIC MOOD [1916]

As the election of 1916 approached, the inevitable calls for TR to run again pressed on him. But Roosevelt was too good a politician to misread the signs. The Republican elders would not forgive his apostasy of 1912, and they controlled the nominating process. So TR, traveling in Trinidad in March, issued this statement to the press denying interest in the nomination. And yet, he was incapable of a Shermanesque statement of absolute refusal: ". . . it would be a mistake to nominate me unless . . ." he wrote. As slim as the prospects were, he held out for some miraculous change of heart, some independent action among the delegates who might be inspired by a yearning for the "heroic." The delegates remained uninspired and nominated Charles Evans Hughes. TR was in no mood for a hopeless third-party run and campaigned in support of Hughes that fall.

I am deeply sensible of the honor conferred on me and of the good-will shown me by the gentlemen who have announced themselves as delegates to be elected in my interest in the Massachusetts presidential primary. Nevertheless I must request, and I now do request and insist, that my name be not brought into the Massachusetts primaries, and I emphatically decline to be a candidate in the primaries of that or of any other State. Months ago I formally notified the authorities of Nebraska, Minnesota, and Michigan to this effect.

I do not wish the nomination.

I am not in the least interested in the political fortunes either of myself or any other man.

I am interested in awakening my fellow countrymen to the need of facing unpleasant facts. I am interested in the triumph of the great principles for which with all my heart and soul I have striven and shall continue to strive.

I will not enter into any fight for the nomination and I will not permit any factional fight to be made in my behalf. Indeed, I will go further and say that it would be a mistake to nominate me unless the country has in its mood something of the heroic—unless it feels not only devotion to ideals but the purpose measurably to realize those ideals in action.

This is one of those rare times which come only at long intervals in a nation's history, where the action taken determines the basis of the life of the generations that follow. Such times were those from 1776 to 1789, in the days of Washington, and from 1858 to 1865, in the days of Lincoln.

It is for us of to-day to grapple with the tremendous national and international problems of our own hour in the spirit and with the ability shown by those who upheld the hands of Washington and Lincoln. Whether we do or do not accomplish this feat will largely depend on the action taken at the Republican and Progressive conventions next June.

Nothing is to be hoped for from the present administration, and the struggles between the President and his party leaders in Congress are to-day merely struggles as to whether the nation shall see its governmental representatives adopt an attitude of a little more or a little less hypocrisy and follow a policy of slightly less baseness. All that they offer us is a choice between degrees of hypocrisy and degrees of infamy.

But disgust with the unmanly failure of the present administration, I believe, does not, and I know ought not to, mean that the American people will vote in a spirit of mere protest. They ought not to, and I believe they will not, be content merely to change the present administration for one equally timid, equally vacillating, equally lacking in vision, in moral integrity, and in high resolve. They should desire, and I believe they do desire, public servants and public policies signifying more than adroit cleverness in escaping action behind clouds of fine words, in refusal to face real internal needs, and in complete absorption of every faculty in devising constantly shifting hand-to-mouth and day-to-day measures for escape from our international duty by the abandonment of our national honor—measures due to sheer dread of various foreign powers, tempered by a sometimes harmonizing and sometimes conflicting dread of various classes of voters, especially hyphenated voters, at home.

We must clarify and define our policies; we must show that our belief in our governmental ideals is so real that we wish to make them count in the world at large and to make the necessary sacrifice in order that they shall count. Surely we, of this great Republic, have a contribution to make to the cause of humanity and we cannot make it unless we first show that we can secure prosperity and fair dealing among our own men and women. I believe that in a crisis so grave it is impossible too greatly to magnify the needs of the country or too strongly to dwell on the necessity of minimizing and subordinating the desires of individuals. . . .

June is a long way off. Many things may occur between now and then. It is utterly impossible to say now with any degree of certainty who should be nominated at Chicago. The crying, the vital need now is that the men who next June assemble at Chicago from the forty-eight States, and express the view of the entire country, shall act with the sane and lofty devotion to the interest of our nation as a whole which was shown by the original Continental Congress. They should approach their task unhampered by any pledge except to bring to its accomplishment every ounce of courage, intelligence, and integrity they possess.

The president at work in the White House, 1903.

4

ON PATRIOTISM AND NATIONAL DEFENSE

TRUE AMERICANISM

A mix of traditional American political values and sentiments, like separation of church and state and Fourth
of July flag waving, captures the Roosevelt philosophy
of patriotism. Preachy and overcooked, his writing on patriotism, nevertheless, won large and appreciative audiences. The
following essay also illustrates the long-standing American
unease with "foreign" customs and insistence on the melting-pot
Americanization of the immigrant. The "undersized man of letters" referred to here is undoubtedly Henry James, whom TR
despised. He once described James as a "miserable little snob."
James, in turn, thought TR an "ominous jingo." The essay
appeared in The Forum, in April 1894. Since then generations of candidates for office, from town councilmen to presidential nominees, have borrowed liberally from the sentiment and
imitated the style.

◆◇◆

Patriotism was once defined as "the last refuge of a scoundrel"; and somebody has recently remarked that when Dr. Johnson gave this definition he was ignorant of the infinite possibilities contained in the word "reform." Of course both gibes were quite justifiable, in so far as they were aimed at people who use noble names to cloak base purposes. Equally of course the man shows little wisdom and a low sense of duty who fails to see that love of country is one of the elemental virtues, even though scoundrels play upon it for their own selfish ends; and, inasmuch as abuses continually grow up in civic life as in all other kinds of life, the statesman is indeed a weakling who hesitates to reform these abuses because the word "reform" is often on the lips of men who are silly or dishonest.

What is true of patriotism and reform is true also of Americanism. There are plenty of scoundrels always ready to try to belittle reform movements or to bolster up existing iniquities in the name of Americanism; but this does not alter the fact that the man who can do most in this country is and must be the man whose Americanism is most sincere and intense. Outrageous though it is to use a noble idea as the cloak for evil, it is still worse to assail the noble idea itself because it can thus be used. The men who do iniquity in the name of patriotism, of reform, of Americanism, are merely one small division of the class that has always existed and will always exist — the class of hypocrites and demagogues, the class that is always prompt to steal the watchwords of righteousness and use them in the interests of evil-doing.

❧ ❧ ❧

We shall never be successful over the dangers that confront us; we shall never achieve true greatness, nor reach the lofty ideal which the founders and preservers of our mighty Federal Republic have set before us, unless we are Americans in heart and soul, in spirit and purpose, keenly alive to the responsibility implied in the very name of American, and proud beyond measure of the glorious privilege of bearing it.

There are two or three sides to the question of Americanism, and two or three senses in which the word "Americanism" can be used to express the antithesis of what is unwholesome and undesirable. In the first place wish to be broadly American and national, as opposed to being local or sectional. We do not wish, in politics, in literature, or in art, to develop that unwholesome parochial spirit, that over-exaltation of the little community at the expense of the great nation, which produces what has been described as the patriotism of the village, the patriotism of the belfry. Politically, the indulgence of this spirit was the chief cause of the calamities which befell the ancient republics of Greece, the medieval republics of Italy, and the petty States of Germany as it was in the last century. It is the spirit of provincial patriotism, the inability to take a view of broad adhesion to the whole nation that has been the chief among the causes that have produced such anarchy in the South American States, and which have resulted in presenting to us not one great Spanish-American federal nation stretching from the Rio Grande to Cape Horn, but a squabbling multitude of revolution-ridden States, not one of which stands even in the second rank as a power. However, politically this question of American nationality has been settled once for all. We are no longer in danger of repeating in our history the shameful and contemptible disasters that have befallen the Spanish possessions on this continent since they threw off the yoke of Spain. Indeed, there is, all through our life, very much less of this parochial spirit than there was formerly. Still there is an occasional outcropping here and there; and it is just as well that we should keep steadily in mind the futility of talking of a Northern literature or a Southern literature, an Eastern or a Western school of art or science. Joel Chandler Harris is emphatically a national writer; so is Mark Twain. They do not write merely for Georgia or Missouri or California any more than for Illinois or Connecticut; they write as Americans and for all people who can read English. St. Gaudens lives in New York; but his work is just as distinctive of Boston or Chicago. It is of very great consequence that we should have a full and ripe literary development in the United States, but it is not of the least consequence whether New York, or Boston, or Chicago, or San Francisco becomes the literary or artistic centre of the United States.

There is a second side of this question of a broad Americanism, however. The patriotism of the village or the belfry is bad, but the lack of all patriotism is even worse. There are philosophers who assure us that, in the future, patriotism will be regarded not as virtue at all, but merely as a mental stage in the journey toward a state of feeling when our patriotism will include the whole human race and all the world. This may be so; but the age of which these philosophers speak is still several aeons distant. In fact, philosophers of this type are so very advanced that they are of no practical service to the present generation. It may be, that in ages so remote that we cannot now understand any of the feelings of those who will dwell in them, patriotism will no longer be regarded as a virtue, exactly as it may be that in those remote ages people will look down upon and disregard monogamic marriage; but as things now are and have been for two or three thousand years past, and are likely to be for two or three thousand years to come, the words "home" and "country" mean a great deal. Nor do they show any tendency to lose their significance. At present, treason, like adultery, ranks as one of the worst of all possible crimes.

One may fall very far short of treason and yet be an undesirable citizen in the community. The man who becomes Europeanized, who loses his power of doing good work on this side of the water, and who loses his love for his native land, is not a traitor; but he is a silly and undesirable citizen. He is as emphatically a noxious element in our body politic as is the man who comes here from abroad and remains a foreigner. Nothing will more quickly or more surely disqualify a man from doing good work in the world than the acquirement of that flaccid habit of mind which its possessors style cosmopolitanism.

It is not only necessary to Americanize the immigrants of foreign birth who settle among us, but it is even more necessary for those among us who are by birth and descent already Americans not to throw away our birthright, and, with incredible and contemptible folly, wander back to bow down before the alien gods whom our forefathers forsook. It is hard to believe that there is any necessity to warn Americans that, when they seek to model themselves on the lines of other civilizations, they make themselves the butts of all right-thinking men; and yet the necessity certainly exists to give this warning to many of our citizens who pride themselves on their standing in the world of art and letters, or, perchance, on what they would style their social leadership in the community. It is always better to be an original than an imitation, even when the imitation is of something better than the original; but what shall we say of the fool who is content to be an imitation of something worse? Even if the weaklings who seek to be other than Americans were right in deeming other nations to be better than their own, the fact yet remains that to be a first-class American is fifty-fold better than to be a second-class imitation of a Frenchman or Englishman. As a matter of fact, however, those of our countrymen who do believe in American inferiority are always individuals who, however cultivated, have some organic weakness in their moral or mental make-up; and the great mass of our people, who are robustly patriotic, and who have sound, healthy minds, are justified in regarding these feeble renegades with a half-impatient and half-amused scorn.

We believe in waging relentless war on rank-growing evils of all kinds, and it makes no difference to us if they happen to be of purely native growth. We grasp at any good, no matter whence it comes. We do not accept the evil attendant upon another system of government as an adequate excuse for that attendant upon our own; the fact that the courtier is a scamp does not render the demagogue any the less a scoundrel. But it remains true that, in spite of all our faults and short-comings, no other land offers such glorious possibilities to the man able to take advantage of them, as does ours; it remains true that no one of our people can do any work really worth doing unless he does it primarily as an American. It is because certain classes of our people still retain their spirit of colonial dependence on, and exaggerated deference to, European opinion, that they fail to accomplish what they ought to. It is precisely along the lines where we have worked most independently that we have accomplished the greatest results; and it is in those professions where there has been no servility to, but merely a wise profiting by foreign experience, that we have produced our greatest men. Our soldiers and statesmen and orators; our explorers, our wilderness-winners, and commonwealth-builders; the men who have made our laws and seen that they were executed; and the other men whose energy and ingenuity have created our marvelous material prosperity—all these have been men who have drawn wisdom from the experience of every age and nation, but who have nevertheless thought, and worked, and conquered, and lived, and died, purely as Americans; and on the whole they have done better work than has been done in any other country during the short period of our national life.

On the other hand, it is on those professions where our people have striven hardest to mold themselves in conventional European forms that they have succeeded least; and this holds true to the present day, the failure being of course most conspicuous where the man takes up his abode in Europe; where he becomes a second rate European, because over-civilized, over-sensitive, over-refined, and has lost the hardihood and manly courage by which alone he can conquer in the keen struggle of our national life. The painter who goes to Paris, not merely to get two or three years' thorough training in his art, but with the intention of following in the ruts worn deep by ten thousand earlier travelers instead of striking off to rise or fall on a new line, thereby forfeits all chance of doing the best work. He must content himself with aiming at that kind of mediocrity which consists in doing fairly well what has already been done better. . . . Thus it is with the undersized man of letters, who flees his country because he, with his delicate, effeminate sensitiveness, finds the conditions of life on this side of the water crude and raw; in other words, because he finds that he cannot play a man's part among men, and so goes where he will be sheltered from the winds that harden stouter souls. This *emigrée* may write graceful and pretty verses, essays, novels; but he will never do work to compare with that of his brother, who is strong enough to stand on his own feet, and do his work as an American.

❦ ❦ ❦

The third sense in which the word "Americanism" may be employed is with reference to the Americanizing of the newcomers to our shores. We must Americanize them in every way, in speech, in political ideas and principles, and in their way of looking at the relations between Church and State. We welcome the German or the Irishman who becomes an American. We have no use for the German or Irishman who remains such. We do not wish German-Americans and Irish-Americans who figure as such in our social and political life; we want only Americans, and, provided they are such, we do not care whether they are of native or of Irish or of German ancestry. We have no room in any healthy American community for a German-American vote or an Irish-American vote, and it is contemptible demagogy to put plans into any party platform with the purpose of catching such a vote. We have no room for any people who do not act and vote simply as Americans, and as nothing else. Moreover, we have as little use for people who carry religious prejudices into our politics as for those who carry prejudices of caste or nationality. We stand unalterably in favor of the public-school system in its entirety. We believe that English, and no other language, is that in which all the school exercises should be conducted. We are against any division of the school fund, and against any appropriation of public money for sectarian purposes. We are against any recognition whatever by the State in any shape or form of State-aided parochial schools. But we are equally opposed to any discrimination against or for a man because of his creed. We demand that all citizens, Protestant and Catholic, Jew and Gentile, shall have fair treatment in every way; that all alike shall have their rights guaranteed them. The very reasons that make us unqualified in our opposition to State-aided sectarian schools make us equally bent that, in the management of our public schools, the adherents of each creed shall be given exact and equal justice, wholly without regard to their religious affiliations; that trustees, superintendents, teachers, scholars, all alike shall be treated without any reference whatsoever to the creed they profess. We maintain that it is an outrage, in voting for a man for any position, whether State or national, to take into account his religious faith, provided only he is a good American. When a secret society does what in some places the American Protective Association seems to have done, and tries to proscribe Catholics both politically and socially, the members of such society show that they themselves are as utterly un-American, as alien to our school of political thought, as the worst immigrants who land on our shores. Their conduct is equally base and contemptible; they are the worst foes of our public-school system, because they strengthen the hands of its ultramontane enemies; they should receive the hearty condemnation of all Americans who are truly patriotic.

The mighty tide of immigration to our shores has brought in its train much of good and much of evil; and whether the good or the evil shall predominate depends mainly on whether these newcomers do or do not throw themselves heartily into our national life, cease to be Europeans, and become Americans like the rest of us. More than a third of the people of the Northern States are of foreign birth or parentage. An immense number of them have become completely Americanized, and these stand on exactly the same plane as the descendants of any Puritan, Cavalier, or Knickerbocker among us, and do their full and honorable share of the nation's work. But where immigrants, or the sons of immigrants, do not heartily and in good faith throw in their lot with us, but cling to the speech, the customs, the ways of life, and the habits of thought of the Old World which they have left, they thereby harm both themselves and us. If they remain alien elements, unassimilated, and with interests separate from ours, they are mere obstructions to the current of our national life, and, moreover, can get no good from it themselves. In fact, though we ourselves also suffer from their perversity, it is they who really suffer most. It is an immense benefit to the European immigrant to change him into an American citizen. To bear the name of American is to bear the most honorable titles; and whoever does not so believe has no business to bear the name at all, and, if he comes from Europe, the sooner he goes back there the better. Besides, the man who does not become Americanized nevertheless fails to remain a European, and becomes nothing at all.

❦ ❦ ❦

From his own standpoint, it is beyond all question the wise thing for the immigrant to become thoroughly Americanized. Moreover, from our standpoint, we have a right to demand it. We freely extend the hand of welcome and of good-fellowship to every man, no matter what his creed or birthplace, who comes here honestly intent on becoming a good United States citizen like the rest of us; but we have a right, and it is our duty to demand that he shall indeed become so and shall not confuse the issues with which we are struggling by introducing among us Old-World quarrels and prejudices. There are certain ideas which he must give up. For instance, he must learn that American life is incompatible with the existence of any form of anarchy, or of any secret society having murder for its aim, whether at home or abroad; and he must learn that we exact full religious toleration and the complete separation of Church and State. Moreover, he must not bring in his Old-World religious, race, and national antipathies, but must merge them into love for our common country, and must take pride in the things which we can all take pride in. He must revere only our flag; not only must it come first, but no other flag should even come second. He must learn to celebrate Washington's birthday rather than that of the Queen or Kaiser, and the Fourth of July instead of St. Patrick's Day. Our political and social questions must be settled on their own merits, and not complicated by quarrels between England and Ireland, or France and Germany, with which we have nothing to do; it is an outrage to fight an American political campaign with reference to questions of European politics. Above all, the immigrant must learn to talk and think and *be* United States.

WASHINGTON'S FORGOTTEN MAXIM
[Naval War College Address]

Only a few weeks after his coveted appointment as assistant secretary of the navy, TR addressed the Naval War College in Newport, Rhode Island, on June 2, 1897. His urgent message was the necessity, for the sake of peace and national honor, of building a stronger navy, and his audience was amply receptive. Given his reputation and recent appointment, the speech received broad national press coverage. In the face of the already evident tensions concerning Spanish behavior in Cuba, it was widely applauded by expansionists across the country. In the months that followed, Roosevelt, with astonishing success, did all he could to convert exhortation into policy.

A century has passed since Washington wrote "To be prepared for war is the most effectual means to promote peace." We pay to this maxim the lip loyalty we so often pay to Washington's words; but it has never sunk deep into our hearts. Indeed of late years many persons have refused it even the poor tribute of lip loyalty, and prate about the iniquity of war as if somehow that was a justification for refusing to take the steps which can alone in the long run prevent war or avert the dreadful disasters it brings in its train. The truth of the maxim is so obvious to every man of really far-sighted patriotism that its mere statement seems trite and useless; and it is not over-creditable to either our intelligence or our love of country that there should be, as there is, need to dwell upon and amplify such a truism.

In this country there is not the slightest danger of an over-development of warlike spirit, and there never has been any such danger. In all our history there has never been a time when preparedness for war was any menace to peace. On the contrary, again and again we have owed peace to the fact that we were prepared for war; and in the only contest which we have had with a European power since the Revolution, the War of 1812, the struggle and all its attendant disasters were due solely to the fact that we were not prepared to face, and were not ready instantly to resent, an attack upon our honor and interest; while the glorious triumphs at sea which redeemed that war were due to the few preparations which we had actually made. We are a great peaceful nation; a nation of merchants and manufacturers, of farmers and mechanics; a nation of workingmen, who labor incessantly with head or hand. It is idle to talk of such a nation ever being led into a course of wanton aggression or conflict with military powers by the possession of a sufficient navy.

The danger is of precisely the opposite character. If we forget that in the last resort we can only secure peace by being ready and willing to fight for it, we may some day have bitter cause to realize that a rich nation which is slothful, timid, or unwieldy is an easy prey for any people which still retains those most valuable of all qualities, the soldierly virtues. We but keep to the traditions of Washington, to the traditions of all the great Americans who struggled for the real greatness of America, when we strive to build up those fighting qualities for the lack of which in a nation, as in an individual, no refinement, no culture, no wealth, no material prosperity, can atone.

Preparation for war is the surest guaranty for peace. Arbitration is an excellent thing, but ultimately those who wish to see this country at peace with foreign nations will be wise if they place reliance upon a first-class fleet of first-class battleships rather than on any arbitration treaty which the wit of man can devise. Nelson said that the British fleet was the best negotiator in Europe, and there was much truth in the saying. Moreover, while we are sincere and earnest in our advocacy of peace, we must not forget that an ignoble peace is worse than any war. . . .

Peace is a goddess only when she comes with sword girt on thigh. The ship of state can be steered safely only when it is always possible to bring her against any foe with "her leashed thunders gathering for the leap." A really great people, proud and high-spirited, would face all the disasters of war rather than purchase that base prosperity which is bought at the price of national honor. All the great masterful races have been fighting races, and the minute that a race loses the hard fighting virtues, then, no matter what else it may retain, no matter how skilled in commerce and finance, in science or art, it has lost its proud right to stand as the equal of the best. Cowardice in a race, as in an individual, is the unpardonable sin, and a willful failure to prepare for danger may in its effects be as bad as cowardice. The timid man who cannot fight, and the selfish, short-sighted, or foolish man who will not take the steps that will enable him to fight, stand on almost the same plane.

❧ ❧ ❧

We of the United States have passed most of our few years of national life in peace. We honor the architects of our wonderful material prosperity; we appreciate the necessity of thrift, energy, and business enterprise, and we know that even these are of no avail without the civic and social virtues. But we feel, after all, that the men who have dared greatly in war, or the work which is akin to war, are those who deserve best of the country. The men of Bunker Hill and Trenton, Saratoga and Yorktown, the men of New Orleans and Mobile Bay, Gettysburg and Appomattox are those to whom we owe most. None of our heroes of peace, save a few great constructive statesmen, can rank with our heroes of war. The Americans who stand highest on the list of the world's worthies are Washington, who fought to found the country which he afterward governed, and Lincoln, who saved it through the blood of the best and bravest in the land; Washington, the soldier and statesman, the man of cool head, dauntless heart, and iron will, the greatest of good men and the best of great men; and Lincoln, sad, patient, kindly Lincoln, who for four years toiled and suffered for the people, and when his work was done laid down his life that the flag which had been rent in sunder might once more be made whole and without a seam.

It is on men such as these, and not on the advocates of peace at any price, or upon those so short-sighted that they refuse to take into account the possibility of war, that we must rely in every crisis which deeply touches the true greatness and true honor of the Republic. The United States has never once in the course of its history suffered harm because of preparation for war, or because of entering into war. But we have suffered incalculable harm, again and again, from a foolish failure to prepare for war or from reluctance to fight when to fight was proper. The men who to-day protest against a navy, and protest also against every movement to carry out the traditional policy of the country in foreign affairs, and to uphold the honor of the flag, are themselves but following in the course of those who protested against the acquisition of the great West, and who failed to make proper preparations for the war of 1812, or refused to support it after it had been made. They are . . . brothers to the men whose short-sightedness and supine indifference prevented any reorganization of the *personnel* of the navy during the middle of the century, so that we entered upon the Civil War with captains seventy years old. They are close kin to the men who, when the Southern States seceded, wished to let the Union be disrupted in peace rather than restored through the grim agony of armed conflict.

I do not believe that any considerable number of our citizens are stamped with this timid lack of patriotism. There are some *doctrinaires* whose eyes are so firmly fixed on the golden vision of universal peace that they cannot see the grim facts of real life until they stumble over them, to their own hurt, and, what is much worse, to the possible undoing of their fellows. There are some educated men in whom education merely serves to soften the fibre and to eliminate the higher, sterner qualities which tell for national greatness; and these men prate about love for mankind, or for another country, as being in some hidden way a substitute for love of their own country. What is of more weight, there are not a few men of means who have made the till their fatherland, and who are always ready to balance a temporary interruption of money-making, or a temporary financial and commercial disaster, against the self-sacrifice necessary in upholding the honor of the nation and the glory of the flag.

But after all these people, though often noisy, form but a small minority of the whole. They would be swept like chaff before the gust of popular fury which would surely come if ever the nation really saw and felt a danger or an insult. The real trouble is that in such a case this gust of popular fury would come too late. Unreadiness for war is merely rendered more disastrous by readiness to bluster; to talk defiance and advocate a vigorous policy in words, while refusing to back up these words by deeds, is cause for humiliation. It has always been true, and in this age it is more than ever true, that it is too late to prepare for war when the time for peace has passed. The short-sightedness of many people, the good-humored indifference to facts of others, the sheer ignorance of a vast number, and the selfish reluctance to insure against future danger by present sacrifice among yet others—these are the chief obstacles to building up a proper navy and carrying out a proper foreign policy.

ɭ ɭ ɭ

Tame submission to foreign aggression of any kind is a mean and unworthy thing; but it is even meaner and more unworthy to bluster first, and then either submit or else refuse to make those preparations which can alone obviate the necessity for submission. I believe with all my heart in the Monroe Doctrine, and I believe also that the great mass of the American people are loyal to it; but it is worse than idle to announce our adherence to this doctrine and yet to decline to take measures to show that ours is not mere lip loyalty. We had far better submit to interference by foreign powers with the affairs of this continent than to announce that we will not tolerate such interference, and yet refuse to make ready the means by which alone we can prevent it. In public as in private life, a bold front tends to insure peace and not strife. If we possess a formidable navy, small is the chance indeed that we shall ever be dragged into a war to uphold the Monroe Doctrine. If we do not possess such a navy, war may be forced on us at any time.

It is certain, then, that we need a first-class navy. It is equally certain that this should not be merely a navy for defense. Our chief harbors should, of course, be fortified and put in condition to resist the attack of an enemy's fleet; and one of our prime needs is an ample force of torpedo boats to use primarily for coast defense. But in war the mere defensive never pays, and can never result in anything but disaster. It is not enough to parry a blow. The surest way to prevent its repetition is to return it. No master of the prize ring ever fought his way to supremacy by mere dexterity in avoiding punishment. He had to win by inflicting punishment. If the enemy is given the choice of time and place to attack, sooner or later he will do irreparable damage, and if he is at any point beaten back, why, after all, it is merely a repulse, and there are no means of following it up and making it a rout. We cannot rely upon coast protection alone. Forts and heavy land guns and torpedo boasts are indispensable, and the last, on occasion, may be used for offensive purposes also. But in the present state of naval and military knowledge we must rely mainly, as all great nations always have relied, on the battleship, the fighting ship of the line. Gunboats and light cruisers serve an excellent purpose, and we could not do without them. In time of peace they are the police of the seas; in time of war they would do some harrying of commerce, and a great deal of scouting and skirmishing; but our main reliance must be on the great armored battle-ships with their heavy guns and shot-proof vitals. In the last resort we must trust to the ships whose business it is to fight and not to run, and who can themselves go to sea and strike at the enemy when they choose, instead of waiting peacefully to receive his blow when and where he deems it best to deliver it. If in the event of war our fleet of battle-ships can destroy the hostile fleet, then our coasts are safe from the menace of serious attack; even a fight that ruined our fleet would probably so shatter the hostile fleet as to do away with all chance of invasion; but if we have no fleet wherewith to meet the enemy on the high seas, or to anticipate his stroke by our own, then every city within reach of the tides must spend men and money in preparation for an attack that may not come, but which would cause crushing and irredeemable disaster if it did come.

Still more it is necessary to have a fleet of great battleships if we intend to live up to the Monroe Doctrine, and to insist upon its observance in the two Americas and the islands on either side of them. If a foreign power, whether in Europe or Asia, should determine to assert its position in those lands wherein we feel that our influence should be supreme, there is but one way in which we can effectively interfere. Diplomacy is utterly useless where there is no force behind it; the diplomat is the servant, not the master, of the soldier. The prosperity of peace, commercial and material prosperity, gives no weight whatever when the clash of arms comes. Even great naked strength is useless if there is no immediate means through which that strength can manifest itself. If we mean to protect the people of the lands who look to us for protection from tyranny and aggression; if we mean to uphold our interests in the teeth of the formidable Old World powers, we can only do it by being ready at any time, if the provocation is sufficient, to meet them on the seas, where the battle for supremacy must be fought. Unless we are prepared so to meet them, let us abandon all talk of devotion to the Monroe Doctrine or to the honor of the American name.

This nation cannot stand still if it is to retain its self-respect, and to keep undimmed the honorable traditions inherited from the men who with the sword founded it and by the sword preserved it. We ask that the work of upbuilding the navy, and of putting the United States where it should be put among maritime powers, go forward without a break. We ask this not in the interest of war, but in the interest of peace. No nation should ever wage war wantonly, but no nation should ever avoid it at the cost of the loss of national honor. A nation should never fight unless forced to; but it should always be ready to fight. The mere fact that it is ready will generally spare it the necessity of fighting. If this country now had a fleet of twenty battle-ships their existence would make it all the more likely that we should not have war. It is very important that we should, as a race, keep the virile fighting qualities and should be ready to use them at need; but it is not at all important to use them unless there is need. One of the surest ways to attain these qualities is to keep our navy in first-class trim. There never is, and never has been, on our part a desire to use a weapon because of its being well-tempered. There is not the least danger that the possession of a good navy will render this country overbearing toward its neighbors. The direct contrary is the truth.

An unmanly desire to avoid a quarrel is often the surest way to precipitate one; and utter unreadiness to fight is even surer. If at the time of our trouble with Chili, six years ago, we had not already possessed the nucleus of the new navy we should almost certainly have been forced into fighting, and even as it was, trouble was only averted because of the resolute stand then taken by the President and by the officers of the navy who were on the spot. If at that time the Chileans had been able to get ready the battle-ship which was building for them, a war would almost certainly have followed, for we had no battle-ship to put against it.

If in the future we have war, it will almost certainly come because of some action, or lack of action, on our part in the way of refusing to accept responsibilities at the proper time, or failing to prepare for war when war does not threaten. An ignoble peace is even worse than an unsuccessful war; but an unsuccessful war would leave behind it a legacy of bitter memories which would hurt our national development for a generation to come. It is true that no nation could actually conquer us, owing to our isolated position; but we would be seriously harmed, even materially, by disasters that stopped far short of conquest; and in these matters, which are far more important than things material, we could readily be damaged beyond repair. No material loss can begin to compensate for the loss of national self-respect. The damage to our commercial interests by the destruction of one of our coast cities would be as nothing compared to the humiliation which would be felt by every American worthy of the name if we had to submit to such an injury without amply avenging it. It has been finely said that "a gentleman is one who is willing to lay down his life for little things"; that is for those things which seem little to the man who cares only whether shares rise or fall in value, and to the timid *doctrinaire* who preaches timid peace from his cloistered study.

AMERICA'S PART OF THE WORLD'S WORK

*Even as governor of New York, TR continued to focus public
attention on national issues, especially those arising out of the
war with Spain. In 1898 the liberated Filipinos, with "ingrati-
tude" shocking to Americans, revolted against rule by their lib-
erators. The insurrection proved more durable than the war. At
a Republican gathering, a Lincoln Club dinner in New York in
February 1899, Roosevelt insisted on ratifying American possession of the islands and meeting what he believed were those
American obligations that victory had earned.*

The last year has been the year of all others most important to the future of
this country since the close of the Civil War. It has seen one of the most
righteous wars of modern times brought to a triumphant conclusion. And I
am glad to feel, when I am speaking to the Republican Club, that I can take
for my text to-night the admirable speech delivered in the Senate of the
United States by the Republican senator from the State of New York,
Senator Thomas C. Platt, in support of the ratification of the treaty—a
speech admirable in temper and in tone, in which all of us as Republicans
may take pride; a speech, also, which set forth in the broadest spirit the reasons why all patriotic Americans should desire the ratification of the treaty,
no matter what their views might be as to the question of expansion in the
abstract. But, indeed, in this matter, while we must shape our national
course as a whole in accordance with a well-settled policy, we must meet
such an exigency as it arises in a spirit of wise patriotism.

No sensible man will advocate our plunging rashly into a course of international knight-errantry; none will advocate our setting deliberately to work to
build up a great colonial empire. But neither will any brave and patriotic man
bid us shrink from doing our duty merely because this duty involves the certainty of strenuous effort and the possibility of danger. Some men of high reputation, from high motives, have opposed the ratification of the treaty just as they
had previously opposed the war; just as some other men whose motives were
equally high in 1861 opposed any effort to restore the Union by force of arms.
The error was almost as great in the one case as in the other, and will be so
adjudged by history. But back of the high motives of these men lay the two great
impulses—the impulses now in 1899 as in 1861—the impulses of sloth and fear;
and well it was for us that the administration and the Senate disregarded them.

We should not lightly court danger and difficulty, but neither should we
shirk from facing them, when in some way or other they must be met. We

are a great nation and we are compelled, whether we will or not, to face the responsibilities that must be faced by all great nations. It is not in our power to avoid meeting them. All that we can decide is whether we shall meet them well or ill. There are social reformers who tell us that in the far distant future the necessity for fighting will be done away with, just as there are social reformers who tell us that in that long-distant time the necessity for work—or, at least, for painful, laborious work—will be done away with. But just at present the nation, like the individual, which is going to do anything in the world must face the fact, that in order to do it, it must work and may have to fight. And it is only thus that great deeds can be done, and the highest and purest form of happiness acquired. Remember that peace itself, that peace after which all men crave, is merely the realization in the present of what has been bought by strenuous effort in the past. Peace represents stored-up effort of our father or of ourselves in the past. It is not a means— it is an end. You do not get peace by peace; you get peace as the result of effort. If you strive to get it by peace you will lose it, that is all. If we ever grow to regard peace as a permanent condition; if we ever grow to feel that we can afford to let the keen, fearless, virile qualities of heart and mind and body be lost, then we will prepare the way for inevitable and shameful disaster in the future.

Peace is of true value only if we use it in part to make ready to face with untroubled heart, with fearless front, whatever the future may have in store for us. The peace which breeds timidity and sloth is a curse and not a blessing. The law of worthy national life, like the law of worthy individual life, is, after all, fundamentally, the law of strife. It may be strife military, it may be strife civil; but certain it is that only through strife, through labor and painful effort, by grim energy and by absolute courage, we move on to better things.

We now have certain duties in the West and East Indies. We cannot with honor shirk these duties. On the one hand we must undertake them, and on the other we must not fail to perform them in a way that will redound to the advantage of the people of the islands, no less than to our national renown.

It is, I am sure, the desire of every American that the people of each island, as rapidly as they show themselves fit for self-government, shall be endowed with a constantly larger measure of self-government. But it would be criminal folly to sacrifice the real welfare of the islands, and to fail to do our own manifest duty, under the plea of carrying out some doctrinaire idea which, if it had been lived up to, would have made the entire North American continent, as now found, the happy hunting-ground of savages. It is the idlest of chatter to speak of savages as being fit for self-government, and though it is occasionally heard from excellent and well-meaning people, people who believe what they say, it usually covers another motive behind— it means that people are afraid to undertake a great task, and cover up their fear by using some term which will give it the guise of philanthropy. If we refrain from doing our part of the world's work, it will not alter the fact that work has got to be done, only it will have to be done by some stronger race, because we will have shown ourselves weaklings. I do not speak merely from the standpoint of American interests, but from the standpoint of civilization and humanity.

It is infinitely better for the whole world that Russia should have taken Turkestan, that France should have taken Algiers, and that England should have taken India. The success of an Algerian or of a Sepoy revolt would be a hideous calamity to all mankind, and those who abetted it, directly or indirectly, would be traitors to civilization. And so exactly the same reasoning applies to our own dealings with the Philippines. We must treat them with absolute justice, but we must treat them also with firmness and courage. They must be made to realize that justice does not proceed from a sense of weakness on our part, that we are the masters. Weakness in any form or shape, as you gentlemen, who all your lives have upheld the honor of the flag ashore and afloat, know, is the unpardonable sin in dealing with such a problem as that with which we are confronted in the Philippines. The insurrection must be stamped out as mercifully as possible; but it must be stamped out.

We have put an end to a corrupt medieval tyranny, and by that very fact we have bound ourselves to see that no savage anarchy takes its place. What the Spaniard has been taught the Malay must learn—that the American flag is to float unchallenged where it floats now. But remembering this, that when this has been accomplished our task has only just begun. Where we have won entrance by the prowess of our soldiers we must deserve to continue by the righteousness, the wisdom, and the even-handed justice of our rule. The American administrators in the Philippines, as in Cuba and Porto Rico, must be men chosen for signal capacity and integrity; men who will administer the provinces on behalf of the entire nation from which they come, and for the sake of the entire people to which they go. If we permit our public service in the Philippines to become the prey of the spoils politicians, if we fail to keep it up to the highest standard, we shall be guilty of an act, not only of wickedness, but of weak and short-sighted folly, and we shall have begun to tread the path which was trod by Spain to her own bitter humiliation. Let us not deceive ourselves. We have a great duty to perform and we shall show ourselves a weak and a poor-spirited people if we fail to set about doing it, or if we fail to do it aright. We are bound to face the situations that arise with courage, and we are no less bound to see that where the sword wins the land, the land shall be kept by the rule of righteous law. We have taken upon ourselves, as in honor bound, a great task, befitting a great nation, and we have a right to ask of every citizen, of every true American, that he shall with heart and hand uphold the leaders of the nation as from a brief and glorious war they strive to a lasting peace that shall redound not only to the interests of the conquered people, not only to the honor of the American public, but to the permanent advancement of civilization and of all mankind.

THE STRENUOUS LIFE

On April 10, 1899, Governor Roosevelt addressed the Hamilton Club of Chicago with his prescription for how the United States should take its place in the world. Rooseveltian prejudices abound in this call for the manly, the courageous, the muscular "life of strife." Roosevelt's unembarrassed and not very restrained call for expansionist world activism led some contemporaries in his own Republican party to see him as a possibly dangerous jingo should he achieve national office.

In speaking to you, men of the greatest city of the West, men of the State which gave to the country Lincoln and Grant, men who preeminently and distinctly embody all that is most American in the American character, I wish to preach, not the doctrine of ignoble ease, but the doctrine of the strenuous life, the life of toil and effort, of labor and strife; to preach that highest form of success which comes, not to the man who desires mere easy peace, but to the man who does not shrink from danger, from hardship, or from bitter toil, and who out of these wins the splendid ultimate triumph.

A life of slothful ease, a life of that peace which springs merely from lack either of desire or of power to strive after great things, is as little worthy of a nation as of an individual. I ask only that what every self-respecting American demands from himself and from his sons shall be demanded of the American nation as a whole. . . . A mere life of ease is not in the end a very satisfactory life, and, above all, it is a life which ultimately unfits those who follow it for serious work in the world. . . .

As it is with the individual, so it is with the nation. It is a base untruth to say that happy is the nation that has no history. Thrice happy is the nation that has a glorious history. Far better it is to dare mighty things, to win glorious triumphs, even though checkered by failure, than to take rank with those poor spirits who neither enjoy much nor suffer much, because they live in the gray twilight that knows not victory nor defeat. If in 1861 the men who loved the Union had believed that peace was the end of all things, and war and strife the worst of all things, and had acted up to their belief, we would have saved hundreds of thousands of lives, we would have saved hundreds of millions of dollars. Moreover, besides saving all the blood and treasure we then lavished, we would have prevented the heartbreak of many women, the dissolution of many homes, and we would have spared the country those months of gloom and shame when it seemed as if our armies marched only to defeat. We could have avoided all this suffering simply by shrinking from strife. And if we had thus avoided it, we would have shown that we were weaklings, and that we were unfit to stand among the great nations of the earth. Thank God for the iron in the blood of our fathers, the men who upheld the wisdom of Lincoln, and bore sword or rifle in the armies of Grant! Let us, the children of the men who proved themselves equal to the mighty days, let us, the children of the men who carried the great Civil War to a triumphant conclusion, praise the God of our fathers that the ignoble counsels of peace were rejected; that the suffering and loss, the blackness of sorrow and despair, were unflinchingly faced, and the years of strife endured; for in the end the slave was freed, the Union restored, and the mighty American republic placed once more as a helmeted queen among nations.

We of this generation do not have to face a task such as that our fathers faced, but we have our tasks, and woe to us if we fail to perform them! We cannot, if we would, play the part of China, and be content to rot by inches in ignoble ease within our borders, taking no interest in what goes on beyond them, sunk in a scrambling commercialism; heedless of the higher life, the life of aspiration, of toil and risk, busying ourselves only with the wants of our bodies for the day, until suddenly we should find, beyond a shadow of question, what China has already found, that in this world the nation that has trained itself to a career of unwarlike and isolated ease is bound, in the end, to go down before other nations which have not lost the manly and adventurous qualities. If we are to be a really great people, we must strive in good faith to play a great part in the world. We cannot avoid meeting great issues. All that we can determine for ourselves is whether we shall meet them well or ill. In 1898 we could not help being brought face to face with the problem of war with Spain. All we could decide was whether we should shrink like cowards from the contest, or enter into it as beseemed a brave and high-spirited people; and, once in, whether failure or success should crown our banners. So it is now. We cannot avoid the responsibilities that confront us in Hawaii, Cuba, Porto Rico, and the Philippines. All we can decide is whether we shall meet them in a way that will redound to the national credit, or whether we shall make of our dealings with these new problems a dark and shameful page in our history. To refuse to deal with them at all merely amounts to dealing with them badly. We have a given problem to solve. If we undertake the solution, there is, of course, always danger that we may not solve it aright; but to refuse to undertake the solution simply renders it certain that we cannot possibly solve it aright.

❧ ❧ ❧

We cannot sit huddled within our own borders and avow ourselves merely an assemblage of well-to-do hucksters who care nothing for what happens beyond. Such a policy would defeat even its own end; for as the nations grow to have ever wider and wider interests, and are brought into closer and closer contact, if we are to hold our own in the struggle for naval and commercial supremacy, we must build up our power without our own borders. We must build the isthmian canal, and we must grasp the points of vantage which will enable us to have our say in deciding the destiny of the oceans of the East and the West.

So much for the commercial side. From the standpoint of international honor the argument is even stronger. The guns that thundered off Manila and Santiago left us echoes of glory, but they also left us a legacy of duty. If we drove out a medieval tyranny only to make room for savage anarchy, we had better not have begun the task at all. It is worse than idle to say that we have no duty to perform, and can leave to their fates the islands we have conquered. Such a course would be the course of infamy. It would be followed at once by utter chaos in the wretched islands themselves. Some stronger manlier power would have to step in and do the work, and we would have shown ourselves weaklings, unable to carry to successful completion the labors that great and high-spirited nations are eager to undertake.

The work must be done; we cannot escape our responsibility and if we are worth our salt, we shall be glad of the chance to do the work—glad of the chance to show ourselves equal to one of the great tasks set modern civilization. But let us not deceive ourselves as to the importance of the task. Let us not be misled by vainglory into underestimating the strain it will put on our powers. Above all, let us, as we value our own self-respect, face the responsibilities with proper seriousness, courage, and high resolve. We must demand the higher order of integrity and ability in our public men who are to grapple with these new problems. We must hold to a rigid accountability those public servants who show unfaithfulness to the interests of the nation or inability to rise to the high level of the new demands upon our strength and our resources.

❦ ❦ ❦

Now, apply all this to our public men of to-day. Our army has never been built up as it should be built up. I shall not discuss with an audience like this the puerile suggestion that a nation of seventy millions of freemen is in danger of losing its liberties from the existence of an army of one hundred thousand men, three fourths of whom will be employed in certain foreign islands, in certain coast fortresses, and on Indian reservations. No man of good sense and stout heart can take such a proposition seriously. If we are such weaklings as the proposition implies, then we are unworthy of freedom in any event. To no body of men in the United States is the country so much indebted as to the splendid officers and enlisted men of the regular army and navy. There is no body from which the country has less to fear, and none of which it should be prouder, none which it should be more anxious to upbuild.

Our army needs complete reorganization—not merely enlarging—and the reorganization can only come as the result of legislation. A proper general staff should be established, and the positions of ordnance, commissary, and quartermaster officers should be filled by detail from the line. Above all, the army must be given the chance to exercise in large bodies. Never again should we see, as we saw in the Spanish war, major-generals in command of divisions who had never before commanded three companies together in the field. Yet, incredible to relate, Congress has shown a queer inability to learn some of the lessons of the war. There were large bodies of men in both branches who opposed the declaration of war, who opposed the ratification of peace, who opposed the upbuilding of the army, and who even opposed the purchase of armor at a reasonable price for the battle-ships and cruisers, thereby putting an absolute stop to the building of any new fighting-ships for the navy. If, during the years to come, any disaster should befall our arms, afloat or ashore, and thereby any shame come to the United States, remember that the blame will lie upon the men whose names appear upon the roll-calls of Congress on the wrong side of these great questions. On them will lie the burden of any loss of our soldiers and sailors, of any dishonor to the flag; and upon you and the people of this country will lie the blame if you do not repudiate, in no unmistakable way, what these men have done. The blame will not rest upon the untrained commander of untried troops, upon the civil officers of a department the organization of which has been left utterly inadequate, or upon the admiral with an insufficient number of ships; but upon the public men who have so lamentably failed in forethought as to refuse to remedy these evils long in advance, and upon the nation that stands behind those public men.

№ № №

In the West Indies and the Philippines alike we are confronted by most difficult problems. It is cowardly to shrink from solving them in the proper way; for solved they must be, if not by us, then by some stronger and more manful race. If we are too weak, too selfish, or too foolish to solve them, some bolder and abler people must undertake the solution. Personally, I am far too firm a believer in the greatness of my country and the power of my countrymen to admit for one moment that we shall ever be driven to the ignoble alternative.

The problems are different for the different islands. Porto Rico is not large enough to stand alone. We must govern it wisely and well, primarily in the interest of its own people. Cuba, is, in my judgment, entitled ultimately to settle for itself whether it shall be an independent state or an integral portion of the mightiest of republics. But until order and stable liberty are secured, we must remain in the island to insure them, and infinite tact, judgment, moderation, and courage must be shown by our military and civil representatives in keeping the island pacified, in relentlessly stamping out brigandage, in protecting all alike, and yet in showing proper recognition to the men who have fought for Cuban liberty. The Philippines offer a yet graver problem. Their population includes half-caste and native Christians, warlike Moslems, and wild pagans. Many of their people are utterly unfit for self-government, and show no signs of becoming fit. Others may in time become fit but at present can only take part in self- government under a wise supervision, at once firm and beneficent. We have driven Spanish tyranny from the islands. If we now let it be replaced by savage anarchy, our work has been for harm and not for good. I have scant patience with those who fear to undertake the task of governing the Philippines, and who openly avow that they do fear to undertake it, or that they shrink from it because of the expense and trouble; but I have even scanter patience with those who make a pretense of humanitarianism to hide and cover their timidity, and who cant about "liberty" and the "consent of the governed," in order to excuse themselves for their unwillingness to play the part of men. Their doctrines, if carried out, would make it incumbent upon us to leave the Apaches of Arizona to work out their own salvation, and to decline to interfere in a single Indian reservation. Their doctrines condemn your forefathers and mine for ever having settled in these United States.

England's rule in India and Egypt has been of great benefit to England, for it has trained up generations of men accustomed to look at the larger and loftier side of public life. It has been of even greater benefit to India and Egypt. And finally, and most of all, it has advanced the cause of civilization. So, if we do our duty aright in the Philippines, we will add to that national renown which is the highest and finest part of national life, will greatly benefit the people of the Philippine Islands, and, above all, we will play our part well in the great work of uplifting mankind. But to do this work, keep ever in mind that we must show in a very high degree the qualities of courage, of honesty, and of good judgment. Resistance must be stamped out. The first and all-important work to be done is to establish the supremacy of our flag.

We must put down armed resistance before we can accomplish anything else, and there should be no parleying, no faltering, in dealing with our foe. As for those in our own country who encourage the foe, we can afford contemptuously to disregard them; but it must be remembered that their utterances are not saved from being treasonable merely by the fact that they are despicable.

When once we have put down armed resistance, when once our rule is acknowledged, then an even more difficult task will begin, for then we must see to it that the islands are administered with absolute honesty and with good judgment. If we let the public service of the islands be turned into the prey of the spoils politician, we shall have begun to tread the path which Spain trod to her own destruction. We must send out there only good and able men, chosen for their fitness, and not because of their partisan service, and these men must not only administer impartial justice to the natives and serve their own government with honesty and fidelity, but must show the utmost tact and firmness, remembering that, with such people as those with whom we are to deal, weakness is the greatest of crimes, and that next to weakness comes lack of consideration for their principles and prejudices.

I preach to you, then, my countrymen, that our country calls not for the life of ease but for the life of strenuous endeavor. The twentieth century looms before us big with the fate of many nations. If we stand idly by, if we seek merely swollen, slothful ease and ignoble peace, if we shrink from the hard contests where men must win at hazard of their lives and at the risk of all they hold dear, then the bolder and stronger peoples will pass us by, and will win for themselves the domination of the world. Let us therefore boldly face the life of strife, resolute to do our duty well and manfully; resolute to uphold righteousness by deed and by word; resolute to be both honest and brave, to serve high ideals, yet to use practical methods. Above all, let us shrink from no strife, moral or physical, within or without the nation, provided we are certain that the strife is justified, for it is only through strife, through hard and dangerous endeavor, that we shall ultimately win the goal of true national greatness.

AMERICA THE UNREADY

In his autobiography, published by Scribner's in 1913, Roosevelt made an argument for preparedness by reflecting on his experience as assistant secretary of the navy in 1898. That TR virtually reorganized the navy and issued war orders to Commodore Dewey, taking advantage of the secretary's absence, constitutes what must be considered one of the most astonishing chapters in the history of government bureaucracy.

I suppose the United States will always be unready for war, and in consequence will always be exposed to great expense, and to the possibility of the gravest calamity, when the nation goes to war. This is no new thing. Americans learn only from catastrophes and not from experience.

There would have been no war in 1812 if, in the previous decade, America, instead of announcing that "peace was her passion," instead of acting on the theory that unpreparedness averts war, had been willing to go to the expense of providing a fleet of a score of ships of the line. However, in that case, doubtless the very men who in the actual event deplored the loss of life and waste of capital which their own supineness had brought about would have loudly inveighed against the "excessive and improper cost of armaments"; so it all came to about the same thing in the end.

There is no more thoroughgoing international Mrs. Gummidge, and no more utterly useless and often utterly mischievous citizen, than the peace-at-any-price, universal-arbitration type of being, who is always complaining either about war or else about the cost of the armaments which act as the insurance against war. There is every reason why we should try to limit the cost of armaments, as these tend to grow excessive, but there is also every reason to remember that in the present stage of civilization a proper armament is the surest guaranty of peace—and is the only guaranty that war, if it does come, will not mean irreparable and overwhelming disaster. In the spring of 1897 President McKinley appointed me assistant secretary of the navy. I owed the appointment chiefly to the efforts of Senator H. C. Lodge, of Massachusetts, who doubtless was actuated mainly by his long and close friendship for me, but also—I like to believe—by his keen interest in the navy. The first book I had ever published, fifteen years previously, was *The History of the Naval War of 1812*; and I have always taken the interest in the navy which every good American ought to take. At the time I wrote the book, in the early eighties, the navy had reached its nadir, and we were then utterly incompetent to fight Spain or any other power that had a navy at all.

Shortly afterward we began timidly and hesitatingly to build up a fleet. It is amusing to recall the roundabout steps we took to accomplish our purpose. In the reaction after the colossal struggle of the Civil War our strongest and most capable men had thrown their whole energy into business, into money-making, into the development, and above all the exploitation and exhaustion at the most rapid rate possible, of our natural resources—mines, forests, soil, and rivers. These men were not weak men, but they permitted themselves to grow short-sighted and selfish; and while many of them down at the bottom possessed the fundamental virtues, including the fighting virtues, others were purely of the glorified huckster or glorified pawnbroker type—which when developed to the exclusion of everything else makes about as poor a national type as the world has seen. This unadulterated huckster or pawnbroker type is rarely keenly sympathetic in matters of social and industrial justice, and is usually physically timid and likes to cover an unworthy fear of the most just war under high-sounding names.

It was reinforced by the large mollycoddle vote—the people who are soft physically and morally, or who have a twist in them which makes them acidly cantankerous and unpleasant as long as they can be so with safety to their bodies. In addition there are the good people with no imagination and no foresight, who think war will not come, but that if it does come armies and navies can be improvised—a very large element, typified by a senator I knew personally who, in a public speech, in answer to a question as to what we would do if America were suddenly assailed by a first-class military power, answered that "we would build a battleship in every creek." Then, among the wise and high-minded people who in self-respecting and genuine fashion strive earnestly for peace, there are the foolish fanatics always to be found in such a movement and always discrediting it—the men who form the lunatic fringe in all reform movements.

All these elements taken together made a body of public opinion so important during the decades immediately succeeding the Civil War as to put a stop to any serious effort to keep the nation in a condition of reasonable military preparedness. The representatives of this opinion then voted just as they now do when they vote against battleships or against fortifying the Panama Canal. It would have been bad enough if we had been content to be weak, and, in view of our weakness, not to bluster. But we were not content with such a policy. We wished to enjoy the incompatible luxuries of an unbridled tongue and an unready hand. There was a very large element which was ignorant of our military weakness, or, naturally enough, unable to understand it; and another large element which liked to please its own vanity by listening to offensive talk about foreign nations. Accordingly, too many of our politicians, especially in Congress, found that the cheap and easy thing to do was to please the foolish peace people by keeping us weak, and to please the foolish violent people by passing denunciatory resolutions about international matters—resolutions which would have been improper even if we had been strong. Their idea was to please both the mollycoddle vote and the vote of the international tail-twisters by upholding, with pretended ardor and mean intelligence, a national policy of peace with insult.

I abhor unjust war. I abhor injustice and bullying by the strong at the expense of the weak, whether among nations or individuals. I abhor violence and bloodshed. I believe that war should never be resorted to when, or so long as, it is honorably possible to avoid it. I respect all men and women who from high motives and with sanity and self-respect do all they can to avert war. I advocate preparation for war in order to avert war; and I should never advocate war unless it were the only alternative to dishonor. I describe the folly of which so many of our people were formerly guilty, in order that we may in our own day be on our guard against similar folly.

We did not at the time of which I write take our foreign duties seriously, and as we combined bluster in speech with refusal to make any reparation whatsoever for action, we were not taken seriously in return. Gradually a slight change for the better occurred, the writings of Captain [Alfred Thayer] Mahan [on the importance of naval power] playing no small part therein. We built some modern cruisers to start with; the people who felt that battleships were wicked compromising with their misguided consciences by saying that the cruisers could be used "to protect our commerce"—which they could not be, unless they had battleships to back them. Then we attempted to build more powerful fighting vessels, and as there was a section of the public which regarded battleships as possessing a name immorally suggestive of violence, we compromised by calling the new ships armored cruisers, and making them combine with exquisite nicety all the defects and none of the virtues of both types. Then we got to the point of building battleships. But there still remained a public opinion, as old as the time of Jefferson, which thought that in the event of war all our problem ought to be one of coast defense, that we should do nothing except repel attack; an attitude about as sensible as that of a prize-fighter who expected to win by merely parrying instead of hitting. To meet the susceptibilities of this large class of well-meaning people, we provided for the battleships under the name of "coast-defense battleships"; meaning thereby that we did not make them quite as seaworthy as they ought to have been, or with quite as much coal capacity as they ought to have had. Then we decided to build real battleships. But there still remained a lingering remnant of public opinion that clung to the coast-defense theory, and we met this in beautiful fashion by providing for "sea-going coast-defense battleships"—the fact that the name was a contradiction in terms being of very small consequence compared to the fact that we did thereby get real battleships.

Our men had to be trained to handle the ships singly and in fleet formation, and they had to be trained to use the new weapons of precision with which the ships were armed. Not a few of the older officers, kept in the service under our foolish rule of pure seniority promotion, were not competent for the task; but a proportion of the older officers were excellent, and this was true of almost all the younger officers. They were naturally first-class men, trained in the admirable naval school at Annapolis. They were overjoyed that at last they were given proper instruments to work with, and they speedily grew to handle these ships individually in the best fashion. They were fast learning to handle them in squadron and fleet formation; but when the war with Spain broke out, they had as yet hardly grasped the principles of modern scientific naval gunnery.

Soon after I began to work as assistant secretary of the navy I became convinced that the war would come. The revolt in Cuba had dragged its weary length until conditions in the island had become so dreadful as to be a standing disgrace to us for permitting them to exist. There is much that I sincerely admire about the Spanish character; and there are few men for whom I have felt greater respect than for certain gentlemen of Spain whom I have known. But Spain attempted to govern her colonies on archaic principles which rendered her control of them incompatible with the advance of humanity and intolerable to the conscience of mankind. In 1898 the so-called war in Cuba had dragged along for years with unspeakable horror, degradation, and misery. It was not "war" at all, but murderous oppression. Cuba was devastated.

During those years, while we continued at "peace," several hundred times as many lives were lost, lives of men, women and children, as were lost during the three months' "war" which put an end to this slaughter and opened a career of peaceful progress to the Cubans. Yet there were misguided professional philanthropists who cared so much more for names than for facts that they preferred a "peace" of continuous murder to a "war" which stopped the murder and brought real peace. Spain's humiliation was certain, anyhow; indeed, it was more certain without war than with it, for she could not permanently keep the island, and she minded yielding to the Cubans more than yielding to us. Our own direct interests were great, because of the Cuban tobacco and sugar, and especially because of Cuba's relation to the projected Isthmian Canal. But even greater were our interests from the standpoint of humanity. Cuba was at our very doors. It was a dreadful thing for us to sit supinely and watch her death-agony. It was our duty, even more from the standpoint of national honor than from the standpoint of national interest, to stop the devastation and destruction. Because of these considerations I favored war; and to-day, when in retrospect it is easier to see things clearly, there are few humane and honorable men who do not believe that the war was both, just and necessary.

The big financiers and the men generally who were susceptible to touch on the money nerve, and who cared nothing for national honor if it conflicted even temporarily with business prosperity, were against the war. The more fatuous type of philanthropist agreed with them. The newspapers controlled by, or run in the interests of, these two classes deprecated war, and did everything in their power to prevent any preparation for war. As a whole the people in Congress were at that time (and are now) a shortsighted set as regards international matters. There were a few men, Senators Cushman K. Davis, for instance, and John Morgan, who did look ahead; and Senator H. C. Lodge, who throughout this quarter of a century of service in the Senate and House has ever stood foremost among those who uphold with far-sighted fearlessness and strict justice to others our national honor and interest; but most of the congressmen were content to follow the worst of all possible courses, that is, to pass resolutions which made war more likely, and yet to decline to take measures which would enable us to meet the war if it did come.

However, in the Navy Department we were able to do a good deal, thanks to the energy and ability of some of the bureau chiefs, and to the general good tone of the service. I soon found my natural friends and allies in such men as Evans, Taylor, Sampson, Wainwright, Brownson, Schroeder, Bradford, Cowles, Cameron, Wilson, O'Neil, and others like them. I used all the power there was in my office to aid these men in getting the material ready. I also tried to gather from every source information as to who the best men were to occupy the fighting positions.

Sound naval opinion was overwhelmingly in favor of Dewey to command one squadron. I was already watching him, for I had been struck by an incident in his past career. It was at a time when there was threat of trouble with Chile. Dewey was off the Argentine, and was told to get ready to move to the other coast of South America. If the move became necessary, he would have to have coal, and yet if he did not make the move, the coal would not be needed. In such a case a man afraid of responsibility always acts rigidly by the regulations and communicates with the department at home to get authority for everything he does; and therefore he usually accomplishes nothing whatever, but is able to satisfy all individuals with red-tape minds by triumphantly pointing out his compliance with the regulations. In a crisis, the man worth his salt is the man who meets the needs of the situation in whatever way is necessary. Dewey purchased the coal and was ready to move at once if need arose. The affair blew over; the need to move did not occur; and for some time there seemed to be a chance that Dewey would get into trouble over having purchased the coal, for our people are like almost all other peoples in requiring responsible officers under such conditions to decide at their own personal peril, no matter which course they follow. However, the people higher up ultimately stood by Dewey.

The incident made me feel that here was a man who could be relied upon to prepare in advance, and to act promptly, fearlessly, and on his own responsibility when the emergency arose. Accordingly I did my best to get him put in command of the Asiatic fleet, the fleet where it was most essential to have a man who would act without referring things back to the home authorities.

🌿 🌿 🌿

When the *Maine* was blown up in Havana Harbor, war became inevitable. A number of the peace-at-any-price men of course promptly assumed the position that she had blown herself up; but investigation showed that the explosion was from outside. And, in any event, it would have been impossible to prevent war. The enlisted men of the navy, who often grew bored to the point of desertion in peace, became keyed up to a high pitch of efficiency, and crowds of fine young fellows, from the interior as well as from the seacoast, thronged to enlist. The navy officers showed alert ability and unwearied industry in getting things ready. There was one deficiency, however, which there was no time to remedy, and of the very existence of which, strange to say, most of our best men were ignorant. Our navy had no idea how low our standard of marksmanship was. We had not realized that the modern battle-ship had become such a complicated piece of mechanism that the old methods of training in marksmanship were as obsolete as the old muzzle-loading broadside guns themselves. Almost the only man in the navy who fully realized this was our naval attaché at Paris, Lieutenant Sims. He wrote letter after letter pointing out how frightfully backward we were in marksmanship. I was much impressed by his letters; but Wainwright was about the only other man who was. And as Sims proved to be mistaken in his belief that the French had taught the Spaniards how to shoot, and as the Spaniards proved to be much worse even than we were, in the service generally Sims was treated as an alarmist. But although I at first partly acquiesced in this view, I grew uneasy when I studied the small proportion of hits to shots made by our vessels in battle. When I was President I took up the matter, and speedily became convinced that we needed to revolutionize our whole training in marksmanship. Sims was given the lead in organizing and introducing the new system; and to him more than to any other one man was due the astonishing progress made by our fleet in this respect, a progress which made the fleet, gun for gun, at least three times as effective, in point of fighting efficiency, in 1908 as it was in 1902. The shots that hit are the shots that count!

Like the people, the government was for a long time unwilling to prepare for war, because so many honest but misguided men believed that the preparation itself tended to bring on the war. I did not in the least share this feeling, and whenever I was left as acting secretary I did everything in my power to put us in readiness. I knew that in the event of war Dewey could be slipped like a wolfhound from a leash; I was sure that if he were given half a chance he would strike instantly and with telling effect; and I made up my mind that all I could do to give him that half-chance should be done. I was in the closest touch with Senator Lodge throughout this period, and either consulted him about or notified him of all the moves I was taking. By the end of February I felt it was vital to send Dewey (as well as each of our other commanders who were not in home waters) instructions that would enable him to be in readiness for immediate action. On the afternoon of Saturday, February 25, when I was acting secretary, Lodge called on me just as I was preparing the order, which (as it was addressed to a man of the right stamp) was of much importance to the subsequent operations. Admiral Dewey speaks of the incident as follows, in his autobiography:

> The first real step [as regards active naval preparations] was taken on February 25, when telegraphic instructions were sent to the Asiatic, European, and South Atlantic squadrons to rendezvous at certain convenient points where, should war break out, they would be most available.
>
> The message to the Asiatic squadron bore the signature of that Assistant Secretary who had seized the opportunity while Acting Secretary to hasten preparations for a conflict which was inevitable. As Mr. Roosevelt reasoned, precautions for readiness would cost little in time of peace, and yet would be invaluable in case of war. His cablegram was as follows:

"Washington, February 25, '98.
DEWEY, HONG KONG:
Order the squadron, except the Monocacy, to Hong Kong. Keep full of coal. In the event of declaration of war Spain [*sic*], your duty will be to see that the Spanish squadron does not leave the Asiatic coast, and then offensive operations in Philippine Islands. Keep Olympia until further orders.
ROOSEVELT."

(The reference to keeping the *Olympia* until further orders was due to the fact that I had been notified that she would soon be recalled to the United States.)

All that was needed with Dewey was to give him the chance to get ready, and then to strike, without being hampered by orders from those not on the ground. Success in war depends very largely upon choosing a man fit to exercise such powers, and then giving him the powers.

It would be instructive to remember, if only we were willing to do so, the fairly comic panic which swept in waves over our seacoast, first when it became evident that war was about to be declared, and then when it was declared. The public waked up to the sufficiently obvious fact that the government was in its usual state—perennial unreadiness for war. There-upon the people of the seaboard district passed at one bound from unreasoning confidence that war never could come to unreasoning fear as to what might happen now that it had come. That acute philosopher, Mr. Dooley,[1] proclaimed that in the Spanish War we were in a dream, but that the Spaniards were in a trance. This just about summed up the facts. Our people had for decades scoffed at the thought of making ready for possible war. Now, when it was too late, they not only backed every measure, wise and unwise, that offered a chance of supplying a need that ought to have been met before, but they also fell into a condition of panic apprehension as to what the foe might do.

For years we had been saying, just as any number of our people now say, that no nation would venture to attack us. Then when we did go to war with an exceedingly feeble nation, we, for the time being, rushed to the other extreme of feeling, and attributed to this feeble nation plans of offensive warfare which it never dreamed of making, and which, if made, it would have been wholly unable to execute. Some of my readers doubtless remember the sinister intentions and unlimited potentialities for destruction with which the fertile imagination of the yellow press endowed the armored cruiser *Viscaya* when she appeared in American waters just before war was declared. The state of nervousness along much of the seacoast was funny in view of the lack of foundation for it; but it offered food for serious thought as to what would happen if we ever became engaged with a serious foe.

---

[1] Dooley was a popular fictional political commentator created by Finley Peter Dunne.

SELF-DEFENSE WITHOUT MILITARISM

Deeply concerned about the United States' lack of preparation to enter the world war (and he thought the nation had been sufficiently provoked by the Germans), TR frequently spoke of Woodrow Wilson's irresponsible failure to arm the country. He calls here for a Swiss-style universal military training adapted to American democratic practice. He had no patience with the pacifist; he valued the "big stick," and he liked to point to the pacific years of his term in office as compared to those that followed as evidence that power could protect the peace. It is an argument that served repeatedly in the twentieth century, not always with the results Roosevelt confidently hoped for. This essay was published as part of a collection called America and the World War *by Scribner's in 1915.*

The other day one of the typical ultrapacifists or peace-at-any-price men put the ultrapacifist case quite clearly, both in a statement of his own and by a quotation of what he called the "golden words" of Mr. Bryan at Mohonk. . . .

The "golden words" of Mr. Bryan were as follows:

> I believe that this nation could stand before the world today and tell the world that it did not believe in war, that it did not believe that it was the right way to settle disputes, that it had no disputes which it was not willing to submit to the judgement of the world. If this nation did that, it not only would not be attacked by any other nation of the earth, but it would become the supreme power in the world.

Of course, it is to be assumed that Mr. Bryan means what he says. If he does, then he is willing to submit to arbitration the question whether the Japanese have or have not the right to send unlimited numbers of immigrants to this shore. If Mr. Bryan does not mean this, among other specific things, then the "golden words" in question represent merely the emotionalism of the professional orator. Of course, if Mr. Bryan means what he says, he also believes that we should not have interfered in Cuba and Cuba ought now to be the property of Spain. He also believes that we ought to have permitted Colombia to reconquer and deprive of their independence the people of Panama, and that we should not have built the Panama Canal. He also believes that California and Texas ought now to be parts of Mexico, enjoying whatever blessings complete abstinence from foreign war has secured that country during the last three years. He also believes that the Declaration of Independence was an arbitrable matter and that the United States ought now to be a dependency of Great Britain. Unless Mr. Bryan does believe all of these things then his "golden words" represent only a rhetorical flourish. He is secretary of state and the right-hand man of President Wilson, and President Wilson is completely responsible for whatever he says and for the things he does—or rather which he leaves undone.

❧ ❧ ❧

No man can possibly be more anxious for peace than I am. I ask those individuals who think of me as a firebrand to remember that during the seven and a half years I was President not a shot was fired at any soldier of a hostile nation by any American soldier or sailor, and there was not so much as a threat of war. Even when the state of Panama threw off the alien yoke of Colombia and when this nation, acting as was its manifest duty, by recognizing Panama as an independent state stood for the right of the governed to govern themselves on the Isthmus, as well as for justice and humanity, there was not a shot fired by any of our people at any Colombian. The blood recently shed at Vera Cruz, like the unpunished wrongs recently committed on our people in Mexico, had no parallel during my administration. When I left the presidency there was not a cloud on the horizon— and one of the reasons why there was not a cloud on the horizon was that the American battle fleet had just returned from its sixteen months' trip around the world, a trip such as no other battle fleet of any power had ever taken, which it had not been supposed could be taken, and which exercised a greater influence for peace than all the peace congresses of the last fifty years. With Lowell I most emphatically believe that peace is not a gift that tarries long in the hands of cowards; and the fool and the weakling are no improvement on the coward. . . .

Of all the nations of the world we are the one that combines the greatest amount of wealth with the smallest ability to defend that wealth. Surely one does not have to read history very much or ponder over philosophy a great deal in order to realize the truth that the one certain way to invite disaster is to be opulent, offensive, and unarmed. There is utter inconsistency between the ideal of making this nation the foremost commercial power in the world and of disarmament in the face of an armed world. There is utter inconsistency between the ideal of making the nation a power for international righteousness and at the same time refusing to make us a power efficient in anything save empty treaties and emptier promises.

I do not believe in a large standing army. Most emphatically I do not believe in militarism. Most emphatically I do not believe in any policy of aggression by us. But I do believe that no man is really fit to be the free citizen of a free republic unless he is able to bear arms and at need to serve with efficiency in the efficient army of the republic. This is no new thing with me. For years I have believed that the young men of the country should know how to use a rifle, and should have a short period of military training which, while not taking them for any length of time from civil pursuits, would make them quickly capable of helping defend the country in case of need. When I was governor of New York, acting in conjunction with the administration at Washington under President McKinley, I secured the sending abroad of one of the best officers in the New York National Guard, Colonel William Cary Sanger, to study the Swiss system. As President I had to devote my attention chiefly to getting the navy built up. But surely the sight of what has happened abroad ought to awaken our people to the need of action, not only as regards our navy but as regards our land-forces also.

Australia has done well in this respect. But Switzerland has worked out a comprehensive scheme with practical intelligence. She has not only solved the question of having men ready to fight, but she has solved the question of having arms to give these men. At present England is in more difficulty about arms than about men, and some of her people when sent to the front were armed with hunting-rifles. Our own shortcomings are far greater. Indeed, they are so lamentable that it is hard to believe that our citizens as a whole know them. To equip half the number of men whom even the British now have in the field would tax our factories to the limit. In Switzerland, during the last two or three years of what corresponds to our high-school work the boy is thoroughly grounded in the rudiments of military training, discipline, and marksmanship. When he graduates he is put for some four to six months in the army to receive exactly the training he would get in time of war. After that he serves eight days a year and in addition often joins with his fellows in practicing at a mark. He keeps his rifle and accoutrements in his home and is responsible for their condition. Efficiency is the watchword of Switzerland, and not least in its army. At the outbreak of this terrible war Switzerland was able to mobilize her forces in the corner of her territory between France and Germany as quickly as either of the great combatants could theirs; and no one trespassed upon her soil.

❦ ❦ ❦

There is no reason whatever why Americans should be unwilling or unable to do what Switzerland has done. We are a far wealthier country than Switzerland and could afford without the slightest strain the very trifling expense and the trifling consumption of time rendered necessary by such a system. It has really nothing in common with the universal service in the great conscript armies of the military powers. No man would be really taken out of industry. On the contrary, the average man would probably be actually benefitted as far as doing his life-work is concerned. The system would be thoroughly democratic in its workings. No man would be exempted from the work and all would have to perform the work alike. It would be entirely possible to arrange that there should be a certain latitude as to the exact year when the four or six months' service was given.

❧ ❧ ❧

It may well be that the Swiss on an average can be made into good troops quicker than our own men; but most assuredly there would be numbers of Americans who would not be behind the Swiss in such a matter. A body of volunteers of the kind I am describing would of course not be as good as a body of regulars of the same size, but they would be immeasurably better than the average soldiers produced by any system we now have or ever have had in connection with our militia. Our regular army would be strengthened by them at the very beginning and would be set free in its entirety for immediate aggressive action; and in addition a levy in mass of the young men of the right age would mean that two or three million troops were put into the field, who, although not as good as regulars, would at once be available in numbers sufficient to overwhelm any expeditionary force which it would be possible for any military power to send to our shores. The existence of such a force would render the immediate taking of cities like San Francisco, New York, or Boston an impossibility and would free us from all danger from sudden raids and make it impossible even for an army corps to land with any prospect of success.

Our people are so entirely unused to things military that it is probably difficult for the average man to get any clear idea of our shortcomings. Unlike what is true in the military nations of the Old World, here the ordinary citizen takes no interest in the working of our War Department in time of peace. No President gains the slightest credit for himself by paying attention to it. Then when a crisis comes and the War Department breaks down, instead of the people accepting what has happened with humility as due to their own fault during the previous two or three decades, there is a roar of wrath against the unfortunate man who happens to be in office at the time.

❧ ❧ ❧

I advocate that our preparedness take such shape as to fit us to resist aggression, not to encourage us in aggression. I advocate preparedness that will enable us to defend our own shores and to defend the Panama Canal and Hawaii and Alaska, and prevent the seizure of territory at the expense of any commonwealth of the western hemisphere by any military power of the Old World.

The African hunter, 1909.

5

AFRICAN HUNTER

When he left the presidency, TR indulged his ambition to hunt big game in Africa in 1909. With his son Kermit he spent many months shooting and collecting specimens, keeping careful lists of species and numbers killed. Some of these trophies he gathered for the Smithsonian Institution. His safari covered hundreds of miles, from Mombasa on the Indian Ocean to Khartoum and on to Egypt. The account of his adventures in Africa was published in Scribner's magazine in 1909 and 1910 and as a book, African Game Trails, in 1910, from which the following two selections were taken.

◆◆◆

LION-HUNTING ON THE KAPITI PLAINS

The dangerous game of Africa are the lion, buffalo, elephant, rhinoceros, and leopard. The hunter who follows any of these animals always does so at a certain risk to life or limb; a risk which it is his business to minimize by coolness, caution, good judgment, and straight shooting. The leopard is in point of pluck and ferocity more than the equal of the other four; but his small size always renders it likely that he will merely maul and not kill a man. My friend Carl Akeley, of Chicago, actually killed bare-handed a leopard which sprang on him. He had already wounded the beast twice, crippling it in one front and one hind paw; whereupon it charged, followed him as he tried to dodge the charge, and struck him full just as he turned. It bit him in one arm, biting again and again as it worked up the arm from the wrist to the elbow; but Akeley threw it, holding its throat with the other hand, and flinging its body to one side. It luckily fell on its side with its two wounded legs uppermost, so that it could not tear him. He fell forward with it and crushed in its chest with his knees until he distinctly felt one of its ribs crack; this, said Akeley, was the first moment when he felt he might conquer. Redoubling his efforts, with knees and hand, he actually choked and crushed the life out of it, although his arm was badly bitten. A leopard will charge at least as readily as one of the big beasts, and is rather more apt to get his charge home, but the risk is less to life than to limb.

There are other animals often or occasionally dangerous to human life which are, nevertheless, not dangerous to the hunter. Crocodiles are far greater pests, and far more often man-eaters, than lions or leopards; but their shooting is not accompanied by the smallest element of risk. Poisonous snakes are fruitful sources of accident, but they are actuated only by fear and the anger born of fear. The hippopotamus sometimes destroys boats and kills those in them; but again there is no risk in hunting him. Finally, the hyena, too cowardly ever to be a source of danger to the hunter, is sometimes a dreadful curse to the weak and helpless. The hyena is a beast of unusual strength and enormous power in his jaws and teeth, and thrice over would be dreaded were fang and sinew driven by a heart of the leopard's cruel courage. But though the creature's foul and evil ferocity has no such backing as that yielded by the angry daring of the spotted cat, it is yet fraught with a terror all its own; for on occasion the hyena takes to man-eating after its own fashion. Carrion-feeder though it is, in certain places it will enter native huts and carry away children or even sleeping adults; and where famine or disease has worked havoc among a people, the hideous spotted beasts become bolder and prey on the survivors.

🌿 🌿 🌿

During the last few decades, in Africa, hundreds of white hunters, and thousands of native hunters, have been killed or wounded by lions, buffaloes, elephants, and rhinos. All are dangerous game; each species has to its grue-some credit a long list of mighty hunters slain or disabled. Among those com-petent to express judgment there is the widest difference of opinion as to the comparative danger in hunting the several kinds of animals. . . . A man who has shot but a dozen or a score of these various animals, all put together, is not entitled to express any but the most tentative opinion as to their relative prowess and ferocity; yet on the whole it seems to me that the weight of opin-ion among those best fitted to judge is that the lion is the most formidable opponent of the hunter, under ordinary conditions. This is my own view.

🌿 🌿 🌿

Everywhere throughout the country we were crossing were signs that the lion was lord and that his reign was cruel. There were many lions, for the game on which they feed was extraordinarily abundant. They occasionally took the ostriches or stock of the settlers, ravaged the herds and flocks of the natives, but not often; for their favorite food was yielded by the swarm-ing herds of kongoni and zebras, on which they could prey at will. Later we found that in this region they rarely molested the buffalo, even where they lived in the same reed beds; and this though elsewhere they habitually prey on the buffalo. But where zebras and hartbeests could be obtained without effort, it was evidently not worth their while to challenge such formidable quarry. Every "kill" I saw was a kongoni or a zebra; probably I came across fifty of each. One zebra kill, which was not more than eighteen hours old (after the lapse of that time vultures and marabous, not to speak of the hye-nas and jackals, leave only the bare bones), showed just what had occurred. The bones were all in place, and the skin still on the lower legs and head. The animal was lying on its belly, the legs spread out, the neck vertebrae crushed; evidently the lion had sprung clean on it, bearing it down by his weight while he bit through the back of the neck, and the zebra's legs had spread out as the body yielded under the lion. One fresh kongoni kill showed no marks on the haunches, but a broken neck and claw marks on the face and withers; in this case the lion's hind legs had remained on the ground, while with his fore paws he grasped the kongoni's head and shoul-ders, holding it until the teeth splintered the neck-bone.

One day we started from the ranch-house in good season for an all-day lion-hunt. Besides Kermit and myself, there was a fellow guest, Medlicott, and not only our host [Sir Alfred Pease], but our hostess and her daughter; and we were joined by Percival at lunch, which we took under a great fig-tree, at the foot of a high, rocky hill. Percival had with him a little mongrel bulldog, and a Masai "boy," a fine, bold-looking savage, with a handsome head-dress and the usual formidable spear; master, man, and dog evidently all looked upon any form of encounter with lions simply in the light of a spree.

After lunch we began to beat down a long donga, or dry watercourse—a creek, as we should call it in the Western plains country. The watercourse with low, steep banks wound in curves, and here and there were patches of brush, which might contain anything in the shape of lion, cheetah, hyena, or wild dog. Soon we came upon lion spoor in the sandy bed; first the foot-prints of a big male, then those of a lioness. We walked cautiously along each side of the donga, the horses following close behind so that if the lion were missed we could gallop after him and round him up on the plain. The dogs—for besides the little bull, we had a large brindled mongrel named Ben, whose courage belied his looks—began to show signs of scenting the lion; and we beat out each patch of brush, the natives shouting and throwing in stones, while we stood with the rifles where we could best command any probable exit. After a couple of false alarms the dogs drew toward one patch, their hair bristling, and showing such eager excitement that it was evident something big was inside; and in a moment one of the boys called, "simba" (lion), and pointed with his finger. It was just across the little ravine, there about four yards wide and as many feet deep; and I shifted my position, peering eagerly into the bushes for some moments before I caught a glimpse of tawny hide; as it moved, there was a call to me to "shoot," for at that distance, if the lion charged, there would be scant time to stop it; and I fired into what I saw. There was a commotion in the bushes, and Kermit fired; and immediately afterward there broke out on the other side, not the hoped-for big lion, but two cubs the size of mastiffs. Each was badly wounded and we finished them off; even if unwounded they were too big to take alive.

This was a great disappointment, and as it was well on in the afternoon, and we had beaten the country most apt to harbor our game, it seemed unlikely that we would have another chance. Percival was on foot and a long way from his house, so he started for it; and the rest of us also began to jog homeward. But Sir Alfred, although he said nothing, intended to have another try. After going a mile or two he started off to the left at a brisk canter; and we, the other riders, followed, leaving behind our gun-bearers, saises, and porters. A couple of miles away was another donga, another shal-low watercourse with occasional big brush patches along the winding bed;

and toward this we cantered. Almost as soon as we reached it our leader found the spoor of two big lions; and with every sense acock, we dismounted and approached the first patch of tall bushes. We shouted and threw in stones, but nothing came out; and another small patch showed the same result. Then we mounted our horses again, and rode toward another patch a quarter of a mile off. I was mounted on Tranquility, the stout and quiet sorrel.

This patch of tall, thick brush stood on the hither bank—that is, on our side of the watercourse. We rode up to it and shouted loudly. The response was immediate, in the shape of loud gruntings, and crashings through the thick brush. We were off our horses in an instant, I throwing the reins over the head of mine; and without delay the good old fellow began placidly grazing, quite unmoved by the ominous sounds immediately in front.

I sprang to one side; and for a second or two we waited, uncertain whether we should see the lions charging out ten yards distant or running away. Fortunately, they adopted the latter course. Right in front of me, thirty yards off, there appeared, from behind the bushes which had first screened him from my eyes, the tawny, galloping form of a big maneless lion. Crack! the Winchester spoke; and as the soft-nosed bullet ploughed forward through his flank the lion swerved so that I missed him with the second shot; but my third bullet went through the spine and forward into his chest. Down he came, sixty yards off, his hind quarters dragging, his head up, his ears back, his jaws open and lips drawn up in a prodigious snarl, as he endeavored to turn to face us. His back was broken; but of this we could not at the moment be sure, and if it had merely been grazed, he might have recovered, and then, even though dying, his charge might have done mischief. So Kermit, Sir Alfred and I fired, almost together, into his chest. His head sank, and he died.

This lion had come out on the left of the bushes; the other, to the right of them, had not been hit, and we saw him galloping off across the plain, six or eight hundred yards away. A couple more shots missed, and we mounted our horses to try to ride him down. The plain sloped gently upward for three-quarters of a mile to a low crest or divide, and long before we got near him he disappeared over this. Sir Alfred and Kermit were tearing along in front and to the right, with Miss Pease close behind; while Tranquility carried me, as fast as he could, on the left, with Medlicott near me. On topping the divide Sir Alfred and Kermit missed the lion, which had swung to the left, and they raced ahead too far to the right. Medlicott and I, however, saw the lion, loping along close behind some kongoni; and this enabled me to get up to him as quickly as the lighter men on the faster horses. The going was now slightly downhill, and the sorrel took me along very well, while Medlicott, whose horse was slow, bore to the right and joined the other two men. We gained rapidly, and, finding out this, the lion suddenly halted and came to bay in a slight hollow, where the grass was rather long. The plain seemed flat, and we could see the lion well from horseback; but, especially when he lay down, it was most difficult to make him out on foot, and impossible to do so when kneeling.

We were about a hundred and fifty yards from the lion, Sir Alfred, Kermit, Medlicott, and Miss Pease off to one side, and slightly above him on the slope, while I was on the level, about equidistant from him and them. Kermit and I tried shooting from the horses; but at such a distance this was not effective. Then Kermit got off, but his horse would not let him shoot; and when I got off I could not make out the animal through the grass with sufficient distinctness to enable me to take aim. Old Ben the dog had arrived, and barking loudly, was strolling about near the lion, which paid him not the slightest attention. At this moment my black sais, Simba, came running up to me and took hold of the bridle; he had seen the chase from the line of march and had cut across to join me. There was no other sais or gun-bearer anywhere near, and his action was plucky, for he was the only man afoot, with the lion at bay. Lady Pease had also ridden up and was an interested spectator only some fifty yards behind me.

Now, an elderly man with a varied past which includes rheumatism does not vault lightly into the saddle; as his sons, for instance, can; and I had already made up my mind that in the event of the lion's charging it would be wise for me to trust to straight powder rather than to try to scramble into the saddle and get under way in time. The arrival of my two companions settled matters. I was not sure of the speed of Lady Pease's horse; and Simba was on foot and it was of course out of the question for me to leave him. So I said, "Good, Simba, now we'll see this thing through," and gentle-mannered Simba smiled a shy appreciation of my tone, though he could not understand the words. I was still unable to see the lion when I knelt, but he was now standing up, looking first at one group of horses and then at the other, his tail lashing to and fro, his head held low, and his lips dropped over his mouth in peculiar fashion, while his harsh and savage growling rolled thunderously over the plain. Seeing Simba and me on foot, he turned toward us, his tail lashing quicker and quicker. Resting my elbow on Simba's bent shoulder, I took steady aim and pressed the trigger; the bullet went in between the neck and shoulder, and the lion fell over on is side, one fore leg in the air. He recovered in a moment and stood up, evidently very sick, and once more faced me, growling hoarsely. I think he was on the eve of charging. I fired again at once, and this bullet broke his back just behind the shoulders; and with the next I killed him outright, after we had gathered round him.

These were two good-sized maneless lions, and very proud of them I was. I think Sir Alfred was at least as proud, especially because we had performed the feat alone, without any professional hunters being present. "We were all amateurs, only gentlemen riders up," said Sir Alfred. It was late before we got the lions skinned. Then we set off toward the ranch, two porters carrying each lion-skin, strapped to a pole; and two others carrying the cub-skins. Night fell long before we were near the ranch; but the brilliant tropic moon lighted the trail. The stalwart savages who carried the bloody lion-skins swung along at a faster walk as the sun went down and the moon rose higher; and they began to chant in unison, one uttering a single word or sentence, and the others joining in a deep-toned, musical chorus. The men on a safari, and indeed African natives generally, are always excited over the death of a lion, and the hunting tribes then chant their rough hunting-songs, or victory songs, until the monotonous, rhythmical repetitions make them grow almost frenzied. The ride home through the moonlight, the vast barren landscape shine like silver on either hand, was one to be remembered; and above all, the sight of our trophies and of their wild bearers.

ELEPHANT-HUNTING ON MOUNT KENIA

On July 24 [1909], in order to ship our fresh accumulations of specimens and trophies, we once more went into Nairobi. It was a pleasure
again to see its tree-bordered streets and charming houses bowered in
vines and bushes, and to meet once more the men and women who dwelt
in the houses. I wish it were in my power to thank individually the members of the many East African households of which I shall always cherish
warm memories of friendship and regard.

❧ ❧ ❧

Most of the time in Nairobi we were the guests of ever-hospitable
[W. N.] McMillan, in his low, cool house, with its broad, vine-shaded
veranda, running around all four sides, and its garden fragrant and brilliant with innumerable flowers. Birds abounded, singing beautifully; the
bulbuls were the most noticeable singers, but there were many others.
The dark ant-eating chats haunted the dusky roads on the outskirts of the
town, and were interesting birds; they were usually found in parties,
flirted their tails up and down as they sat on bushes or roofs or wires,
sang freely in chorus until after dusk, and then retired to holes in the
ground for the night. A tiny owl with a queer little voice called continually not only after nightfall, but in the bright afternoons. Shrikes spitted
insects on the spines of the imported cactus in the gardens.

It was race week, and the races, in some of which Kermit rode, were
capital fun. The white people—army officers, government officials, farmers
from the country round about, and their wives—rode to the races on
ponies or even on camels, or drove up in rickshaws, in gharries, in bullock tongas, occasionally in automobiles, most often in two-wheel carts or
rickety hacks drawn by mules and driven by a turbaned Indian or a
native in a cotton shirt. There were Parsees, and Goanese dressed just like
the Europeans. There were many other Indians, their picturesque women-
kind gaudy in crimson, blue, and saffron. The constabulary, Indian and
native, were in neat uniforms and well set up, though often barefooted.
Straight, slender Somalis with clear-cut features were in attendance on
the horses. Native negroes, of many different tribes, flocked to the race-
course and its neighborhood. The Swahilis, and those among the others
who aspired toward civilization, were well clad, the men in half-
European costume, the women in flowing, parti-colored robes. But most
of them were clad, or unclad, just as they always had been. Wakamba, with

filed teeth, crouched in circles on the ground. Kikuyu passed, the men each with a blanket hung round the shoulders, and girdles of chains, and armlets and anklets of solid metal; the older women bent under burdens they carried on the back, half of them in addition with babies slung somewhere round them, while now and then an unmarried girl would have her face painted with ochre and vermilion. A small party of Masai warriors kept close together, each clutching his shining, long-bladed war spear, their hair daubed red and twisted into strings. A large band of Kavirondo, stark naked, with a shield and spear and head-dress of nodding plumes, held a dance near the race-track. As for the races themselves, they were carried on in the most sporting spirit, and only the Australian poet Patterson could adequately write of them.

❧ ❧ ❧

We were in the Kikuyu country. On our march we met several parties of natives. I had been much inclined to pity the porters, who had but one blanket apiece; but when I saw the Kikuyus, each with nothing but a smaller blanket, and without the other clothing and the tents of the porters, I realized how much better off the latter were simply because they were on a white man's safari. At Neri boma we were greeted with the warmest hospitality by the district commissioner, Mr. Browne. Among other things, he arranged a great Kikuyu dance in our honor. Two thousand warriors, and many women, came in; as well as a small party of Masai moran. The warriors were naked, or half-naked; some carried gaudy blankets, others girdles of leopard-skin; their ox-hide shields were colored in bold patterns, their long-bladed spears quivered and gleamed. Their faces and legs were painted red and yellow; the faces of the young men who were about to undergo the rite of circumcision were stained a ghastly white, and their bodies fantastically painted. The warriors wore bead neck-laces and waist-belts and armlets of brass and steel, and spurred anklets of monkey-skin. Some wore head-dresses made out of a lion's mane or from the long black-and-white fur of the Colobus monkey; others had plumes stuck in their red-daubed hair. They chanted in unison a deep-toned chorus, and danced rhythmically in rings, while the drums throbbed and the horns blared; and they danced by us in column, springing and chanting. The women shrilled applause, and danced in groups by themselves. The Masai circled and swung in a panther-like dance of their own, and the measure, and their own fierce singing and calling, maddened them until two of their number, their eyes staring, their faces working, went into fits of berserker frenzy, and were disarmed at once to prevent mischief. Some of the tribesmen held wilder dances still in the evening, by the light of fires that blazed in a grove where their thatched huts stood.

The second day after reaching Neri the clouds lifted and we dried our damp clothes and blankets. Through the bright sunlight we saw in front of us the high rock peaks of Kenia, and shining among them the fields of everlasting snow which feed her glaciers; for beautiful, lofty Kenia is one of the glacier-bearing mountains of the equator. Here Kermit and Tarlton went northward on a safari of their own, while . . . I headed for Kenia itself. For two days we travelled through a well-peopled country. The fields of corn—always called mealies in Africa—of beans, and sweet potatoes, with occasional plantations of bananas, touched one another in almost uninterrupted succession. In most of them we saw the Kikuyu women at work with their native hoes; for among the Kikuyus, as among other savages, the woman is the drudge and beast of burden. Our trail led by clear, rushing streams, which formed the headwaters of the Tana; among the trees fringing their banks were graceful palms, and there were groves of tree—ferns here and there on the sides of the gorges.

On the afternoon of the second day we struck upward among the steep foot-hills of the mountain, riven by deep ravines. We pitched camp in an open glade, surrounded by the green wall of tangled forest, the forest of the tropical mountainsides.

The trees, strange of kind and endless in variety, grew tall and close, laced together by vine and creeper, while underbrush crowded the space between their mossy trunks, and covered the leafy mould beneath. Toward dusk crested ibis flew overhead with harsh clamor, to seek their night roosts; parrots chattered, and a curiously homelike touch was given by the presence of a thrush in color and shape almost exactly like our robin. Monkeys called in the depths of the forest, and after dark tree-frogs piped and croaked, and the tree-hyraxes uttered their wailing cries.

Elephants dwelt permanently in this mountainous region of heavy woodland. On our march thither we had already seen their traces in the "shambas," as the cultivated fields of the natives are termed; for the great beasts are fond of raiding the crops at night, and their inroads often do serious damage. In this neighborhood their habit is to live high up in the mountains, in the bamboos, while the weather is dry; the cows and calves keeping closer to the bamboos than the bulls. A spell of wet weather, such as we had fortunately been having, drives them down in the dense forest which covers the lower slopes. Here they may either pass all their time, or at night they may go still father down, into the open valley where the shambas lie; or they may occasionally still do what they habitually did in the days before the white hunters came, and wander far away, making migrations that are sometimes seasonal, and sometimes irregular and unaccountable.

No other animal, not the lion himself, is so constant a theme of talk, and a subject of such unflagging interest round the camp-fires of African hunters and in the native villages of the African wilderness, as the elephant. Indeed the elephant has always profoundly impressed the imagination of mankind. It is, not only to hunters, but to naturalists, and to all people who possess any curiosity about wild creatures and the wild life of nature, the most interesting of all animals. Its huge bulk, its singular form, the value of its ivory, its great intelligence—in which it is only matched, if at all, by the highest apes, and possibly by one or two of the highest carnivora—and its varied habits, all combine to give it an interest such as attaches to no other living creature below the rank of man.

🌿 🌿 🌿

For two days after reaching our camp in the open glade on the mountainside it rained. We were glad of this, because it meant that the elephants would not be in the bamboos, and Cuninghame and the 'Ndorobo went off to hunt for fresh signs. Cuninghame is as skillful an elephant-hunter as can be found in Africa, and is one of the very few white men able to help even the wild bushmen at their work. By the afternoon of the second day they were fairly well satisfied as to the whereabouts of the quarry.

The following morning a fine rain was till falling when Cuninghame, Heller, and I started on our hunt; but by noon it had stopped. Of course we went in single file and on foot; not even a bear-hunter from the cane-brakes of the lower Mississippi could ride through that forest. We left our home camp standing, taking blankets and a coat and change of underclothing for each of us, and two small Whymper tents, with enough food for three days; I also took my wash kit and a book from the Pigskin Library. First marched the 'Ndorobo guides, each with his spear, his blanket round his shoulders, and a little bundle of corn and sweet potato. Then came Cuninghame, followed by his gun-bearer. Then I came, clad in khaki-colored flannel shirt and khaki trousers buttoning down the legs, with hobnailed shoes and a thick slouch-hat; I had intended to wear rubber-soled shoes, but the soaked ground was too slippery. My two gun-bearers followed, carrying the Holland and the Springfield. Then came Heller, at the head of a dozen porters and skinners; he and they were to fall behind when we actually struck fresh elephant spoor, but to follow our trail by the help of a Dorobo who was left with them.

For three hours our route lay along the edge of the woods. We climbed into and out of deep ravines in which groves of tree-ferns clustered. We waded through streams of swift water, whose course was broken by cataract and rapid. We passed through shambas, and by the doors of little hamlets of thatched beehive huts. We met flocks of goats and hairy, fat-tailed sheep guarded by boys; strings of burden-bearing women stood meekly to one side to let us pass; parties of young men sauntered by, spear in hand.

Then we struck into the great forest, and in an instant the sun was shut from sight by the thick screen of wet foliage. It was a riot of twisted vines, interlacing the trees and bushes. Only the elephant paths, which, of every age, crossed and recrossed it hither and thither, made it possible. One of the chief difficulties in hunting elephants in the forest is that it is impossible to travel, except very slowly and with much noise, off these trails, so that it is sometimes very difficult to take advantage of the wind; and although the sight of the elephant is dull, both its sense of hearing and its sense of smell are exceedingly acute.

Hour after hour we worked our way onward through tangled forest and matted jungle. There was little sign of bird or animal life. A troop of long-haired black-and-white monkeys bounded away among the tree-tops. Here and there brilliant flowers lightened the gloom. We ducked under vines and climbed over fallen timber. Poisonous nettles stung our hands. We were drenched by the wet boughs which we brushed aside. Mosses and ferns grew rank and close. The trees were of strange kinds. There were huge trees with little leaves, and small trees with big leaves. There were trees with bare, fleshy limbs, that writhed out through the neighboring branches, bearing sparse clusters of large frontage. In places the forest was low, the trees thirty or forty feet high, the bushes that chocked the ground between fifteen or twenty feet high. In other places mighty monarchs of the wood, straight and tall, towered aloft to an immense height; among them were trees whose smooth, round holes were spotted like sycamores, while far above our heads their gracefully spreading branches were hung with vines like mistletoe and draped with Spanish moss; trees whose surfaces were corrugated and knotted as if they were made of bundles of great creepers; and giants whose buttressed trunks were four times a man's length across. . . .

As evening fell we pitched camp by the side of a little brook at the bottom of a ravine, and dined ravenously on bread, mutton, and tea. The air was keen, and under our blankets we slept in comfort until dawn. Breakfast was soon over and camp struck; and once more we began our cautious progress through the dim, cool archways of the mountain forest.

Two hours after leaving camp we came across the fresh trail of a small herd of perhaps ten or fifteen elephant cows and calves, but including two big herd bulls. At once we took up the trail. Cuninghame and his bush people consulted again and again, scanning every track and mark with minute attention. The signs showed that the elephants had fed in the shambas early in the night, had then returned to the mountain, and stood in one place resting for several hours, and had left this sleeping-ground some time before we reached it. After we had followed the trail a short while we made the experiment of trying to force our own way through the jungle, so as to get the wind more favorable; but our progress was too slow and noisy, and we returned to the path the elephants had beaten. Then the 'Ndorobo went ahead, traveling noiselessly and at speed. One of them was clad in a white blanket, and another in a red one, which were conspicuous; but they were too silent and cautious to let the beasts see them, and could tell exactly where they were and what they were doing by the sounds. When these trackers waited for us they would appear before us like ghosts; once one of them dropped down from the branches above, having climbed a tree with monkey-like agility to get a glimpse of the great game.

At last we could hear the elephants, and under Cuninghame's lead we walked more cautiously than ever. The wind was right, and the trail of one elephant led close alongside that of the rest of the herd, and parallel thereto. It was about noon. The elephants moved slowly, and we listened to the boughs crack, and now and then to the curious internal rumblings of the great beasts. Carefully, every sense on the alert, we kept pace with them. My double-barrel was in my hands, and, whenever possible, as I followed the trail, I stepped in the huge footprints of the elephant, for where such a weight had pressed there were no sticks left to crack under my feet. It made our veins thrill thus for half an hour to creep stealthily along, but a few rods from the herd, never able to see it, because of the extreme denseness of the cover, but always hearing first one and then another of its members, and always trying to guess what each one might do, and keeping ceaselessly ready for whatever might befall. A flock of hornbills flew up with noisy clamor, but the elephants did not heed them.

At last we came in sight of the mighty game. The trail took a twist to one side, and there, thirty yards in front of us, we made out part of the gray and massive head of an elephant resting his tusks on the branches of a young tree. A couple of minutes passed before, by cautious scrutiny, we were able to tell whether the animal was a cow or a bull, and whether, if a bull, it carried heavy enough tusks. Then we saw that it was a big bull with good ivory. It turned its head in my direction and I saw its eye; and I fired a little to one side of the eye, at a spot which I thought would lead to the brain. I struck exactly where I aimed, but the head of an elephant is enormous and the brain small, and the bullet missed it. However, the shock momentarily stunned the beast. He stumbled forward, half falling, and as he recovered I fired with the second barrel, again aiming for the brain. This time the bullet sped true, and as I lowered the rifle from my shoulder, I saw the great lord of the forest come crashing to the ground.

But at that very instant, before there was a moment's time in which to reload, the thick bushes parted immediately on my left front, and through them surged the vast bulk of a charging bull elephant, the matted mass of tough creepers snapping like packthread before his rush. He was so close that he could have touched me with his trunk. I leaped to one side and dodged behind a tree trunk, opening the rifle, throwing out the empty shells, and slipping in two cartridges. Meanwhile Cuninghame fired right and left, at the same time throwing himself into the bushes on the other side. Both his bullets went home, and the bull stopped short in his charge, wheeled, and immediately disappeared in the thick cover. We ran forward, but the forest had closed over his wake. We heard him trumpet shrilly, and then all sounds ceased.

The 'Ndorobo, who had quite properly disappeared when this second bull charged, now went forward, and soon returned with the report that he had fled at speed, but was evidently hard hit, as there was much blood on the spoor. If we had been only after ivory we should have followed him at once; but there was no telling how long a chase he might lead us; and as we desired to save the skin of the dead elephant entire, there was no time whatever to spare. It is a formidable task, occupying many days, to preserve an elephant for mounting in a museum, and if the skin is to be properly saved, it must be taken off without an hour's unnecessary delay.

So back we turned to where the dead tusker lay, and I felt proud indeed as I stood by the immense bulk of the slain monster and put my hand on the ivory. The tusks weighed a hundred and thirty pounds the pair. There was the usual scene of joyful excitement among the gun-bearers — who had behaved excellently — and among the wild bush people who had done the tracking for us; and, as Cuninghame had predicted, the old Masai Dorobo, from pure delight, proceeded to have hysterics on the body of the dead elephant. The scene was repeated when Heller and the porters appeared half an hour later. Then, chattering like monkeys, and as happy as possible, all porters, gun-bearers, and 'Ndorobo alike, began the work of skinning and cutting up the quarry, under the leadership and supervision of Heller and Cuninghame, and soon they were all splashed with blood from head to foot. One of the trackers took off his blanket and squatted stark naked inside the carcass the better to use his knife. Each laborer rewarded himself by cutting off strips of meat for his private store, and hung them in red festoons from the branches round about. There was no let-up in the work until it was stopped by darkness.

Our tents were pitched in a small open glade a hundred yards from the dead elephant. The night was clear, the stars shone brightly, and in the west the young moon hung just above the line of tall tree-tops. Fires were speedily kindled and the men sat around them, feasting and singing in a strange minor tone until late in the night. The flickering light left them at one moment in black obscurity, and the next brought into bold relief their sinewy crouching figures, their dark faces, gleaming eyes and flashing teeth. When they did sleep, two of the 'Ndorobo slept so close to the fire as to burn themselves; an accident to which they are prone, judging from the many scars of old burns on their legs. I toasted slices of elephant's heart on a pronged stick before the fire, and found it delicious; for I was hungry, and the night was cold. We talked of our success and exulted over it, and made our plans for the morrow; and then we turned in under our blankets for another night's sleep.

Next morning some of the 'Ndorobo went off on the trail of Cuninghame's elephant to see if it had fallen, but found that it had travelled steadily, though its wounds were probably mortal. There was no object in my staying, for Heller and Cuninghame would be busy for the next ten days, and would ultimately have to use all the porters in taking off and curing the skin, and transporting it to Neri; so I made up my mind to go down to the plains for a hunt by myself. Taking one porter to carry my bedding, and with my gun-bearers and a Dorobo as guide, I struck off through the forest for the main camp, reaching it early in the afternoon. Thence I bundled off a safari to Cuninghame and Heller, with food for a week, and tents and clothing; and then enjoyed the luxury of a shave and a warm bath. Next day was spent in writing and in making preparations for my own trip. A Kikuyu chief, clad in a cloak of hyrax-skins and carrying his war spear, came to congratulate me on killing the elephant and to present me with a sheep. Early the following morning everything was in readiness; the bull-necked porters lifted their loads, I stepped out in front, . . . and in ten hours' march we reached Neri boma with its neat buildings, its trees, and its well-kept flower-beds.

On the evening of September 6 we were all together again at Meru boma, on the northeastern slopes of Kenia. . . . Thanks to the unfailing kindness of the commissioner, Mr. Horne, we were given full information of the elephant in the neighborhood. He had no 'Ndorobo, but among the Wa-Meru, a wild martial tribe, who lived close around him, there were a number of hunters, or at least of men who knew the forest and the game, and these had been instructed to bring in any news.

We had, of course, no idea that elephant would be found close at hand. But next morning, about eleven, Horne came to our camp with four of his black scouts, who reported that three elephants were in a patch of thick jungle beside the shambas, not three miles away. Horne said that the elephants were cows, that they had been in the neighborhood some days, devastating the shambas, and were bold and fierce, having charged some men who sought to drive them away from the cultivated fields; its curious to see how little heed these elephants pay to the natives. I wished a cow for the museum, and also another bull. So off we started at once, Kermit carrying his camera. I slipped on my rubber-soled shoes, and had my gun-bearers accompany me bare-footed, with the Holland and Springfield rifles. We followed footpaths among the fields until we reached the edge of the jungle in which the elephants stood. . . .

On account of the wind we had to go well to one side before entering the jungle. Then in we went in a single file, Cuninghame and Tarlton leading, with a couple of our naked guides. The latter showed no great desire to get too close, explaining that the elephants were "very fierce." Once in the jungle, we trod as quietly as possible, threading our way along the elephant trails, which crossed and recrossed one another. Evidently it was a favorite haunt, for the sign was abundant, both old and new. In the impenetrable cover it was quite impossible to tell just where the elephants were, and twice we sent one of the savages up a tree to locate the game. The last time the watcher, who stayed in the tree, indicated by signs that the elephant were not far off; and his companions wished to lead us round to where the cover was a little lower and thinner. But to do so would have given them our wind, and Cuninghame refused, taking into his own hands the management of the stalk. I kept my heavy rifle at the ready, and on we went, in watchful silence, prepared at any moment for a charge. We could not tell at what second we might catch our first glimpse at very close quarters of "the beast that hath between his eyes the serpent for a hand," and, when thus surprised, the temper of "the huge earth-shaking beast" is sometimes of the shortest.

Cuninghame and Tarlton stopped for a moment to consult; Cuninghame stooped, and Tarlton mounted his shoulders and stood upright, steadying himself by my hand. Down he came and told us that he had seen a small tree shake seventy yards distant; although upright on Cuninghame's shoulders he could not see the elephant itself. Forward we stole for a few yards, and then a piece of good luck befell us, for we came on the trunk of a great fallen tree, and scrambling up, we found ourselves perched in a row six feet above the ground. The highest part of the trunk was near the root, farthest from where the elephants were; and though it offered precarious footing, it also offered the best lookout. Thither I balanced, and looking over the heads of my companions I at once made out the elephant. At first I could see nothing but the shaking branches, and one huge ear occasionally flapping. Then I made out the ear of another beast, and then the trunk of a third was uncurled, lifted, and curled again; it showered its back with earth. The watcher we had left behind in the tree-top coughed; the elephants stood motionless, and up went the biggest elephant's trunk, feeling for the wind; the watcher coughed again, and then the bushes and saplings swayed and parted as three black bulks came toward us. The cover was so high that we could not see their tusks, only the tops of their heads and their backs being visible. The leader was the biggest, and at it I fired when it was sixty yards away, and nearly broadside on, but heading slightly toward me. I had previously warned every one to kneel. The recoil of the heavy rifle made me rock, as I stood unsteadily on my perch, and I failed to hit the brain. But the bullet, only missing the brain by an inch or two, brought the elephant to its knees; as it rose I floored it with the second barrel. The blast of the big rifle, by the way, was none too pleasant for the other men on the log and made Cuninghame's nose bleed. Reloading, I fired twice at the next animal, which was now turning. It stumbled and nearly fell, but at the same moment the first one rose again, and I fired both barrels into its head, bringing it once more to the ground. Once again it rose—an elephant's brain is not an easy mark to hit under such conditions—but as it moved slowly off, half stunned, I snatched the little Springfield rifle, and this time shot true, sending the bullet into its brain. As it fell I took another shot at the wounded elephant, now disappearing in the forest, but without effect.

On walking up to our prize it proved to be not a cow, but a good-sized adult (but not old) herd bull, with thick, short tusks weighing about forty pounds apiece. Ordinarily, of course, a bull, not a cow, is what one desires, although on this occasion I needed a cow to complete the group for the National Museum. However, Heller and Cuninghame spent the next few days in preserving the skin, which I afterward gave to the University of California; and I was too much pleased with our luck to feel inclined to grumble. We were back in camp five hours after leaving it. Our gun-bearers usually felt it incumbent on them to keep a dignified bearing while in our company. But the death of an elephant is always a great event; and one of the gun-bearers, as they walked ahead of us campward, soon began to improvise a song, reciting the success of the hunt, the death of the elephant, and the power of the rifles; and gradually, as they got farther ahead, the more light-hearted among them began to give way to their spirits and they came into camp frolicking, gambolling, and dancing as if they were still the naked savages that they had been before they became the white man's followers.

Two days later Kermit got his bull. He and Tarlton had camped about ten miles off in a magnificent forest, and late the first afternoon received news that a herd of elephants was in the neighborhood. They were off by dawn, and in a few hours came on the herd. It consisted chiefly of cows and calves, but there was one big master-bull, with fair tusks. It was open forest with long grass. By careful stalking they got within thirty yards of the bull, behind whom was a line of cows. Kermit put both barrels of his heavy double 450 into the tusker's head, but without even staggering him; and as he walked off Tarlton also fired both barrels into him, with no more effect; then, as he slowly turned, Kermit killed him with a shot in the brain from the 405 Winchester. Immediately the cows lifted their ears, and began trumpeting and threatening; if they had come on in a body at that distance, there was not much chance of turning them or of escaping from them; and after standing stock-still for a minute or two, Kermit and Tarlton stole quietly off for a hundred yards, and waited until the anger of the cows cooled and they had moved away, before going up to the dead bull. Then they followed the herd again, and Kermit got some photos which, as far as I know, are better than any that have ever before been taken of wild elephant. He took them close up, at imminent risk of a charge.

The following day the two hunters rode back to Meru, making a long circle. The elephants they saw were not worth shooting, but they killed the finest rhinoceros we had yet seen. . . . He was a bull, with a thirty-inch horn.

By this time Cuninghame and Heller had finished the skin and skeleton of the bull they were preserving. Near the carcass Heller trapped an old male leopard, a savage beast; its skin was in fine shape, but it was not fat, and weighed just one hundred pounds. Now we all joined, and shifted camp to a point eight or nine miles distant from Meru boma, and fifteen hundred feet lower among the foot-hills. It was much hotter at this lower level; palms were among the trees that bordered the streams. On the day we shifted camp Tarlton and I rode in advance to look for elephants, followed by our gun-bearers and half a dozen wild Meru hunters, each carrying a spear or a bow and arrows. When we reached the hunting-grounds, open country with groves of trees and patches of jungle, the Meru went off in every direction to find elephant. We waited their return under a tree by a big stretch of cultivated ground. The region was well peopled, and all the way down the path had led between fields which the Meru women were tilling with their adze-like hoes, and banana-plantations where among the bananas other trees had been planted and the yam-vines trained up their trunks. These cool, shady banana-plantations, fenced in with tall hedges and bordered by rapid brooks, were really very attractive. Among them were scattered villages of conical thatched huts, and level places plastered with cow dung on which the grain was threshed; it was then stored in huts raised on posts. There were herds of cattle and flocks of sheep and goats, and among the burdens the women bore we often saw huge bottles of milk. In the shambas there were platforms and sometimes regular thatched huts placed in the trees; these were for the watchers who were to keep the elephants out of the shambas at night. Some of the natives wore girdles of banana-leaves, looking, as Kermit said, much like the pictures of savages in Sunday-school books.

In addition we killed, with the Fox shotgun, Egyptian geese, yellow-billed mallards, francolins, spur-fowl, and sand-grouse for the pot, and certain other birds for specimens.

Kermit and I kept about a dozen trophies for ourselves; otherwise we shot nothing that was not used either as a museum specimen or for meat—usually for both purposes. We were in hunting-grounds practically as good as any that have ever existed; but we did not kill a tenth, nor a hundredth, part of what we might have killed had we been willing. The mere size of the bag indicates little as to a man's prowess as a hunter, and almost nothing as to the interest or value of his achievement.

LIST OF GAME SHOT WITH THE RIFLE DURING THE TRIP

	By T. R.	By K. R.		By T. R.	By K. R.
Lion	9	8	Big gazelle		
Leopard	—	3	Grant's	5	3
Cheetah	—	7	Roberts's	4	6
Hyena	5	4	Notata	8	1
Elephant	8	3	Thomson's gazelle	11	9
Square-mouthed rhino	5	4	Gerenuk	3	2
Hook-lipped Rhino	8	3	Klipspringer	1	3
Hippopotamus	7	1	Oribi	18	8
Wart-hog	8	4	Duiker	3	2
Common zebra	15	4	Steinbuck	4	2
Big or Grevy's zebra	5	5	Dikdik	1	1
Giraffe	7	2	Baboon	—	3
Buffalo	6	4	Red ground-monkey	1	—
Giant eland	1	2	Green monkey	—	1
Common eland	5	2	Black-and-white		
Bongo	—	2	monkey	5	4
Kudu	—	2	Serval	—	1
Situtunga	—	1	Jackal	—	1
Bushbuck			Aardwolf	—	1
East African	2	4	Ratel	—	1
Uganda harnessed	1	2	Porcupine	—	2
Nile harnessed	3	3	Ostrich	2	—
Sable	—	3	Great bustard	4 (1 on wing)	3
Roan	4	5			(1 on wing)
Oryx	10	3	Lesser bustard	1	1
Wildebeest	5	2	Kavirondo crane	2 (on wing)	—
Neumann's hartbeest	—	3	Flamingo	—	4
Coke's hartbeest	10	3	Whale-headed stork	1	1
Big hartbeest			Marabou	1	1
Jackson's	14	7	Saddle-billed stork	1 (on wing)	—
Uganda	1	3	Ibis stork	2 (on wing)	—
Nilotic	8	4	Pelican	1	—
Topi	12	3	Guinea-fowl	5	5
Common water-buck	5	3	Francolin	1	2
Singsing water-buck	6	6	Fish-eagle	—	1
Common kob	10	6	Vulture	—	2
Vaughn's kob	1	2	Crocodile	1	3
White-eared kob	3	2	Monitor	—	1
Saddle-backed lechwi			Python	3	—
(Mrs. Gray's)	3	1			
Bohor reedbuck	10	4	**TOTAL**	**296**	**216**
Chanler's buck	3	4			
Impala	7	5	**GRAND TOTAL**		**512**

TR with Colonel Rondon, co-leader of the Brazilian expedition, 1913.

6

AMAZON EXPLORER

DOWN AN UNKNOWN RIVER

*A*fter his unsuccessful presidential campaign in 1912, TR undertook an expedition of exploration in the interior of Brazil from late fall 1913 to the spring of 1914. The expedition included his son Kermit and two army officers, Colonel Candido Mariano da Silva Rondon and Lieutenant João Lyra, sent by the Brazilian government. The adventure was difficult and dangerous—not only because of the journey itself, but because one member of the exploring party was murdered by another. The effort, to TR's great satisfaction, did produce significant new geographical data, and a grateful Brazilian government named the newly explored tributary of the Amazon "Rio Roosevelt." This account of the trek down the unknown river was first published by Scribner's in 1914.

◆◇◆

The mightiest river in the world is the Amazon. It runs from west to east, from the sunset to the sunrise, from the Andes to the Atlantic. The main stream flows almost along the equator, while the basin which contains its affluents extends many degrees north and south of the equator. The gigantic equatorial river-basin is filled with an immense forest, the largest in the world, with which no other forest can be compared save those of western Africa and Malaysia. We were within the southern boundary of this great equatorial forest, on a river which was not merely unknown but unguessed at, no geographer having ever suspected its existence. This river flowed northward toward the equator, but whither it would go, whether it would turn one way or another, the length of its course, where it would come out, the character of the stream itself, and the character of the dwellers along its banks—all these things were yet to be discovered.

ꕤ ꕤ ꕤ

On the morning of March 22 we started in our six canoes. We made ten kilometres. Twenty minutes after starting we came to the first rapids. Here every one walked except the three best paddlers, who took the canoes down in succession—an hour's job. Soon after this we struck a bees' nest in the top of a tree overhanging the river; our steersman climbed out and robbed it, but, alas! lost the honey on the way back. We came to a small steep fall which we did not dare run in our overladen clumsy and cranky dugouts. Fortunately, we were able to follow a deep canal which led off for a kilometre, returning just below the falls, fifty yards from where it had started. Then, having been in the boats and in motion only one hour and a half, we came to a long stretch of rapids which it took us six hours to descend, and we camped at the foot. Everything was taken out of the canoes, and they were run down in succession. At one difficult and perilous place they were let down by ropes; and even thus we almost lost one.

We went down the right bank. On the opposite bank was an Indian village, evidently inhabited only during the dry season. The marks on the stumps of trees showed that these Indians had axes and knives; and there were old fields in which maize, beans, and cotton had been grown. The forest dripped and steamed. Rubber-trees were plentiful. At one point the tops of a group of tall trees were covered with yellow-white blossoms. Others bore red blossoms. Many of the big trees, of different kinds, were buttressed at the base with great thin walls of wood. Others, including both palms and ordinary trees, showed an even stranger peculiarity. The trunk, near the base, but sometimes six or eight feet from the ground, was split into a dozen or twenty branches or small trunks which sloped outward in tent-like shape, each becoming a root. The larger trees of this type looked as if their trunks were seated on the tops of the pole frames of Indian tepees. At one point in the stream, to our great surprise, we saw a flying-fish. It skimmed the water like a swallow for over twenty yards.

Although we made only ten kilometres we worked hard all day. The last canoes were brought down and moored to the bank at nightfall. Our tents were pitched in the darkness.

Next day we made thirteen kilometres. We ran, all told, a little over an hour and three-quarters. Seven hours were spent in getting past a series of rapids at which the portage, over rocky and difficult ground, was a kilometre long. The canoes were run down empty—a hazardous run, in which one of them upset.

Yet while we were actually on the river, paddling and floating downstream along the reaches of swift, smooth water, it was very lovely. When we started in the morning the day was overcast and the air was heavy with vapor. Ahead of us the shrouded river stretched between dim walls of forest, half seen in the mist. Then the sun burned up the fog and loomed through it in a red splendor that changed first to gold and then to molten white. In the dazzling light, under the brilliant blue of the sky, every detail of the magnificent forest was vivid to the eye; the great trees, the network of bush-ropes, the caverns of greenery where thick-leaved vines covered all things else. Wherever there was a hidden boulder the surface of the current was broken by waves. In one place, in midstream, a pyramidal rock thrust itself six feet above the surface of the river.

A kilometre and a half after leaving this camp we came on a stretch of big rapids. The river here twists in loops, and we had heard the roaring of these rapids the previous afternoon. Then we passed out of earshot of them; but Antonio Correa, our best waterman, insisted all along that the roaring meant rapids worse than any we had encountered for some days. "I was brought up in the water, and I know it like a fish, and all its sounds," said he. He was right. We had to carry the loads nearly a kilometre that afternoon, and the canoes were pulled out on the bank so that they might be in readiness to be dragged overland next day. Rondon, Lyra, Kermit, and Antonio Correa explored both sides of the river. On the opposite or left bank they found the mouth of a considerable river, bigger than the Rio Kermit [named for TR's son], flowing in from the west and making its entrance in the middle of the rapids. This river we christened the Taunay, in honor of a distinguished Brazilian, an explorer, a soldier, a senator, who was also a writer of note. Kermit had with him two of his novels, and I had read one of his books dealing with a disastrous retreat during the Paraguayan war.

Next morning, the 25th, the canoes were brought down. A path was chopped for them and rollers laid; and half-way down the rapids Lyra and Kermit, who were overseeing the work as well as doing their share of the pushing and hauling, got them into a canal of smooth water, which saved much severe labor. As our food-supply lowered we were constantly more desirous of economizing the strength of the men. One day more would complete a month since we had embarked on the Duvida—as we had started in February, the lunar and calendar months coincided. We had used up over half our provisions. We had come only a trifle over one hundred and sixty kilometres, thanks to the character and number of the rapids. We believed we had three or four times the distance yet to go before coming to a part of the river where we might hope to meet assistance, either from rubber-gatherers or from Pyrineus [a Brazilian army lieutenant], if he were really coming up the river which we were going down. If the rapids continued to be as they had been it could not be much more than three weeks before we were in straits for food, aside from the ever-present danger of accident in the rapids; and if our progress were no faster than it had been—and we were straining to do our best—we would in such event still have several hundreds of kilometres of unknown river before us. We could not even hazard a guess at what was in front. The river was now a really big river, and it seemed impossible that it could flow either into the Gy-Parana or the Tapajos. It was more probable that it was the headwaters of the Aripuanan, a river which . . . was not even named on the excellent English map of Brazil I carried. Nothing but the mouth had been known to any geographer; but the lower course had long been known to rubber-gatherers, and recently a commission from the government of Amazonas had part way ascended one branch of it—not as far as the rubber-gatherers had gone, and, as it turned out, not the branch we came down.

Two of our men were down with fever. Another man, Julio, a fellow of powerful frame, was utterly worthless, being an inborn, lazy shirk with the heart of a ferocious cur in the body of a bullock. The others were good men, some of them very good indeed. They were under the immediate supervision of Pedrinho Craveiro, who was first-class in every way. . . .

In mid-afternoon we were once more in the canoes; but we had paddled with the current only a few minutes, we had gone only a kilometre, when the roar of rapids in front again forced us to haul up to the bank. As usual, Rondon, Lyra, and Kermit, with Antonio Correa, explored both sides while camp was being pitched. The rapids were longer and steeper descent than the last, but on the opposite or western side there was a passage down which we thought we could get the empty dugouts at the cost of dragging them only a few yards at one spot. The loads were to be carried down the hither bank, for a kilometre, to the smooth water. The river foamed between great rounded masses of rock, and at one point there was a sheer fall of six or eight feet. We found and ate wild pineapples. Wild beans were in flower. At dinner we had a toucan and a couple of parrots, which were very good.

All next day was spent by Lyra in superintending our three best watermen as they took the canoes down the west side of the rapids, to the foot, at the spot to which the camp had meantime been shifted. In the forest some of the huge sipas, or rope vines, which were as big as cables, bore clusters of fragrant flowers. The men found several honey-trees, and fruits of various kinds, and small coconuts; they chopped down an ample number of palms, for the palm-cabbage; and, most important of all, they gathered a quantity of big Brazil-nuts, which when roasted tasted like the best of chestnuts and are nutritious; and they caught a number of big piranhas, which were good eating. So we all had a feast, and everybody had enough to eat and was happy. . . .

Next morning we went about three kilometres before coming to some steep hills, beautiful to look upon, clad as they were in dense, tall, tropical forest, but ominous of new rapids. Sure enough, at their foot we had to haul up and prepare for a long portage. The canoes we ran down empty. Even so, we were within an ace of losing two, the lashed couple in which I ordinarily journeyed. In a sharp bend of the rapids, between two big curls, they were swept among the boulders and under the matted branches which stretched out from the bank. They filled, and the racing current pinned them where they were, one partly on the other. All of us had to help get them clear. Their fastenings were chopped asunder with axes. Kermit and half a dozen of the men, stripped to the skin, made their way to a small rock island in the little falls just above the canoes, and let down a rope which we tied to the outermost canoe. The rest of us, up to our armpits and barely able to keep our footing as we slipped and stumbled among the boulders in the swift current, lifted and shoved while Kermit and his men pulled the rope and fastened the slack to a half-submerged tree. Each canoe in succession was hauled up the little rock island, baled, and then taken down in safety by two paddlers. It was nearly four o'clock before we were again ready to start, having been delayed by a rain-storm so heavy that we could not see across the river. Ten minutes' run took us to the head of another series of rapids; the exploring party returned with the news that we had an all-day's job ahead of us; and we made camp in the rain, which did not matter much, as we were already drenched through. It was impossible, with the wet wood, to make a fire sufficiently hot to dry all our soggy things, for the rain was still falling. A tapir was seen from our boat, but, as at the moment we were being whisked round in a complete circle by a whirlpool, I did not myself see it in time to shoot.

Next morning we went down a kilometre, and then landed on the other side of the river. The canoes were run down, and the loads carried to the other side of a little river coming in from the west, which Colonel Rondon christened Cherrie River. Across this we went on a bridge consisting of a huge tree felled by Macairo, one of our best men. Here we camped, while Rondon, Lyra, Kermit, and Antonio Correa explored what was ahead. They were absent until mid-afternoon. Then they returned with the news that we were among ranges of low mountains, utterly different in formation from the high plateau region to which the first rapids, those we had come to on the 2d of March, belonged. Through the first range of these mountains the river ran in a gorge, some three kilometres long, immediately ahead of us. The ground was so rough and steep that it would be impossible to drag the canoes over it and difficult enough to carry the loads; and the rapids were so bad, containing several falls, one of at least ten metres in height, that it was doubtful how many of the canoes we could get down them. Kermit, who was the only man with much experience of rope work, was the only man who believed we could get the canoes down at all; and it was, of course, possible that we should have to build new ones at the foot to supply the place of any that were lost or left behind. In view of the length and character of the portage and of all the unpleasant possibilities that were ahead and of the need of keeping every pound of food, it was necessary to reduce weight in every possible way and to throw away everything except the barest necessities.

We thought we had reduced our baggage before; but now we cut to the bone. . . .

The last thee days of March we spent in getting to the foot of the rapids in the gorge. Lyra and Kermit, with four of the best watermen, handled the empty canoes. The work was not only difficult and laborious in the extreme, but hazardous; for the walls of the gorge were so sheer that at the worst places they had to cling to narrow shelves on the face of the rock, while letting the canoes down with ropes. Meanwhile Rondon surveyed and cut a trail for the burden-bearers, and superintended the portage of the loads.

🌿 🌿 🌿

On April 2 we once more started, wondering how soon we should strike other rapids in the mountains ahead, and whether in any reasonable time we should, as the aneroid [barometer] indicated, be so low down that we should necessarily be in a plain where we could make a journey of at least a few days without rapids. We had been exactly a month going through an uninterrupted succession of rapids. During that month we had come only about one hundred and ten kilometres, and had descended nearly one hundred and fifty metres—the figures are approximate but fairly accurate. We had lost four of the canoes with which we started, and one other, which we had built, and the life of one man; and the life of a dog which by its death had in all probability saved the life of Colonel Rondon. In a straight line northward toward our supposed destination, we had not made more than a mile and a quarter a day; at the cost of bitter toil for most of the party, of much risk for some of the party, and of some risk and some hardship for all the party. Most of the camaradas [companions] were downhearted, naturally enough, and occasionally asked one of us if we really believed that we should ever get out alive; and we had to cheer them up as best we could.

There was no change in our work for the time being. We made but three kilometres that day. Most of the party walked all the time; but the dugouts carried the luggage until we struck the head of the series of rapids which were to take up the next two or three days. The river rushed through a wild gorge, a chasm or canyon, between two mountains. Its sides were very steep, mere rock walls, although in most places so covered with the luxuriant growth of the trees and bushes that clung in the crevices and with green moss that the naked rock was hardly seen. Rondon, Lyra, and Kermit, who were in front, found a small level spot with a beach of sand, and sent back word to camp there while they spent several hours in exploring the country ahead. The canoes were run down empty, and the loads carried painfully along the face of the cliffs; so bad was the trail that I found it rather hard to follow, although carrying nothing but my rifle and cartridge bag. The explorers returned with the information that the mountains stretched ahead of us, and that there were rapids as far as they had gone. We could only hope that the aneroid was not hopelessly out of kilter, and that we should, therefore, fairly soon find ourselves in comparatively level country. The severe toil, on a rather limited food-supply, was telling on the strength as well as on the spirits of the men; Lyra and Kermit, in addition to their other work, performed as much actual physical labor as any of them.

Next day, the 3d of April, we began the descent of these sinister rapids of the chasm. Colonel Rondon had gone to the summit of the mountain in order to find a better trail for the burden-bearers, but it was hopeless, and they had to go along the face of the cliffs. Such an exploring expedition as that in which we were engaged of necessity involves hard and dangerous labor and perils of many kinds. To follow downstream an unknown river, broken by innumerable cataracts and rapids, rushing through mountains of which the existence has never even been guessed, bears no resemblance whatever to following even a fairly dangerous river which has been thoroughly explored and has become in some sort a highway, so that experienced pilots can be secured as guides, while the portages have been pioneered and trails chopped out, and every dangerous feature of the rapids is known before-hand. In this case no one could foretell that the river would cleave its way through steep mountain chains, cutting narrow clefts in which the cliff walls rose almost sheer on either hand. When a rushing river thus "canyons," as we used to say out West, and the mountains are very steep, it becomes almost impossible to bring the canoes down the river itself and utterly impossible to portage them along the cliff sides, while even to bring the loads over the mountain is a task of extraordinary labor and difficulty. Moreover, no one can tell how many times the task will have to be repeated or when it will end or whether the food will hold out; every hour of work in the rapids is fraught with the possibility of the gravest disaster, and yet it is imperatively necessary to attempt it; and all this is done in an uninhabited wilderness, or else a wilderness tenanted only by unfriendly savages, where failure to get through means death by disease and starvation. Wholesale disasters to South American exploring parties have been frequent.

❦ ❦ ❦

Under such conditions whatever is evil in men's natures comes to the front. On this day a strange and terrible tragedy occurred. One of the camaradas, a man of pure European blood, was the man named Julio, of whom I have already spoken. He was a very powerful fellow and had been importunately eager to come on the expedition; and he had the reputation of being a good worker. But, like so many men of high standing, he had had no idea of what such an expedition really meant, and under the strain of toil, hardship, and danger his nature showed its true depths of selfishness, cowardice, and ferocity. He shirked all work. He shammed sickness. Nothing could make him do his share; and yet unlike his self-respecting fellows he was always shamelessly begging for favors. Kermit was the only one of our party who smoked; and he was continually giving a little tobacco to some of the camaradas, who worked especially well under him. The good men did not ask for it; but Julio, who shirked every labor, was always, and always in vain, demanding it. Colonel Rondon, Lyra, and Kermit each tried to get work out of him, and in order to do anything with him had to threaten to leave him in the wilderness. He threw all his tasks on his comrades, and moreover, he stole their food as well as ours. On such an expedition the theft of food comes next to murder as a crime, and should by rights be punished as such. We could not trust him to cut down palms or gather nuts, because he would stay out and eat what ought to have gone into the common store. Finally, the men on several occasions themselves detected him stealing their food. Alone of the whole party, and thanks to the stolen food, he had kept in full flesh and bodily vigor.

One of our best men was a huge negro named . . . Paishon—a corporal and acting sergeant in the engineer corps. He had, by the way, literally torn his trousers to pieces, so that he wore only the tatters of a pair of old drawers until I gave him my spare trousers when we lightened loads. He was a stern disciplinarian. One evening he detected Julio stealing food and smashed him in the mouth. Julio came crying to us, his face working with fear and malignant hatred; but after investigation he was told that he had gotten off uncommonly light. The men had three or four carbines, which were sometimes carried by those who were not their owners.

On this morning, at the outset of the portage, Pedrinho discovered Julio stealing some of the men's dried meat. Shortly afterward Paishon rebuked him for, as usual, lagging behind. By this time we had reached the place where the canoes were tied to the bank and then taken down one at a time. We were sitting down, waiting for the last loads to be brought along the trail. Pedrinho was still in the camp we had left. Paishon had just brought in a load, left it on the ground with his carbine beside it, and returned on the trail for another load. Julio came in, put down his load, picked up the carbine, and walked back on the trail, muttering to himself but showing no excitement. We thought nothing of it, for he was always muttering; and occasionally one of the men saw a monkey or big bird and tried to shoot it, so it was never surprising to see a man with a carbine.

In a minute we heard a shot; and in a short time three or four of the men came up the trail to tell us that Paishon was dead, having been shot by Julio, who had fled into the woods. Colonel Rondon and Lyra were ahead; I sent a messenger for them, directed [George] Cherrie [an American member of the group] and Kermit to stay where they were and guard the canoes and provisions, and started down the trail with the doctor—an absolutely cool and plucky man, with a revolver but no rifle—and a couple of the camaradas. We soon passed the dead body of poor Paishon. He lay in a huddle, in a pool of his own blood, where he had fallen, shot through the heart. I feared that Julio had run amuck, and intended merely to take more lives before he died, and that he would begin with Pedrinho, who was alone and unarmed in the camp we had left. Accordingly I pushed on, followed by my companions, looking sharply right and left; but when we came to the camp the doctor quietly walked by me, remarking: "My eyes are better than yours, colonel; if he is in sight I'll point him out to you, as you have the rifle." However, he was not there, and the others soon joined us with the welcome news that they had found the carbine.

The murderer had stood to one side of the path and killed his victim, when a dozen paces off, with deliberate and malignant purpose. Then evidently his murderous hatred had at once given way to his innate cowardice, and perhaps hearing some one coming along the path, he fled in panic terror into the wilderness. A tree had knocked the carbine from his hand. His footsteps showed that after going some rods he had started to return, doubtless for the carbine, but had fled again, probably because the body had then been discovered. It was questionable whether or not he would live to reach the Indian villages, which were probably his goal. He was not a man to feel remorse—never a common feeling; but surely that murderer was in a living hell, as, with fever and famine leering at him from the shadows, he made his way through the empty desolation of the wilderness. Franca, the cook, quoted out of the melancholy proverbial philosophy of the people the proverb, "No man knows the heart of anyone"; and then expressed with deep conviction a weird ghostly belief I had never encountered before: "Paishon is following Julio now, and will follow him until he dies; Paishon fell forward on his hands and knees, and when a murdered man falls like that his ghost will follow the slayer as long as the slayer lives."

We did not attempt to pursue the murderer. We could not legally put him to death, although he was a soldier who in cold blood had just deliberately killed a fellow soldier. If we had been near civilization we would have done our best to bring him in and turn him over to justice. But we were in the wilderness, and how many weeks' journey was ahead of us we could not tell. Our food was running low, sickness was beginning to appear among the men, and both their courage and their strength were gradually ebbing. Our first duty was to save the lives and the health of the men of the expedition who had honestly been performing, and had still to perform, so much perilous labor. If we brought the murderer in he would have to be guarded night and day on an expedition where there were always loaded firearms about, and where there would continually be opportunity and temptation for him to make an effort to seize food and a weapon and escape, perhaps murdering some other good man. He could not be shackled while climbing along the cliff slopes; he could not be shackled in the canoes, where there was always chance of upset and drowning; and standing guard would be an additional and severe penalty on the weary, honest men already exhausted by overwork. The expedition was in peril, and it was wise to take every chance possible that would help secure success. Whether the murderer lived or died in the wilderness was of no moment compared with the duty of doing everything to secure the safety of the rest of the party. For the two days following we were always on the watch against his return, for he could have readily killed some one else by rolling rocks down on any of the men working on the cliff sides or in the bottom of the gorge. But we did not see him until the morning of the third day. We had passed the last of the rapids of the chasm, and the four boats were going downstream when he appeared behind some trees on the bank and called out that he wished to surrender and be taken aboard; for the murderer was an arrant craven at heart, a strange mixture of ferocity and cowardice. Colonel Rondon's boat was far in advance; he did not stop nor answer. I kept on in similar fashion with the rear boats, for I had no intention of taking the murderer aboard, to the jeopardy of the other members of the party, unless Colonel Rondon told me that it would have to be done in pursuance of his duty, as an officer of the army and a servant of the government of Brazil. At the first halt Colonel Rondon came up to me and told me that this was his view of his duty, but that he had not stopped because he wished first to consult me as the chief of the expedition. I answered that for the reasons enumerated above I did not believe that in justice to the good men of the expedition we should jeopardize their safety by taking the murderer along, and that if the responsibility were mine I should refuse to take him; but that he, Colonel Rondon, was the superior officer of both the murderer and of all the other enlisted men and army officers on the expedition, and in return was responsible for his actions to his own governmental superiors and to the laws of Brazil; and that in view of this responsibility he must act as his sense of duty bade him. Accordingly, at the next camp he sent back two men, expert woodsmen, to find the murderer and bring him in. They failed to find him.

I have anticipated my narrative because I do not wish to recur to the horror more than is necessary. I now returned to my story. After we found that Julio had fled, we returned to the scene of the tragedy. The murdered man lay with a handkerchief thrown over his face. We buried him beside the place where he fell. With axes and knives the camaradas dug a shallow grave while we stood by with bared heads. Then reverently and carefully we lifted the poor body which but half an hour before had been so full of vigorous life. Colonel Rondon and I bore the head and shoulders. We laid him in the grave, and heaped a mound over him, and put a rude cross at his head. We fired a volley for a brave and loyal soldier who had died doing his duty. The we left him forever, under the great trees beside the lonely river.

That day we got only half-way down the rapids. There was no good place to camp. But at the foot of one steep cliff there was a narrow, boulder-covered slope where it was possible to sling hammocks and cook; and a slanting spot was found for my cot, which had sagged until by this time it looked like a broken-backed centiped. It rained a little during the night, but not enough to wet us much. Next day Lyra, Kermit, and Cherrie finished their job, and brought the four remaining canoes to camp, one leaking badly from the battering on the rocks. We then went downstream a few hundred yards, and camped on the opposite side; it was not a good camping-place, but it was better than the one we left.

The men were growing constantly weaker under the endless strain of exhausting labor. Kermit was having an attack of fever, and Lyra and Cherrie had touches of dysentery, but all three continued to work. While in the water trying to help with an upset canoe I had by my own clumsiness bruised my leg against a boulder; and the resulting inflammation was somewhat bothersome. I now had a sharp attack of fever, but thanks to the excellent care of the doctor, was over it in about forty-eight hours; but Kermit's fever grew worse and he too was unable to work for a day or two. We could walk over the portages, however. A good doctor is an absolute necessity on an exploring expedition in such a country as that we were in, under penalty of a frightful mortality among the members; and the necessary risks and hazards are so great, the chances of disaster so large, that there is no warrant for increasing them by the failure to take all feasible precautions.

🌿 🌿 🌿

One day Trigueiro [Kermit's dog] failed to embark with the rest of us, and we had to camp where we were next day to find him. Easter Sunday we spent in the fashion with which we were altogether too familiar. We only ran in a clear course for ten minutes all told, and spent eight hours in portaging the loads past rapids down which the canoes were run; the balsa was almost swamped. This day we caught twenty-eight big fish, mostly piranhas, and everybody had all he could eat for dinner and for breakfast the following morning.

The forenoon of the following day was a repetition of this wearisome work; but late in the afternoon the river began to run in long and quiet reaches. We made fifteen kilometres, and for the first time in several weeks camped where we did not hear the rapids. The silence was soothing and restful. The following day, April 14, we made a good run of some thirty-two kilometres. We passed a little river which entered on our left. We ran two or three light rapids and portaged the loads by another. The river ran in long and usually tranquil stretches. In the morning when we started the view was lovely. There was a mist, and for a couple of miles the great river, broad and quiet, ran between the high walls of tropical forest, the tops of the giant trees showing dim through the haze. Different members of the party caught many fish, and shot a monkey and a couple of jacu-tinga—birds kin to a turkey but the size of a fowl—so we again had a camp of plenty. The dry season was approaching, but there were still heavy, drenching rains. On this day the men found some new nuts of which they liked the taste; but the nuts proved unwholesome and half of the men were very sick and unable to work the following day. In the balsa only two were left fit to do anything, and Kermit plied a paddle all day long.

Accordingly, it was a rather sorry crew that embarked the following morning, April 15. But it turned out a red-letter day. The day before, we had come across cuttings, a year old, which were probably but not certainly made by pioneer rubber men. But on this day—during which we made twenty-five kilometres—after running two hours and a half we found on the left bank a board on a post with the initials J. A., to show the farthest-up point which a rubber man had reached and claimed as his own. An hour farther down we came on a newly built house in a little planted clearing; and we cheered heartily. No one was at home, but the house of palm thatch was clean and cool. A couple of dogs were on watch, and the belongings showed that a man, and a woman, and a child lived there and had only just left. Another hour brought us to a similar house where dwelt an old black man who showed the innate courtesy of the Brazilian peasant. We came on these rubber men and their houses in about latitude ten degrees twenty-four minutes. . . .

Six weeks had been spent in steadily slogging our way down through the interminable series of rapids. It was astonishing, when we were on a river of about the size of the upper Rhine or Elbe, to realize that no geographer had any idea of its existence. But, after all, no civilized man of any grade had ever been on it. . . .

We had passed the period when there was a chance of peril, of disaster, to the whole expedition. There might be risk ahead to individuals, and some difficulties and annoyances for all of us; but there was no longer the least likelihood of any disaster to the expedition as a whole. We now no longer had to face continual anxiety, the need of constant economy with food, the duty of labor with no end in sight, and bitter uncertainty as to the future.

It was time to get out. The wearing work, under very unhealthy conditions, was beginning to tell on every one. Half of the camaradas had been down with fever and were much weakened; only a few of them retained their original physical and moral strength. Cherrie and Kermit had recovered; but both Kermit and Lyra still had bad sores on their legs from the bruises received in the water work. I was in worse shape. The after-effects of the fever still hung on; and the leg which had been hurt while working in the rapids with the sunken canoe had taken a turn for the bad and developed an abscess. The good doctor, to whose unwearied care and kindness I owe much, had cut it open and inserted a drainage-tube; an added charm being given the operation and the subsequent dressings by the enthusiasm with which the piums and boroshudas [insects] took part therein. I could hardly hobble and was pretty well laid up. But "there aren't no 'stop, conductor,' while a battery's changing ground." No man has any business to go on such a trip as ours unless he will refuse to jeopardize the welfare of his associates by any delay caused by a weakness or ailment of his. It is his duty to go forward, if necessary on all fours, until he drops. Fortunately, I was put to no such test. I remained in good shape until we had passed the last of the rapids of the chasms. When my serious trouble came we had only canoe-riding ahead of us. It is not ideal for a sick man to spend the hottest hours of the day stretched on the boxes in the bottom of a small open dugout, under the well-nigh intolerable heat of the torrid sun of the mid-tropics, varied by blinding, drenching downpours of rain; but I could not be sufficiently grateful for the chance. Kermit and Cherrie took care of me as if they had been trained nurses; and Colonel Rondon and Lyra were no less thoughtful.

The north was calling strongly to the three men of the north—Rocky Dell farm to Cherrie, Sagamore Hill to me, and to Kermit the call was stronger still. After nightfall we could now see the Dipper well above the horizon—upside down, with the two pointers pointing to a north star below the world's rim; but the Dipper, with all its stars. In our home country spring had now come, the wonderful northern spring of long glorious days, of brooding twilights, of cool delightful nights. Robin and bluebird, meadow-lark and song-sparrow, were singing in the mornings at home; the maple buds were red; wind-flowers and bloodroot were blooming while the last patches of snow still lingered; the rapture of the hermit-thrush in Vermont, the serene golden melody of the wood-thrush on Long Island, would be heard before we were there to listen. Each man to his home, and to his true love! Each was longing for the homely things that were so dear to him, for the home people who were dearer still, and for the one who was dearest of all.

On a hunting trip in the western United States, 1905.

7

AMERICAN WILDERNESS HUNTER

THE LORDLY BUFFALO

TR the informed naturalist, comfortable with Darwin's terminology and a keen observer of land and animals, here reveals his passion and pleasure in hunting. He regrets wholesale slaughter of the buffalo of the 1870s but defends it as necessary for the spread of settlement. He harbors no reservations, however, about the excitement and satisfaction of his own hunting of the animal in a more sporting and controlled manner. Not long after this hunting trip, Roosevelt organized the Boone and Crockett Club in New York City in 1887 and became its first president. Among other goals the club was intended to promote both the preservation of large game in the United States and the "manly sport" of hunting it with rifle. This selection is from Hunting Trips of a Ranchman, published in 1885 by G. P. Putnam's Sons.

◆◇◆

Gone forever are the mighty herds of the lordly buffalo. A few solitary individuals and small bands are still to be found scattered here and there in the wilder parts of the plains; and, though most of these will be very soon destroyed, others will for some years fight off their doom and lead a precarious existence either in remote and almost desert portions of the country near the Mexican frontier, or else in the wildest and most inaccessible fastnesses of the Rocky Mountains; but the great herds, that for the first three-quarters of this century formed the distinguishing and characteristic feature of the Western plains, have vanished forever.

It is only about a hundred years ago that the white man, in his march westward, first encroached upon the lands of the buffalo, for these animals had never penetrated in any number to the Appalachian chain of mountains. Indeed, it was after the beginning of the century before the inroads of the whites upon them grew at all serious. Then, though constantly driven westward, the diminution in their territory, if sure, was at least slow, although growing progressively more rapid. Less than a score of years ago the great herds, containing many millions of individuals, ranged over a vast expanse of country that stretched in an unbroken line from near Mexico to far into British America; in fact, over almost all the plains that are now known as the cattle region. But since that time their destruction has gone on with appalling rapidity and thoroughness; and the main factors in bringing it about have been the railroads, which carried hordes of hunters into the land and gave them means to transport their spoils to market. Not quite twenty years since, the range was broken in two, and the buffalo herds in the middle slaughtered or thrust aside; and thus there resulted two ranges, the northern and the southern. The latter was the larger but, being more open to the hunters, was the sooner to be depopulated; and the last of the great southern herds was destroyed in 1878, though scattered bands escaped and wandered into the desolate wastes to the southwest. Meanwhile, equally savage war was waged on the northern herds, and five years later the last of these was also destroyed or broken up. The bulk of this slaughter was done in the dozen years from 1872 to 1883; never before in all history were so many large wild animals of one species slain in so short a space of time.

The extermination of the buffalo has been a veritable tragedy of the animal world. Other races of animals have been destroyed within historic times, but these have been species of small size, local distribution, and limited numbers, usually found in some particular island or group of islands; while the huge buffalo, in countless myriads, ranged over the greater part of a continent. Its nearest relative, the Old World aurochs, formerly found all through the forests of Europe, is almost as near the verge of extinction, but with the latter the process has been slow and has extended over a period of a thousand years, instead of being compressed into a dozen. The destruction of the various larger species of South African game is much more local, and is proceeding at a much slower rate. It may truthfully be said that the sudden and complete extermination of the vast herds of the buffalo is without a parallel in historic times.

No sight is more common on the plains than that of a bleached buffalo skull; and their countless numbers attest the abundance of the animal at a time not so very long past. On those portions where the herds made their last stand, the carcasses, dried in the clear, high air, or the mouldering skeletons, abound. Last year, in crossing the country around the heads of the Big Sandy, O'Fallon Creek, Little Beaver, and Box Alder, these skeletons or dried carcasses were in sight from every hillock, often lying over the ground so thickly that several score could be seen at once. A ranchman who at the same time had made a journey of a thousand miles across northern Montana, along the Milk River, told me that, to use his own expression, during the whole distance he was never out of sight of a dead buffalo, and never in sight of a live one.

Thus, though gone, the traces of the buffalo are still thick over the land. Their dried dung is found everywhere, and is in many places the only fuel afforded by the plains; their skulls, which last longer than any other part of the animal, are among the most familiar of objects to the plainsman; their bones are in many districts so plentiful that it has become a regular industry, followed by hundreds of men (christened "bone-hunters" by the frontiersmen), to go out with wagons and collect them in great numbers for the sake of the phosphates they yield; and Bad Lands, plateaus, and prairies alike, are cut up in all directions by the deep ruts which were formerly buffalo trails.

The rapid and complete extermination of the buffalo affords an excellent instance of how a race that has thriven and multiplied for ages under conditions of life to which it has slowly fitted itself by a process of natural selection continued for countless generations, may succumb at once when these surrounding conditions are varied by the introduction of one or more new elements, immediately becoming the chief forces with which it has to contend in the struggle for life. The most striking characteristics of the buffalo, and those which had been found most useful in maintaining the species until the white man entered upon the scene, were its phenomenal gregariousness—surpassed by no other four-footed beast, and only equaled, if equaled at all, by one or two kinds of South African antelope—its massive bulk, and unwieldy strength. The fact that it was a plains and not a forest or mountain animal was at that time also greatly in its favor. Its toughness and hardy endurance fitted it to contend with purely natural forces: to resist cold and the winter blasts, or the heat of a thirsty summer, to wander away to new pastures when the feed on the old was exhausted, to plunge over the broken ground, and to plough its way through snowdrifts or quagmires. But one beast of prey existed sufficiently powerful to conquer it when full grown and in health; and this, the grizzly bear, could only be considered an occasional foe. The Indians were its most dangerous enemies, but they were without horses, and their weapons, bows and arrows, were only available at close range; so that a slight degree of speed enabled a buffalo to get out of the way of their human foes when discovered, and on the open plains a moderate development of the senses was sufficient to warn them of the approach of the latter before they had come up to the very close distance required for their primitive weapons to take effect. Thus the strength, size, and gregarious habits of the brute were sufficient for a protection against most foes; and a slight degree of speed and moderate development of the senses served as adequate guards against the grizzlies and bow-bearing foot Indians. Concealment, and the habit of seeking lonely and remote places for a dwelling, would have been of no service.

But the introduction of the horse, and shortly afterward the incoming of white hunters carrying long-range rifles, changed all this. The buffaloes' gregarious habits simply rendered them certain to be seen and made it a matter of perfect ease to follow them up; their keeping to the open plains heightened their conspicuousness, while their senses were too dull to discover their foes at such a distance as to nullify the effects of the long rifles; their speed was not such as to enable them to flee from a horseman; and their size and strength merely made them too clumsy either to escape from or to contend with their foes. Add to this the fact that their hides and flesh were valuable, and it is small wonder that, under the new order of things, they should have vanished with such rapidity.

The incoming of the cattlemen was another cause of the completeness of their destruction. Wherever there is good feed for a buffalo, there is good feed for a steer or cow; and so the latter have penetrated into all the pastures of the former; and of course the cowboys follow. A cowboy is not able to kill a deer or antelope unless in exceptional cases, for they are too fleet, too shy, or keep themselves too well hidden. But a buffalo neither tries nor is able to do much in the way of hiding itself; its senses are too dull to give it warning in time; and it is not so swift as a horse, so that a cowboy, riding round in the places where cattle, and therefore buffalo, are likely to be, is pretty sure to see any of the latter that may be about, and then can easily approach near enough to be able to overtake them when they begin running. The size and value of the animal make the chase after it very keen. Hunters will follow the trail of a band for days, when they would not follow that of deer or antelope for a half-hour.

🌿 🌿 🌿

While the slaughter of the buffalo has been in places needless and brutal, and while it is greatly to be regretted that the species is likely to become extinct, and while, moreover, from a purely selfish standpoint, many, including myself, would rather see it continue to exist as the chief feature in the unchanged life of the Western wilderness; yet, on the other hand, it must be remembered that its continued existence in any numbers was absolutely incompatible with anything but a very sparse settlement of the country; and that its destruction was the condition precedent upon the advance of white civilization in the West, and was a positive boon to the more thrifty and industrious frontiersmen. Where the buffalo were plenty, they ate up all the grass that could have supported cattle. The country over which the huge herds grazed during the last year or two of their existence was cropped bare, and the grass did not grow to its normal height and become able to support cattle for in some cases two, in others three, seasons. Every buffalo needed as much food as an ox or cow; and if the former abounded, the latter perforce would have to be scarce. Above all, the extermination of the buffalo was the only way of solving the Indian question. As long as this large animal of the chase existed, the Indians simply could not be kept on reservations, and always had an ample supply of meat on hand to support them in the event of a war; and its disappearance was the only method of forcing them to at least partially abandon their savage mode of life. From the standpoint of humanity at large, the extermination of the buffalo has been a blessing. The many have been benefitted by it; and I suppose the comparatively few of us who would have preferred the continuance of the old order of things, merely for the sake of our own selfish enjoyment, have no right to complain.

The buffalo is more easily killed than any other kind of plains game; but its chase is very far from being the tame amusement it has lately been represented. It is genuine sport; it needs skill, marksmanship, and hardihood in the man who follows it, and if he hunts on horseback, it needs also pluck and good riding. It is no way akin to various forms of so-called sport in vogue in parts of the East, such as killing deer in a lake or by fire-hunting, or even by watching at a runway. No man who is not of an adventurous temper, and able to stand rough food and living, will penetrate to the haunts of the buffalo. The animal is so tough and tenacious of life that it must be hit in the right spot; and care must be used in approaching it, for its nose is very keen, and though its sight is dull, yet, on the other hand, the plains it frequents are singularly bare of cover; while, finally, there is just a faint spice of danger in the pursuit, for the bison, though the least dangerous of all bovine animals, will, on occasions, turn upon the hunter, and though its attack is, as a rule, easily avoided, yet in rare cases it manages to charge home. A ranchman of my acquaintance once, many years ago, went out buffalo-hunting on horseback, together with a friend who was unused to the sport, and who was mounted on a large, untrained, nervous horse. While chasing a bull, the friend's horse became unmanageable, and when the bull turned, proved too clumsy to get out of the way, and was caught on the horns, one of which entered its flank, while the other inflicted a huge, bruised gash across the man's thigh, tearing the muscles all out. Both horse and rider were flung to the ground with tremendous violence. The horse had to be killed, and the man died in a few hours from the shock, loss of blood, and internal injuries. Such an accident, however, is very exceptional.

❦ ❦ ❦

One September I determined to take a short trip after bison. At that time I was staying in a cow-camp a good many miles up the river from my ranch; there were then no cattle south of me, where there are now very many thousand head, and the buffalo had been plentiful in the country for a couple of winters past, but the last of the herds had been destroyed or driven out six months before, and there were only a few stragglers left. It was one of my first hunting trips; previously, I had shot with the rifle very little, and that only at deer or antelope. I took as a companion one of my best men, named Ferris . . . ; we rode a couple of ponies, not very good ones, and each carried his roll of blankets and a very small store of food in a pack behind the saddle.

Leaving the cow-camp early in the morning, we crossed the Little Missouri and for the first ten miles threaded our way through the narrow defiles and along the tortuous divides of a great tract of Bad Lands. Although it was fall and the nights were cool, the sun was very hot in the middle of the day, and we jogged along at a slow pace, so as not to tire our ponies. Two or three blacktail deer were seen, some distance off, and, when we were a couple of hours on our journey, we came across the fresh track of a bull buffalo. Buffalo wander a great distance, for, though they do not go fast, yet they may keep traveling, as they graze, all day long; and though this one had evidently passed but a few hours before, we were not sure we would see him. His tracks were easily followed as long as he had kept to the soft creek bottom, crossing and recrossing the narrow wet ditch which wound its way through it; but when he left this and turned up a winding coulee that branched out in every direction, his hoofs scarcely made any marks in the hard ground. We rode up the ravine, carefully examining the soil for nearly half an hour, however; finally, as we passed the mouth of a little side coulee, there was a plunge and crackle through the bushes at its head, and a shabby-looking old bull bison galloped out of it and, without an instant's hesitation, plunged over a steep bank into a patch of rotten, broken ground which led around the base of a high butte. So quickly did he disappear that we had not time to dismount and fire. Spurring our horses we galloped up to the brink of the cliff down which he had plunged; it was remarkable that he should have gone down it unhurt. From where we stood we could see nothing; so, getting our horses over the broken ground as fast as possible, we ran to the butte and rode around it, only to see the buffalo come out of the broken land and climb up the side of another butte over a quarter of a mile off. In spite of his great weight and cumbersome, heavy-looking gait, he climbed up the steep bluff with ease and even agility, and when he had reached the ridge stood and looked back at us for a moment; while so doing he held his head high up, and at that distance his great shaggy mane and huge forequarter made him look like a lion. In another second he again turned away and made off; and being evidently very shy and accustomed to being harassed by hunters, must have traveled a long distance before stopping, for we followed his trail for some miles, until it got on such hard, dry ground that his hoofs did not leave a scrape in the soil, and yet did not again catch so much as a glimpse of him.

It was late in the afternoon before we saw any game; then we made out in the middle of a large plain three black specks, which proved to be buffalo — old bulls. Our horses had come a good distance, under a hot sun, and, as they had had no water except from the mudhole in the morning, they were in no condition for running. They were not very fast, anyhow; so, though the ground was unfavorable, we made up our minds to try to creep up to the buffalo. We left the ponies in a hollow half a mile from the game, and started off on our hands and knees, taking advantage of every sage-brush as cover. After a while we had to lie flat on our bodies and wriggle like snakes; and while doing this I blundered into a bed of cactus, and filled my hands with the spines. After taking advantage of every hollow, hillock, or sage-brush, we got without about a hundred and twenty-five or fifty yards of where the three bulls were unconsciously feeding, and as all between was bare ground I drew up and fired. It was the first time I ever shot a buffalo, and, confused by the bulk and shaggy hair of the beast, I aimed too far back at one that was standing nearly broadside on toward me. The bullet told on his body with a loud crack, the dust flying up from his hide; but it did not work him any immediate harm, or in the least hinder him from making off; and away went all three, with their tails up, disappearing over a light rise in the ground.

Much disgusted, we trotted back to where the horses were picketed, jumped on them, a good deal out of breath, and rode after the flying game. We thought that the wounded one might turn out and leave the others; and so followed them, though they had over a mile's start. For seven or eight miles we loped our jaded horses along at a brisk pace, occasionally seeing the buffalo far ahead; and finally, when the sun had just set, we saw that all three had come to a stand in a gentle hollow. There was no cover anywhere near them; and, as a last desperate resort, we concluded to try to run them on our worn-out ponies. As we cantered toward them they faced us for a second and then turned round and made off, while with spurs and quirts we made the ponies put on a burst that enabled us to close in with the wounded one just about the time that the lessening twilight had almost vanished; while the rim of the full moon rose above the horizon. The pony I was on could barely hold his own, after getting up within sixty or seventy yards of the wounded bull; my companion, better mounted, forged ahead, a little to one side. The bull saw him coming and swerved from his course, and by cutting across I was able to get nearly up to him. The ground over which we were running was fearful, being broken into holes and ditches, separated by hillocks; in the dull light, and at the speed we were going, no attempt could be made to guide the horses, and the latter, fagged out by their exertions, floundered and pitched forward at every stride, hardly keeping their legs. When up within twenty feet I fired my rifle, but the darkness, and especially the violent labored motion of my pony, made me miss; I tried to get in closer, when suddenly up went the bull's tail, and, wheeling, he charged me with lowered horns. My pony, frightened into momentary activity, spun round and tossed up his head; I was holding the rifle in both hands, and the pony's head, striking it, knocked it violently against my forehead, cutting quite a gash, from which, heated as I was, the blood poured into my eyes. Meanwhile the buffalo, passing me, charged my companion, and followed him as he made off, and, as the ground was very bad, for some little distance his lowered head was unpleasantly near the tired pony's tail. I tried to run in on him again, but my pony stopped short, dead beat; and by no spurring could I force him out of a slow trot. My companion jumped off and took a couple of shots at the buffalo, which missed in the dim moonlight; and to our unutterable chagrin the wounded bull labored off and vanished in the darkness. I made after him on foot, in hopeless and helpless wrath, until he got out of sight.

Our horses were completely done out; we did not mount them again, but led them slowly along, trembling, foaming, and sweating. The ground was moist in places, and after an hour's search we found in a reedy hollow a little mud-pool with water so slimy that it was almost gelatinous. Thirsty though we were, for we had not drunk for twelve hours, neither man nor horse could swallow more than a mouthful or two of this water. We unsaddled the horses, and made our beds by the hollow, each eating a biscuit; there was not a twig with which to make a fire, nor anything to which we might fasten the horses. Spreading the saddle-blankets under us, and our own over us, we lay down, with the saddles as pillows, to which we had been obliged to lariat our steeds.

The ponies stood about, almost too tired to eat; but in spite of their fatigue they were watchful and restless, continually snorting or standing with their ears forward, peering out into the night; wild beasts, or some such things, were about. The day before we had had a false alarm from supposed hostile Indians, who turned out to be merely half-breed Crees; and, as we were in a perfectly lonely part of the wilderness, we knew we were in the domain of both white and red horse-thieves, and that the latter might, in addition to our horses, try to take our scalps. It was some time before we dozed off, waking up with a start whenever we heard the horses stop grazing and stand motionless with heads raised, looking out into the darkness. But at last, tired out, we fell sound asleep.

About midnight we were rudely wakened by having our pillows whipped out from under our heads; and as we started from the bed we saw, in the bright moonlight, the horses galloping madly off with the saddles, tied to the lariats, whose other ends were around their necks, bounding and trailing after them. Our first thought was that they had been stampeded by horse-thieves, and we rolled over and crouched down in the grass with our rifles; but nothing could be seen, except a shadowy four-footed form in the hollow, and in the end we found that the horses must have taken alarm at a wolf or wolves that had come up to the edge of the bank and looked over at us, not being able at first to make out what we were.

We did not expect to find the horses again that night, but nevertheless took up the broad trail made by the saddles as they dragged through the dewy grass, and followed it well in the moonlight. Our task proved easier than we had feared; for they had not run much over half a mile, and we found them standing close together and looking intently round when we came up. Leading them back we again went to sleep; but the weather was rapidly changing, and by three o'clock a fine rain began to come steadily down, and we cowered and shivered under our wet blankets till morning. At the first streak of dawn, having again eaten a couple of biscuits, we were off, glad to bid good-by to the inhospitable pool in whose neighborhood we had spent such a comfortless night. A fine, drizzling mist shrouded us and hid from sight all distant objects; and at times there were heavy downpours of rain. Before we had gone any distance we became what is termed by back-woodsmen or plainsmen "turned round," and the creeks suddenly seemed to be running the wrong way; after which we traveled purely by the compass.

For some hours we kept a nearly straight course over the formless, shape-less, plain, drenched through and thoroughly uncomfortable; then, as we rose over a low divide, the fog lifted for a few minutes, and we saw several black objects slowly crossing some rolling country ahead of us, and a glance satisfied us they were buffalo. The horses were picketed at once, and we ran up as near the game as we dared, and then began to stalk them, creeping for-ward on our hands and knees through the soft muddy prairie soil, while a smart shower of rain blew in our faces, as we advanced up wind. The coun-try was favorable, and we got within less than a hundred yards of the near-est, a large cow, though we had to creep along so slowly that we were chilled through, and our teeth chattered behind our blue lips. To crown my misfor-tunes, I now made one of those misses which a man to his dying day always looks back upon with wonder and regret. The rain was beating in my eyes, and the drops stood out in the sights of the rifle so that I could hardly draw a bead; and I either overshot or else at the last moment must have given a nervous jerk and pulled the rifle clear off the mark. At any rate, I missed clean, and the whole band plunged down into a hollow and were off before, with my stiffened and numbed fingers, I could get another shot; and in wet, sullen misery we plodded back to the ponies.

All that day the rain continued, and we passed another wretched night. Next morning, however, it had cleared off, and as the sun rose brightly we forgot our hunger and sleepiness, and rode cheerily off up a large dry creek, in whose bottom pools of rain-water still stood. During the morning, how-ever, our ill luck continued. My companion's horse almost trod on a rattle-snake, and narrowly escaped being bitten. While riding along the face of a steeply inclined bluff the sandy soil broke away under the ponies' hoofs, and we slid and rolled down to the bottom, where we came to in a heap, horses and men. Then while galloping through a brush-covered bottom my pony put both forefeet in a hole made by the falling and uprooting of a tree, and turned a complete somersault, pitching me a good ten feet beyond his head. And, finally, while crossing what looked like the hard bed of a dry creek, the earth gave way under my horse as if he had stepped on a trap-door and let him down to his withers in soft, sticky mud. I was off at once and floundered to the bank, loosening the lariat from the saddle-bow; and both of us turning to with a will and bringing the other pony into our aid, hauled him out by the rope, pretty nearly strangling him in so doing; and he looked rather a melancholy object as he stood up, trembling and shaking, and plastered with mire from head to tail.

🌿 🌿 🌿

Shortly after midday we left the creek bottom, and skirted a ridge of broken buttes, cut up by the gullies and winding ravines, in whose bottoms grew bunch-grass. While passing near the mouth and to leeward of one of these ravines both ponies threw up their heads and snuffed the air, turning their muzzles toward the head of the gully. Feeling sure that they had smelt some wild beast, either a bear or a buffalo, I slipped off my pony and ran quickly but cautiously up along the valley. Before I had gone a hundred yards, I noticed in the soft soil at the bottom the round prints of a bison's hoofs; and immediately afterward got a glimpse of the animal himself, as he fed slowly up the course of the ravine, some distance ahead of me. The wind was just right, and no ground could have been better for stalking. Hardly needing to bend down, I walked up behind a small sharp-crested hillock and, peeping over, there below me, not fifty yards off, was a great bison bull. He was walking along, grazing as he walked. His glossy fall coat was in fine trim and shone in the rays of the sun, while his pride of bearing showed him to be in the lusty vigor of his prime. As I rose above the crest of the hill, he held up his head and cocked his tail to the air. Before he could go off, I put the bullet in behind his shoulder. The wound was an almost immediately fatal one, yet with surprising agility for so large and heavy an animal, he bounded up the opposite side of the ravine, heedless of two more balls, both of which went into his flank and ranged forward, and disappeared over the ridge at a lumbering gallop, the blood pouring from his mouth and nostrils. We knew he could not go far, and trotted leisurely along on his bloody trail; and in the next gully we found him stark dead, lying almost on his back, having pitched over the side when he tried to go down it. His head was a remarkably fine one, even for a fall buffalo. He was lying in a very bad position, and it was most tedious and tiresome work to cut it off and pack it out. The flesh of a cow or calf is better eating than is that of a bull; but the so-called hump meat—that is, the strip of steak on each side of the backbone—is excellent, and tender and juicy. Buffalo meat is with difficulty to be distinguished from ordinary beef. At any rate, the flesh of this bull tasted uncommonly good to us, for we had been without fresh meat for a week; and until a healthy, active man has been without it for some little time, he does not know how positively and almost painfully hungry for flesh he becomes, no matter how much farinaceous food he may have. And the very toil I had been obliged to go through, in order to procure the head, made me feel all the prouder of it when at last it was in my possession.

STILL-HUNTING ELK ON THE MOUNTAINS

*The account of this hunting adventure illustrates well the skill of
Roosevelt the writer. He draws the reader into the experience of
the hunt, transmitting the energy and excitement of the
encounter. At the same time he never loses his irrepressible
habit of recording a naturalist's observations of animal habits
and habitat. The image of the bull moose as a dangerous
antagonist that TR uses in this story is one to which he will
return during his 1912 presidential campaign. This selection is
from* Hunting Trips of a Ranchman, *published in 1885 by
G. P. Putnam's Sons.*

After the buffalo, the elk are the first animals to disappear from a country
when it is settled. This arises from their size and consequent conspicuousness, and the eagerness with which they are followed by hunters; and also
because of their gregariousness and their occasional fits of stupid panic, during whose continuance hunters can now and then work great slaughter in a
herd. Five years ago elk were abundant in the valley of the Little Missouri,
and in fall were found wandering in great bands of over a hundred individuals each. But they have now vanished completely, except that one or two
may still lurk in some of the most remote and broken places where there are
deep, wooded ravines.

Formerly, the elk were plentiful all over the plains, coming down into
them in great bands during the fall months and traversing their entire
extent. But the incoming of hunters and cattlemen has driven them off the
ground as completely as the buffalo; unlike the latter, however, they are still
common in the dense woods that cover the Rocky Mountains and the other
great Western chains. In the old days, running elk on horseback was a
highly esteemed form of plains sport; but now that it has become a beast of
the timber and the craggy ground, instead of a beast of the open, level
prairie, it is followed almost solely on foot and with the rifle. Its sense of
smell is very acute, and it has good eyes and quick ears; and its wariness
makes it under ordinary circumstances very difficult to approach. But it is
subject to fits of panic folly, and during their continuance great numbers can
be destroyed. A band places almost as much reliance upon the leaders as
does a flock of sheep; and if the leaders are shot down, the others will huddle together in a terrified mass, seemingly unable to make up their minds in
which direction to flee. When one, more bold than the rest, does at last step
out, the hidden hunters at once shooting it down will produce a fresh panic.

I have known of twenty elk (or wapiti, as they are occasionally called) being thus procured out of one band. And at times they show a curious indifference to danger, running up on a hunter who is in plain sight, or standing still for a few fatal seconds to gaze at one that unexpectedly appears.

In spite of its size and strength and great branching antlers, the elk is but little more dangerous to the hunter than is an ordinary buck. Once, in coming up to a wounded one, I had it strike at me with its forefeet, bristling up the hair on the neck, and making a harsh, grating noise with its teeth; as its back was broken it could not get at me, but the savage glare in its eyes left me no doubt as to its intentions. Only in a single instance have I ever known of a hunter being regularly charged by one of these great deer. He had struck a band of elk and wounded an old bull, which, after going a couple of miles, received another ball and then separated from the rest of the herd and took refuge in a dense patch of small timber. The hunter went in on its trail and came upon it lying down; it jumped to its feet, and, with hair all bristling, made a regular charge upon its pursuer, who leaped out of the way behind a tree just in time to avoid it. It crashed past through the undergrowth without turning, and he killed it with a third and last shot. But this was a very exceptional case, and in most instances the elk submits to death with hardly an effort at resistance; it is by no means as dangerous an antagonist as is a bull moose.

The elk is unfortunately one of those animals seemingly doomed to total destruction at no distant date. Already its range has shrunk to far less than one-half its former size. Originally it was found as far as the Atlantic seaboard; I have myself known of several sets of antlers preserved in the house of a Long Island gentleman, whose ancestors had killed the bearers shortly after the first settlement of New York. Even so late as the first years of this century, elk were found in many mountainous and densely wooded places east of the Mississippi: in New York, Pennsylvania, Virginia, Kentucky, Tennessee, and all of what were then the Northwestern States and Territories. The last individual of the race in the Adirondacks was killed in 1834; in Pennsylvania, not till nearly thirty years later; while a very few are still to be found in northern Michigan. Elsewhere they must now be sought far to the west of the Mississippi; and even there they are almost gone from the great plains, and are only numerous in the deep mountain forests. Wherever it exists the skin-hunters and meat-butchers wage the most relentless and unceasing war upon it for the sake of its hide and flesh, and their unremitting persecution is thinning out the herds with terrible rapidity.

The gradual extermination of this, the most stately and beautiful animal of the chase to be found in America, can be looked upon only with unmixed regret by every sportsman and lover of nature. Excepting the moose, it is the largest and, without exception, it is the noblest of the deer tribe. No other species of true deer, in either the Old or the New World, comes up to it in size and in the shape, length, and weight of its mighty antlers; while the grand, proud carriage and lordly bearing of an old bull make it perhaps the most majestic-looking of all the animal creation. The open plains have already lost one of their great attractions, now that we no more see the long lines of elk trotting across them; and it will be a sad day when the lordly, antlered beasts are no longer found in the wild, rocky glens and among the lonely woods of towering pines that cover the great Western mountain chains.

The elk has other foes besides man. The grizzly will always make a meal of one if he gets a chance; and against his ponderous weight and savage prowess hoofs and antlers avail but little. Still he is too clumsy and easily avoided ever to do very much damage in the herds. Cougars, where they exist, work more havoc. A bull elk in rutting season, if on his guard, would with ease beat off a cougar; but the sly, cunning cat takes its quarry unawares, and once the cruel fangs are fastened in the game's throat or neck, no plunging or struggling can shake if off. The gray timber-wolves also join in twos and threes to hunt down and ham-string the elk, if other game is scare. But these great deer can hold their own and make head against all their brute foes; it is only when pitted against Man the destroyer that they succumb in the struggle of life.

I have never shot any elk in the immediate neighborhood of [the Dakota ranchland] where my cattle range; but I have had very good sport with them in a still wider and more western region; and this I will now describe.

We went into the mountains with a pack-train, leaving the ranch wagon at the place where we began to go up the first steep rise. There were two others, besides myself, in the party; one of them, the teamster, a weather-beaten old plainsman, who possessed a most extraordinary stock of miscel-laneous misinformation upon every conceivable subject, and the other my ranch foreman, Merrifield. None of us had ever been within two hundred miles of the Bighorn range before; so that our hunting trip had the added zest of being also an exploring expedition.

Each of us rode one pony, and the packs were carried on four others. We were not burdened by much baggage. Having no tent, we took the canvas wagon-sheet instead; our bedding, plenty of spare cartridges, some flour, bacon, coffee, sugar, and salt, and a few very primitive cooking utensils completed the outfit.

❦ ❦ ❦

It was on the second day of our journey into the mountains, while leading the pack-ponies down the precipitous side of a steep valley, that I obtained my first sight of elk. The trail wound through a forest of tall, slender pines, standing very close together, and with dead trees lying in every direction. The narrow trunks or overhanging limbs threatened to scrape off the packs at every moment, as the ponies hopped and scrambled over the fallen trunks; and it was difficult work, and most trying to the temper, to keep them going alone straight and prevent them from wandering off to one side or the other. At last we got out into a succession of small, open glades, with boggy spots in them; the lowest glade was of some size, and as we reached it we saw a small band of cow elk disappearing into the woods on its other edge. I was riding a restive horse, and when I tried to jump off to shoot, it reared and turned round before I could get my left foot out of the stirrup; when I at last got free I could get a glimpse of but one elk; vanishing behind a dead trunk, and my hasty shot missed. I was a good deal annoyed at this, my opening experience with mountain game, feeling that it was an omen of misfortune; but it did not prove so, for during the rest of my two weeks' stay, I with one exception got every animal I fired at.

A beautiful clear mountain brook ran through the bottom of the valley, and in an open space by its side we pitched camp. We were entirely out of fresh meat, and after lunch all three of us separated to hunt. . . . The teamster went upstream, Merrifield went down, while I followed the tracks of the band of cows and calves that we had started in the morning; their trail led along the wooded hillcrests parallel to the stream and therefore to Merrifield's course.

❦ ❦ ❦

The band I was following had, as is their custom, all run together into a wedge-shaped mass when I fired, and crashed off through the woods in a bunch during the first moments of alarm. The footprints in the soil showed that they had in the beginning taken a plunging gallop, but after a few strides had settled into the swinging, ground-covering trot that is the elk's most natural and characteristic gait. A band of elk, when alarmed, is likely to go twenty miles without halting; but these had probably been very little molested, and there was a chance that they would not go far without stopping. After getting through the first grove, the huddled herd had straightened itself out into single file, and trotted off in a nearly straight line. A mile or two of ground having been passed over in this way, the animals had slackened their pace into a walk, evidently making up their minds that they were out of danger. Soon afterward they had begun to go slower, and to scatter out on each side, browsing or grazing.

It was not difficult work to follow up the band at first. While trotting their sharp hoofs came down with sufficient force to leave very distinct footprints, and moreover, the trail was the more readily made out as all the animals trod nearly in each other's steps. But when the band spread out the tracking was much harder, as each single one, walking slowly along, merely made here and there a slight scrape in the soil or a faint indentation in the bed of pine-needles. Besides, I had to advance with the greatest caution, keeping the sharpest lookout in front and on all sides of me. Even as it was, though I got very close up to my game, they were on foot before I saw them and I did not get a standing shot. While carefully looking to my footsteps I paid too little heed to the rifle which I held in my right hand, and let the barrel tap smartly on a tree-trunk. Instantly there was a stamp and movement among the bushes ahead and to one side of me; the elk had heard but had neither seen nor smelt me; and a second afterward I saw the indistinct shadowy outlines of the band as they trotted downhill, from where their beds had been made on the very summit of the crest, taking a course diagonal to mine. I raced forward and also downhill, behind some large mossy boulders, and cut them fairly off, the band passing directly ahead of me and not twenty yards away, at a slashing trot, which a few of them changed for a wild gallop as I opened fire. I was so hemmed in by the thick tree-trunks, and it was so difficult to catch more than a fleeting glimpse of each animal, that though I fired four shots I only brought down one elk, a full-grown cow, with a broken neck, dead in its tracks; but I also broke the hind leg of a bull calf.

❧ ❧ ❧

After thrusting the hunting-knife into the throat of the cow I followed the trail of the band; and in an open glade, filled with all sage-brush, came across and finished the wounded calf. Meanwhile the others ran directly across Merrifield's path, and he shot two. This gave us much more meat than we wished, nor would we have shot as many, but neither of us could reckon upon the other's getting as much game, and flesh was a necessity. Leaving Merrifield to skin and cut up the dead animals, I walked back to camp, where I found the teamster, who had brought in the hams and tongues of two deer he had shot, and sent him back with a pack-pony for the hides and meat of the elk. Elk tongues are most delicious eating, being juicy, tender, and well flavored; they are excellent to take out as a lunch on a long hunting trip.

We now had more than enough meat in camp and did not shoot at another cow or calf elk while on the mountains, though we saw quite a number; the last day of my stay I was within fifty yards of two that were walking quietly through a very dense, swampy wood. But it took me some time longer before I got any fine heads.

One day Merrifield and I went out together and had a rather exciting chase after some bull elk. The previous evening, toward sunset, I had seen three bulls trotting off across an open glade toward a great stretch of forest and broken ground, up near the foot of the rocky peaks. Next morning, early, we started off to hunt through this country. The walking was hard work, especially up and down the steep cliffs, covered with slippery pine-needles; or among the windfalls, where the rows of dead trees lay piled up across one another in the wildest confusion. We saw nothing until we came to a large patch of burnt ground, where we at once found the soft, black soil marked up by elk hoofs; nor had we penetrated into it more than few hundred yards before we came to tracks made but a few minutes before, and almost instantly afterward saw three bull elk, probably those I had seen on the preceding day. We had been running briskly uphill through the soft, heavy loam, in which our feet made no noise but slipped and sank deeply; as a consequence, I was all out of breath and my hand so unsteady that I missed my first shot. Elk, however, do not vanish with the instantaneous rapidity of frightened deer, and these three trotted off in a direction quartering to us. I doubt if I ever went through more violent exertion than in the next ten minutes. We raced after them at full speed, opening fire; I wounded all three, but none of the wounds were immediately disabling. They trotted on and we panted afterward, slipping on the wet earth, pitching headlong over charred stumps, leaping on dead logs that broke beneath our weight, more than once measuring our full length on the ground, halting and firing whenever we got a chance. At last one bull fell; we passed him by after the others, which were still running uphill. The sweat streamed into my eyes and made furrows in the sooty mud that covered my face, from having fallen full length down on the burnt earth; I sobbed for breath as I toiled at a shambling trot after them, as nearly done out as could well be. At this moment they turned downhill. It was a great relief; a man who is too done up to go a step uphill can still run fast enough down; with a last spurt I closed in near enough to fire again; one elk fell; the other went off at a walk. We passed the second elk and I kept on alone after the third, not able to go at more than a slow trot myself, and too much winded to dare risk a shot at any distance. He got out of the burnt patch, going into some thick timber in a deep ravine; I closed pretty well, and rushed after him into a thicket of young evergreens.

The first one shot down was already dead. The second was only wounded, though it could not rise. When it saw us coming it sought to hide from us by laying its neck flat on the ground, but when we came up close it raised its head and looked proudly at us, the heavy mane bristling up on the neck, while its eyes glared and its teeth grated together. I felt really sorry to kill it. Though these were both well-grown elks, their antlers, of ten points, were small, twisted, and ill shaped; in fact, hardly worth preserving, except to call to mind a chase in which during a few minutes I did as much downright hard work as it has not often fallen to my lot to do. The burnt earth had blackened our faces and hands till we looked like negroes.

No sportsman can ever feel much keener pleasure and self-satisfaction than when, after a successful stalk and good shot, he walks up to a grand elk lying dead in the cool shade of the great evergreens, and looks at the massive and yet finely moulded form, and at the mighty antlers which are to serve in the future as the trophy and proof of his successful skill. Still-hunting the elk on the mountains is as noble a kind of sport as can well be imagined; there is nothing more pleasant and enjoyable, and at the same time it demands that the hunter shall bring into play many manly qualities. There have been few days of my hunting life that were so full of unalloyed happiness as were those spent on the Bighorn range. From morning till night I was on foot, in cool, bracing air, now moving silently through the vast, melancholy pine forests, now treading the brink of high, rocky precipices, always amid the most grand and beautiful scenery; and always after as noble and lordly game as is to be found in the Western world.

HUNTING THE GRIZZLY

Bear-hunting in the wild landscape of the Rocky Mountains represents a long journey for TR, who as a frail young boy struggled for breath. The young Roosevelt had vowed to build his weak and sickly body to robust good health. Clearly, he succeeded. In this account, which appeared in The Wilderness Hunter, *first published in 1893 by G. P. Putnam's Sons, note TR's interest in and knowledge of birds, reflecting a lifelong concern for ornithology.*

If out in the late fall or early spring, it is often possible to follow a bear's trail in the snow, having come upon it either by chance or hard hunting, or else having found where it leads from some carcass on which the beast has been feeding. In the pursuit one must exercise great caution, as at such times the hunter is easily seen a long way off, and game is always especially watchful for any foe that may follow its trail.

Once I killed a grizzly in this manner. It was early in the fall, but snow lay on the ground, while the gray weather boded a storm. My camp was in a bleak, wind-swept valley, high among the mountains which form the divide between the headwaters of the Salmon and Clark's Fork of the Columbia. All night I had lain in my buffalo bag, under the lee of a windbreak of branches, in the clump of fir-trees where I had halted the preceding evening. At my feet ran a rapid mountain torrent, its bed choked with ice-covered rocks; I had been lulled to sleep by the stream's splashing murmur, and the loud moaning of the wind along the naked cliffs. At dawn I rose and shook myself free of the buffalo-robe, coated with hoar-frost. The ashes of the fire were lifeless; in the dim morning the air was bitter cold. I did not linger a moment, but snatched up my rifle, pulled on my fur cap and gloves and strode off up a side ravine; as I walked I ate some mouthfuls of venison, left over from supper.

Two hours of toil up the steep mountain brought me to the top of a spur. The sun had risen, but was hidden behind a bank of sullen clouds. On the divide I halted, and gazed out over a vast landscape, inconceivably wild and dismal. Around me towered the stupendous mountain masses which make up the backbone of the Rockies. From my feet, as far as I could see, stretched a rugged and barren chaos of ridges and detached rock masses. Behind me, far below, the stream wound like a silver ribbon, fringed with dark conifers and the changing, dying foliage of poplar and quaking aspen. In front the bottoms of the valleys were filled with the sombre evergreen forest, dotted here and there with black, ice-skimmed tarns; and the dark spruces clustered also in the higher gorges and were scattered thinly along the mountain-sides. The snow which had fallen lay in drifts and streaks, while where the wind had scope it was blown off and the ground left bare.

For two hours I walked onward across the ridges and valleys. Then among some scattered spruces, where the snow lay to the depth of half a foot, I suddenly came on the fresh, broad trail of a grizzly. The brute was evidently roaming restlessly about in search of a winter den, but willing, in passing, to pick up any food that lay handy. At once I took the trail, traveling above and to one side, and keeping a sharp lookout ahead. The bear was going across wind, and this made my task easy. I walked rapidly, though cautiously; and it was only in crossing the large patches of bare ground that I had to fear making a noise. Elsewhere the snow muffled my footsteps, and made the trail so plain that I scarcely had to waste a glance upon it, bending my eyes always to the front.

At last, peering cautiously over a ridge crowned with broken rocks, I saw my quarry, a big, burly bear, with silvered fur. He had halted on an open hillside, and was busily digging up the caches of some rock gophers or squirrels. He seemed absorbed in his work, and the stalk was easy. Slipping quietly back, I ran toward the end of the spur, and in ten minutes struck a ravine, of which one branch ran past within seventy yards of where the bear was working. In this ravine was a rather close growth of stunted evergreens, affording good cover, although in one or two places I had to lie down and crawl through the snow. When I reached the point for which I was aiming, the bear had just finished rooting, and was starting off. A slight whistle brought him to a standstill, and I drew a bead behind his shoulder, and low down, resting the rifle across the crooked branch of a dwarf spruce. At the crack he ran off at speed, making no sound, but the thick spatter of blood splashes, showing clear on the white snow, betrayed the mortal nature of the wound. For some minutes I followed the trail; and then, topping a ridge, I saw the dark bulk lying motionless in a snow-drift at the foot of a low rock wall, down which he had tumbled.

The usual practice of the still-hunter who is after grizzly is to toll it to baits. The hunter either lies in ambush near the carcass, or approaches it stealthily when he thinks the bear is at its meal.

One day while camped near the Bitter Root Mountains in Montana I found that a bear had been feeding on the carcass of a moose which lay some five miles from the little open glade in which my tent was pitched, and I made up my mind to try to get a shot at it that afternoon. I stayed in camp till about three o'clock, lying lazily back on the bed of sweet-smelling evergreen boughs, watching the pack-ponies as they stood under the pines on the edge of the open, stamping now and then, and switching their tails. The air was still, the sky a glorious blue; at that hour in the afternoon even the September sun was hot. The smoke from the smouldering logs of the camp-fire curled thinly upward. Little chipmunks scuttled out from their holes to the packs, which lay in a heap on the ground, and then scuttled madly back again. A couple of drab-colored whiskey-jacks, with bold mien and fearless bright eyes, hopped and fluttered round, picking up the scraps, and uttering an extraordinary variety of notes, mostly discordant; so tame were they that one of them lit on my outstretched arm as I half dozed, basking in the sunshine.

When the shadows began to lengthen, I shouldered my rifle and plunged into the woods. At first my route lay along a mountainside; then for half a mile over a windfall, the dead timber piled about in crazy confusion. After that I went up the bottom of a valley by a little brook, the ground being carpeted with a sponge of soaked moss. At the head of this brook was a pond covered with water-lilies; and a scramble through a rocky pass took me into a high, wet valley, where the thick growth of spruce was broken by occasional strips of meadow. In this valley the moose carcass lay, well at the upper end.

In moccasined feet I trod softly through the soundless woods. Under the dark branches it was already dusk, and the air had the cool chill of evening. As I neared the clump where the body lay, I walked with redoubled caution, watching and listening with strained alertness. Then I heard a twig snap; and my blood leaped, for I knew the bear was at his supper. In another moment I saw his shaggy, brown form. He was working with all his awkward giant strength, trying to bury the carcass, twisting it to one side and other with wonderful ease. Once he got angry and suddenly gave it a tremendous cuff with his paw; in his bearing he had something half humorous, half devilish. I crept up within forty yards; but for several minutes he would not keep his head still. Then something attracted his attention in the forest, and he stood motionless looking toward it, broadside to me, with his fore paws planted on the carcass. This gave me my chance. I drew a very fine bead between his eye and ear, and pulled the trigger. He dropped like a steer when struck with a poleaxe.

If there is a good hiding-place handy it is better to lie in wait at the carcass. One day on the headwaters of the Madison, I found that a bear was coming to an elk I had shot some days before; and I at once determined to ambush the beast when he came back that evening. The carcass lay in the middle of a valley a quarter of a mile broad. The bottom of this valley was covered by an open forest of tall pines; a thick jungle of smaller evergreens marked where the mountains rose on either hand. There were a number of large rocks scattered here and there, one, of very convenient shape, being only some seventy or eighty yards from the carcass. Up this I clambered. It hid me perfectly, and on its top was a carpet of soft pine-needles, on which I could lie at my ease.

Hour after hour passed by. A little black woodpecker with a yellow crest ran nimbly up and down the tree-trunks for some time and then flitted away with a party of chickadees and nuthatches. Occasionally a Clark's crow soared about overhead or clung in any position to the swaying end of a pine branch, chattering and screaming. Flocks of crossbills, with wavy flight and plaintive calls, flew to a small mineral lick near by, where they scraped the clay with their queer little beaks.

As the westering sun sank out of sight beyond the mountains these sounds of bird life gradually died away. Under the great pines the evening was still with the silence of primeval desolation. The sense of sadness and loneliness, the melancholy of the wilderness, came over me like a spell. Every slight noise made my pulses throb as I lay motionless on the rock gazing intently into the gathering gloom. I began to fear that it would grow too dark to shoot before the grizzly came.

Suddenly, and without warning, the great bear stepped out of the bushes and trod across the pine-needles with such swift and silent footsteps that its bulk seemed unreal. It was very cautious, continually halting to peer around; and once it stood up on its hind legs and looked long down the valley toward the red west. As it reached the carcass I put a bullet between its shoulders. It rolled over, while the woods resounded with its savage roaring. Immediately it struggled to its feet and staggered off; and fell again to the next shot, squalling and yelling. Twice this was repeated; the brute being one of those bears which greet every wound with a great outcry, and sometimes seem to lose their feet when hit—although they will occasionally fight as savagely as their more silent brethren. In this case, the wounds were mortal, and the bear died before reaching the edge of the thicket.

I spent much of the fall of 1889 hunting on the head-waters of the Salmon and Snake in Idaho, and along the Montana boundary-line from the Big Hole Basin and the head of the Wisdom River to the neighborhood of Red Rock Pass and to the north and west of Henry's Lake. During the last fortnight my companion was the old mountain-man . . . always called either "Hank" or "Griff." He was a crabbedly honest old fellow, and a very skillful hunter; but he was worn out with age and rheumatism, and his temper had failed even faster than his bodily strength. He showed me a greater variety of game than I had seen before in so short a time; nor did I ever before or after make so successful a hunt. But he was an exceedingly disagreeable companion on account of his surly, moody ways. I generally had to get up first, to kindle the fire, and make ready breakfast, as he was very quarrelsome. Finally, during my absence from camp one day, while not very far from Red Rock Pass, he found my whiskey-flask, which I kept purely for emergencies, and drank all the contents. When I came back he was quite drunk. This was unbearable, and after some high words I left him, and struck off homeward through the woods on my own account. We had with us four pack and saddle horses; and of these I took a very intelligent and gentle little bronco mare, which possessed the invaluable trait of always staying near camp, even when not hobbled. I was not hampered with much of an outfit, having only my buffalo sleeping-bag, a fur coat, and my washing kit, with a couple of spare pairs of socks and some handkerchiefs. A frying-pan, some salt, flour, baking-powder, a small chunk of salt pork, and a hatchet, made up a light pack, which, with the bedding, I fastened across the stock-saddle by means of a rope and a spare packing cinch. My cartridges and knife were in my belt; my compass and matches, as always, in my pocket. I walked, while the little mare followed almost like a dog, often without my having to hold the lariat which served as halter.

The country was for the most part fairly open, as I kept near the foot-hills where glades and little prairies broke the pine forest. The trees were of small size. There was no regular trail, but the course was easy to keep, and I had no trouble of any kind save on the second day. That afternoon I was following a stream which at last "canyoned up"; that is, sank to the bottom of a canyon-like ravine impassable for a horse. I started up a side valley, intending to cross from its head coulees to those of another valley which would lead in below the canyon.

However, I got enmeshed in the tangle of winding valleys at the foot of the steep mountains, and as dusk was coming on I halted and camped in a little open spot by the side of a small, noisy brook, with crystal water. The place was carpeted with soft, wet, green moss, dotted red with the kinnikinic-berries, and at its edge, under the trees where the ground was dry, I threw down the buffalo bed on the mat of sweet-smelling pine-needles. Making camp took but a moment. I opened the pack, tossed the bedding on a smooth spot, knee-haltered the little mare, dragged up a few dry logs, and then strolled off, rifle on shoulder, through the frosty gloaming, to see if I could pick up a grouse for supper.

For half a mile I walked quickly and silently over the pine-needles, across a succession of slight ridges separated by narrow, shallow valleys. The forest here was composed of lodge-pole pines, which on the ridges grew close together, with tall slender trunks, while in the valleys the growth was more open. Though the sun was behind the mountains there was yet plenty of light by which to shoot, but it was fading rapidly.

At last, as I was thinking of turning toward camp, I stole up to the crest of one of the ridges, and looked over into the valley some sixty yards off. Immediately I caught the loom of some large, dark object; and another glance showed me a big grizzly walking slowly off with his head down. He was quartering to me, and I fired into his flank, the bullet, as I afterward found, ranging forward and piercing one lung. At the shot he uttered a loud, moaning grunt, and plunged forward at a heavy gallop, while I raced obliquely down the hill to cut him off. After going a few hundred feet he reached a laurel thicket, some thirty yards broad, and two or three times as long, which he did not leave. I ran up to the edge and there halted, not liking to venture into the mass of twisted, close-growing stems and glossy foliage. Moreover, as I halted, I heard him utter a peculiar, savage kind of whine from the heart of the brush. Accordingly, I began to skirt the edge, standing on tiptoe and gazing earnestly to see if I could not catch a glimpse of his hide. When I was at the narrowest part of the thicket, he suddenly left it directly opposite, and then wheeled and stood broadside to me on the hillside, a little above. He turned his head stiffly toward me; scarlet strings of froth hung from his lips; his eyes burned like embers in the gloom.

I held true, aiming behind the shoulder, and my bullet shattered the point or lower end of his heart, taking out a big nick. Instantly the great bear turned with a harsh roar of fury and challenge, blowing the bloody foam from his mouth, so that I saw the gleam of his white fangs; and then he charged straight at me, crashing and bounding through the laurel bushes, so that it was hard to aim. I waited till he came to a fallen tree, raking him as he topped it with a ball, which entered his chest and went through the cavity of his body, but he neither swerved nor flinched, and at the moment I did not know that I had struck him. He came steadily on, and in another second was almost upon me. I fired for his forehead, but my bullet went low, entering his open mouth, smashing his lower jaw and going into the neck. I leaped to one side almost as I pulled the trigger; and through the hanging smoke the first thing I saw was his paw as he made a vicious side blow at me. The rush of his charge carried him past. As he struck he lurched forward, leaving a pool of bright blood where his muzzle hit the ground; but he recovered himself and made two or three jumps onward, while I hurriedly jammed a couple of cartridges into the magazine, my rifle holding only four, all of which I had fired. Then he tried to pull up, but as he did so his muscles seemed suddenly to give way, his head drooped, and he rolled over and over like a shot rabbit. Each of my first three bullets had inflicted a mortal wound.

It was already twilight, and I merely opened the carcass, and then trotted back to camp. Next morning I returned and with much labor took off the skin. The fur was very fine, the animal being in excellent trim, and unusually bright-colored. Unfortunately, packing it out I lost the skull, and had to supply its place with one of plaster. The beauty of the trophy, and the memory of the circumstances under which I procured it, make me value it perhaps more highly than any other in my house.

This is the only instance in which I have been regularly charged by a grizzly. On the whole, the danger of hunting these great bears has been much exaggerated. At the beginning of the present century, when white hunters first encountered the grizzly, he was doubtless an exceedingly savage beast, prone to attack without provocation, and a redoubtable foe to persons armed with the clumsy, small-bore, muzzle-loading rifles of the day. He has been hunted for sport and hunted for his pelt and hunted for the bounty and hunted as a dangerous enemy to stock, until, save in the very wildest districts, he has learned to be more wary than a deer and to avoid man's presence almost as carefully as the most timid kind of game. Except in rare cases he will not attack of his own accord, and, as a rule, even when wounded, his object is escape rather than battle.

Still, when fairly brought to bay, or when moved by a sudden fit of ungovernable anger, the grizzly is a very dangerous antagonist.

🌿 🌿 🌿

It is always well to have two men in following a wounded bear under such conditions. This is not necessary, however, and a good hunter, rather than lose his quarry, will, under ordinary circumstances, follow and attack it, no matter how tangled the fastness in which it has sought refuge; but he must act warily and with the utmost caution and resolution, if he wishes to escape a terrible and probably fatal mauling. An experienced hunter is rarely rash, and never heedless; he will not, when alone, follow a wounded bear into a thicket, if by the exercise of patience, skill, and knowledge of the game's habits he can avoid the necessity; but it is idle to talk of the feat as something which ought in no case to be attempted. While danger ought never to be needlessly incurred, it is yet true that the keenest zest in sport comes from its presence, and from the consequent exercise of the qualities necessary to overcome it. The most thrilling moments of an American hunter's life are those in which, with every sense on the alert, and with nerves strung to the highest point, he is following alone into the heart of its forest fastness the fresh and bloody footprints of an angered grizzly; and no other triumph of American hunting can compare with the victory to be thus gained.

The Badlands ranchman, 1885.

RANCHMAN AND COWBOY

IN COWBOY LAND

Among TR's fondest memories were those of his days in the Dakota territory in the 1880s doing the work of a cowboy. He was greeted in the Badlands as a dude from the East but quickly earned the respect and even the admiration of the tough-skinned and range-hardened men of the cattle country. This description of cowboy life from his autobiography, published by Charles Scribner's Sons in 1913, shows to advantage his keen eye for detail and his ability to draw the reader into his adventure.

◆◇◆

In those days on a cow-ranch the men were apt to be away on the various round-ups at least half the time. It was interesting and exciting work, and except for the lack of sleep on the spring and summer round-ups it was not exhausting work; compared to lumbering or mining or blacksmithing, to sit in the saddle is an easy form of labor. The ponies were of course grass-fed and unshod. Each man had his own string of nine or ten. One pony would be used for the morning work, one for the afternoon, and neither would again be used for the next three days. A separate pony was kept for night riding.

The spring and early summer round-ups were especially for the branding of calves. There was much hard work and some risk on a round-up, but also much fun. The meeting-place was appointed weeks beforehand, and all the ranchmen of the territory to be covered by the round-up sent their representatives. There were no fences in the West that I knew, and their place was taken by the cowboy and the branding-iron. The cattle wandered free. Each calf was branded with the brand of the cow it was following. Sometimes in winter there was what we called line riding; that is, camps were established and the line riders travelled a definite beat across the desolate waste of snow, to and fro from one camp to another, to prevent the cattle from drifting. But as a rule nothing was done to keep the cattle in any one place. In the spring there was a general round-up in each locality. Each outfit took part in its own round-up and all the outfits of a given region combined to send representatives to the two or three round-ups that covered the neighborhoods near by into which their cattle might drift. For example, our Little Missouri round-up generally worked down the river from a distance of some fifty or sixty miles above my ranch toward the Kildeer Mountains, about the same distance below. In addition we would usually send representatives to the Yellowstone round-up, and to the round-up along the upper Little Missouri, and, moreover, if we heard that cattle had drifted, perhaps toward the Indian reservation southeast of us, we would send a wagon and rider after them.

At the meeting-point, which might be in the valley of a half-dry stream or in some broad bottom of the river itself, or perchance by a couple of ponds under some queerly shaped butte that was a landmark for the region roundabout, we would all gather on the appointed day. The chuck-wagons, containing the bedding and food, each drawn by four horses and driven by the teamster-cook, would come jolting and rattling over the uneven sward. Accompanying each wagon were eight or ten riders, the cow-punchers, while their horses, a band of a hundred or so, were driven by the two herders, one of whom was known as the day wrangler and one as the night wrangler. The men were lean, sinewy fellows, accustomed to riding half-broken horses at any speed over any country by day or by night. They wore flannel shirts, with loose handkerchiefs knotted round their necks, broad hats, high-heeled boots with jingling spurs, and sometimes leather chaps, although often they merely had their trousers tucked into the tops of their high boots. There was a good deal of rough horse-play, and, as with any other gathering of men or boys of high animal spirits, the horse-play sometimes became very rough indeed; and as the men usually carried revolvers, and as there were occasionally one or two noted gun-fighters among them, there was now and then a shooting affray. A man who was a coward or who shirked his work had a bad time, of course; a man could not afford to let himself be bullied or treated as a butt; and, on the other hand, if he was "looking for a fight," he was certain to find it. But my own experience was that if a man did not talk until his associates knew him well and liked him, and if he did his work, he never had any difficulty in getting on. In my own round-up district I speedily grew to be friends with most of the men. When I went among strangers I always had to spend twenty-four hours in living down the fact that I wore spectacles, remaining as long as I could judiciously deaf to any side-remarks about "four-eyes," unless it became evident that my being quiet was misconstrued and that it was better to bring matters to a head at once.

If, for instance, I was sent off to represent the Little Missouri brands on some neighboring round-up, such as the Yellowstone, I usually showed that kind of diplomacy which consists in not uttering one word that can be avoided. I would probably have a couple of days' solitary ride, mounted on one horse and driving eight or ten others before me, one of them carrying my bedding. Loose horses drive best at a trot, or canter, and if a man is travelling alone in this fashion it is a good thing to have them reach the camp-ground sufficiently late to make them desire to feed and sleep where they are until morning. In consequence I never spent more than two days on the journey from whatever the point was at which I left the Little Missouri, sleeping the one night for as limited a number of hours as possible.

As soon as I reached the meeting-place I would find out the wagon to which I was assigned. Riding to it, I turned my horses into the saddle-band and reported to the wagon boss, or, in his absence, to the cook—always a privileged character, who was allowed and expected to order men around. He would usually grumble savagely and profanely about my having been put with his wagon, but this was merely conventional on his part; and if I sat down and said nothing he would probably soon ask me if I wanted anything to eat, to which the correct answer was that I was not hungry and would wait until meal-time. The bedding-rolls of the riders would be strewn round the grass, and I would put mine down a little outside the ring, where I would not be in any one's way, with my six or eight branding-irons beside it. The men would ride in, laughing and talking with one another, and perhaps nodding to me. One of their number, usually the wagon foreman, might put some question to me as to what brands I represented, but no other word would be addressed to me, nor would I be expected to volunteer any conversation. Supper would consist of bacon, Dutch oven bread, and possibly beef; once I won the good graces of my companions at the outset by appearing with two antelope which I had shot. After supper I would roll up in my bedding as soon as possible, and the others would follow suit at their pleasure.

At three in the morning or thereabouts, at a yell from the cook, all hands would turn hurriedly out. Dressing was a simple affair. Then each man rolled and corded his bedding—if he did not, the cook would leave it behind and he would go without any for the rest of the trip—and came to the fire, where he picked out a tin cup, tin plate, and knife and fork, helped himself to coffee and to whatever food there was, and ate it standing or squatting as best suited him. Dawn was probably breaking by this time, and the trampling of unshod hoofs showed that the night wrangler was bringing in the pony-herd. Two of the men would then run ropes from the wagon at right angles to one another, and into this as a corral the horses would be driven. Each man might rope one of his own horses, or more often point it out to the most skillful roper of the outfit, who would rope it for him—for if the man was an unskillful roper and roped the wrong horse or roped the horse in the wrong place there was a chance of the whole herd stampeding. Each man then saddled and bridled his horse. This was usually followed by some resolute bucking on the part of two or three of the horses, especially in the early days of each round-up. The bucking was always a source of amusement to all the men whose horses did not buck and these fortunate ones would gather round giving ironical advice, and especially adjuring the rider not to "go to leather"—that is, not to steady himself in the saddle by catching hold of the saddle-horn.

As soon as the men had mounted, the whole outfit started on the long circle, the morning circle. Usually the ranch foreman who bossed a given wagon was put in charge of the men of one group by the round-up foreman; he might keep his men together until they had gone some ten or fifteen miles from camp, and then drop them in couples at different points. Each couple made its way toward the wagon, gathering all the cattle it could find. The morning's ride might last six or eight hours, and it was still longer before some of the men got in. Singly and in twos and threes they appeared from every quarter of the horizon, the dust rising from the hoofs of the steers and bulls, the cows and calves, they had collected. Two or three of the men were left to take care of the herd while the others changed horses, ate a hasty dinner, and then came out to the afternoon work. This consisted of each man in succession being sent into the herd, usually with a companion, to cut out the cows of his brand or brands which were followed by unbranded calves, and also to cut out any mavericks or unbranded yearlings. We worked each animal gently out to the edge of the herd, and then with a sudden dash took it off at a run. It was always desperately anxious to break back and rejoin the herd. There was much breakneck galloping and twisting and turning before its desire was thwarted and it was driven to join the rest of the cut—that is, the other animals which had been cut out, and which were being held by one or two other men. Cattle hate being alone, and it was no easy matter to hold the first one or two that were cut out; but soon they got a little herd of their own, and then they were contented. When the cutting out had all been done, the calves were branded, and all misadventures of the "calf wrestlers," the men who seized, threw, and held each calf when roped by the mounted roper, were hailed with yelling laughter. Then the animals which for one reason or another it was desired to drive along with the round-up were put into one herd and left in charge of a couple of night guards, and the rest of us would loaf back to the wagon for supper and bed.

By this time I would have been accepted as one of the rest of the outfit, and all strangeness would have passed off, the attitude of my fellow cow-punchers being one of friendly forgiveness even toward my spectacles. Night guards for the cattle-herd were then assigned by the captain of the wagon, or perhaps by the round-up foreman, according to the needs of the case, the guards standing for two hours at a time from eight in the evening till four in the morning. The first and last watches were preferable, because sleep was not broken as in both of the other two. If things went well, the cattle would soon bed down and nothing further would occur until morning, when there was a repetition of the work, the wagon moving each day eight or ten miles to some appointed camping-place.

Each man would picket his night horse near the wagon, usually choosing the quietest animal in his string for that purpose, because to saddle and mount a "mean" horse at night is not pleasant. When utterly tired, it was hard to have to get up for one's trick at night herd. Nevertheless, on ordinary nights the two hours round the cattle in the still darkness were pleasant. The loneliness, under the vast empty sky, and the silence, in which the breathing of the cattle sounded loud, and the alert readiness to meet any emergency which might suddenly arise out of the formless night, all combined to give one a sense of subdued interest. Then, one soon got to know the cattle of marked individuality, the ones that led the others into mischief; and one also grew to recognize the traits they all possessed in common, and the impulses which, for instance, made a whole herd get up toward midnight, each beast turning round and then lying down again. But by the end of the watch each rider had studied the cattle until it grew monotonous, and heartily welcomed his relief guard. A newcomer, of course, had any amount to learn, and sometimes the simplest things were those which brought him to grief.

One night early in my career I failed satisfactorily to identify the direction in which I was to go in order to reach the night herd. It was a pitch-dark night. I managed to get started wrong, and I never found either the herd or the wagon again until sunrise, when I was greeted with withering scorn by the injured cow-puncher, who had been obliged to stand double guard because I failed to relieve him.

There were other misadventures that I met with where the excuse was greater. The punchers on night guard usually rode round the cattle in reverse directions; calling and singing to them if the beasts seemed restless, to keep them quiet. On rare occasions something happened that made the cattle stampede, and then the duty of the riders was to keep with them as long as possible and try gradually to get control of them.

One night there was a heavy storm, and all of us who were at the wagons were obliged to turn out hastily to help the night herders. After a while there was a terrific peal of thunder, the lightning struck right by the herd, and away all the beasts went, heads and horns and tails in the air. For a minute or two I could make out nothing except the dark forms of the beasts running on every side of me, and I should have been very sorry if my horse had stumbled, for those behind would have trodden me down. Then the herd split, part going to one side, while the other part seemingly kept straight ahead, and I galloped as hard as ever beside them. I was trying to reach the point—the leading animals—in order to turn them, when suddenly there was a tremendous splashing in front. I could dimly make out that the cattle immediately ahead and to one side of me were disappearing, and the next moment the horse and I went off a cut bank into the Little Missouri. I bent away back in the saddle, and though the horse almost went down he just recovered himself, and, plunging and struggling through water and quicksand, we made the other side. Here I discovered that there was another cowboy with the same part of the herd that I was with; but almost immediately we separated. I galloped hard through a bottom covered with big cottonwood trees, and stopped the part of the herd that I was with, but very soon they broke on me again, and repeated this twice. Finally toward morning the few I had left came to a halt.

It had been raining hard for some time. I got off my horse and leaned against a tree, but before long the infernal cattle started on again, and I had to ride after them. Dawn came soon after this, and I was able to make out where I was and head the cattle back, collecting other little bunches as I went. After a while I came on a cowboy on foot carrying his saddle on his head. He was my companion of the previous night. His horse had gone full speed into a tree and killed itself, the man, however, not being hurt. I could not help him, as I had all I could do to handle the cattle. When I got them to the wagon, most of the other men had already come in and the riders were just starting on the long circle. One of the men changed my horse for me while I ate a hasty breakfast and then we were off for the day's work.

As only about half of the night herd had been brought back, the circle riding was particularly heavy, and it was ten hours before we were back at the wagon. We then changed horses again and worked the whole herd until after sunset, finishing just as it grew too dark to do anything more. By this time I had been nearly forty hours in the saddle, changing horses five times, and my clothes had thoroughly dried on me, and I fell asleep as soon as I touched the bedding. Fortunately some men who had gotten in late in the morning had had their sleep during the daytime, so that the rest of us escaped night guard and were not called until four next morning. Nobody ever gets enough sleep on a round-up.

RANCHING IN THE BADLANDS

"Civilization" is an important word to TR. It recurs again and again in his writing, often to rationalize the advance of white and Western interests in the world. He also expresses here a tough-minded attitude about relations with Indians. While acknowledging depredations committed by whites, he scorns the "sentimental nonsense" that settlers of the West stole the land from the Indians. This piece is drawn from one of TR's earliest works, Hunting Trips of a Ranchman, *published by G. P. Putnam's Sons in 1885 and often reprinted.*

The great middle plains of the United States, parts of which are still scantily peopled by men of Mexican parentage, while other parts have been but recently won from the warlike tribes of Horse Indians, now form a broad pastoral belt, stretching in a north and south line from British America to the Rio Grande. Throughout this great belt of grazing-land almost the only industry is stock-raising, which is here engaged in on a really gigantic scale; and it is already nearly covered with the ranches of the stockmen, except on those isolated tracts (often themselves of great extent) from which the red men look hopelessly and sullenly out upon their old hunting-grounds, now roamed over by the countless herds of long-horned cattle. The northern portion of this belt is that which has been most lately thrown open to the whites; and it is with this part only that we have to do.

The Northern cattle plains occupy the basin of the Upper Missouri; that is, they occupy all of the land drained by the tributaries of that river, and by the river itself, before it takes its long trend to the southeast. They stretch from the rich wheat-farms of central Dakota to the Rocky Mountains, and southward to the Black Hills and the Bighorn chain, thus including all of Montana, northern Wyoming, and extreme western Dakota. The character of this rolling, broken, plains country is everywhere much the same. It is a high, nearly treeless region, of light rainfall, crossed by streams which are sometimes rapid torrents and sometimes merely strings of shallow pools. In places, it stretches out into deserts of alkali and sagebrush or into nearly level prairies of short grass, extending many miles without a break; elsewhere there are rolling hills, sometimes of considerable height; and in other places the ground is rent and broken into the most fantastic shapes, partly by volcanic action and partly by the action of water in a dry climate. These latter portions form the famous Bad Lands. Cottonwood trees fringe the streams or stand in groves on the alluvial bottoms of the rivers; and some of the steep hills and canyon sides are clad with pines or stunted cedars. In the early spring, when the young blades first sprout, the land looks green and bright; but during the rest of the year there is no such appearance of freshness, for the short bunch-grass is almost brown, and the gray-green sagebush, bitter and withered-looking, abounds everywhere, and gives a peculiarly barren aspect to the landscape.

It is but little over half a dozen years since these lands were won from the Indians. They were their only remaining great hunting-grounds, and toward the end of the last decade all of the Northern plains tribes went on the war-path in a final desperate effort to preserve them. After bloody fighting and protracted campaigns, they were defeated, and the country thrown open to the whites, while the building of the Northern Pacific Railroad gave immi-gration an immense impetus. There were great quantities of game, especially buffalo, and the hunters who thronged in to pursue the huge herds of the latter were the rough forerunners of civilization. No longer dreading the Indians and having the railway on which to transport the robes, they fol-lowed the buffalo in season and out, until, in 1883, the herds were practi-cally destroyed. But, meanwhile, the cattlemen formed the vanguard of the white settlers. Already the hardy Southern stockmen had passed up with their wild-looking herds to the very border of the dangerous land, and even into it, trusting to luck and their own prowess for their safety; and the instant the danger was even partially removed, their cattle swarmed north-ward along the streams. Some Eastern men, seeing the extent of the grazing country, brought stock out by the railroad, and the short-horned beasts became almost as plenty as the wilder-looking Southern steers. At the pre-sent time, indeed, the cattle of these Northern ranges show more shorthorn than longhorn blood.

🌿 🌿 🌿

The cattle rove free over the hills and prairies, picking up their own living even in winter, all the animals of each herd having certain distinctive brands on them. But little attempt is made to keep them within definite bounds, and they wander whither they wish, except that the ranchmen generally com-bine to keep some of their cowboys riding lines to prevent them straying away altogether. The missing ones are generally recovered in the annual round-ups, when the calves are branded. These round-ups, in which many outfits join together, and which cover hundreds of miles of territory, are the busiest periods of the year for the stockmen, who then, with their cowboys, work from morning till night. In winter, little is done except a certain amount of line-riding.

The cowboys form a class by themselves, and are now quite as typical representatives of the wilder side of Western life as were a few years ago the skin-clad hunters and trappers. They are mostly of native birth, and although there are among them wild spirits from every land, yet the latter soon become undistinguishable from their American companions, for these plainsmen are far from being so heterogeneous as is commonly supposed. On the contrary, all have a curious similarity to each other; existence in the West seems to put the same stamp upon each and every one of them. Sinewy, hardy, self-reliant, their life forces them to be both daring and adventurous, and the passing over their heads of a few years leaves printed on their faces certain lines which tell of dangers quietly fronted and hardships uncomplainingly endured. They are far from being as lawless as they are described; though they sometimes cut queer antics when, after many months of lonely life, they come into a frontier town in which drinking and gambling are the only recognized forms of amusement, and where pleasure and vice are considered synonymous terms. On the round-ups, or when a number get together, there is much boisterous, often foul-mouthed, mirth; but they are rather silent, self-contained men when with strangers, and are frank and hospitable to a degree. The Texans are perhaps the best at the actual cowboy work. They are absolutely fearless riders and understand well the habits of the half-wild cattle, being unequalled in those most trying times when, for instance, the cattle are stampeded by a thunder-storm at night, while in the use of the rope they are only excelled by the Mexicans. On the other hand, they are prone to drink, and, when drunk, to shoot. Many Kansans, and others from the Northern States, have also taken up the life of late years, and though these scarcely reach, in point of skill and dash, the standard of the Southerners, who may be said to be born in the saddle, yet they are to the full as resolute and even more trustworthy. My own foremen were originally Eastern backwoodsmen.

ᘜ ᘜ ᘜ

My own ranches, the Elkhorn and the Chimney Butte, lie along the eastern border of the cattle country, where the Little Missouri flows through the heart of the Bad Lands. This, like most other plains rivers, has a broad, shallow bed, through which in times of freshets runs a muddy torrent that neither man nor beast can pass; at other seasons of the year it is very shallow, spreading out into pools, between which the trickling water may be but a few inches deep. Even then, however, it is not always easy to cross, for the bottom is filled with quicksands and mud-holes. The river flows in long sigmoid curves through an alluvial valley of no great width. The amount of this alluvial land enclosed by a single bend is called a bottom, which may be either covered with cottonwood trees or else be simply a great grass meadow. From the edges of the valley the land rises abruptly in steep high buttes, whose crests are sharp and jagged. This broken country extends back from the river for many miles, and has been called always, by Indians, French voyageurs, and American trappers alike, the "Bad Lands," partly from its dreary and forbidding aspect and partly from the difficulty experienced in traveling through it.

❦ ❦ ❦

In spite of their look of savage desolation, the Bad Lands make a good cattle country, for there is plenty of nourishing grass and excellent shelter from the winter storms. The cattle keep close to them in the cold months, while in the summertime they wander out on the broad prairies stretching back of them, or come down the river-bottoms.

My home-ranch stands on the river brink. From the low, long veranda, shaded by leafy cottonwoods, one looks across sand-bars and shallows to a strip of meadowland, behind which rises a line of sheer cliffs and grassy plateaus. This veranda is a pleasant place in the summer evenings when a cool breeze stirs along the river and blows in the faces of the tired men, who loll back in their rocking-chairs (what true American does not enjoy a rocking chair?), book in hand—though they do not often read the books, but rock gently to and fro, gazing sleepily out at the weird-looking buttes opposite, until their sharp lines grow indistinct and purple in the afterglow of the sunset. The story-high house of hewn logs is clean and neat, with many rooms, so that one can be alone if one wishes to. The nights in summer are cool and pleasant, and there are plenty of bearskins and buffalo-robes, trophies of our own skill, with which to bid defiance to the bitter cold of winter. In summertime, we are not much within doors, for we rise before dawn and work hard enough to be willing to go to bed soon after nightfall. The long winter evenings are spent sitting round the hearthstone, while the pine logs roar and crackle, and the men play checkers or chess, in the firelight. The rifles stand in the corners of the room or rest across the elk-antlers which jut out from over the fireplace. From the deer-horns ranged along the walls and thrust into the beams and rafters hang heavy overcoats of wolfskin or coonskin, and otter-fur or beaver-fur caps and gauntlets. Rough board shelves hold a number of books, without which some of the evenings would be long indeed.

The charm of ranch life comes in its freedom and the vigorous open-air existence it forces a man to lead. Except when hunting in bad ground, the whole time away from the house is spent in the saddle, and there are so many ponies that a fresh one can always be had. These ponies are of every size and disposition, and rejoice in names as different as their looks. Hackamore, Wire Fence, Steel Trap, War Cloud, Pinto, Buckskin, Circus, and Standing Jimmie are among those that, as I write, are running frantically round the corral in the vain effort to avoid the rope, wielded by the dexterous and sinewy hand of a broad-hatted cowboy.

A ranchman is kept busy most of the time, but his hardest work comes during the spring and fall round-ups, when the calves are branded or the beeves gathered for market. Our round-up district includes the Beaver and Little Beaver creeks (both of which always contain running water, and head up toward each other) and as much of the river, nearly two hundred miles in extent, as lies between their mouths. All the ranches along the lines of these two creeks and the river space between join in sending from one to three or four men to the round-up, each man taking eight ponies; and for every six or seven men there will be a four-horse wagon to carry the blankets and mess-kit. The whole, including perhaps forty or fifty cowboys, is under the head of one first-class foreman, styled the captain of the round-up. Beginning at one end of the line, the round-up works along clear to the other. Starting at the head of one creek, the wagons and the herd of spare ponies go down ten or twelve miles, while the cowboys, divided into small parties, scour the neighboring country, covering a great extent of territory, and in the evening come into the appointed place with all the cattle they have seen. This big herd, together with the pony herd, is guarded and watched all night, and driven during the day. At each home-ranch (where there is always a large corral fitted for the purpose) all the cattle of that brand are cut out from the rest of the herd, which is to continue its journey; and the cows and calves are driven into the corral, where the latter are roped, thrown, and branded. In throwing the rope from horseback, the loop, held in the right hand, is swung round and round the head by a motion of the wrist; when on foot, the hand is usually held by the side, the loop dragging on the ground. It is a pretty sight to see a man who knows how to use the rope; again and again an expert will catch fifty animals by the leg without making a misthrow. But unless practice is begun very young, it is hard to become really proficient.

Cutting out cattle, next to managing a stampeded herd at night, is that part of the cowboy's work needing the boldest and most skillful horsemanship. A young heifer or steer is very loath to leave the herd, always tries to break back into it, can run like a deer, and can dodge like a rabbit; but a thorough cattle-pony enjoys the work as much as its rider, and follows a beast like a four-footed fate through every double and turn. The ponies for the cutting-out or afternoon work are small and quick; those used for the circle-riding in the morning have need rather to be strong and rangey.

The work on a round-up is very hard, but although the busiest it is also the pleasantest part of a cowboy's existence. His food is good, though coarse, and his sleep is sound indeed; while the work is very exciting, and is done in company under the stress of an intense rivalry between all the men, both as to their own skill and as to the speed and training of their horses. Clumsiness and, still more, the slightest approach to timidity expose a man to the roughest and most merciless raillery; and the unfit are weeded out by a very rapid process of natural selection. When the work is over for the day the men gather round the fire for an hour or two to sing songs, talk, smoke, and tell stories; and he who has a good voice, or, better still, can play a fiddle or banjo, is sure to receive his meed of most sincere homage.

Though the ranchman is busiest during the round-up, yet he is far from idle at other times. He rides round among the cattle to see if any are sick, visits any outlying camp of his men, hunts up any bands of ponies which may stray—and they are always straying—superintends the haying, and, in fact, does not often find that he has too much leisure on his hands. Even in winter he has work which must be done. His ranch supplies milk, butter, eggs, and potatoes, and his rifle keeps him, at least intermittently, in fresh meat; but coffee, sugar, flour, and whatever else he may want has to be hauled in, and this is generally done when the ice will bear. Then fire-wood must be chopped; or, if there is a good vein of coal, as on my ranch, the coal must be dug out and hauled in. Altogether, though the ranchman will have time enough to take shooting trips, he will be very far from having time to make shooting a business, as a stranger who comes for nothing else can afford to do.

There are now no Indians left in my immediate neighborhood, though a small party of harmless Grosventres occasionally passes through; yet it is but six years since the Sioux surprised and killed five men in a log station just south of me, where the Fort Keogh trail crosses the river; and, two years ago, when I went down on the prairies toward the Black Hills, there was still danger from Indians. That summer the buffalo-hunters had killed a couple of Crows, and while we were on the prairie a long-range skirmish occurred near us between some Cheyennes and a number of cowboys. In fact, we ourselves were one day scared by what we thought to be a party of Sioux;

but, on riding toward them, they proved to be half-breed Crees who were more afraid of us than we were of them.

During the past century a good deal of sentimental nonsense has been talked about our taking the Indians' land. Now, I do not mean to say for a moment that gross wrong has not been done the Indians, both by government and individuals, again and again. The government makes promises impossible to perform, and then fails to do even what it might toward their fulfillment; and where brutal and reckless frontiersmen are brought into contact with a set of treacherous, revengeful and fiendishly cruel savages a long series of outrages by both sides is sure to follow. But as regards taking the land, at least from the Western Indians, the simple truth is that the latter never had any real ownership in it at all. Where the game was plenty, there they hunted; they followed it when it moved away to new hunting-grounds, unless they were prevented by stronger rivals, and to most of the land on which we found them they had no stronger claim than that of having a few years previously butchered the original occupants. When my cattle came to the Little Missouri, the region was only inhabited by a score or so of white hunters; their title to it was quite as good as that of most Indian tribes to the lands they claim; yet nobody dreamed of saying that these hunters owned the country. Each would eventually have kept his own claim of 160 acres, and no more. The Indians should be treated in just the same way that we treat the white settlers. Give each his little claim; if, as would generally happen, he declined this, why, then let him share the fate of the thousands of white hunters and trappers who have lived on the game that the settlement of the country has exterminated, and let him, like these whites, who will not work, perish from the face of the earth which he cumbers.

The doctrine seems merciless, and so it is; but it is just and rational for all that. It does not do to be merciful to a few at the cost of justice to the many. The cattlemen at least keep herds and build houses on the land; yet I would not for a moment debar settlers from the right of entry to the cattle country, though their coming in means in the end the destruction of us and our industry.

For we ourselves and the life that we lead will shortly pass away from the plains as completely as the red and white hunters who have vanished from before our herds. The free, open-air life of the ranchman, the pleasantest and healthiest life in America, is from its very nature ephemeral. The broad and boundless prairies have already been bounded and will soon be made narrow. It is scarcely a figure of speech to say that the tide of white settlement during the last few years has risen over the West like a flood; and the cattlemen are but the spray from the crest of the wave, thrown far in advance, but soon to be overtaken. As the settlers throng into the lands and seize the good ground, especially that near the streams, the great fenceless ranches, where the cattle and their mounted herdsmen wandered unchecked over hundreds of thousands of acres, will be broken up and divided into corn land, or else into small grazing farms where a few hundred head of stock are closely watched and taken care of. Of course the most powerful ranches, owned by wealthy corporations or individuals, and already firmly rooted in the soil, will long resist this crowding; in places, where the ground is not suited to agriculture, or where, through the old Spanish land-grants, the title has been acquired to a great tract of territory, cattle ranching will continue for a long time, though in a greatly modified form; elsewhere, I doubt if it lasts out the present century.

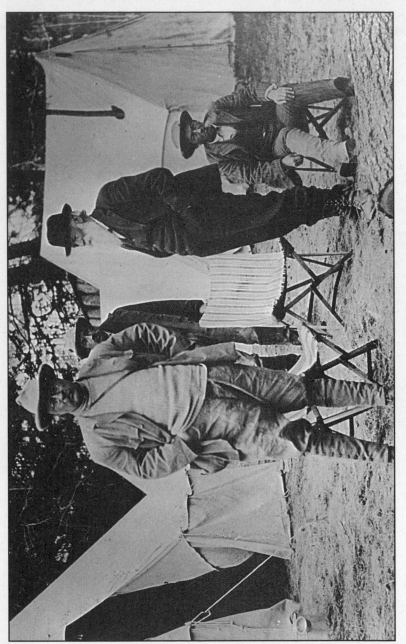

TR with John Burroughs, American naturalist, 1903.

9

CONSERVATIONIST AND NATURALIST

FORESTRY AND BUSINESS

*T*he management of forests and other natural resources has long been the focus of national political debate, a debate TR did much to define during his presidency. As a naturalist, ranchman, and hunter, TR had a lifelong interest in conservation, and as president he was deeply committed to an activist role for government in this field. As with many other issues, TR here attempted to reconcile the public interest with the interests of the business community from which he and the Republican party drew much support. This address to the Forest Congress was delivered in Washington on January 5, 1905. Before the year was out, TR had succeeded in establishing a forestry service in the Department of Agriculture to further the work of conservation.

◆◇◆

It is a pleasure to greet all of you here this afternoon, but of course especially the members of the American Forest Congress. You have made, by your coming, a meeting which is without parallel in the history of forestry. And, Mr. Secretary,[1] I must take this opportunity of saying to you what you so amply deserve, that no man in this country has done so much as you have done in the last eight years to make it possible to take a business view from the standpoint of all the country of just such questions as this. It is not many years since such a meeting as this would have been regarded as chimerical; the thought of it would have been regarded as absolutely chimerical. In the old pioneer days the American had but one thought about a tree, and that was to cut it down; and the mental attitude of the nation toward the forests was largely conditioned upon the fact that the life-work of the earlier generations of our people had been of necessity to hew down the forests, for they had to make clearings on which to live; and it was not until half a century of our national life had passed that any considerable body of American citizens began to live under conditions where the tree ceased to be something to be cleared off the earth. It always takes time to get the mind of a people accustomed to any change in conditions, and it took a long time to get the mind of our people, as a whole, accustomed to the fact that they had to alter their attitude toward the forests. For the first time the great business and the forest interests of the nation have joined together, through delegates altogether worthy of the organizations they represent, to consider their individual and their common interests in the forest. This congress may well be called a meeting of forest users, for that the users of the forest come together to consider how best to combine use with preservation is the significant fact of the meeting, the fact full of powerful promise for the forests of the future.

The producers, the manufacturers, and the great common carriers of the nation had long failed to realize their true and vital relation to the great forests of the United States, and the forests and industries both suffered from that failure. The suffering of the industries in such case comes after the destruction of the forests, but it is just as inevitable as that destruction. If the forest is destroyed it is only a question of a relatively short time before the business interests suffer in consequence. All of you know that there is opportunity in any new country for the development of the type of temporary inhabitant whose idea is to skin the country and go somewhere else. You all know, and especially those of you from the West, the individual

---

[1] TR refers here to Secretary of Agriculture James Wilson.

whose idea of developing the country is to cut every stick of timber off of it and then leave a barren desert for the home-makers who comes in after him. That man is a curse and not a blessing to the country. The prop of the country must be the business man who intends so to run his business that it will be profitable for his children after him. That is the type of business that it is worth while to develop. The time of indifference and misunderstanding has gone by. Your coming is a very great step toward the solution of the forest problem—a problem which cannot be settled until it is settled right. And it cannot be settled right until the forces which bring that settlement about come, not from the government, not even from the newspapers and from the public sentiment in general, but from the active, intelligent, and effective interest of the men to whom the forest is important from the business point of view, because they use it and its product, and whose interest is therefore concrete instead of general and diffuse. I do not in the least underrate the power of an awakened public opinion; but in the final test it will be the attitude of the industries of the country which more than anything else will determine whether or not our forests are to be preserved. It is because of their recognition of that prime material fact that so much has been accomplished, Mr. Wilson, by those interested under you and in the other departments of the government in the preservation of the forests. We want the active and zealous help of every man far-sighted enough to realize the importance from the standpoint of the nation's welfare in the future of preserving the forests; but that help by itself will not avail. It will not even be the main factor in bringing about the result toward which we are striving; the main factor must come from the intelligence of the business interests concerned, so that the manufacturer, the railway man, the miner, the lumberman, the dealer in lumber, shall appreciate that it is of direct interest to them to preserve through use instead of waste, the great resources upon which they depend for the successful development of their business. This is true because by far the greater part of all our forests must pass into the hands of forest users, whether directly or through the government, which will continue to hold some of them, but only as trustee. The forest is for use, and its users will decide its future. It was only a few years ago that the practical lumberman felt that the forest expert was a man who wished to see the forests preserved as bric-a-brac, and the American business man was not prepared to do much from the bric-a-brac standpoint. Now, I think, we have got a working agreement between the forester and the business man whose business is the use of the forest. We have got them to come together with the understanding that they must work for a common end, work to see the forest preserved for use. The great significance of this congress comes from the fact that henceforth the movement for the conservative use of the forest is to come mainly from within, not from without; from the men who are actively interested in the use of the forest in one way or another, even more than from those whose interest is philanthropic and general. The difference means, as the difference in such a case always does mean, to a large extent the difference between mere agitation and actual execution, between the hope of accomplishment and the thing done. We believe that at last forces have been set in motion which will convert the once distant prospect of the conservation of the forest by wise use into the practical accomplishment of that great end; and of this most hopeful and significant fact the coming together of this congress is the sufficient proof.

※ ※ ※

If the present rate of forest destruction is allowed to continue, with nothing to offset it, a timber famine in the future is inevitable. Fire, wasteful and destructive forms of lumbering, and the legitimate use, taken together, are destroying our forest resources far more rapidly than they are being replaced. It is difficult to imagine what such a timber famine would mean to our resources. And the period of recovery from the injuries which a timber famine would entail would be measured by the slow growth of the trees themselves. Remember that you can prevent such a timber famine occurring by wise action taken in time, but once the famine occurs there is no possible way of hurrying the growth of the trees necessary to relieve it. You have got to act in time or else the nation would have to submit to prolonged suffering after it had become too late for forethought to avail. Fortunately, the remedy is a simple one, and your presence here to-day is a most encouraging sign that there will be such forethought. It is the great merit of the Department of Agriculture in the forest work that its efforts have been directed to enlist the sympathy and co-operation of the users of wood, water, and grass, and to show that forestry will and does pay, rather than to exhaust itself in the futile attempt to introduce conservative methods by any other means. I believe most emphatically in sentiment, but I want the sentiment to be put in co-operation with the business interests, and that is what is being done. The policy is one of helpfulness throughout, and never of hostility or coercion toward any legitimate interest whatsoever. In the very nature of things it can make little progress apart from you. Whatever it may be possible for the government to accomplish, its work must ultimately fail unless your interest and support give it permanence and power. It is only as the producing and commercial interests of the country come to realize that they need to have trees growing up in the forest not less than they need the product of the trees cut down that we may hope to see the permanent prosperity of both safely secured.

This statement is true not only as to forests in private ownership, but as to the national forests as well. Unless the men from the West believe in forest preservation the Western forests cannot be preserved. We here at the head-quarters of the National Government recognize that absolutely. We believe, we know, that it is essential for the well-being of the people of the States of the great plains, the States of the Rockies, the States of the Pacific slope, that the forests shall be preserved, and we know also that our belief will count for nothing unless the people of those States themselves wish to pre-serve the forests. If they do we can help materially; we can direct their efforts, but we cannot save the forests unless they wish them to be saved.

I ask, with all the intensity that I am capable of, that the men of the West remember the sharp distinction I have just drawn between the man who skins the land and the man who develops the country. I am going to work with, and only with, the man who develops the country. I am against the land-skinner every time. Our policy is consistent to give to every portion of the public domain its highest possible amount of use, and of course that can be given only through the hearty co-operation of the Western people. I would like to add one word as to the creation of a national forest service which I have recommended repeatedly in messages to Congress, and espe-cially in my last. I wish to see all the forest work of the government concen-trated in the Department of Agriculture. It is folly to scatter such work, as I have said over and over again, and the policy which this Administration is trying to carry out through the creation of such a service is that of making the national forests more actively and more permanently useful to the people of the West, and I am heartily glad to know that the Western sentiment sup-ports more and more vigorously the policy of setting aside national forests, the creation of a national forest service, and especially the policy of increas-ing the permanent usefulness of these forest lands to all who come in contact with them. With what is rapidly getting to be a practically unbroken senti-ment in the West behind such a forest policy, with what is rapidly getting to be a practically unbroken support by the great stable interests behind the general policy of the conservative use of the forests, we have a right to feel that we have entered on an era of great and lasting progress. Only entered upon it; much, very much, remains to be done; and as in every other depart-ment of human activity our debt of gratitude will be due, not to the amiable but short-sighted optimist who thinks you have made a good beginning and the end may take care of itself; still less to the man who sits at one side and says how poorly the work is being done by those who are doing it; but to the men who try, each in his own place, practically to forward this great work. That is the type of man who is going to do the work, and it is because I believe that we have enlisted the active, practical sympathy of just that kind of man in this work that I believe the future of this policy to be bright and the permanence of our timber-supplies more nearly assured than at any previous time in our history. To the men represented in this congress this great result is primarily due. In closing, I wish to thank you who are here, not merely for what you are doing in this particular movement, but for the fact that you are illustrating what I hope I may call the typically American method of meeting questions of great and vital importance to the nation — the method of seeing whether the individuals particularly concerned cannot by getting together and co-operating with the government do infinitely more for themselves than it would be possible for any government under the sun to do for them. I believe in the future of this movement, because I think you have the right combination of qualities — the quality of individual initiative, the quality of individual resourcefulness, combined with the quality that enables you to come together for mutual help, and having so come, to work with the government; and I pledge you in the fullest measure the support of the government in what you are doing.

THE CONSERVATION OF WILD LIFE

It is difficult to decide whether the fact that this essay seems so timely more than seventy-five years after it was written is a mark of progress in conservation or of a lack thereof. For TR, knowledge of birds and animals was a lifetime's avocation. His outrage at the large-scale slaughter of game requires some rationalization, given the long lists of kills he carefully tallied after hunting trips only a few years earlier. Although he would undoubtedly have provided such rationalization, with all the necessary distinctions, on request, none appears here. This book review appeared in the January 20, 1915, issue of The Outlook.

Forty years ago John Ruskin gave a series of lectures on "Greek and English Birds," which he later gathered into a volume under the title of *Love's Meinie* — a title showing affectation of course, for Ruskin was as affected as Carlyle; and no small part of the contents of the volume exhibits affectation carried to the verge of mental unsoundness. But it is beautifully written — else it would not be Ruskin's. It shows the delight in nature which can never be felt save by the man whose pulses throb with sheer delight in the spring scents of budding things, in the music of birds, the rustling of trees, the running of brooks, and in the wind-flaws on glassy lakes; a delight which can never be interpreted to others unless by one who is also master of the great art of putting fine thoughts into simple, clear, and noble words.

It also contains a characteristically amusing, and by no means wholly unjust, attack on modern science. In comparing it with the crass ignorance of the average upper-class Englishman he says:

> It is vulgar in a far worse way by its arrogance and materialism. In general the scientific natural history of a bird consists of four articles — first, the name and estate of the gentleman whose gamekeeper shot the last that was seen in England; secondly, two or three stories of doubtful origin, printed in every book on the subject of birds for the last fifty years; thirdly, an account of the feathers, from the comb to the rump, with enumerations of the colors which are never more to be seen on the living bird of English eyes; and, lastly, a discussion of the reasons why none of the twelve names which former naturalists have given to the bird are of any further use, and why the present author has given it a thirteenth, which is to be universally, and to the end of time, accepted.

With the stricture on modern scientific terminology contained in the last clause I cordially agree. But of far greater practical importance is the lesson to be inferred from the first and third "articles." It is deeply discreditable to the people of any country calling itself civilized that as regards many of the grandest or most beautiful or most interesting forms of wild life once to be found in the land we should now be limited to describing, usually in the dryest of dry books, the physical characteristics which when living they possessed, and the melancholy date at which they ceased to live.

Ever since man in recognizably human shape made his appearance on this planet he has been an appreciable factor in the destruction of other forms of animal life, and he has been a potent factor ever since he developed the weapons known to the savages of the last few tens of thousands of years. But modern weapons have given a tremendous impetus to this destruction. Never before were such enormous quantities of big beasts and large birds slain as in the nineteenth century. Never before was there such extensive and wasteful slaughter of strange and beautiful forms of wild life as in the century which saw the greatest advance in material civilization and the most rapid spread of the civilized peoples throughout all the world.

Toward the end of that century a few civilized nations wakened to a sense of shame at what was going on. Enlightened men and women here and there began to take efficient action to restrain this senseless destruction of that which, once destroyed, could never be replaced. Gradually they roused a more general sentiment, and now there is a considerable body of public opinion in favor of keeping for our children's children, as a priceless heritage, all the delicate beauty of the lesser and all the burly majesty of the mightier forms of wild life. We are fast learning that trees must not be cut down more rapidly than they are replaced; we have taken forward steps in learning that wild beasts and birds are by right not the property merely of the people alive to-day, but the property of the unborn generations, whose belongings we have no right to squander; and there are even faint signs of our growing to understand that wild flowers should be enjoyed unplucked where they grow, and that it is barbarism to ravage the woods and fields, rooting out the mayflower and breaking branches of dogwood as ornaments for automobiles filled with jovial but ignorant picnickers from cities.

In the present century the new movement gathered head. Men began to appreciate the need of preserving wild life, not only because it was useful, but also because it was beautiful. Song- birds, shore-birds, water-fowl, birds of all kinds, add by voice and action to the joy of living of most men and women to whom the phrase "joy of living" has any real meaning. Such stately or lovely wild creatures as moose, wapiti, deer, hartbeest, zebra, gazelle, when protected give ample commercial returns, and, moreover, add to the landscape just as waterfalls and lofty pine-trees and towering crags add to the landscape. Fertile plains, every foot of them tilled, are of the first necessity; but great natural playgrounds of mountain, forest, cliff-walled lake, and brawling brook are also necessary to the full and many-sided development of a fine race. In just the same way the homely birds of farm and lawn and the wild creatures of the waste should all be kept. It is utterly untrue to say, as demagogues and selfish materialists sometimes unite in saying, that "the game belongs to the people"—meaning the loafers and market gunners who wish to kill it, and the wealthy and lazy gourmands who wish to eat it, without regard to the future. It is true that the game belongs to the people; but this rightly means the people who are to be born a hundred years hence just as much as the people who are alive to-day. In the same way, persons who own land, and, above all, persons who merely visit or pass through land, have no more right wantonly or carelessly to destroy birds or deface scenery than they have to pollute waters or burn down forests or let floods through levees. The sooner we appreciate these facts, the sooner we shall become a really civilized people.

Laws to protect small and harmless wild life, especially birds, are indispensable. Such laws cannot be enacted or enforced until public opinion is back of them; and associations like the Audubon Societies do work of incalculable good in stirring, rousing, and giving effect to this opinion; and men like Mr. [William T.] Hornaday [author of *Wild Life Conservation*] render all of us their debtors by the way they efficiently labor for this end, as well as for what comes only next in importance, the creation of sanctuaries for the complete protection of the larger, shyer, and more persecuted forms of wild life. This country led the way in establishing the Yellowstone Park as such a sanctuary; the British and German Empires followed, and in many ways have surpassed us. There are now many such sanctuaries and refuges in North America, middle and South Africa, and even Asia, and the results have been astounding. Many of the finer forms of animal life, which seemed on the point of vanishing, are now far more numerous than fifteen years ago, having by their rapid increase given proof of the abounding vigor of nature's fertility where nature is unmarred by man. But very much remains to be done, and there is need of the most active warfare against the forces of greed, carelessness, and sheer brutality, which, if left unchecked, would speedily undo all that has been accomplished, and would inflict literally irreparable damage.

The books before me are powerful weapons in this warfare for light against darkness. Mr. Hornady's volume, in which he has been assisted by

Mr. Walcott, consists chiefly of lectures delivered before the admirable Forest School of Yale University. It is really a full technical treatise which should be owned and constantly used by every man and woman who is alive to our needs in this matter. He shows how much has been accomplished in creating the right type of popular opinion. He is able to tell what we have accomplished in the creation of great National playgrounds, the National parks, which are National game-preserves. The Yellowstone, Glacier, Mount Olympus, Grand Canyon, Sequoia, and other parks represent one of the best bits of National achievement which our people have to their credit of recent years. The National forests should also be made game reserves. No sale of game or market hunting should be allowed anywhere; fortunately, the infamous traffic in millinery feathers has now been forbidden. The Federal migratory bird law is a capital piece of legislation. Mr. Hornaday shows the imperative need of protecting our shore-birds; he shows the economic value of birds to the farmer; he deals with what must, alas! be called just severity with the attitude of the average "sportsman" toward wild life.

One of the most interesting and pleasant phases of the movement of which Mr. Hornaday is one of the leaders is that which deals with the rapidity with which animals accustom themselves to protection and multiply when given the chance to do so. In New York and New England whitetail deer have enormously increased in numbers during the last thirty years. In Vermont the deer were absolutely exterminated forty years ago. Then a dozen were introduced from the Adirondacks. These have thriven and multiplied literally over a thousandfold. In forty years the original twelve individuals have increased to such an extraordinary degree that at present hunting under proper restriction is permitted, and five or six thousand deer are killed annually, without diminution of the stock. Mr. Hornaday is an entirely sane and rational man; he heartily approves of hunting, of sport carried on in legitimate fashion, as it can be, without any diminution of the amount of game. He shows that in the case of the Yellowstone elk it is urgently desirable that there should be a great increase in the killing, especially of cows; for in the absence of a sufficient number of natural foes they have increased until they now die by thousands each winter of starvation. (By the way, I venture to point out that when the cougars in the Yellowstone dwell away from the deer, antelope, and sheep, and prey only on elk, they do no damage.) Our prime duty, at present, as regards the immense majority of large or beautiful or useful mammals and the birds, is to protect them from excessive killing, or, indeed, from all killing. But when genuinely protected, birds and mammals increase so rapidly that it becomes imperative to kill them. If, under such circumstances, their numbers are not kept down by legitimate hunting—and some foolish creatures protest even against legitimate hunting—it would be necessary to have them completely exterminated by paid butchers. But the foolish sentimentalists who do not see this are not as yet the really efficient foes of wild life and of sensible movements for its preservation. The game-hog, the man who commercializes the destruction of game, and the wealthy epicure—all of these, backed by the selfish ignorance which declines to learn, are the real foes with whom we must contend. The true lovers of the chase, true sportsmen, true believers in hunting as a manly and vigorous pastime, recognize these men as their worst foes; and the great array of men and women who do not hunt, but who love wild creatures, who love all nature, must discriminate sharply between the two classes.

The Audubon Societies, which have done so much good work, have rarely done a better piece of work than in publishing the charming little book *Alaskan Bird Life,* which has been edited by Ernest Ingersoll. It has been prepared for free distribution among the people of Alaska. Surely, societies that do such work are entitled to the heartiest support from all good citizens. Let school-teachers have it free by all means; give it as a prize to exceptional pupils; but let the average man or woman pay something for such a first-class little volume. It is a book of really exceptional merit; no bird-lover in the United States or Canada—not to speak of Alaska—can afford not to have it in his or her library. It is all excellent; but best of all are the portions contributed by Mr. E. W. Nelson. Mr. Nelson is one of our best field-ornithologists, and also, one of our best closet scientific systematists; and to extraordinary powers of observation, and intense love of the wilderness of wild creatures, he adds the ability to write with singular power and charm. Nothing better of its kind has ever been done than his account in this little volume of the bird life, at all seasons of the year, in the Yukon Valley and on the islands and along the seacoast. His ear is as good as his eye. He is the first writer to do justice to the musical notes, especially the love notes, of the "sou-sou-southerly" duck, which in winter we know so well on Long Island Sound. He tells of the Lapland longspur, singing on the wing like a bobolink; and of the noisy cock ptarmigan crowing his challenge as he springs a few yards in the air when he is still the dominant figure on the snowy spring plains, before the hosts of water-fowl arrive. Mr. Nelson is the first observer graphically and fully to portray the life history of the strange emperor-goose. He is almost the first observer to describe the songs—for they are songs—of the shore-birds; and particularly attractive is his description of the aerial love-dance and love-song of the tiny and gentle semi-palmated sandpiper. I cannot forbear quoting his account of the bird chorus that greets the oncoming of one of the spring storms:

The evening before the onset of one of these spring storms was commonly heralded on the tundra, even in the clearest weather, by wonderful outbursts of cries from the larger water-fowl, and these would continue for half an hour before the birds settled down for the night. Thousands of birds took part in producing the tremendous chorus. It was made up of the notes of numberless loons in small ponds joined with the rolling cries of cranes, the bugling of flocks of swans on the large ponds, the clanging of innumerable geese, the hoarse calls of various ducks, and the screams of gulls and terns, all in a state of great excitement, apparently trying to outdo one another in strength of voice. The result was a volume of wildly harmonious music, so impressive that these concerts still remain among my most vivid memories of the north.

These ornithological sketches by Mr. Nelson are masterpieces of vivid and truthful portrayal of wild nature. They are as well done, from the standpoint of the nature-lover and the man of letters, as Hudson's delightful *Naturalist in La Plata* and *Idle Days in Patagonia*. These two volumes of Hudson's are literature, just as White's *Selborne* and Burrough's writing are literature. Nelson writes with as strong charm as Hudson; he has the same love and understanding of wild life, and in addition he is a trained scientific man of the first class and an adventurous wanderer in the wilderness. A man who combines such qualities is very rare, and it is a pity not to utilize him to the utmost. Some first-class publishing firm, like Scribner's, should insist upon Mr. Nelson's writing an American ornithology which would take rank as both a literary and a scientific classic.

The third volume [*Menschen und Tiere in Deutsch Sudwest*] is Mr. [Adolf] Fischer's sketch of men and beasts in German southwestern Africa. He describes the fell destruction, the almost complete annihilation, of the wonderful big-game fauna of these southwestern African wastes by the white hunters and the black and yellow men whom they armed in the nineteenth century. It was a butchery so appallingly wasteful that it is melancholy to read of it. He also describes the steps taken by the German Government during the last decade to undo this wrong, especially by the establishment of carefully guarded game reserves. As in our country, as soon as the effort was seriously made it was entirely successful; eland, kudu, wildebeests, zebras, and many other wild creatures have once again begun to grow plentiful, and on these reserves are gradually losing their fear of man. Mr. Fischer's account of the desert and its dwellers shows keen sympathy and understanding. The mighty wilderness creatures of Africa surpass those of all the other continents in size, beauty, strangeness, number, and variety; and to allow this magnificent fauna to be needlessly butchered to satisfy the ignoble greed of hide and trophy hunters is a crime against our children's children. There are vast tracts of country that are useless for agriculture and of most use as game-preserves managed in the interest of all people, both those existing and the unborn. England and Germany have done a fine work in the interest of civilization by their preservation of the African fauna in sanctuaries and by good game-laws well enforced.

This is one of the many, many reasons why the present dreadful war [World War I] fills me with sadness. The men, many of whom I have known — Germans, Englishmen, Frenchmen, Belgians — who have been opening the Dark Continent to civilization, and who on the whole and of recent years have done their work so wisely, are now destroying one another and ruining the work that has been done. I knew many of the men, Englishmen and Germans, who have done most for the creation and success of these game-preserves — Schilling, Hamilton, Jackson, Gotzen, Harry Johnston, Buxton. In all essentials they resembled one another. The admirable work they did was of the same character, alike in the British and in the German possessions. It is cruel to think that their splendid purposes and energies should now be twisted into the paths of destruction.

WOLVES AND WOLF-HOUNDS

*Roosevelt's hunting stories had broad appeal for their combina-
tion of instruction and adventure. Always the naturalist, he
could not resist detailed description of the habits and habitat of
animal life, as in this piece from* The Wilderness Hunter *published in 1893 by G. P. Putnam's Sons.*

The wolf is the archetype of ravin, the beast of waste and desolation. It is
still found scattered thinly throughout all the wilder portions of the United
States, but has everywhere retreated from the advance of civilization.

Wolves show an infinite variety in color, size, physical formation, and
temper. Almost all the varieties intergrade with one another, however, so
that it is very difficult to draw a hard-and-fast line between any two of
them. Nevertheless, west of the Mississippi there are found two distinct
types. One is the wolf proper, or big wolf, specially akin to the wolves of
the Eastern States. The other is the little coyote, or prairie-wolf. The coyote and the big wolf are found together in almost all the wilder districts
from the Rio Grande to the valleys of the upper Missouri and the upper
Columbia. Throughout this region there is always a sharp line of demar-
cation, especially in size, between the coyotes and the big wolves of any
given district; but in certain districts the big wolves are very much larger
than their brethren in other districts. In the upper Columbia country, for
instance, they are very large; along the Rio Grande they are small. Doctor
Hart Merriam informs me that, according to his experience, the coyote is
largest in southern California. In many respects the coyote differs altogether
in habits from its big relative. For one thing, it is far more tolerant of man.
In some localities coyotes are more numerous around settlements, and
even in the close vicinity of large towns, than they are in the frowning and
desolate fastness haunted by their grim elder brother.

Big wolves vary far more in color than the coyotes do. I have seen
white, black, red, yellow, brown, gray, and grizzled skins, and others representing every shade between, although usually each locality has its pre-
vailing tint. The grizzled, gray, and brown often have precisely the coat of
the coyote. The difference in size among wolves of different localities, and
even of the same locality, is quite remarkable, and so, curiously enough, is
the difference in the size of the teeth, in some cases even when the body of
one wolf is as big as that of another. I have seen wolves from Texas and
New Mexico which were undersized, slim animals with rather small tusks,

in no way to be compared to the long-toothed giants of their race that dwell in the heavily timbered mountains of the Northwest and in the far North. As a rule, the teeth of the coyote are relatively smaller than those of the gray wolf.

Formerly wolves were incredibly abundant in certain parts of the country, notably on the great plains, where they were known as buffalo-wolves, and were regular attendants on the great herds of the bison. Every traveler and hunter of the old days knew them as among the most common sights of the plains, and they followed the hunting parties and emigrant trains for the sake of the scraps left in camp. Now, however, there is no district in which they are really abundant. The wolfers, or professional wolf-hunters, who killed them by poisoning for the sake of their fur, and the cattlemen, who likewise killed them by poisoning because of their raids on the herds, have doubtless been the chief instruments in working their decimation on the plains. In the 70s, and even in the early 80s, many tens of thousands of wolves were killed by the wolfers in Montana and northern Wyoming and western Dakota. Nowadays the surviving wolves of the plains have learned caution; they no longer move abroad at midday, and still less do they dream of hanging on the footsteps of hunter and traveler. Instead of being one of the most common they have become one of the rarest sights of the plains. A hunter may wander far and wide through the plains for months nowadays and never see a wolf, though he will probably see many coyotes. However, the diminution goes on, not steadily but by fits and starts, and, moreover, the beasts now and then change their abodes and appear in numbers in places where they have been scarce for a long period. In the present winter of 1892-93 big wolves are more plentiful in the neighborhood of my ranch than they have been for ten years, and have worked some havoc among the cattle and young horses. The cowboys have been carrying on the usual vindictive campaign against them; a number have been poisoned, and a number of others have fallen victims to their greediness, the cowboys surprising them when gorged to repletion on the carcass of a colt or calf and in consequence unable to run, so that they are easily ridden down, roped, and then dragged to death.

Yet even the slaughter wrought by man in certain localities does not seem adequate to explain the scarcity or extinction of wolves throughout the country at large. In most places they are not followed any more eagerly than are the other large beasts of prey, and they are usually followed with less success. Of all animals the wolf is the shyest and hardest to slay. It is almost or quite as difficult to still-hunt as the cougar, and is far more difficult to kill with hounds, traps, or poison; yet it scarcely holds its own as well as the great cat, and it does not begin to hold its own as well as the bear, a beast certainly more readily killed, and one which produces fewer young at a birth. Throughout the East the black bear is common in many localities from which the wolf has vanished completely. It at present exists in very scanty numbers in northern Maine and the Adirondacks; is almost or quite extinct in Pennsylvania; lingers here and there in the mountains from West Virginia to east Tennessee, and is found in Florida; but is everywhere less abundant than the bear. It is possible that this destruction of the wolves is due to some disease among them, perhaps to hydrophobia, a terrible malady, from which it is known that they suffer greatly at times. Perhaps the bear is helped by its habit of hibernating, which frees it from most dangers during winter; but this cannot be the complete explanation, for in the South it does not hibernate, and yet holds its own as well as in the North. What makes it all the more curious that the American wolf should disappear sooner than the bear is that the reverse is the case with the allied species of Europe, where the bear is much sooner killed out of the land.

Indeed the differences of this sort between nearly related animals are literally inexplicable. Much of the difference in temperament between such closely allied species as the American and European bears and wolves is doubtless due to their surroundings and to the instincts they have inherited through many generations; but for much of the variation it is not possible to offer any explanation. In the same way there are certain physical differences for which it is very hard to account, as the same conditions seem to operate in directly reverse ways with different animals. No one can explain the process of natural selection which has resulted in the otter of America being larger than the otter of Europe, while the badger is smaller; in the mink being with us a much stouter animal than its Scandinavian and Russian kinsman, while the reverse is true of our sable or pine-marten.

ভ ভ ভ

The difference even among the wolves of different sections of our own country is very notable. It may be true that the species as a whole is rather weak and less ferocious than the European wolf; but it is certainly not true of the wolves of certain localities. The great timber-wolf of the central and northern chains of the Rockies and coast ranges is in every way a more formidable creature than the buffalo-wolf of the plains, although they intergrade. The skins and skulls of the wolves of northwestern Montana and Washington which I have seen were quite as large and showed quite as stout claws and teeth as the skins and skulls of Russian and Scandinavian wolves, and I believe that these great timber-wolves are in every way as formidable as their Old World kinsfolk. However, they live where they come in contact with a population of rifle-bearing frontier hunters, who are very different from European peasants or Asiatic tribesmen; and they have, even when most hungry, a wholesome dread of human beings. Yet I doubt if an unarmed man would be entirely safe should he, while alone in the forest in mid-winter, encounter a fair-sized pack of ravenously hungry timber-wolves.

A full-grown dog-wolf of the northern Rockies, in exceptional instances, reaches a height of thirty-two inches and a weight of 130 pounds; a big buffalo-wolf of the upper Missouri stands thirty or thirty-one inches at the shoulder and weighs about 110 pounds. A Texan wolf may not reach over eighty pounds. The bitch wolves are smaller; and moreover there is often great variation even in the wolves of closely neighboring localities.

The wolves of the Southern plains were not often formidable to large animals, even in the days when they most abounded. They rarely attacked the horses of the hunter, and indeed were but little regarded by these experienced animals. They were much more likely to gnaw off the lariat with which the horse was tied than to try to molest the steed himself. They preferred to prey on young animals, or on the weak and disabled. They rarely molested a full-grown cow or steer, still less a full-grown buffalo, and, if they did attack such an animal, it was only when emboldened by numbers. In the plains of the upper Missouri and Saskatchewan the wolf was, and is, more dangerous, while in the northern Rockies his courage and ferocity attain their highest pitch.

🌿 🌿 🌿

The big timber-wolves of the northern Rocky Mountains attack every four-footed beast to be found where they live. They are far from contenting themselves with hunting deer and snapping up the pigs and sheep of the farm. When the weather gets cold and food scarce they band together in small parties, perhaps of four or five individuals, and then assail anything, even a bear or a panther. A bull elk or bull moose, when on its guard, makes a most dangerous fight; but a single wolf will frequently master the cow of either animal, as well as domestic cattle and horses. In attacking such large game, however, the wolves like to act in concert, one springing at the animal's head, and attracting its attention, while the other hamstrings it. Nevertheless, one such big wolf will kill an ordinary horse. A man I knew, who was engaged in packing into the Coeur d'Alenes, once witnessed such a feat on the part of a wolf. He was taking his pack-train down into a valley when he saw a horse grazing therein; it had been turned loose by another packing outfit because it became exhausted. He lost sight of it as the trail went down a zigzag, and while it was thus out of sight he suddenly heard it utter the appalling scream, unlike and more dreadful than any other sound, which a horse only utters in extreme fright or agony. The scream was repeated, and as he came in sight again he saw that a great wolf had attacked the horse. The poor animal had been bitten terribly in its haunches and was cowering upon them, while the wolf stood and looked at it a few paces off. In a moment or two the horse partially recovered and made a desperate bound forward, starting at full gallop. Immediately the wolf was after it, overhauled it in three or four jumps, and then seized it by the hock, while its legs were extended, with such violence as to bring it completely back on its haunches. It again screamed piteously; and this time with a few savage snaps the wolf hamstrung and partially disembowelled it, and it fell over, having made no attempt to defend itself. I have heard of more than one incident of this kind. If a horse is a good fighter, however, as occasionally, though not often, happens, it is a most difficult prey for any wild beast, and some veteran horses have no fear of wolves whatsoever, well knowing that they can either strike them down with their forefeet or repulse them by lashing out behind.

Wolves are cunning beasts and will often try to lull their prey into unsuspicion by playing round and cutting capers. I once saw a young deer and a wolf cub together near the hut of the settler who had captured both. The wolf was just old enough to begin to feel vicious and bloodthirsty and to show symptoms of attacking the deer. On the occasion in question he got loose and ran toward it, but it turned and began to hit him with its forefeet, seemingly in sport; whereat he rolled over on his back before it, and acted like a puppy at play. Soon it turned and walked off; immediately the wolf, with bristling hair, crawled after, and with a pounce seized it by the haunch, and would doubtless have murdered the bleating, struggling creature, had not the bystanders interfered.

Where there are no domestic animals, wolves feed on almost anything from a mouse to an elk. They are redoubted enemies of foxes. They are easily able to overtake them in fair chase, and kill numbers. If the fox can get into the underbrush, however, he can dodge around much faster than the wolf, and so escape pursuit. Sometimes one wolf will try to put a fox out of a cover while another waits outside to snap him up. Moreover, the wolf kills even closer kinsfolk than the fox. When pressed by hunger it will undoubtedly sometimes seize a coyote, tear it in pieces and devour it, although during most of the year the two animals live in perfect harmony. I once myself, while out in the deep snow, came across the remains of a coyote that had been killed in this manner. Wolves are also very fond of the flesh of dogs, and if they get a chance promptly kill and eat any dog they can master—and there are but few that they cannot. Nevertheless, I have been told of one instance in which a wolf struck up an extraordinary friendship with a strayed dog, and the two lived and hunted together for many months, being frequently seen by the settlers of the locality. This occurred near Thompson's Falls, Montana.

🌿 🌿 🌿

Though I have never known wolves to attack a man, yet in the wilder portion of the far Northwest I have heard them come around camp very close, growling so savagely as to make one almost reluctant to leave the camp-fire and go out into the darkness unarmed. Once I was camped in the fall near a lonely little lake in the mountains, by the edge of quite a broad stream. Soon after nightfall three or four wolves came around camp and kept me awake by their sinister and dismal howling. Two or three times they came so close to the fire that I could hear them snap their jaws and growl, and at one time I positively thought that they intended to try to get into camp, so excited were they by the smell of the fresh meat. After a while they stopped howling; and then all was silent for an hour or so. I let the fire go out and was turning into bed when I suddenly heard some animal of considerable size come down to the stream nearly opposite me and begin to splash across, first wading, then swimming. It was pitch-dark and I could not possibly see, but I felt sure it was a wolf. However, after coming half-way over it changed its mind and swam back to the opposite bank; nor did I see or hear anything more of the night marauders.

🌿 🌿 🌿

The true way to kill wolves, however, is to hunt them with greyhounds on the great plains. Nothing more exciting than this sport can possibly be imagined. It is not always necessary that the greyhound should be of absolutely pure blood. Prize-winning dogs of high pedigree often prove useless for the purpose. If by careful choice, however, a ranchman can get together a pack composed both of the smooth-haired greyhound and the rough-haired Scotch deerhound, he can have excellent sport. The greyhounds sometimes do best if they have a slight cross of bulldog in their veins, but this is not necessary. If once a greyhound can be fairly entered to the sport and acquires confidence, then its wonderful agility, its sinewy strength and speed, and the terrible snap with which its jaws come together render it a most formidable assailant. Nothing can possibly exceed the gallantry with which good greyhounds, when their blood is up, fling themselves on a wolf or any other foe. There does not exist, and there never has existed, on the wide earth a more perfect type of dauntless courage than such a hound.

※ ※ ※

During the last decade many ranchmen in Colorado, Wyoming, and Montana have developed packs of greyhounds able to kill a wolf unassisted. Greyhounds trained for this purpose always seize by the throat; and the light dogs used for coursing jack-rabbits are not of much service, smooth or rough-haired greyhounds and deerhounds standing over thirty inches at the shoulder and weighing over ninety pounds being the only ones that, together with speed, courage, and endurance, possess the requisite power.

One of the most famous packs in the West was that of the Sun River Hound Club, in Montana, started by the stockmen of Sun River to get rid of the curse of wolves which infested the neighborhood and worked very serious damage to the herds and flocks. The pack was composed of both greyhounds and deerhounds, the best being from the kennels of Colonel Williams and of Mr. Van Hummel, of Denver; they were handled by an old plainsman and veteran wolf-hunter named Porter. In the season of '86 the astonishing number of 146 wolves were killed with these dogs. Ordinarily, as soon as the dogs seized a wolf, and threw or held it, Porter rushed in and stabbed it with his hunting-knife; one day, when out with six hounds, he thus killed no less than twelve out of the fifteen wolves started, though one of the greyhounds was killed and all the others were cut and exhausted. But often the wolves were killed without his aid. The first time the two biggest hounds—deerhounds or wire-haired greyhounds—were tried, when they had been at the ranch only three days, they performed such a feat. A large wolf had killed and partially eaten a sheep in a corral close to the ranch-house, and Porter started on the trail, and followed him at a jog-trot nearly ten miles before the hounds sighted him. Running but a few rods, he turned viciously to bay, and the two great greyhounds struck him like stones hurled from a catapult, throwing him as they fastened on his throat; they held him down and strangled him before he could rise, two other hounds getting up just in time to help at the end of the worry.

Ordinarily, however, no two greyhounds or deerhounds are a match for a gray wolf, but I have known of several instances in Colorado, Wyoming, and Montana in which three strong veterans have killed one. The feat can only be performed by big dogs of the highest courage, who all act together, rush in at top speed, and seize by the throat; for the strength of the quarry is such that otherwise he will shake off the dogs, and then speedily kill them by rapid snaps with his terribly armed jaws. Where possible, half a dozen dogs should be slipped at once, to minimize the risk of injury to the pack: unless this is done, and unless the hunter helps the dogs in the worry, accidents will be frequent and an occasional wolf will be found able to beat off, maiming or killing, a lesser number of assailants. Some hunters prefer the smooth greyhound, because of its great speed, and others the wire-coated animal, the rough deerhound, because of its superior strength; both, if of the right kind, are dauntless fighters.

Colonel Williams' greyhounds have performed many noble feats in wolf-hunting. He spent the winter of 1875 in the Black Hills, which at that time did not contain a single settler and fairly swarmed with game. Wolves were especially numerous and very bold and fierce, so that the dogs of the party were continually in jeopardy of their lives. On the other hand they took an ample vengeance, for many wolves were caught by the pack. Whenever possible, the horsemen kept close enough to take an immediate hand in the fight, if the quarry was a full-grown wolf, and thus save the dogs from the terrible punishment they were otherwise certain to receive. The dogs invariably throttled, rushing straight at the throat, but the wounds they themselves received were generally in the flank or belly; in several instances these wounds resulted fatally. Once or twice a wolf was caught and held by two greyhounds until the horsemen came up; but it took at least five dogs to overcome and slay unaided a big timber-wolf. Several times the feat was performed by a party of five, consisting of two greyhounds, one rough-coated deerhound, and two cross-bloods; and once by a litter of seven young greyhounds, not yet come to their full strength.

Once or twice the so-called Russian wolf-hounds, or silky-coated grey-hounds, the "borzois," have been imported and tried in wolf-hunting on the Western plains; but hitherto they have not shown themselves equal, at either running or fighting, to the big American-bred greyhounds of the type produced by Colonel Williams and certain others of our best Western breeders. Indeed I have never known any foreign greyhounds, whether Scotch, English, or from Continental Europe, to perform such feats of courage, endurance, and strength, in chasing and killing dangerous game, as the home-bred greyhounds of Colonel Williams.

CAMERA SHOTS AT BIG GAME

*It was while enjoying—or tolerating—the leisure afforded by
the vice presidency that TR wrote this preface to A. G. Wallihan's*
Camera Shots at Big Game *in May 1901. While Roosevelt's
admiration is genuine, it is difficult to imagine him substituting
camera for rifle in his own wilderness adventures. His early concern for conservation and his defense of sports hunting are evident
here. The tension would endure.*

It is a pleasure to write an introduction to Mr. Wallihan's really noteworthy
book, for his photographs of wild game possess such peculiar value that all
lovers, whether of hunting or of natural history, should be glad to see them
preserved in permanent form. The art and practice of photographing wild
animals in their native haunts has made great progress in recent years. It is
itself a branch of sport, and hunting with the camera has many points of
superiority when compared to hunting with the rifle. But, even under favorable conditions, very few men have the skill, the patience, the woodcraft and
plainscraft which enabled Mr. Wallihan to accomplish so much; and, moreover, the conditions as regards most of our big-game animals are continually
changing for the worse. The difficulties of getting really good and characteristic photographs are such as to be practically insuperable where game is
very scarce and very shy, and throughout most of the United States game is
steadily growing scarcer and shyer. Photographs in a game-preserve, no
matter how large this preserve, are, of course, not quite the same thing.

The elk have now almost everywhere diminished in numbers so that it
would be very difficult indeed to get pictures like some of Mr. Wallihan's,
and though the blacktail and the antelope last better, yet they, too, can
nowhere be found as they were but a dozen years ago. The cougar pictures
have an especial value. Where cougars are plentiful it is easier to take their
photographs than in the case of deer, and there are a number of localities in
the Rockies where they are still fairly abundant; but they are steadily growing scarcer, and where they have become really scarce the work of the photographer becomes one of such hopeless labor, the chance for success is so
very small, as to be practically prohibitive. There are still cougars east of the
Mississippi, but nowadays it would be a simple impossibility for any man to
take of them such pictures as Mr. Wallihan has taken of the Colorado
cougars. Moreover, even where cougars are plentiful, the photographer
might work a lifetime before getting such a remarkable picture as that of the
cougar jumping in mid-air. As I know from practical experience, it is

exceedingly difficult, even when the cougar has been treed, to get a really fine photograph, as it is not possible to choose the conditions of ground and light in advance.

Mr. Wallihan's hunting was in northwestern Colorado and western Wyoming —regions where I have often followed the game he describes. There are no whitetail deer in the country he covered, the buffalo were extinct before he began work with his camera, and he never had luck with bears. But his series of elk, antelope, blacktail, and mountain-lion pictures leave little to be desired. It is, by the way, difficult to determine whether to use the ordinary vernacular names of these animals, or their book names, which are better in themselves, but which unfortunately have not been popularly adopted. The elk, for instance, has no resemblance to the animal properly called the elk in the Old World, which is the blood brother of the moose, nor yet to the other animals improperly called elk in Asia and Africa. The blacktail of the Rocky Mountains is not the true blacktail of the Pacific coast. The antelope is not an antelope at all, occupying an entirely unique position as the only hollow-horned ruminant which annually sheds its horns. It would be far better if the three could be known as wapiti, mule-deer, and prongbuck. But unfortunately they are rarely known by these titles in common speech. With the cougar the case is a little different. It is sometimes called cougar among the ranchmen, and the names of panther and mountain-lion, by which it is known respectively in the East and in the West, are so misleading that it is best to drop them and give it the proper title.

The elk, or wapiti, were still plentiful in northwestern Colorado a decade ago, going in large herds. The merciless persecution they have suffered for the sake of their flesh, hide, antlers, and teeth has resulted in the species being reduced to a few hundred individuals. The Wyoming elk are travelling the same path, although the existence of the great protected nursery and breeding-ground in the Yellowstone National Park has delayed the process and gives us reasonable hope that the animals will never become entirely extinct. The part played by true sportsmen, worthy of the name, in this extinction has been nil, and indeed very little appreciable harm has been done by any men who have merely hunted in season for trophies. The real damage has come from the professional hunters and their patrons. In a wild frontier country it is too much to expect that the settlers will not occasionally kill meat for their own use, though every effort should be made to educate them to the knowledge that a wapiti or deer free in the woods will, by attracting tourists, bring into the neighborhood many times as much money as the dead carcass would represent. The professional game-butchers, however, have no excuse of any kind. They kill the animal for the hide and for the flesh. Moreover, the horns are strikingly ornamental and are freely purchased by a certain class of wealthy people who wholly lack the skill and hardihood necessary to those who would themselves be hunters, and who have not the good taste to see that antlers properly have their chief value as trophies. Nothing adds more to a hall or a room than fine antlers when they have been shot by the owner, but there is always an element of the absurd in a room furnished with trophies of the chase which the owner has acquired by purchase. Even less defensible is it either to kill or to put a premium upon the killing of this noble and beautiful creature for the sake of its teeth. Yet the habit of wearing elk's teeth on watch-chains and the like has been responsible for no small amount of slaughter. The Audubon Societies have done useful work in trying to prevent the destruction of song-birds and waders for millinery purposes. It would be well if some similar society would wage war against the senseless fashion of wearing elk's teeth when the wearer has not shot the animal; for such a fashion simply becomes one cause of extermination.

The mule, or Rocky Mountain blacktail, deer is in some localities migratory. This is the case in Colorado, where the winter and summer ranges of the deer are wholly distinct, and where during the migrations the animals follow well-established trails leading over and among the mountains and across the streams. Some of Mr. Wallihan's most beautiful pictures are those taken of deer crossing a stream. In dealing with the pronghorn antelope, on the other hand, a shy and far-sighted creature of the dry, open prairie, almost the only chance consisted in catching the game when it came to drink. Incidentally it will be seen that Mr. Wallihan in his description lays stress upon the superior keenness of vision of the antelope as compared to the deer. Mr. Wallihan is a very close and accurate observer, as indeed it was necessary he should be in order to obtain such results as he has obtained. His remarks on the comparative dullness of the deer's eyesight are in accord not only with my experience, but with those of almost every first-class hunter whom I have met. Yet I have known book authorities to assert the contrary. Of course it is all a matter of comparison. A deer's vision is better than that of a buffalo, and, I believe, better than that of a bear, and a motion catches its eye at once. But the antelope has better sight by far than any other game, and will be brought to a condition of alert suspicion by the sight of a man at a distance so great that he would be practically certain to escape observation from a deer.

In Mr. Wallihan's cougar-hunting he had the good fortune to be associated with Mr. Frank Wells, a first-class hunter with an excellent pack of hounds. Mr. Wells is not only a good hunter, but a good observer. He has written two or three pieces about cougars and cougar-hunting which are filled with refreshing common sense, in striking contrast to the average tales on the subject. More nonsense has been talked and written about the cougar than about any other American beast. Even experienced hunters often gravely talk of cougars ten and eleven feet long. As Mr. Wells has pointed out, these figures are never even approximated. The animal is variable in size, and very rarely a monster old male will reach the length of eight feet; but by no system of fair measurement will any cougar ever be found to go more than a very few inches over this limit, and even an eight-foot cougar is a giant of its kind. Hardly one in a hundred reaches such a length. The cougar is very destructive to deer and colts as well as calves, sheep, young elk, etc. When pressed by hunger, big cougars will kill full-grown elk, horses, and cattle; but they are cowardly beasts, and not only is it a wholly exceptional circumstance for them to attack any human being unprovoked, but they do not even make an effective fight against man when cornered. They rarely charge, and, as far as I know, never from any distance. A small number of really good fighting dogs can kill a cougar, and it readily trees even before dogs that would be quite incapable of mastering it. If man or dog comes close up, there is of course danger from the formidable jaws and sharp claws; but commonly the danger is only to the pack. Only in very rare cases is there any to the hunter. Owing to the cougar habits, the only method of pursuing it which offers any reasonable chance of success is with hounds. It is occasionally killed by accident without hounds, but under such circumstances the chances of success are so small as not to warrant even the most skillful hunter making a practice of pursuing it in this manner.

Mr. Wallihan is not only a good photographer, but a lover of nature and of the wild life of the wilderness. His pictures and his descriptions are good in themselves as records of a fascinating form of life which is passing away. Moreover, they should act as spurs to all of us to try to see that this life does not wholly vanish. It will be a real misfortune if our wild animals disappear from mountain, plain, and forest, to be found only, if at all, in great game-preserves. It is to the interest of all of us to see that there is ample and real protection for our game as for our woodlands. A true democracy, really alive to its opportunities, will insist upon such game preservation, for it is to the interest of our people as a whole. More and more, as it becomes necessary to preserve the game, let us hope that the camera will largely supplant the rifle. It is an excellent thing to have a nation proficient in marksmanship, and it is highly undesirable that the rifle should be wholly laid by. But the shot is, after all, only a small part of the free life of the wilderness. The chief attractions lie in the physical hardihood for which the life calls, the sense of limitless freedom which it brings, and the remoteness and wild charm and beauty of primitive nature. All of this we get exactly as much in hunting with the camera as in hunting with the rifle; and of the two, the former is the kind of sport which calls for the higher degree of skill, patience, resolution, and knowledge of the life history of the animal sought.

TR with his wife, Edith Carow Roosevelt, 1908.

10

ON WOMEN

WOMEN AND THE HOME

"Hard duty well done" is a theme that runs through much of the writing of TR, as in this address to the National Congress of Mothers, which met in Washington in March 1905. Roosevelt had supported equal rights for women, including equality of educational opportunity, legal rights, and suffrage. All this he thought would serve them well in their roles as wives and mothers. More advanced in his views than most men of his day, TR nevertheless held very traditional views about the role of women in society. In this talk Roosevelt also addressed his deep and continuing concern that Americans were not producing children in adequate supply.

◆◇◆

In our modern industrial civilization there are many and grave dangers to counterbalance the splendors and the triumphs. It is not a good thing to see cities grow at disproportionate speed relative to the country; for the small landowners, the men who own their little homes, and therefore to a very large extent the men who till farms, the men of the soil, have hitherto made the foundation of lasting national life in every State; and, if the foundation becomes either too weak or too narrow, the superstructure, no matter how attractive, is in imminent danger of failing.

But far more important than the question of the occupation of our citizens is the question of how their family life is conducted. No matter what that occupation may be, as long as there is a real home and as long as those who make up the home do their duty to one another, to their neighbors and to the State, it is of minor consequence whether the man's trade is plied in the country or the city, whether it calls for the work of the hands or for the work of the head.

But the nation is in a bad way if there is no real home, if the family is not of the right kind; if the man is not a good husband and father, if he is brutal or cowardly or selfish, if the woman has lost her sense of duty, if she is sunk in vapid self-indulgence or has let her nature be twisted so that she prefers a sterile pseudo-intellectuality to that great and beautiful development of character which comes only to those whose lives know the fullness of duty done, or effort made and self-sacrifice undergone.

In the last analysis the welfare of the State depends absolutely upon whether or not the average family, the average man and woman and their children, represent the kind of citizenship fit for the foundation of a great nation; and if we fail to appreciate this we fail to appreciate the root morality upon which all healthy civilization is based.

No piled-up wealth, no splendor of material growth, no brilliance of artistic development, will permanently avail any people unless its home life is healthy, unless the average man possesses honesty, courage, common sense, and decency, unless he works hard and is willing at need to fight hard; and unless the average woman is a good wife, a good mother, able and willing to perform the first and greatest duty of womanhood, able and willing to bear, and to bring up as they should be brought up, healthy children, sound in body, mind, and character, and numerous enough so that the race shall increase and not decrease.

There are certain old truths which will be true as long as this world endures, and which no amount of progress can alter. One of these is the truth that the primary duty of the husband is to be the home-maker, the bread-winner for his wife and children, and that the primary duty of the woman is to be the helpmate, the housewife, and mother. The woman should have ample educational advantages; but save in exceptional cases the man must be, and she need not be, and generally ought not to be, trained for a lifelong career as the family bread-winner; and, therefore, after a certain point the training of the two must normally be different because the duties of the two are normally different. This does not mean inequality of function, but it does mean that normally there must be dissimilarity of function. On the whole, I think the duty of the woman the more important, the more difficult, and the more honorable of the two; on the whole I respect the woman who does her duty even more than I respect the man who does his.

No ordinary work done by man is either as hard or as responsible as the work of a woman who is bringing up a family of small children; for upon her time and strength demands are made not only every hour of the day, but often every hour of the night. She may have to get up night after night to take care of a sick child, and yet must by day continue to do all her household duties as well; and if the family means are scant she must usually enjoy even her rare holidays taking her whole brood of children with her. The birth-pangs make all men the debtors of all women. Above all our sympathy and regard are due to the struggling wives among those whom Abraham Lincoln called the plain people, and whom he so loved and trusted; for the lives of these women are often led on the lonely heights of quiet, self-sacrificing heroism.

Just as the happiest and most honorable and most useful task that can beset any man is to earn enough for the support of his wife and family, for the bringing up and starting in life of his children, so the most important, the most honorable and desirable task which can beset any woman is to be a good and wise mother in a home marked by self-respect and mutual forbearance, by willingness to perform duty, and by refusal to sink into self-indulgence or avoid that which entails effort and self-sacrifice. Of course there are exceptional men and exceptional women who can do and ought to do much more than this, who can lead and ought to lead great careers of outside usefulness in addition to—not as substitutes for—their home work; but I am not speaking of exceptions; I am speaking of the average citizens, the average men and women who make up the nation.

Inasmuch as I am speaking to an assemblage of mothers I shall have nothing whatever to say in praise of an easy life. Yours is the work which is never ended. No mother has an easy time, and most mothers have very hard times, and yet what true mother would barter her experience of joy and sorrow in exchange for a life of cold selfishness, which insists upon perpetual amusement and the avoidance of care, and which often finds its fit dwelling-place in some flat designed to furnish with the least possible expenditure of effort the maximum of comfort and of luxury, but in which there is literally no place for children?

The woman who is a good wife, a good mother, is entitled to our respect as is no one else; but she is entitled to it only because, and so long as, she is worthy of it. Effort and self-sacrifice are the laws of worthy life for a man as for the woman; though neither the effort nor the self-sacrifice may be the same for the one as for the other. I do not in the least believe in the patient Griselda type of woman, in the woman who submits to gross and long-continued ill treatment, any more than I believe in a man who tamely submits to wrongful aggression. No wrong-doing is so abhorrent as wrong-doing by a man toward the wife and the children who should arouse every tender feeling in his nature. Selfishness toward them, the lack of tenderness toward them, lack of consideration for them, above all, brutality in any form toward them, should arouse the heartiest scorn and indignation in every upright soul.

I believe in the woman's keeping her self-respect just as I believe in the man's doing so. I believe in her rights just as much as I believe in the man's, and indeed a little more; and I regard marriage as a partnership, in which each partner is in honor bound to think of the rights of the other as well as of his or her own. But I think that the duties are even more important than the rights; and in the long run I think that the reward is ampler and greater for duty well done, than for the insistence upon individual rights, necessary though this, too, must often be. Your duty is hard, your responsibility great; but greatest of all is your reward. I do not pity you in the least. On the contrary, I feel respect and admiration for you.

Into the woman's keeping is committed the destiny of the generations to come after us. In bringing up your children you mothers must remember that while it is essential to be loving and tender, it is no less essential to be wise and firm. Foolishness and affection must not be treated as interchangeable terms; and besides training your sons and daughters in the softer and milder virtues you must seek to give them those stern and hardy qualities which in after-life they will surely need. Some children will go wrong in spite of the best training; and some will go right even when their surroundings are most unfortunate; nevertheless an immense amount depends upon the family training. If you mothers through weakness bring up your sons to be selfish and to think only of themselves, you will be responsible for much sadness among the women who are to be their wives in the future. If you let your daughters grow up idle, perhaps under the mistaken impression that as you yourselves have had to work hard they shall know only enjoyment, you are preparing them to be useless to others and burdens to themselves. Teach boys and girls alike that they are not to look forward to lives spent in avoiding difficulties, but to lives spent in overcoming difficulties. Teach them that work, for themselves and also for others, is not a curse, but a blessing; seek to make them happy, to make them enjoy life, but seek also to make them face life with the steadfast resolution to wrest success from labor and adversity, and to do their whole duty before God and to man. Surely she who can thus train her sons and her daughters is thrice fortunate among women.

There are many good people who are denied the supreme blessing of children, and for these we have the respect and sympathy always due to those who, from no fault of their own, are denied any of the other great blessings of life. But the man or woman who deliberately forgoes these blessings, whether from viciousness, coldness, shallow-heartedness, self-indulgence, or mere failure to appreciate aright the difference between the all-important and the unimportant—why, such a creature merits contempt as hearty as any visited upon the soldier who runs away in battle, or upon the man who refuses to work for the support of those dependent upon him, and who, though able-bodied, is yet content to eat in idleness the bread which others provide.

The existence of women of this type forms one of the most unpleasant and unwholesome features of modern life. If anyone is so dim of vision as to fail to see what a thoroughly unlovely creature such a woman is, I wish he would read Judge Robert Grant's novel *Unleavened Bread*, ponder seriously the character of Selma, and think of the fate that would surely overcome any nation which developed its average and typical woman along such lines. Unfortunately, it would be untrue to say that this type exists only in American novels. That it also exists in American life is made unpleasantly evident by the statistics as to the dwindling families in some localities. It is made evident in equally sinister fashion by the census statistics as to divorce, which are fairly appalling; for easy divorce is now, as it ever has been, a bane to any nation, a curse to society, a menace to the home, an incitement to married unhappiness, and to immorality, an evil thing for men, and a still more hideous evil for women. These unpleasant tendencies in our American life are made evident by articles such as those which I actually read not long ago in a certain paper, where a clergyman was quoted, seemingly with approval, as expressing the general American attitude when he said that the ambition of any save a very rich man should be to rear two children only, so as to give his children an opportunity "to taste a few of the good things of life."

This man, whose profession and calling should have made him a moral teacher, actually set before others the ideal, not of training children to do their duty, not of sending them forth with stout hearts and ready minds to win triumphs for themselves and their country, not of allowing them the opportunity and giving them the privilege of making their own place in the world, but, forsooth, of keeping the number of children so limited that they might "taste a few good things"! The way to give a child a fair chance in life is not to bring it up in luxury, but to see that it has the kind of training that will give it strength of character. Even apart from the vital question of national life, and regarding only the individual interest of the children themselves, happiness in the true sense is a hundredfold more apt to come to any given member of a healthy family of healthy-minded children, well brought up, well educated, but taught that they must shift for themselves, must win their own way, and by their own exertions make their own positions of usefulness, than it is apt to come to those whose parents themselves have acted on and have trained their children to act on the selfish and sordid theory that the whole end of life is "to taste a few good things."

The intelligence of the remark is on a par with its morality, for the most rudimentary mental process would have shown the speaker that if the average family in which there are children contained but two children the nation as a whole would decrease in population so rapidly that in two or three generations it would very deservedly be on the point of extinction, so that the people who had acted on this base and selfish doctrine would be giving place to others with braver and more robust ideals. Nor would such a result be in any way regrettable; for a race that practiced such doctrine—that is, a race that practiced race suicide—would thereby conclusively show that it was unfit to exist, and that it had better give place to people who had not forgotten the primary laws of their being.

To sum up, then, the whole matter is simple enough. If either a race or an individual prefers the pleasures of mere effortless ease, of self-indulgence, to the infinitely deeper, the infinitely higher pleasures that come to those who know the toil and the weariness, but also the joy, of hard duty well done, why, that race or that individual must inevitably in the end pay the penalty of leading a life both vapid and ignoble. No man and no woman really worthy of the name can care for the life spent solely or chiefly in the avoidance of risk and trouble and labor. Save in exceptional cases the prizes worth having in life must be paid for, and the life worth living must be a life of work for a worthy end, and ordinarily of work more for others than for oneself.

The man is but a poor creature whose effort is not rather for the betterment of his wife and children than for himself; and as for the mother, her very name stands for loving unselfishness and self-abnegation, and, in any society fit to exist, is fraught with associations which render it holy.

The woman's task is not easy—no task worth doing is easy—but in doing it, and when she has done it, there shall come to her the highest and holiest joy known to mankind; and having done it, she shall have the reward prophesied in Scripture; for her husband and her children, yes, and all people who realize that her work lies at the foundation of all national happiness and greatness, shall rise up and call her blessed.

WOMEN IN SCIENCE

*There are few better examples of TR's odd and fascinating
habit of combining the old-fashioned and the modern than this
short piece on the rights of women. It was part of the review of
a book by H. J. Mozans on the right of women to scientific education that TR wrote for* The Outlook *in January 1914.*

Most of the so-called arguments against giving woman the chance
which is given to the lowest men are in essence identical with the arguments formerly used by the favored classes among men against giving
equality of opportunity to the majority of male mankind who were below
them. Unfortunately the enfranchised man usually takes some time before
he realizes that the woman, his helpmate, cannot justly be denied the
rights which it were injustice for him not to receive.

The opponents of giving to woman her rights of course vary widely in
nature. Some of them are made opponents chiefly by the excesses of foolish or immoral advocates of the movement among the women themselves.
Every such movement, every democratic movement or movement for
social or industrial reform, must have its leaders and its martyrs, and
unfortunately every such movement also develops a few fools and a few
knaves, who give an alloy of base metal to the pure gold of the leadership
and the martyrdom. There are foolish women and women who are worse
than foolish who in advocating justice to woman seek to release her from
her physical obligations to humanity and her moral obligations to society.
Advocates of this type who demand that woman shall cease doing her
prime duty as wife and mother, as the bearer and rearer of children, are
not only foolish but wicked.

❦ ❦ ❦

When the reforms have been accomplished and the period of excitement has passed, there is no more reason for believing that woman will
shirk her duties because she has acquired rights than for believing that
the average man in a democracy will be less dutiful than the average man
in a despotism. The argument both from theory and experience is identical
in the two cases.

❦ ❦ ❦

The progress of woman, or, in other words, the progress of man in helping himself by doing justice to the woman who labors beside him, has been more rapid in some countries than in others, and at some times than at others. Italy has borne an honorable distinction in the advance, standing far above France, England, and Germany, and, for the matter of that, beyond the United States until very recent times. Five centuries ago that very remarkable woman Christine de Pizan (whose learning was so wide that it included the ability to write a standard military text-book) spoke as follows:

> I say to thee again, and doubt never the contrary, that if it were the custom to put the little maidens to the school, and they were made to learn the sciences as they do to the men-children, that they should learn as perfectly, and they should be as well entered into the subtleties of all the arts and sciences as men be. And peradventure, there should be more of them, for I have teached heretofore that by how much women have the body more soft than the men have, and less able to do divers things, by so much they have the understanding more sharp as they apply it."

In the Italy of the Middle Ages there were great schools of medicine for women at Salerno and Bologna. Yet the University of Paris persecuted women during those very centuries because they dared to try to serve their fellow women in their hours of sorest need! And but a generation ago the University of London, with blind selfishness and obscurantism, declined to allow women to study surgery or medicine. Vassar, the pioneer college for women, is not fifty years old.

🌿 🌿 🌿

Nowadays few men of the first rank, few men indeed aside from cheap dealers in paradoxes, deny woman's right to as good an education as any man can obtain. We marvel that our predecessors a century or even half a century ago should have failed to see this. Half a century or a century hence our successors will marvel as greatly that we failed to see the indefensibility of denying to woman the other rights necessary to put her on a footing of complete equality with man.

They will marvel no less at the folly and wickedness of the women who have believed that the acquirement of rights will absolve them from the performance of duties. . . . Neither woman nor man can shirk duties under penalty of eventually losing rights, for the possession of the right should be conditioned on the performance of the duty. In any healthy community the prime duty of the woman will ever be that of the wife and mother, just as the prime duty of the man will be to provide the home for wife and children; and this prime duty need interfere no more in one case than in the other with the opportunity to lead, in whatever direction the woman chooses, a life of full and varied interests, which of necessity means a life in which work worth doing is well done.

THE PARASITE WOMAN:
THE ONLY INDISPENSABLE CITIZEN

Ahead of most of his male contemporaries, TR always insisted that marriage must be a full partnership of sharing between man and woman, not a male-dominated relationship. He had no difficulty in simultaneously arguing that the primary role for women was as mothers and wives, who, whatever else they accomplished, must, with the help of their husbands, make a proper home for the rearing of children. He rejected equality of function but insisted on equality of right. Having no patience with advocates of small families, Roosevelt believed that families of more than two children were essential to the health and progress of the nation. And so he often included with his call for women's equal rights a plea that they bear children in numbers adequate to the country's needs. This essay was included in The Foes of Our Own Household, *a collection published in 1917 by the George H. Doran Company.*

Of all species of silliness the silliest is the assertion sometimes made that the woman whose primary life-work is taking care of her home and children is somehow a "parasite woman." It is such a ridiculous inversion of the truth that it ought not to be necessary even to allude to it. Nevertheless, it is acted upon by a large number of selfish, brutal, or thoughtless men, and it is screamed about by a number of foolish women. Therefore a word of common sense on the matter may not be out of place.

There are men so selfish, so short-sighted, or so brutal, that they speak and act as if the fact of the man's earning money for his wife and children, while the woman bears the children, rears them, and takes care of the house for them and for the man, somehow entitles the man to be known as the head of the family, instead of a partner on equal terms with his wife, and entitles him to the exclusive right to dispose of the money and, as a matter of fact, to dispose of it primarily in his own interest.

There are professional feminists and so-called woman's rights women who, curiously enough, seem to accept so much of this male attitude as implies that the partner who earns the money is the superior partner and that therefore the woman, who is physically weaker than the man, should accept as her primary duty the rivaling of him in the money-making business in which he will normally do better than she will; and they stigmatize as parasites the women who do the one great and all-essential work, without which no other activity by either sex amounts to anything.

Apply common sense and common decency to both attitudes. It is entirely right that any woman should be allowed to make any career for herself of which she is capable, whether or not it is a career followed by a man. She has the same right to be a lawyer, a doctor, a farmer, or a storekeeper that the man has to be a poet, an explorer, a politician, or a painter. There are women whose peculiar circumstances or whose peculiar attributes render it advisable that they should follow one of the professions named, just as there are men who can do most good to their fellows by following one of the careers above indicated for men. More than this. It is indispensable that such careers shall be open to women and that certain women shall follow them, if the women of a country, and therefore if the country itself, expect any development. In just the same way, it is indispensable that some men shall be explorers, artists, sculptors, literary men, politicians, if the country is to have its full life. Some of the best farmers are women, just as some of the best exploring work and scientific work has been done by women. There is a real need for a certain number of women doctors and women lawyers. Whether a writer or a painter or a singer is a man or a woman makes not the slightest difference, provided that the work he or she does is good.

All this I not merely admit; I insist upon it. But surely it is a mere statement of fact to add that the primary work of the average man and the average woman—and of all exceptional men and women whose lives are to be really full and happy—must be the great primal work of home-making and home-keeping, for themselves and their children.

The primary work of the man is to earn his own livelihood and the livelihood of those dependent upon him, to do his own business, whether his business is on a farm or in a shop, in the counting-room of a bank or the engine-cab of a train, in a mine or on a fishing-boat, or at the head of a telegraph or telephone line; whether he be an engineer or an inventor, a surgeon or a railway president, or a carpenter or a brakeman. In other words, the man must do his business and do it well in order to support himself and his wife and children and in order that the nation may continue to exist. I appreciate to the full the work of the politician, the poet, the sculptor, and the explorer; and yet it is mere common sense to say that they cannot do any work at all unless their average fellow countryman does his business, whether with hand or brain, pen or pick, in such fashion that the country is on a decent industrial basis. If it is not, nobody will have any house or anything to eat or any means of getting around; and therefore there won't be any poets or politicians. This is not exalting one class at the expense of another. On the contrary it recognizes the absolute need from the standpoint of national greatness and permanent achievement, that there shall be some men in a state the worth of whose activities cannot be and is not measured or expressed by money. But there is also the absolute need that this shall not be true of the average man—and, as a matter of fact, it is a great deal better even if it is not true of the exceptional man—if, in addition to his non-remunerative work, he is able by his activities to pay his way as he goes.

Now, this also applies to women. Exceptional women—like Julia Ward Howe or Harriet Beecher Stowe or Mrs. Homer—are admirable wives and mothers, admirable keepers of the home, and yet workers of genius outside the home. Such types, of course, are rare whether among men or women. There are also exceptional—and less happy, and normally less useful—women whose great service to the state and community is rendered outside the home, and who have no family life; just as is true of exceptional—and normally less happy and less useful—men. But exactly as it is true that no nation will prosper unless the average man is a home-maker; that is, unless at some business or trade or profession, he earns enough to make a home for himself and his wife and children, and is a good husband and father; so no nation can exist at all unless the average woman is the home-keeper, the good wife, and unless she is the mother of a sufficient number of healthy children to insure the race going forward and not backward. The indispensable work for the community is the work of the wife and the mother. It is the most honorable work. It is literally and exactly the vital work, the work which of course must be done by the average woman or the whole nation goes down with a crash.

Foolish men treat this fact as warranting them in all kinds of outcries against what they call "unwomanly" activities, including the outcry against the "higher education." This is nonsense. The woman is entitled to just as much education as the man; and it will not hurt her one particle more than it hurts the man. It may hurt a fool in either case; but no one else. However, justification is given these people who cry against the "higher education" by such utterances as those made the other day by a president of a women's college who fatuously announced, in advocacy of a small birth-rate, that it was better to have one child brought up in the best way than several not thus brought up. In the first place, there is no such antithesis as is thus implied, for, as a matter of fact, children in a family of children are usually better brought up than the only child, or than the child of a two-child family. In the next place, the statement, which must of course be taken to apply to the average individual, is on its face false, and the woman making it is not only unfit to be at the head of a female college, but is not fit to teach the lowest class in a kindergarten, for such teaching is not merely folly, but a peculiarly repulsive type of mean and selfish wickedness. The one-child family as an average ideal of course spells death; and death means the end of all hope. It is only while there is life that there is hope. A caste or a race or a nation, where the average family consists of one child, faces immediate extinction, and therefore it matters not one particle how this child is brought up. But if there are plenty of children then there is always hope. Even if they have not been very well brought up, they *have* been brought up, and so there is something to work on.

Just as the prime work for the average man must be earning his livelihood and the livelihood of those dependent upon him, so the prime work for the average woman must be keeping the home and bearing and rearing her children. This woman is not a parasite on society. She *is* society. Socially, the same standard of moral obligation applies both to her and to the man; and in addition she is entitled to all the chivalry of love and tenderness and reverence, if in gallant and fearless fashion she faces the risk and wearing labor entailed by her fulfillment of duty; but if she shirks her duty she is entitled to no more consideration than the man who shirks his. Unless she does her duty, the whole social system collapses. If she does her duty, she is entitled to all honor.

This last statement is the crucial statement. The one way to honor this indispensable woman, the wife and mother, is to insist that she be treated as the full equal of her husband. The birth-pangs make all men the debtors of all women; and the man is a wretched creature who does not live up to his obligation. Marriage should be a real partnership; a partnership of the soul, the spirit, and the mind, no less than of the body. An immediately practical feature of this partnership should be the full acknowledgment that the woman who keeps the home has exactly the same right to a say in the disposal of the money as the man who earns the money. Earning the money is not one whit more indispensable than keeping the home. Indeed, I am inclined to put it in the second place. The husband who does not give his wife, as a matter of right, her share in the disposal of the common funds is false to his duty. It is not a question of favor at all. Aside from the money to be spent on common account, for the household and the children, the wife has just the same right as the husband to her pin-money, her spending-money. It is not his money that he gives to her as a gift. It is hers as a matter of right. He may earn it; but she earns it because she keeps the house; and she has just as much right to it as he has. This is not a hostile right; it is a right which it is every woman's duty to ask and which it should be every man's pride and pleasure to give without asking. He is a poor creature if he grudges it; and she in her turn is a poor creature if she does not insist upon her rights, just exactly as she is worse than a poor creature if she does not do her duty.

It is the men who insist upon women doing their duty fully, who insist that the primary duty of the woman is in the home, who also have a right to insist that she is just as much entitled to the suffrage as is the man. We believe in equality of right, not in identity of functions. The woman must bear and rear the children, as her first duty to the state; and the man's first duty is to take care of her and the children. In neither case is it the exclusive duty. In neither case does it exclude the performance of other duties. The right to vote no more implies that a woman will neglect her home than that a man will neglect his business. Indeed, as regards one of the greatest and most useful of all professions, that of surgery and medicine, it is probably true that the average doctor's wife has more time for the performance of political duties than the average doctor himself.

There was a capital article recently in *The Britannia*, the official organ of the Women's Social and Political Union in England, by Mrs. Emmeline Pankhurst. She was urging the full performance of duty in the war both by men and by women. In it she denounced the laboring men who did not whole-heartedly do everything in their power to aid the cause of England in the war. She spoke of the fact that working men and women in France could not understand how there could be strikes among workers in England during the war. She insisted that the prime duty during the war was for the men and women alike to put aside all other grievances and make common cause on behalf of the nation, and then to try to make the country a better one for their children to live in. It was a capital article, and it should be read by men and women here just as much as by men and women in England. It is because I believe that the American woman will in time of need and when the facts are brought home to her take such a position as Mrs. Pankhurst has thus taken, that I emphatically believe that she should have the right just as much as the man to vote, and, what is even more important, that she shall be given her full rights in connection with the performance by her as wife and mother of those indispensable duties which make her the one absolutely indispensable citizen of this Republic.

TR with Booker T. Washington at Tuskegee Institute, 1905.

11

ON RACE

THE NEGRO PROBLEM

*I*t is clear that TR spoke to the people of a different time and a different sensibility when he, as president, could refer to the "backward race" and the "forward race" to distinguish between black and white Americans. Nevertheless, when few white leaders dared to, TR did speak for equality of opportunity and of justice. By contrast, the Progressive reforms that marked the early years of the twentieth century remained generally innocent of ideas encouraging racial equality or racial justice. In this February 1905 Lincoln Day talk to the Republican Club of New York City, Roosevelt counseled patience and hoped that the future would be better, but beyond his familiar call to duty there is little in the speech that black Americans could have applauded with enthusiasm.

♦♦♦

In his second inaugural, in a speech which will be read as long as the memory of his nation endures, Abraham Lincoln closed by saying:

> With malice toward none; with charity for all; with firmness in the right, as God gives us to see the right, let us strive on to finish the work we are in; . . . to do all which may achieve and cherish a just and lasting peace among ourselves, and with all nations.

Immediately after his re-election he had already spoken thus:

> The strife of the election is but human nature practically applied to the facts of the case. What has occurred in this case must ever recur in similar cases. Human nature will not change. In any future great national trial, compared with the men of this, we shall have as weak and as strong, as silly and as wise, as bad and as good. Let us, therefore, study the incidents of this as philosophy to learn wisdom from, and none of them as wrongs to be revenged. . . . May not all having a common interest reunite in a common effort to serve our common country? For my own part, I have striven and shall strive to avoid placing any obstacle in the way. So long as I have been here I have not willingly planted a thorn in any man's bosom. While I am deeply sensible to the high compliment of a re-election, and duly grateful, as I trust to Almighty God for having directed my countrymen to a right conclusion, as I think for their own good, it adds nothing to my satisfaction that any other man may be disappointed or pained by the result.
>
> May I ask those who have not differed with me to join with me in this same spirit toward those who have?

This is the spirit in which mighty Lincoln sought to bind up the nation's wounds when its soul was yet seething with fierce hatreds, with wrath, with rancor, with all the evil and dreadful passions provoked by civil war. Surely this is the spirit which all Americans should show now, when there is so little excuse for malice or rancor or hatred, when there is so little of vital consequence to divide brother from brother.

Lincoln, himself a man of Southern birth, did not hesitate to appeal to the sword when he became satisfied that in no other way could the Union be saved, for high though he put peace he put righteousness still higher. He warred for the Union; he warred to free the slave; and when he warred he warred in earnest, for it is a sign of weakness to be half-hearted when blows must be struck. But he felt only love, a love as deep as the tenderness of his great and sad heart, for all his countrymen alike in the North and in the South, and he longed above everything for the day when they should once more be knit together in the unbreakable bonds of eternal friendship.

We of to-day, in dealing with all our fellow citizens, white or colored, North or South, should strive to show just the qualities that Lincoln showed: his steadfastness in striving after the right, and his infinite patience and forbearance with those who saw that right less clearly than he did; his earnest endeavor to do what was best, and yet his readiness to accept the best that was practicable when the ideal best was unattainable; his unceasing effort to cure what was evil, coupled with his refusal to make a bad situation worse by any ill-judged or ill-timed effort to make it better.

The great Civil War in which Lincoln towered as the loftiest figure left us not only a reunited country, but a country which has the proud right to claim as its own glory won alike by those who wore the blue and by those who wore the gray, by those who followed Grant and by those who followed Lee; for both fought with equal bravery and with equal sincerity of conviction, each striving for the light as it was given him to see the light; though it is now clear to all that the triumph of the cause of freedom and of the Union was essential to the welfare of mankind. We are now one people, a people with failings which we must not blink, but a people with great qualities in which we have the right to feel just pride.

All good Americans who dwell in the North must, because they are good Americans, feel the most earnest friendship for their fellow countrymen who dwell in the South, a friendship all the greater because it is in the South that we find in its most acute phase one of the gravest problems before our people: the problem of so dealing with the man of one color as to secure him the rights that no one would grudge him if he were of another color. To solve this problem it is, of course, necessary to educate him to perform the duties a failure to perform which will render him a curse to himself and to all around him.

Most certainly all clear-sighted and generous men in the North appreciate the difficulty and perplexity of this problem, sympathize with the South in the embarrassment of conditions for which she is not alone responsible, feel an honest wish to help her where help is practicable, and have the heartiest respect for those brave and earnest men of the South who, in the face of fearful difficulties, are doing all that men can do for the betterment alike of white and of black. The attitude of the North toward the Negro is far from what it should be and there is need that the North also should act in good faith upon the principle of giving to each man what is justly due him, of treating him on his worth as a man, granting him no special favors, but denying him no proper opportunity for labor and the reward of labor. But the peculiar circumstances of the South render the problem there far greater and far more acute.

Neither I nor any other man can say that any given way of approaching that problem will present in our time even an approximately perfect solution, but we can safely say that there can never be such solution at all unless we approach it with the effort to do fair and equal justice among all men; and to demand from them in return just and fair treatment for others. Our effort should be to secure to each man, whatever his color, equality of opportunity, equality of treatment before the law. As a people striving to shape our actions in accordance with the great law of righteousness we cannot afford to take part in or be indifferent to the oppression or maltreatment of any man who, against crushing disadvantages, has by his own industry, energy, self-respect, and perseverance struggled upward to a position which would entitle him to the respect of his fellows, if only his skin were of a different hue.

Every generous impulse in us revolts as the thought of thrusting down instead of helping up such a man. To deny any man the fair treatment granted to others no better than he is to commit a wrong upon him—a wrong sure to react in the long run upon those guilty of such denial. The only safe principle upon which Americans can act is that of "all men up," not that of "some men down." If in any community the level of intelligence, morality, and thrift among the colored men can be raised, it is humanly speaking sure that the same level among the whites will be raised to an even higher degree; and it is no less sure that the debasement of the blacks will in the end carry with it an attendant debasement of the whites.

The problem is so to adjust the relations between two races of different ethnic type that the rights of neither be abridged nor jeopardied; that the backward race be trained so that it may enter into the possession of true freedom, while the forward race is enabled to preserve unharmed the high civilization wrought out by its forefathers. The working out of this problem must necessarily be slow; it is not possible in offhand fashion to obtain or to confer the priceless boons of freedom, industrial efficiency, political capacity, and domestic morality. Nor is it only necessary to train the colored man; it is quite as necessary to train the white man, for on his shoulders rests a well-nigh unparalleled sociological responsibility. It is a problem demanding the best thought, the utmost patience, the most earnest effort, the broadest charity, of the statesman, the student, the philanthropist; of the leaders of thought in every department of our national life. The church can be a most important factor in solving it aright. But above all else we need for its successful solution the sober, kindly, steadfast, unselfish performance of duty by the average plain citizen in his every-day dealings with his fellows.

The ideal of elemental justice meted out to every man is the ideal we should keep ever before us. It will be many a long day before we attain to it, and unless we show not only devotion to it, but also wisdom and self-restraint in the exhibition of that devotion, we shall defer the time for its realization still further. In striving to attain to so much of it as concerns dealing with men of different colors, we must remember two things.

In the first place, it is true of the colored man, as it is true of the white man, that in the long run his fate must depend far more upon his own effort than upon the efforts of any outside friend. Every vicious, venal, or ignorant colored man is an even greater foe to his own race than to the community as a whole. The colored man's self-respect entitles him to do that share in the political work of the country which is warranted by his individual ability and integrity and the position he has won for himself. But the prime requisite of the race is moral and industrial uplifting.

Laziness and shiftlessness, these, and above all, vice and criminality of every kind, are evils more potent for harm to the black race than all acts of oppression of white men put together. The colored man who fails to condemn crime in another colored man, who fails to co-operate in all lawful ways in bringing colored criminals to justice, is the worst enemy of his own people, as well as an enemy to all the people. Law abiding black men should, for the sake of their race, be foremost in relentless and unceasing warfare against lawbreaking black men. If the standards of private morality and industrial efficiency can be raised high enough among the black race, then its future on this continent is secure. The stability and purity of the home is vital to the welfare of the black race, as it is to the welfare of every race.

In the next place the white man who, if only he is willing, can help the colored man more than all other white men put together, is the white man who is his neighbor, North or South. Each of us must do his whole duty without flinching, and if that duty is national it must be done in accordance with the principles above laid down. But in endeavoring each to be his brother's keeper it is wise to remember that each can normally do most for the brother who is his immediate neighbor. If we are sincere friends of the Negro let us each in his own locality show it by his action therein, and let us each show it also by upholding the hands of the white man, in whatever locality, who is striving to do justice to the poor and the helpless, to be a shield to those whose need for such a shield is great.

The heartiest acknowledgements are due to the ministers, the judges and law officers, the grand juries, the public men, and the great daily newspapers in the South, who have recently done such effective work in leading the crusade against lynching in the South; and I am glad to say that during the last three months the returns, as far as they can be gathered, show a smaller number of lynchings than for any other three months during the last twenty years. Let us uphold in every way the hands of the men who have led in this work, who are striving to do all their work in this spirit.

☙ ☙ ☙

Let us be steadfast for the right; but let us err on the side of generosity rather than on the side of vindictiveness toward those who differ from us as to the method of attaining the right. Let us never forget our duty to help in uplifting the lowly, to shield from wrong the humble; and let us likewise act in a spirit of the broadest and frankest generosity toward all our brothers, all our fellow countrymen; in a spirit proceeding not from weakness but from strength, a spirit which takes no more account of locality than it does of class or of creed; a spirit which is resolutely bent on seeing that the Union which Washington founded and which Lincoln saved from destruction shall grow nobler and greater throughout the ages.

I believe in this country with all my heart and soul. I believe that our people will in the end rise level to every need, will in the end triumph over every difficulty that rises before them. I could not have such confident faith in the destiny of this mighty people if I had it merely as regards one portion of that people. Throughout our land things on the whole have grown better and not worse, and this is as true of one part of the country as it is of another. I believe in the Southerner as I believe in the Northerner. I claim the right to feel pride in his great qualities and in his great deeds exactly as I feel pride in the great qualities and deeds of every other American. For weal or for woe we are knit together, and we shall go up or down together; and I believe that we shall go up and not down, that we shall go forward instead of halting and falling back, because I have an abiding faith in the generosity, the courage, the resolution, and the common sense of all my countrymen.

The Southern States face difficult problems; and so do the Northern States. Some of the problems are the same for the entire country. Others exist in greater intensity in one section; and yet others exist in greater intensity in another section. But in the end they will all be solved; for fundamentally our people are the same throughout this land; the same in the qualities of heart and brain and hand which have made this Republic what it is in the great to-day; which will make it what it is to be in the infinitely greater to-morrow. I admire and respect and believe in and have faith in the men and women of the South as I admire and respect and believe in and have faith in the men and women of the North. All of us alike, Northerners and Southerners,

Easterners and Westerners, can best prove our fealty to the nation's past by the way in which we do the nation's work in the present; for only thus can we be sure that our children's children shall inherit Abraham Lincoln's single-hearted devotion to the great unchanging creed that "righteousness exalteth a nation."

THE EDUCATION OF THE NEGRO

In October 1905 TR addressed the students and faculty of Tuskegee Institute in Alabama, a pioneer school for black students established by Booker T. Washington. As in his Lincoln Day address earlier that year in New York, he suggests hard work, law-abiding behavior, and patience to further the cause of black Americans.

To the white population as well as to the black, it is of the utmost importance that the Negro be encouraged to make himself a citizen of the highest type of usefulness. It is to the interest of the white people that this policy be conscientiously pursued, and to the interest of the colored people that they clearly realize that they have opportunities for economic development here in the South not now offered elsewhere. Within the last twenty years the industrial operations of the South have increased so tremendously that there is a scarcity of labor almost everywhere; so that it is the part of wisdom for all who wish the prosperity of the South to help the Negro to become in the highest degree useful to himself, and therefore to the community in which he lives. The South has always depended, and now depends, chiefly upon her native population for her work. Therefore in view of the scarcity not only of common labor, but of skilled labor, it becomes doubly important to train every available man to be of the utmost use, by developing his intelligence, his skill, and his capacity for conscientious effort. Hence the work of the Tuskegee Normal and Industrial Institute is a matter of the highest practical importance to both the white man and the black man, and well worth the support of both races alike in the South and in the North. Your fifteen hundred students are not only being educated in head and heart, but also trained to industrial efficiency, for from the beginning Tuskegee has placed especial emphasis upon the training of men and women in agriculture, mechanics, and household duties. Training in these three fundamental directions does not embrace all that the Negro, or any other race, needs, but it does cover in a very large degree the field in which the Negro can at present do most for himself and be most helpful to his white neighbors. Every black man who leaves this institute better able to do mechanical or industrial work adds by so much to the wealth of the whole community and benefits all people in the community. The professional and mercantile avenues to success are overcrowded; for the present the best chance of success awaits the intelligent worker at some mechanical trade or on a farm; for this man will almost certainly achieve industrial independence.

I am pleased, but not in the least surprised, to learn that many among the men and women trained at Tuskegee find immediate employment as leaders and workers among their own people, and that their services are eagerly sought by white people for various kinds of industrial work, the demand being much greater than the supply. Viewed from any angle, ignorance is the costliest crop that can be raised in any part of this Union. Every dollar put into the education of either white man or black man, in head, in hand, and in heart, yields rich dividends to the entire community. Merely from the economic standpoint it is of the utmost consequence to all our citizens that institutions such as this at Tuskegee should be a success. But there are other and even higher reasons that entitle it to our support.

In the interest of humanity, of justice, and of self-protection, every white man in America, no matter where he lives, should try to help the Negro to help himself. It is in the interest and for the protection of the white man to see that the Negro is educated. It is not only the duty of the white man, but it is to his interest, to see that the Negro is protected in property, in life, and in all his legal rights. Every time a law is broken, every individual in the community has the moral tone of his life lowered. Lawlessness in the United States is not confined to any one section; lynching is not confined to any one section; and there is perhaps no body of American citizens who have deserved so well of the entire American people as the public men, the publicists, the clergymen, the countless thousands of high-minded private citizens, who have done such heroic work in the South in arousing public opinion against lawlessness in all its forms, and especially against lynching. I very earnestly hope that their example will count in the North as well as in the South, for there are just as great evils to be warred against in one region of our country as in another, though they are not in all places the same evils. And when any body of men in any community stands bravely for what is right, these men not merely serve a useful purpose in doing the particular task to which they set themselves, but give a lift to the cause of good citizenship throughout the Union.

I heartily appreciate what you have done at Tuskegee; and I am sure you will not grudge my saying that it could not possibly have been done save for the loyal support you have received from the white people roundabout; for during the twenty-five years of effort to educate the black man here in the midst of a white community of intelligence and culture, there has never been an outbreak between the races, or any difficulty of any kind. All honor is due to the white men of Alabama, to the white men of Tuskegee, for what they have done. And right here let me say that if in any community a misunderstanding between the races arises, over any matter, infinitely the best way out is to have a prompt, frank, and full conference and consultation between representatives of the wise, decent, cool-headed men among the whites and the wise, decent, cool-headed colored men. Such a conference will always tend to bring about a better understanding, and will be a great help all round.

Hitherto I have spoken chiefly of the obligations existing on the part of the white man. Now remember on the other hand that no help can permanently avail you save as you yourselves develop capacity for self-help. You young colored men and women educated at Tuskegee must by precept and example lead your fellows toward sober, industrious, law-abiding lives. You are in honor bound to join hands in favor of law and order and to war against all crime, and especially against all crime by men of your own race; for the heaviest wrong done by the criminal is the wrong to his own race. You must teach the people of your race that they must scrupulously observe any contract into which they in good faith enter, no matter whether it is hard to keep or not. If you save money, secure homes, become taxpayers, and lead clean, decent, modest lives, you will win the respect of your neighbors of both races. Let each man strive to excel his fellows only by rendering substantial service to the community in which he lives.

The colored people have many difficulties to pass through, but these difficulties will be surmounted if only the policy of reason and common sense is pursued. You have made real and great progress. According to the census the colored people of this country own and pay taxes upon something like three hundred million dollars' worth of property, and have blotted out over fifty per cent of their illiteracy. What you have done in the past is an indication of what you will be able to accomplish in the future under wise leadership. Moral and industrial education is what is most needed, in order that this progress may continue. The race cannot expect to get everything at once. It must learn to wait and bide its time; to prove itself worthy by showing its possession of perseverance, of thrift, of self-control. The destiny of the race is chiefly in its own hands, and must be worked out patiently and persistently along these lines. Remember also that the white man who can be of most use to the colored man is that colored man's neighbor. It is the southern people themselves who must and can solve the difficulties that exist in the South; of course what help the people of the rest of the Union can give them must and will be gladly and cheerfully given. The hope of advancement for the colored man in the South lies in his steady, common-sense effort to improve his moral and material condition, and to work in harmony with the white man in upbuilding the Commonwealth. The future of the South now depends upon the people of both races living up to the spirit and letter of the laws of their several States and working out the destinies of both races, not as races, but as law-abiding American citizens.

RACE DECADENCE

The book review was another of TR's writing vehicles, and he often used it as much to broadcast his own ideas as to criticize the book in question. In this essay he discusses what was for him a long-standing concern that the solid and superior "old stock" of the country would decline, in this case by reluctance to reproduce in adequate numbers. Elsewhere he warned of the dangers to the predominant strain of Nordic blood of mixing with the lesser but apparently attractive immigrant stock. This review also offers an example of his mixing the advocacy for the equality of women and an exhortation to the womanly duties of wife and mother to expand the nation's numbers. The review appeared in The Outlook *in April 1911.*

An Australian writer, Mr. Beale, has written a work on *Racial Decay,* not good in form, but in substance I believe better worth the study of every sincere patriot, not merely in Australia, Great Britain, and Canada, but in the United States of America, than any other book that has been written for years. It sets forth in detail, and illustrates by chart, certain facts which have long been familiar to students and thinkers who care to face the truth, and whose studies and thought are not superficial. But, unfortunately, the facts set forth, though of fundamental importance to the whole people, are so unpleasant that ease-loving persons who do not care for anything that causes them disquiet refuse to look them in the face; and the great bulk of good people are in ignorance of them, or at least wholly fail to appreciate their far-reaching significance.

Mr. Beale deals with the startling decline of the birth-rate in Great Britain, the Australian states, and France, this decline being due to the capital sin, the cardinal sin, against the race and against civilization — willful sterility in marriage. He only touches on the United States incidentally; but every student of the subject knows that the United States shares with the other English-speaking countries the melancholy and discreditable position of coming next to the people of France, among great civilized countries, in that rapid decline of the birth-rate which inevitably signalizes race decay, and which, if unchecked, means racial death. Mr. Beale shows that the decline of the birth-rate in France because of willful sterility in marriage began fifty or sixty years ago, and has continued to such a point that the French race in France for the last decade has been actually decreasing in numbers, the population of France being kept practically level only by the higher birth-rate among immigrants, chiefly Italians and Germans. Among the English-speaking peoples there has long been much complacent pointing at France as a nation that no longer held its own among the peoples of the earth. As a matter of fact, the English-speaking peoples have now all entered on the same course which France has followed until year by year she has become less and less able to rank as the equal of Germany. Moreover, the decline in the birth-rate among the English-speaking peoples has proceeded at an even more rapid rate than in France itself.

※ ※ ※

The American stock is being cursed with the curse of sterility, and it is earning the curse, because the sterility is willful. It is due to moral, and not physiological shortcomings. It is due to coldness, to selfishness, to love of ease, to shrinking from risk, to an utter and pitiful failure in sense of perspective and in power of weighing what really makes the highest joy, and to a rooting out of the sense of duty or a twisting of that sense into improper channels. Moreover, the same racial crime is spreading almost as rapidly among the sons and daughters of immigrants as among the descendants of the native-born. If it were confined to Americans of old stock, while it would be a matter of shame to us who are of the old stock, we could at least feel that the traditions and principles and purposes of the founders of the Republic would find their believers and exponents among their descendants by adoption; and in such case I, for one, would heartily throw in my fate with the men of alien stock who were true to the old American principles rather than with the men of the old American stock who were traitors to the old American principles. But the children of the immigrants show the same willful sterility that is shown by the people of the old stock. It is almost unnecessary to say that the sterility is not physiological—of course disregarding the naturally numerous exceptions—and is in no sense due to the change from Europe to another land. For over two centuries after coming here the descendants of the European settlers were among the most prolific of mankind; and the same is true now of the whites of the southern Appalachian region; while there is probably no race on the face of the earth more prolific than the French of Canada, who have become and continued such during the very centuries which have seen the sterility among their kinsfolk the French of Europe grow until the race is actually going backward in point of numbers.

During the last decade the increase in population of the United States was almost two-thirds by immigration, the increase by birth-rate showing a far lower percentage than ever before. Lincoln rarely ventured to prophesy.

His chief prophecy, which looked far ahead into the future, was about our growth of population, and this has been lamentably falsified by the facts. He prophesied that by this time we would have over two hundred millions of people; and so we would have had if the United States had continued to increase at the rate that it increased during Lincoln's lifetime. As it is, if the present rate of decrease in the birth-rate continues, this country will have become stationary in population by the middle of the century; and so will the English-speaking peoples of the British Empire.

❦ ❦ ❦

It is never safe to prophesy. Neither I nor any one else can say what will happen in the future. But we can speak conditionally. We can say that, if the processes now at work for a generation continue to work in the same manner and at the same rate of increase during the present century, by its end France will not carry the weight in the civilized world that Belgium now does, and the English-speaking peoples will not carry anything like the weight that the Spanish-speaking peoples now do, and the future of the white race will rest in the hands of the German and the Slav. Are Americans really content that this land of promise, this land of the future, this abounding and vigorous nation, shall become decrepit in what ought to be the flower of its early manhood?

❦ ❦ ❦

If there are no children to a marriage, the race vanishes with the generation itself; and if there are only one or two children to a marriage, the vanishing of the race is only put off for a short time. Sterile marriages include those where there are but one or two children, just as they include those where there are no children; willful sterility is as much a crime against the race in the case of the marriage where there are no children. From the standpoint of the race the average three-child marriage must probably also be treated as a sterile marriage; for the one extra child does not, on the average, cover the cases of death, the cases where for proper and legitimate reasons the man or woman does not marry, and the cases where married people through no fault of their own fail to have children. The race cannot go ahead, it will not keep its numbers even, unless the average man and woman who are married and who are capable of having children have a family of four children. These, and these only, are the men and women with whom the whole future of the nation, the whole future of civilization, rests.

I know well every form of cheap sophistry which can be used in answer to this statement. I know well how certain it is that this statement will be twisted out of shape, and how some men, who for their own purpose choose to pretend to misunderstand it, will cause it to be misunderstood by some good men and women who have not thought deeply. But it is a statement which not only must be made, but upon which all true lovers of their country and lovers of mankind should insist with their whole hearts.

No partnership of happiness can ever be such unless it is also a partnership of work; and in this life it is rare indeed that success and happiness come save as the result of willingness to run risk and to face danger as well as work. But woe to the small souls who shrink from facing the great adventure! Shame to those who choose to lead their lives in a round of cheap self-indulgence and vapid excitement! They shall end in the gray twilight which has known neither victory nor defeat, and which therefore means the worst of all possible kinds of defeat, the defeat that comes to those who have not dared to try to win the battle. In the partnership of man and woman the woman risks most, and for that reason we should hold in peculiar abhorrence the man who fails to realize this and to be gentle and tender and loyal in his dealings with her. The birth pangs make all men the debtors of all women; and those men have indeed touched the lowest abyss of brutality and depravity who do not recognize something holy in the names of wife and mother. No man, not even the soldier who does his duty, stands quite on the level with the wife and mother who has done her duty.

I do not believe that there is identity of duties as between man and woman, and I do believe that it is far more important for both to dwell upon their duties than their rights. But I also believe in a full equality of rights; if women wish to vote, I favor it (although I do not think it anything like as important for them or for the state as are many other things that they can and should do); but the extent of my reverence for and belief in a woman who does her duty measures also the depth of my contempt for the woman who shirks her primal and most essential duty. The man who either is responsible for, or acquiesces in, sterility in marriage is even more contemptible than the woman; but he is the only person more contemptible. Exactly as the measure of our regard for the soldier who does his full duty in battle is the measure of our scorn for the coward who flees, so the measure of our respect for the true wife and mother is the measure of our scorn and contemptuous abhorrence for the wife who refuses to be a mother.

❧ ❧ ❧

I hope I shall not be misunderstood, unless willfully. I no more mean that a man and a woman are good citizens merely because they have children than I mean that a man is a good soldier merely because he can fight. In each case the possession of one essential quality does not atone for the lack of other qualities, which are only less essential. Criminals should not have children. Shiftless and worthless people should not marry and have families which they are unable to bring up properly. Such marriages are a curse to the community. But this is only the negative side of the matter; and the positive is always more important than the negative. In our civilization to-day the great danger is that there will be failure to have enough children of the marriages that ought to take place. What we most need is insistence upon the duty of decent people to have enough children, and the sternest condemnation of the practices commonly resorted to in order to secure sterility.

❧ ❧ ❧

Our appeal must be not only to the intellect and the reason; it must be to the heart and the conscience. In this great fundamental matter, vital to the life of the whole nation, our appeal must be to the plain people, to the average man and the average woman; and fundamentally it must be an appeal to character, an earnest prayer that in the souls of all of us the sense of duty may grow and not dwindle, and may be guided by wisdom and inspired by courage. We honor the good man and the good woman who do their duty; and, above all others, we honor the wife and mother, for she is the high priestess of the race, who bears in her strong and tender arms the burden of the destinies of mankind.

Reviewing a manuscript at his desk at Sagamore Hill, 1905.

12

CRITIC OF ARTS AND LETTERS

TOLSTOY

TR had no patience for pacifism, and he took what opportunities he could to defend his views on military power. A better historian than literary critic, he seems here to have missed the point of Tolstoy's work Kreutzer Sonata, *which posits the ideal of chastity as a central theme, hardly suggesting "moral perversion" in the author. The essay appeared in May 1909 in* The Outlook.

One of the comic features of the political campaign last fall [Taft defeated Bryan for the presidency] was the letter which Count Tolstoy wrote on behalf of Mr. Bryan. In this letter Count Tolstoy advocated the election of Mr. Bryan on the ground that he was the representative of the party of peace, of anti-militarism. From the point of view of American politics, the incident possessed no importance beyond furnishing material for the humorous columns of the newspapers. But it had a certain real interest as indicating Count Tolstoy's worth as a moral guide. He advocated Mr. Bryan on the theory that Mr. Bryan represented peace and anti-militarism. Now there was but one point in the platform of either political party in 1908 which contained any element of menace to the peace of the world. This was the plank in the Bryanite platform which demanded the immediate exclusion by law of all Asiatic laborers, and therefore of the Japanese. Coupled with it was the utterly meaningless plank about the navy, which was, however, intended to convey the impression that we ought to have a navy only for the defense of our coasts—that is, a merely "defensive" navy, or, in other words, a quite worthless navy. At the present time there is neither justification nor excuse for such a law—wholly without regard to what the future may show. The exclusion plank in Mr. Bryan's platform represented merely an idle threat, a wanton insult, and it was coupled with what was intended to be a declaration that the policy of upbuilding the navy, which has been so successfully carried on during the past dozen years, would be abandoned. Any man of common sense, therefore, ought to perceive the self-evident fact that the only menace to peace which was contained in any possible action by the American Republic was that contained in the election of Mr. Bryan and the attempt to put into effect his platform. That Count Tolstoy did not see this affords a curious illustration of his complete inability to face facts; of his readiness to turn aside from the truth in the pursuit of any phantom, however foolish; and of the utter fatuity of those who treat him as a philosopher, whose philosophy should be, or could be, translated into action.

Count Tolstoy is a man of genius, a great novelist. *War and Peace, Anna Karenina, The Cossacks, Sebastopol,* are great books. As a novelist he has added materially to the sum of production of his generation. As a professional philosopher and moralist, I doubt if his influence has really been very extensive among men of action; of course it has a certain weight among men who live only in the closet, in the library, and among the high-minded men of this type, who, because of their sheltered lives, naturally reject what is immoral, and do not have to deal with what is fantastic, in Tolstoy's teachings; it is probable that the really lofty side of these teachings gives them a certain sense of spiritual exaltation. But I have no question that whatever little influence Tolstoy has exerted among men of action has told, on the whole, for evil. I do not think his influence over men of action has been great, for I think he has swayed or dominated only the feeble folk and the fantastic folk. No man who possesses both robust common sense and high ideals, and who strives to apply both in actual living, is affected by Tolstoy's teachings, save as he is affected by the teachings of hundreds of other men in whose writings there are occasional truths mixed with masses of what is commonplace or erroneous. Strong men may gain something from Tolstoy's moral teachings, but only on condition that they are strong enough and sane enough to be repelled by those parts of his teachings which are foolish or immoral. Weak persons are hurt by the teachings. Still, I think that the mere fact that these weak persons are influenced sufficiently to be marred means that there was not in them a very great quantity of potential usefulness to mar. In the United States we suffer from grave moral dangers; but they are for the most part dangers which Tolstoy would neither perceive nor know how to combat. Moreover, the real and dreadful evils which do in fact share in his denunciation of and attack upon both good and evil are usually not evils which are of much moment among us. On the other hand, we are not liable to certain kinds of wickedness which there is real danger of his writings inculcating; for it is a lamentable fact that, as is so often the case with a certain type of mystical zealot, there is in him a dark streak which tells of moral perversion. That side of his teachings which is partially manifested in the revolting *Kreutzer Sonata* can do exceedingly little damage in America, for it would appeal only to decadents; exactly as it could have come only from a man who, however high he may stand in certain respects, has in him certain dreadful qualities of the moral pervert.

The usual effect of prolonged and excessive indulgence in Tolstoyism on American disciples is comic rather than serious. One of these disciples, for instance, not long ago wrote a book on American municipal problems which ascribed our ethical and social shortcomings in municipal matters in part to the sin of "militarism." Now the mind of this particular writer in making such a statement was influenced not in the least by what had actually occurred or was occurring in our cities, but by one of Tolstoy's theories which had no possible bearing upon American life. Militarism is a real factor for good or for evil in most European countries. In America it has not the smallest effect one way or the other; it is a negligible quantity. There are undoubtedly states of society where militarism is a grave evil, and there are plenty of circumstances in which the prime duty of man may be to strive against it. But it is not righteous war, not even war itself, which is the absolute evil, the evil which is evil always and under all circumstances. Militarism which takes the form of a police force, municipal or national, may be the prime factor for upholding peace and righteousness. Militarism is to be condemned or not purely according to the conditions. So eating horse-meat is in itself a mere matter of taste; but the early Christian missionaries in Scandinavia found that serious evil sprang from the custom of eating horse-meat in honor of Odin. It is literally true that our very grave municipal problems in New York or Chicago have no more to do with militarism than with eating the meat of horses that have been sacrificed to pagan deities; and a crusade against one habit, as an element in municipal reform, is just about as rational as would be a crusade against the other. Oliver Wendell Holmes said that it had taken a century to remove the lark from American literature; because the poets insisted upon writing, not about the birds they saw, but about the birds they had read of in the writings of other poets. Militarism as an evil in our social life is as purely a figment of the imagination as the skylark in our literature. Moreover, the fact that in spite of this total absence of militarism there is so much that is evil in our life, so much need for reform, ought to show persons who think that the destruction of militarism would bring about the millennium how completely they lack the sense of perspective.

Another disciple used to write poetry in defense of the Mahdi,[1] apparently under the vague impression that this also was a protest against militarism and therefore in line with Tolstoy's teachings—as very possible it was. Now, Mahdism was as hideous an exhibition of bloodthirsty cruelty, governmental tyranny, corruption and inefficiency, and homicidal religious fanaticism as the world has ever seen. Its immediate result was to destroy over half the population in the area where it held sway, and to bring the most dreadful degradation and suffering to the remainder. It represented in the aggregate more wickedness, more wrong-doing, more human suffering, than all the wickedness, wrong-doing, and human suffering in all the Christian communities put together during the same period. It was characteristic of the fantastic perversion of morality which naturally results from the serious acceptance of Tolstoy as a moral teacher that one manifestation of this acceptance should have been a defense of Mahdism. Of course when the Anglo-Egyptian army overthrew Mahdism it conferred a boon upon all mankind, and most of all upon the wretched inhabitants of the Soudan.

---

[1] A radical Muslim sect of the Sudan which revolted against Egyptian control in 1881.

So much for Tolstoyism in America, the only place where I have studied it in action, and where its effect, although insignificant for good, has been not much more significant for evil, being absurd rather than serious. As to the effect in Russia itself, I am not competent to speak. But the history of the Duma proved in the most emphatic way that the greatest danger to liberalism in Russia sprang from the fact that the liberals were saturated with just such folly as that taught by Tolstoy.

☙ ☙ ☙

The important point is that his preaching is compounded of some very beautiful and lofty sentiments, with much that is utterly fantastic, and with some things that are grossly immoral. The Duma fell far short of what its friends in other lands hoped for, just because it showed these very same traits, and because it failed to develop the power for practical common-sense work. There were plenty of members who could utter the loftiest moral sentiments, sentiments quite as lofty as those once uttered by Robespierre; but there was an insufficiency of members able and willing to go to work in practical fashion, able and willing to try to make society measurably better by cutting out the abuses that could be cut out, and by starting things on the right road, instead of insisting upon doing nothing unless they could immediately introduce the millennium and reform all the abuses of society out of hand with a jump. What was needed was a body of men like those who made our Constitution; men accustomed to work with their fellows, accustomed to compromise; men who clung to high ideals; but who were imbued with the philosophy which Abraham Lincoln afterward so strikingly exemplified, and were content to take the best possible where the best absolute could not be secured. This was the spirit of Washington and his associates in one great crisis of our national life, of Lincoln and his associates in the other great crisis. It is the only spirit from which it will ever be possible to secure good results in a free country; and it is the direct negation of Tolstoyism. To minimize the chance of anything but willful misunderstanding, let me repeat that Tolstoy is a great writer, a great novelist; that the unconscious influence of his novels is probably, on the whole, good, even disregarding their long standing as works of art; that even as a professional moralist and philosophical adviser of mankind in religious matters he has some excellent theories and on some points develops a noble and elevating teaching; but that taken as a whole, and if generally diffused, his moral and philosophical teachings, so far as they had any influence at all, would have an influence for bad; partly because on certain points they teach downright immorality, but much more because they tend to be both foolish and fantastic, and if logically applied would mean the extinction of humanity in a generation.

DANTE AND THE BOWERY

*Roosevelt's interests and erudition were as broad as his talent.
In his role as literary critic he offers an interesting commentary
on modern and medieval poetry in an essay that appeared in*
The Outlook *in the summer of 1911.*

It is the conventional thing to praise Dante because he of set purpose "used the language of the market-place," so as to be understanded of the common people; but we do not in practice either admire or understand a man who writes in the language of our own market-place. It must be the Florentine market-place of the thirteenth century—not Fulton Market of to-day. What infinite use Dante would have made of the Bowery! Of course, he could have done it only because not merely he himself, the great poet, but his audience also, would have accepted it as natural. The nineteenth century was more apt than the thirteenth to boast of itself as being the greatest of the centuries; but, save as regards purely material objects, ranging from locomotives to bank buildings, it did not wholly believe in its boasting. A nineteenth-century poet, when trying to illustrate some point he was making, obviously felt uncomfortable in mentioning nineteenth-century heroes if he also referred to those of classic times, lest he should be suspected of instituting comparisons between them. A thirteenth-century poet was not in the least troubled by any such misgivings, and quite simply illustrated his point by allusions to any character in history or romance, ancient or contemporary, that happened to occur to him.

Of all the poets of the nineteenth century, Walt Whitman was the only one who dared use the Bowery—that is, use anything that was striking and vividly typical of the humanity around him—as Dante used the ordinary humanity of his day; and even Whitman was not quite natural in doing so, for he always felt that he was defying the conventions and prejudices of his neighbors, and his self-consciousness made him a little defiant. Dante was not defiant of conventions: the conventions of his day did not forbid him to use human nature just as he saw it, no less than human nature as he read about it. The Bowery is one of the great highways of humanity, a highway of seething life, of varied interest, of fun, of work, of sordid and terrible tragedy; and it is haunted by demons as evil as any that stalk through the pages of the *Inferno*. But no man of Dante's art and with Dante's soul would write of it nowadays; and he would hardly be understood if he did. Whitman wrote of homely things and every-day men, and of their greatness, but his art was not equal to his power and his purpose; and, even as it was, he, the poet, by set intention, of the democracy, is not known to the people as widely as he should be known; and it is only the few—the men like Edward FitzGerald, John Burroughs, and W. E. Henley[2]—who prize him as he ought to be prized.

Nowadays, at the outset of the twentieth century, cultivated people would ridicule the poet who illustrated fundamental truths, as Dante did six hundred years ago, by examples drawn alike from human nature as he saw it around him and from human nature as he read of it. I suppose that this must be partly because we are so self-conscious as always to read a comparison into any illustration, forgetting the fact that no comparison is implied between two men, in the sense of estimating their relative greatness or importance, when the career of each of them is chosen merely to illustrate some given quality that both possess. It is also probably due to the fact that an age in which the critical faculty is greatly developed often tends to develop a certain querulous inability to understand the fundamental truths which less critical ages accept as a matter of course. To such critics it seems improper, and indeed ludicrous, to illustrate human nature by examples chosen alike from the Brooklyn Navy Yard or Castle Garden and the Piraeus, alike from Tammany and from the Roman mob organized by the foes or friends of Caesar. To Dante such feeling itself would have been inexplicable.

Dante dealt with those tremendous qualities of the human soul which dwarf all differences in outward and visible form and station, and therefore, he illustrated what he meant by any example that seemed to him apt. Only the great names of antiquity had been handed down, and so, when he spoke of pride or violence of flattery, and wished to illustrate his thesis by an appeal to the past, he could speak only of great and prominent characters; but in the present of his day most of the men he knew, or knew of, were naturally people of no permanent importance—just as is the case in the present of our own day. Yet the passions of these men were the same as those of the heroes of old, godlike or demonic; and so he unhesitatingly used his contemporaries, or his immediate predecessors, to illustrate his points, without regard to their prominence or lack of prominence. He was not concerned with the differences in their fortunes and careers, with their heroic proportions or lack of such proportions; he was a mystic whose imagination soared so high and whose thoughts plumbed so deeply the far depths of our being that he was also quite simply a realist; for the eternal mysteries were ever before his mind, and, compared to them, the differences between the careers

---

[2] Well-known authors and literary critics of that day.

of the mighty masters of mankind and the careers of even very humble people seemed trivial. If we translate his comparisons into the terms of our day, we are apt to feel amused over the trait of his, until we go a little deeper and understand that we are ourselves to blame, because we have lost the faculty simply and naturally to recognize that the essential traits of humanity are shown alike by big men and by little men, in the lives that are now being lived and in those that are long ended.

Probably no two characters in Dante impress the ordinary reader more than Farinata and Capaneus: the man who raises himself waist-high from out his burning sepulchre, unshaken by torment, and the man who, with scornful disdain, refused to brush from his body the falling flames; the great souls—magnanimous, Dante calls them—whom no torture, no disaster, no failure of the most absolute kind could force to yield or to bow before the dread powers that had mastered them. Dante has created these men, has made them permanent additions to the great figures of the world; they are imaginary only in the sense that Achilles and Ulysses are imaginary—that is, they are now as real as the figures of any men that ever lived. One of them was a mythical hero in a mythical feat, the other a second-rate faction leader in a faction-ridden Italian city of the thirteenth century, whose deeds have not the slightest importance aside from what Dante's mention gives. Yet the two men are mentioned as naturally as Alexander and Caesar are mentioned. Evidently they are dwelt upon at length because Dante felt it his duty to express a peculiar horror for that fierce pride which could defy its overlord, while at the same time, and perhaps unwillingly, he could not conceal a certain shuddering admiration for the lofty courage on which this evil pride was based.

The point I wish to make is the simplicity with which Dante illustrated one of the principles on which he lays most stress, by the example of a man who was of consequence only in the history of the parochial politics of Florence. Farinata will now live forever as a symbol of the soul; yet as an historical figure he is dwarfed beside any one of hundreds of the leaders in our own Revolution and Civil War. Tom Benton, of Missouri, and Jefferson Davis, of Mississippi, were opposed to one another with a bitterness which surpassed that which rived asunder Guelph from Ghibellin, or black Guelph from white Guelph. They played mighty parts in a tragedy more tremendous than any which any medieval city ever witnessed or could have witnessed. Each possessed an iron will and undaunted courage, physical and moral; each led a life of varied interest and danger, and exercised a power not possible in the career of the Florentine. One, the champion of the Union, fought for his principles as unyieldingly as the other fought for what he deemed right in trying to break up the Union. Each was a colossal figure. Each, when the forces against which he fought overcame him—for his latter years Benton saw the cause of disunion triumph in Missouri, just as Jefferson Davis lived to see the cause of union triumph in the Nation—fronted as adverse fate with the frowning defiance, the high heart, and the stubborn will which Dante has commemorated for all time in his hero who "held hell in great scorn." Yet a modern poet who endeavored to illustrate such a point by reference to Benton and Davis would be uncomfortably conscious that his audience would laugh at him. He would feel ill at ease, exactly as he would feel that he was posing, was forced and unnatural, if he referred to the deeds of the evil heroes of the Paris Commune as he would without hesitation refer to the many similar but smaller leaders of riots in the Roman forum.

Dante speaks of a couple of French troubadours, or of a local Sicilian poet, just as he speaks of Euripides; and quite properly, for they illustrate as well what he has to teach; but we of to-day could not possibly speak of a couple of recent French poets or German novelists in the same connection without having an uncomfortable feeling that we ought to defend ourselves from possible misapprehension; and therefore we could not speak of them naturally. When Dante wishes to assail those guilty of crimes of violence, he in one stanza speaks of the torments inflicted by divine justice on Attila (coupling him with Pyrrhus and Sextus Pompey—a sufficiently odd conjunction in itself, by the way), and in the next stanza mentions the names of a couple of local highwaymen who had made travel unsafe in particular neighborhoods. The two highwaymen in question were by no means as important as Jesse James and Billy the Kid; doubtless they were far less formidable fighting men, and their adventures were less striking and varied. Yet think of the way we should feel if a great poet should now arise who would incidentally illustrate the ferocity of the human heart by allusions both to the terrible Hunnish "scourge of God" and to the outlaws who in our own times defied justice in Missouri and New Mexico!

When Dante wishes to illustrate the fierce passions of the human heart, he may speak of Lycurgus, or of Saul; or he may speak of two local contemporary captains, victor or vanquished in obscure struggles between Guelph and Ghibellin; men like Jacopo del Cassero or Buonconte, whom he mentions as naturally as he does Cyrus or Rehoboam. He is entirely right! What one among our own writers, however, would be able simply and naturally to mention Ulrich Dahlgren, or Custer, or Morgan, or Raphael Semmes, or Marion, or Sumter, as illustrating the qualities shown by Habbibal, or Rameses, or William the Conqueror, or by Moses or Hercules? Yet the

Guelph and Ghibelin captains of whom Dante speaks were in no way as important as these American soldiers of the second or third rank. Dante saw nothing incongruous in treating at length of the qualities of all of them; he was not thinking of comparing the genius of the unimportant local leader with the genius of the great sovereign conquerors of the past — he was thinking only of the qualities of courage and daring and of the awful horror of death; and when we deal with what is elemental in the human soul it matters but little whose soul we take. In the same way he mentions a couple of spendthrifts of Padua and Siena, who come to violent ends, just as in the preceding canto he had dwelt upon the tortures undergone by Dionysius and Simon de Montfort, guarded by Nessus and his fellow centaurs. For some reason he hated the spendthrifts in question as the Whigs of Revolutionary South Carolina and New York hated Tarleton, Kruger, Saint Leger, and De Lancey; and to him there was nothing incongruous in drawing a lesson from one couple of offenders more than from another. (It would, by the way, be outside my present purpose to speak of the rather puzzling manner in which Dante confounds his own hatreds with those of heaven, and, for instance, shows a vindictive enjoyment in putting his personal opponent Filippo Argenti in hell, for no clearly adequate reason.)

When he turns from those whom he is glad to see in hell toward those for whom he cares, he shows the same delightful power of penetrating through the externals into the essentials. Cato and Manfred illustrate his point no better than Belacqua, a contemporary Florentine maker of citherns. Alas! what poet to-day would dare to illustrate his argument by introducing Steinway in company with Cato and Manfred! Yet again, when examples of love are needed, he draws them from the wedding-feast at Cana, from the actions of Pylades and Orestes, and from the life of a kindly, honest comb-dealer of Siena who had just died. Could we now link together Peter Cooper and Pylades, without feeling a sense of incongruity? He couples Priscian with a politician of local note who had written an encyclopaedia and a lawyer of distinction who had lectured at Bologna and Oxford; we could not now with such fine unconsciousness bring Evarts and one of the compilers of the Encyclopaedia Britannica into a like comparison.

When Dante deals with the crimes which he most abhorred, simony and barratry, he flails offenders of his age who were of the same type as those who in our days flourish by political or commercial corruption; and he names his offenders, both those just dead and those still living, and puts them, popes and politicians alike, in hell. There have been trust magnates and politicians and editors and magazine-writers in our own country whose lives and deeds were no more edifying than those of the men who lie in the third and the fifth chasm of the eighth circle of the Inferno; yet for a poet to name those men would be condemned as an instance of shocking taste.

One age expresses itself naturally in a form that would be unnatural, and therefore undesirable, in another age. We do not express ourselves nowadays in epics at all; and we keep the emotions aroused in us by what is good or evil in the men of the present in a totally different compartment from that which holds our emotions concerning what was good or evil in the men of the past. An imitation of the letters of the times past, when the spirit has wholly altered, would be worse than useless; and the very qualities that help to make Dante's poem immortal would, if copied nowadays, make the copyist ridiculous. Nevertheless, it would be a good thing if we could, in some measure, achieve the mighty Florentine's high simplicity of soul, at least to the extent of recognizing in those around us the eternal qualities which we admire or condemn in the men who wrought good or evil at any stage in the world's previous history. Dante's masterpiece is one of the supreme works of art that the ages have witnessed; but he would have been the last to wish that it should be treated only as a work of art, or worshipped only for art's sake, without reference to the dread lessons it teaches mankind.

AN ART EXHIBITION

While TR can be described as a modern, a risk taker, open to experiment and innovation, he was also very conventional and oddly conservative. In 1913 the now-famous Armory Show, the International Exhibition of Modern Art, introduced some of the new movements in art to many Americans. TR attended. His judgment about art was not nearly as enduring as his political judgment, but its expression here, with a wonderfully comic moment on cubism, is delightfully reactionary. This selection is from The Outlook, *March 1913.*

The recent "International Exhibition of Modern Art" in New York was really noteworthy. Messrs. Davies, Kuhn, Gregg, and their fellow members of the Association of American Painters and Sculptors did a work of very real value in securing such an exhibition of the works of both foreign and native painters and sculptors. Primarily their purpose was to give the public a chance to see what has recently been going on abroad. No similar collection of the works of European "moderns" has ever been exhibited in this country. The exhibitors were quite right as to the need of showing to our people in this manner the art forces which of late have been at work in Europe, forces which cannot be ignored.

This does not mean that I in the least accept the view that these men take of the European extremists whose pictures were here exhibited. It is true, as the champions of these extremists say, that there can be no life without change, no development without change, and that to be afraid of what is different or unfamiliar is to be afraid of life. It is no less true, however, that change may mean death and not life, and retrogression instead of development. Probably we err in treating most of these pictures seriously. It is likely that many of them represent in the painters the astute appreciation of the power to make folly lucrative which the late P. T. Barnum showed with his faked mermaid. There are thousands of people who will pay small sums to look at a faked mermaid; and now and then one of this kind with enough money will buy a Cubist picture, or a picture of a misshapen nude woman, repellent from every standpoint.

In some ways it is the work of the American painters and sculptors which is of most interest in this collection, and a glance at this work must convince anyone of the real good that is coming out of the new movements, fantastic though many of the developments of these new movements are. There was one note entirely absent from the exhibition, and that was the note of commonplace. There was not a touch of simpering, self-satisfied conventionality anywhere in the exhibition. Any sculptor or painter who had in him something to express and the power of expressing it found the field open to him. He did not have to be afraid because his work was not along ordinary lines. There was no stunting or dwarfing, no requirement that a man whose gift lay in new directions should measure up or down to stereotyped and fossilized standards.

For all of this there can be only hearty praise. But this does not in the least mean that the extremists whose paintings and pictures were represented are entitled to any praise, save, perhaps, that they have helped to break fetters. Probably in any reform movement, any progressive movement, in any field of life, the penalty for avoiding the commonplace is a liability to extravagance. It is vitally necessary to move forward and to shake off the dead hand, often the fossilized dead hand, of the reactionaries; and yet we have to face the fact that there is apt to be a lunatic fringe among the votaries of any forward movement. In this recent art exhibition the lunatic fringe was fully in evidence, especially in the rooms devoted to the Cubists and the Futurists, or Near-Impressionists. I am not entirely certain which of the two latter terms should be used in connection with some of the various pictures and representations of plastic art—and, frankly, it is not of the least consequence. The Cubists are entitled to the serious attention of all who find enjoyment in the colored puzzle-pictures of the Sunday newspapers. Of course there is no reason for choosing the cube as a symbol, except that it is probably less fitted than any other mathematical expression for any but the most formal decorative art. There is no reason why people should not call themselves Cubists, or Octagonists, or Parallelopipedonists, or Knights of the Isosceles Triangle, or Brothers of the Cosine, if they so desire; as expressing anything serious and permanent, one term is as fatuous as another. Take the picture which for some reason is called "A Naked Man Going Down Stairs." There is in my bathroom a really good Navajo rug which, on any proper interpretation of the Cubist theory, is a far more satisfactory and decorative picture. Now, if, for some inscrutable reason, it suited somebody to call this rug a picture of, say, "A Well-Dressed Man Going Up a Ladder," the name would fit the facts just about as well as in the case of the Cubist picture of the "Naked Man Going Down Stairs." From the standpoint of terminology each name would have whatever merit inheres in a rather cheap straining after effect; and from the standpoint of decorative value, of sincerity, and of artistic merit, the Navajo rug is infinitely ahead of the picture.

As for many of the human figures in the pictures of the Futurists, they show that the school would be better entitled to the name of the "Past-ists."

I was interested to find that a man of scientific attainments who had likewise looked at the pictures had been struck, as I was, by their resemblance to the later work of the palaeolithic artists of the French and Spanish caves. There are interesting samples of the strivings for the representation of the human form among artists of many different countries and times, all in the same stage of palaeolithic culture, to be found in a recent number of the "Revue d'Ethnographie." The palaeolithic artist was able to portray the bison, the mammoth, the reindeer, and the horse with spirit and success, while he still stumbled painfully in the effort to portray man. This stumbling effort in his case represented progress, and he was entitled to great credit for it. Forty thousand years later, when entered into artificially and deliberately, it represents only a smirking pose of retrogression, and is not praiseworthy. So with much of the sculpture. A family group of precisely the merit that inheres in a structure made of the wooden blocks in a nursery is not entitled to be reproduced in marble. Admirers speak of the kneeling female figure by [Wilhelm] Lehmbruck—I use "female" advisedly, for although obviously mammalian it is not especially human—as "full of lyric grace," as "tremendously sincere," and "of a jewel-like preciousness." I am not competent to say whether these words themselves represent sincerity or merely a conventional jargon; it is just as easy to be conventional about the fantastic as about the commonplace. In any event one might as well speak of the "lyric grace" of a praying mantis, which adopts much the same attitude; and why a deformed pelvis should be called "sincere," or a tibia of giraffe-like length "precious," seems to a reasonably sane view of the pictures of Matisse a question of pathological rather than artistic significance. This figure and the absurd portrait head of some young lady have the merit that inheres in extravagant caricature. It is a merit, but it is not a high merit. It entitles these pieces to stand in sculpture where nonsense rhymes stand in literature and the sketches of Aubrey Beardsley in a pictorial art. These modern sculptured caricatures in no way approach the gargoyles of Gothic cathedrals, probably because the modern artists are too self-conscious and make themselves ridiculous by pretentiousness. The makers of the gargoyles knew very well that the gargoyles did not represent what was most important in the Gothic cathedrals. They stood for just a little point of grotesque reaction against, and relief from, the tremendous elemental vastness and grandeur of the Houses of God. They were imps, sinister and comic, grim and yet futile, and they fitted admirably into the framework of the theology that found its expression in the towering and wonderful piles which they ornamented.

Very little of the work of the extremists among the European "moderns" seems to be good in and for itself; nevertheless it has certainly helped any number of American artists to do work that is original and serious; and this not only in painting but in sculpture. I wish the exhibition had contained some of the work of the late Marcius-Simons; very few people knew or cared for it while he lived; but not since Turner has there been another man on whose canvas glowed so much of that unearthly "light that never was on land or sea." But the exhibition contained so much of extraordinary merit that it is ungrateful even to mention an omission. To name the pictures one would like to possess—and the bronzes and tanagras and plasters—would mean to make a catalogue of indefinite length. One of the most striking pictures was the "Terminal Yards"—the seeing eye was there, and the cunning hand. I should like to mention all the pictures of the president of the association, Arthur B. Davies. As first-class decorative work of an entirely new type, the very unexpected pictures of Sheriff Bob Chanler have a merit all their own. The "Arizona Desert," the "Canadian Night," the group of girls on the roof of a New York tenement-house, the studies in the Bronx Zoo, the "Heracles," the studies for the Utah monument, the little group called "Gossip," which has something of the quality of the famous fifteenth idyl of Theocritus, the "Pelf," with its grim suggestiveness—these and a hundred others are worthy of study, each of them; I am naming at random those which at the moment I happen to recall. I am not speaking of the acknowledged masters, of Whistler, Puvis de Chavannes, Monet; nor of John's children; nor of Cezanne's old woman with a rosary; nor of Redon's marvelous color-pieces—a worthy critic should speak of these. All I am trying to do is to point out why a layman is grateful to those who arranged this exhibition.

BIBLIOGRAPHY

The Works of Theodore Roosevelt, 20 vols. (New York: Charles Scribner's Sons, 1926), is still the most useful single collection of TR's works, including, as it does, his essays, important speeches, and key state papers. His book-length works, some of which were reprinted in several editions, include the following:

African Game Trails (New York: Charles Scribner's Sons, 1910).

America and the World War (New York: Charles Scribner's Sons, 1915). A collection of essays and speeches.

American Ideals and Other Essays Social and Political (New York: G. P. Putnam's Sons, 1897).

A Book-Lover's Holidays in the Open (New York: Charles Scribner's Sons, 1916). Nature essays.

Fear God and Take Your Own Part, (New York: George H. Doran Company, 1916). A collection of essays.

The Foes of Our Own Household (New York: George H. Doran Company, 1917). Social and political essays.

Gouverneur Morris (Boston: Houghton Mifflin Company, 1888).

Hero Tales from American History, with Henry Cabot Lodge (New York: The Century Company, 1895).

Hunting Trips of a Ranchman (New York: G. P. Putnam's Sons, 1885).

The Naval War of 1812 (New York: G. P. Putnam's Sons, 1882).

New York (New York: Longmans, Green and Company, 1891).

Oliver Cromwell (New York: Charles Scribner's Sons, 1900).

Outdoor Pastimes of an American Hunter (New York: Charles Scribner's Sons, 1905).

Ranch Life and the Hunting Trail (New York: The Century Company, 1888).

The Rough Riders (New York: Charles Scribner's Sons, 1899).

The Strenuous Life. Essays and Addresses (New York: The Century Company, 1900).

Theodore Roosevelt An Autobiography (New York: Macmillan Company, 1913).

Thomas Hart Benton (Boston: Houghton Mifflin Company, 1887).

Through The Brazilian Wilderness (New York: Charles Scribner's Sons, 1914).

The Wilderness Hunter (New York: G. P. Putnam's Sons, 1893).

The Winning of the West, 4 vols. (New York: G. P. Putnam's Sons, 1889-1896)

In every corner of the world, on every subject under the sun, Penguin represents quality and variety—the very best in publishing today.

For complete information about books available from Penguin—including Puffins, Penguin Classics, and Arkana—and how to order them, write to us at the appropriate address below. Please note that for copyright reasons the selection of books varies from country to country.

In the United Kingdom: Please write to *Dept. JC, Penguin Books Ltd, FREEPOST, West Drayton, Middlesex UB7 0BR.*

If you have any difficulty in obtaining a title, please send your order with the correct money, plus ten percent for postage and packaging, to *P.O. Box No. 11, West Drayton, Middlesex UB7 0BR*

In the United States: Please write to *Consumer Sales, Penguin USA, P.O. Box 999, Dept. 17109, Bergenfield, New Jersey 07621-0120.* VISA and MasterCard holders call 1-800-253-6476 to order all Penguin titles

In Canada: Please write to *Penguin Books Canada Ltd, 10 Alcorn Avenue, Suite 300, Toronto, Ontario M4V 3B2*

In Australia: Please write to *Penguin Books Australia Ltd, P.O. Box 257, Ringwood, Victoria 3134*

In New Zealand: Please write to *Penguin Books (NZ) Ltd, Private Bag 102902, North Shore Mail Centre, Auckland 10*

In India: Please write to *Penguin Books India Pvt Ltd, 706 Eros Apartments, 56 Nehru Place, New Delhi 110 019*

In the Netherlands: Please write to *Penguin Books Netherlands bv, Postbus 3507, NL-1001 AH Amsterdam*

In Germany: Please write to *Penguin Books Deutschland GmbH, Metzlerstrasse 26, 60594 Frankfurt am Main*

In Spain: Please write to *Penguin Books S. A., Bravo Murillo 19, 1° B, 28015 Madrid*

In Italy: Please write to *Penguin Italia s.r.l., Via Felice Casati 20, I-20124 Milano*

In France: Please write to *Penguin France S. A., 17 rue Lejeune, F−31000 Toulouse*

In Japan: Please write to *Penguin Books Japan, Ishikiribashi Building, 2−5−4, Suido, Bunkyo-ku, Tokyo 112*

In Greece: Please write to *Penguin Hellas Ltd, Dimocritou 3, GR−106 71 Athens*

In South Africa: Please write to *Longman Penguin Southern Africa (Pty) Ltd, Private Bag X08, Bertsham 2013*